THE COVENANTERS *in* Ireland

A HISTORY OF THE CONGREGATIONS

Cameron Press
2010

Published jointly by the

Church History

and

Bookshop and Publications Committees

of the

Reformed Presbyterian Church of Ireland.

www.rpc.org

Copyright

Cameron Press

2010

ISBN: 978-1-905455-04-1

Cover designed by Mark Thompson

Printed by Trimprint.

36 English Street, Armagh

Copies available from the Covenanter Book Centre

37 Knockbracken Road, Carryduff, Belfast.

www.covenanterbooks.com

FOR CHRIST'S CROWN & COVENANT

The Reformed Presbyterian Church emerged from the crucible of persecution in 17th Century Scotland. The Covenanters of that time, though struggling as a minority against a ruthlessly tyrannical government, nevertheless did not lose their vision of a national, united and reformed church in the British Isles, under the authority of Christ the head and king of the church. The 'National Covenant of Scotland' and the 'Solemn League and Covenant of England, Ireland and Scotland' were intended to bring about this uniformity, but persecution and division ended any practical implementation of their dream.

However the successors of those Covenanters never gave up their aspirations. Today the Reformed Presbyterian Church can be found worshipping and witnessing in Scotland, Northern Ireland, the Republic of Ireland, Australia, Canada, France, Japan, Sudan, and the United States of America. These bodies still hold to the headship of Christ over the nations and over the Church. There are other denominations and fellowships in Ireland, Scotland, North America and even Cyprus, which in a large part also owe their origins to Reformed Presbyterianism.

The Irish Church today still holds to the descending obligation of those 17th Century Covenants, as well as adhering to the Westminster Standards, the denomination's summary of Biblical doctrine and practice. The Reformed Presbyterian Church is Calvinistic in its theology, Presbyterian in its government and follows the simplicity of the synagogue in its worship rather than the complexity of the Temple which has been fulfilled in Christ. In that sense she is possibly more aware of the Christian Church's indebtedness to its Hebrew heritage than many contemporary Christians and she still highly values the 'Older Testament' of God's self-revelation, recognising that the idea of Christ's covenant is the glue that cements both Testaments in an unbreakable bond.

None of this should be taken to imply that the Reformed Presbyterian Church lives in the past. She honours the past and learns from it, but she is aware of the need for on-going witness and reformation in line with the biblical principles referred to above. To mention but three examples:

- The Church engages in various kinds of missionary, evangelistic and social work.
- As with the Reformers, she encourages the use of Bibles and Psalters in contemporary English - the 'vulgar language' (Westminster Confession of Faith 1:8) that is the language commonly spoken by the people.
- The Church also takes a keen interest in all matters which affect the spiritual and moral life of the United Kingdom and Ireland.

The Reformed Presbyterian Church is a small family of like-minded believers - but it still has the big vision of its founders. The 17th Century Covenanters had an influence on the Reformed branch of Christianity which exceeded what might be expected considering their comparatively small numbers, (their contribution to the Westminster Assembly is a case in point). We, their modern successors, must have no less an influence. At a time when the Church in the West is often weak and fragmented and tempted to further compromise or even to abandon Biblical teaching, we must not lose our nerve. The Reformed Presbyterian Church does not claim to be perfect. We do not have all the truth and we can learn from others, but surely the modern Christian Church still needs the principles we espouse. She still needs to acknowledge her Saviour and Lord in all His Kingly fullness. May the Lord Jesus Christ be pleased to use us and this publication in some way towards the accomplishment of that glorious end!

Rev. Barry J. Galbraith. (Moderator of Synod 2010)

'Christ is all' panel from the former Bailiesmills Manse, now in the Meeting House.

*How beautiful upon the mountains are the feet of him
that bringeth good tidings,
that publisheth peace;
that bringeth good tidings of good,
that publisheth salvation;
that saith unto Zion,*

Thy God reigneth!

Isaiah ch. 52 verse 7.

Early 20th Century glass plate photograph of Laymore near Ballymena where Covenanters met to worship

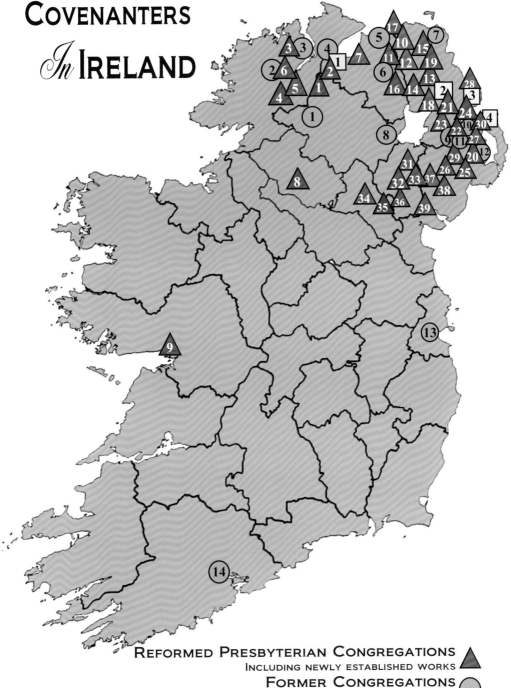

COVENANTERS
In IRELAND

REFORMED PRESBYTERIAN CONGREGATIONS
INCLUDING NEWLY ESTABLISHED WORKS

FORMER CONGREGATIONS
THOSE CONGREGATIONS NOW CLOSED

EASTERN REFORMED SYNOD CONGREGATIONS
THOSE CLOSED OR NOW PART OF THE GENERAL ASSEMBLY
NOT INCLUDING THOSE WHO RETURNED TO THE R. P. SYNOD

MAP

1. BREADY
2. FAUGHAN
3. MILFORD
4. STRANORLAR
5. CONVOY
6. LETTERKENNY
7. LIMAVADY
8. ENNISKILLEN
9. GALWAY
10. BALLYCLABBER
11. BALLYLAGGAN
12. BALLYMONEY
13. CLOUGHMILLS
14. CULLYBACKEY
15. DERVOCK
16. DRIMBOLG
17. GLENMANUS
18. KELLSWATER
19. KILRAUGHTS
20. BAILIESMILLS
21. BALLYCLARE
22. SHAFTESBURY SQUARE
23. TRINITY
24. CARRICKFERGUS
25. DROMARA
26. DROMORE
27. KNOCKBRACKEN
28. LARNE
29. LISBURN
30. NEWTOWNARDS
31. CLARE
32. BALLYLANE
33. BALLENON
34. CREEVAGH
35. FAIRVIEW
36. TULLYVALLEN
37. LOUGHBRICKLAND
38. RATHFRILAND
39. RIVERSIDE, NEWRY

1. MULVIN
2. GORTLEE
3. RAMELTON
4. CLARENDON STREET
5. RINGRASH
6. GARVAGH
7. BUSHMILLS
8. GRANGE
9. GROSVENOR ROAD
10. CREGAGH ROAD
11. BOTANIC AVENUE
12. BALLYMACASHON
13. DUBLIN
14. CORK

1. WATERSIDE
2. ESKYLANE
3. LOUGHMOURNE
4. ANN STREET, N'ARDS

CONTENTS

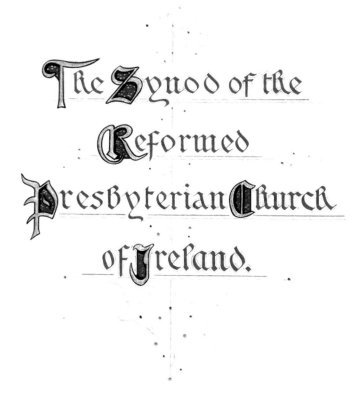

Frontpiece to 1911 Covenant Renewal

FOREWARD

In his book, *The shaping of Ulster Presbyterian belief and practice, 1770-1840*, the historian Dr. Andrew Holmes has observed that there is a 'seemingly unique obsession of Ulster Presbyterians with writing and reading congregational histories'. To a large extent this is a reflection of the importance of the congregation within Presbyterianism and the way in which its identity is intertwined with locality and historic family associations. It is hardly surprising given the way in which historical events have shaped our denomination, that Covenanters are as equally guilty of this fascination with the past. The first known attempt to produce a history of Reformed Presbyterianism in Ireland dates from 1810 when Rev. William Stavely was asked to write an account of the rise and progress of the Covenanters on this island. Sadly there is no evidence that Stavely's undoubted knowledge of this subject was ever committed to print.

It was not until 1984 with the publication of Rev. Professor Adam Loughridge's *Covenanters in Ireland* that a general history of Irish Reformed Presbyterianism appeared. In interweaving chronological narrative with thematic analysis, Professor Loughridge, for many years the energetic and knowledgeable convener of the Church History Committee, provided a scholarly, yet accessible history of the denomination, though inevitably given the scope of his study, he could say little in any depth on individual congregations.

However, as the historical bibliography in this volume reveals, many Reformed Presbyterians, the venerable professor among them, have been active in researching and writing congregational histories. Beginning in 1912 with William Shaw's account of Cullybackey, the histories of approximately half of the Covenanter congregations currently in existence have been produced.

This present work is different from these writings in that it has brought together in a single volume histories of each of the Reformed Presbyterian congregations in Ireland, including congregations no longer in existence, as well as information on home and foreign missions. An especially welcome inclusion is the reissued and updated *fasti* of the Reformed Presbyterian Church in Ireland, first published in 1970.

This book has had a long gestation. It was in the 1940s when, under the direction of the Church History Committee, that the work of actively drawing together histories of each of the congregations of the Reformed Presbyterian Church in Ireland began. The task proved immense and it was not until the mid 1970s that short accounts of each congregation were published in the *Covenanter Witness* in a series entitled 'Where we worship'.

Though much of the groundwork for the present volume was due to the efforts of Professor Loughridge, the final version is the product of many hands. All those who have been involved in the production of this volume deserve enormous credit for their efforts. Many hours of research followed by checking and rechecking have gone into this book which will be the standard work of reference for years to come and a major resource for academic, local and family historians.

This publication appears at a time when there is considerable interest in exploring the history of Reformed Presbyterianism on this island. The *Covenanters in Ulster* project of 2008-09, initiated by Mark Thompson while he was Chairman of the Ulster-Scots Agency, presented the history of the denomination to a wide audience and generated much interest. This year has seen the marking of the 250th anniversary of the foundation of Kellswater, the oldest Reformed Presbyterian congregation in Ireland, and 'the capital of Covenanting' as Professor Loughridge once described it. In 2011 the 200th anniversary of the first meeting of Synod will, God willing be commemorated.

Reformed Presbyterians are especially conscious of the grace of God in preserving the denomination through times of difficulty, trial and persecution. It is undoubtedly the intention of the compilers to record the movement of the Spirit of God among this people over the more than three centuries of distinct Covenanter witness in Ireland.

This book tells our story.

William Roulston
Convener, Reformed Presbyterian Church History Committee

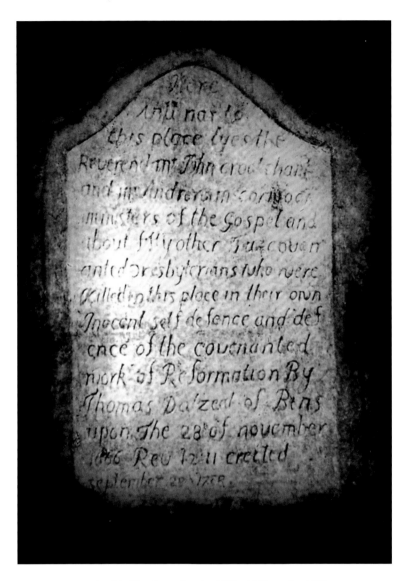

Battle of Rullion Green, Pentland Hills, 28 November 1666
Memorial bears the names of Rev. Andrew McCormick of Magerally and Rev. John Crookshanks of Raphoe,
who both died in the cause of the Covenanted Reformation.

'Here and near to this place lies the Reverend Mr John Crookshank and
Mr Andrew McCormick ministers of the Gospel and About fifty other true covenanted
Presbyterians who were killed in this place in their own Inocent {sic} self defence
and defence of the covenanted work of Reformation By Thomas Dalzeal of Bins
upon the 28 of November 1666 Rev 12. 11
Erected September 28 1738'

HISTORICAL INTRODUCTION
THE SPIRITUAL ROOTS OF
THE REFORMED PRESBYTERIAN
CHURCH OF IRELAND

The Reformed Presbyterian Church was formally constituted in 1763 with the formation of the Reformed Presbytery. The roots of the Church however are to be found in the Scottish Reformation which was established by an Act of Parliament in the summer of 1560. This Reformation came about when young Scottish men, studying in continental Europe, came into contact with the gospel as taught by **Martin Luther** and returned home to preach it in Scotland. The first of these men was **Patrick Hamilton**, who after a few months preaching the gospel was burned at the stake as a Lutheran heretic in 1528. Others were to follow, such as **George Wishart** who was martyred in 1546.

In the persecution of Reformers that characterised Mary Tudor's reign many fled to Geneva and Frankfurt to escape her cruel intentions. Among these refugees was **John Knox** who spent several years in Geneva with John Calvin. He described Geneva as *"the most perfect school of Christ on earth since the days of the apostles"*.

Knox was invited back to Scotland to preach the gospel and promote the work of the Reformation by some Scottish nobles who entered into a solemn covenant to demonstrate their commitment to the cause of Reformation. Knox arrived in Scotland on 1st May 1559. God signally blessed his preaching. By the next summer, such was the impact and acceptance of the gospel that Scotland, formally by an Act of Parliament, rejected Roman Catholicism and accepted the Reformed faith as the religion of the land.

John Knox and his fellow Reformers recognised Jesus Christ as King of His Church and sought to ensure that the church's doctrine, worship and government were consistent with his revealed will as set forth in the Scriptures. Therefore, the Scottish Church became Presbyterian, governed by elders with Presbytery replacing the episcopal hierarchy. John Knox is recognised as the father of Presbyterianism, but when this form of church government came under sustained attack from the episcopal party in the 1570s it was **Andrew Melville** who championed its defence. Thereafter, he became known as the *'Great Champion of Presbyterianism'*.

The Stuart kings, James VI of Scotland and I of England (1578-1625) and Charles I (1625-1649) were opposed to Presbyterianism. They favoured episcopacy which they believed helped to maintain their power base. James coined the slogan, *'no bishop, no king'*. He knew the commitment of the Scottish people to Presbyterianism and so in a subtle way he introduced what could be described as **'creeping episcopacy'**. Perpetual moderators were appointed in 1607 and then bishops in 1612. In 1618 the Articles of Perth were passed which interfered with aspects of worship. Since many of these measures were not rigidly enforced there was little reaction from the population.

When Charles I came to the throne in 1625 he was a firm believer in the *'divine right of kings'*. In this concept of kingship he believed that the king had the absolute right to execute his will in church and state. In the 1630s he began to enforce his policy on Scotland and the north of Ireland where Presbyterianism had by then taken root following the commencement of the Plantation of Ulster in 1610.

The matter came to a head in 1637 when the king imposed an English style prayer book on the Scottish church. When **Dean Hannay** attempted to read the liturgy in the High Kirk of Edinburgh (St Giles' Cathedral) a spontaneous uproar ensued. Negotiations with the king came to nothing. In the crisis the nation responded under the direction of its leaders to enter into covenant with God (**the National Covenant of 1638**) to remain steadfast to King Jesus and the Protestant Reformation. The Presbyterians in Ireland were in sympathy with their Scottish co-religionists, the authorities putting pressure on them to denounce the Covenant by swearing an oath, known as the **Black Oath**. Most refused and many fled back to Scotland to escape fines or imprisonment.

Not long after this Civil War broke out in England between the Crown and Parliament (August 1642). Both sides sought help from the Scottish people.

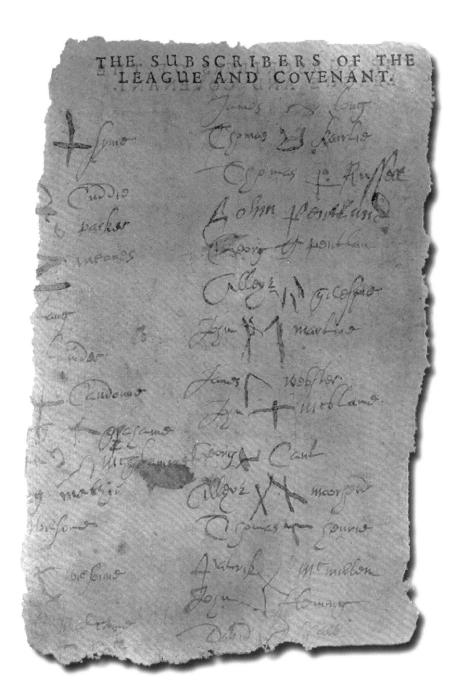

One of the original Covenants survives to this day, signed by the people at Holywood on 8 April, 1644, and is in the collection of the Ulster Museum. It has 67 of the original signatures

S.OLEMNE LEAGUE AND COVENANT For REFORMATION, and Defence of Religion, The Honour and Happinesse of the King, and the Peace and Safety of the three Kingdomes of Scotland, England, and Ireland.

The Scots agreed to help the Parliamentarians (Roundheads) but only on the basis of Covenant **(the Solemn League and Covenant of 1643)**. This Covenant was signed in the three kingdoms of England, Scotland and Ireland and among other things it pledged the signatories to "*the reformation of religion in the kingdoms of England and Ireland in doctrine, worship, discipline and government, according to the Word of God, and the example of the best reformed Churches*". In this Covenant Jesus Christ is recognised as the Head of the Church and the Ruler of the nation.

This period of Scottish church history is known as the Second Reformation, and the Covenanted Presbyterians in Scotland and Ireland experienced many blessings in their churches in the 1640s and 1650s.

Charles I was beheaded by the English in 1649 and the kingdom was governed by the Cromwellian Commonwealth. After Cromwell's death there was a yearning for monarchy again. Charles II was restored to the throne in 1660. Since he had signed the Covenant the Scottish people hoped he would lend his support to the Covenanted Reformation in the three kingdoms and be sympathetic to Presbyterian church government. They were to be bitterly disappointed. No sooner was he on the throne when he declared the Covenants traitorous documents and had them burned in London, Edinburgh and Carrickfergus by the public hangman. His next move was to have the Covenanter leaders arrested and executed including (**James Guthrie** (minister), **Archibald Campbell, Marquis of Argyll** (nobleman), **Archibald Johnston, Lord Warriston** (lawyer). **Samuel Rutherford** (minister and college professor) died before the King's cruel intentions could be implemented.

Charles next moved against the Presbyterian ministers in Scotland and Ireland. They had either to conform to episcopacy or be ejected from their pulpits and deprived of their livelihoods. About one third of the Scottish ministers (350) were ejected along with 61 of the 68 Presbyterian ministers in the north of Ireland.

The Covenanted population continued to follow their ministers to hear the gospel preached at open-air meetings called **'conventicles'** often in shady glens or windswept moors. This stubborn refusal to conform to episcopacy infuriated the king. He unleashed a period of relentless and merciless persecution upon the Covenanters. The barbarity associated with the deaths by drowning of **Margaret Wilson** (aged 18) and **Margaret McLaughan** (aged 65) in the Solway Firth is notorious. It is estimated that 18,000 Covenanters suffered death, banishment or such fines and destruction of property as reduced them to absolute poverty. This persecution continued throughout the reigns of Charles II (1660-1685) and James II (1685-1688). During this period Covenanter ministers like **Donald Cargill**, **Richard Cameron, Alexander Peden** and **James Renwick** continued to preach the gospel faithfully and bear witness fearlessly to the Crown Rights of King Jesus. For example, in 1680 Richard Cameron and some Covenanter friends rode into the village of Sanquhar and read a paper setting forth their principles. In this **'Sanquhar Declaration'** they denounced Charles II for his tyrannical rule and declared that he had forfeited the right to govern. Interestingly, what Cameron and his friends did at Sanquhar, and for which they were branded traitors, the whole nation did in 1688, when James II was declared unfit to govern the three kingdoms and was ousted from the throne.

Relief came when the general population, weary of Stuart tyranny, invited William Prince of Orange and his wife Mary (the daughter of James II) from Holland to take the throne. James fled to Ireland where he found some support but was defeated by William at the Battle of the Boyne in July 1690.

During the period of persecution the ranks of the Covenanted Presbyterians in Scotland and Ireland were decimated, either by persecution or defection. Those who remained faithful to the Crown Rights of King Jesus and the Covenanted Work of Reformation formed themselves into Societies for mutual support and spiritual fellowship. At the Revolution Settlement the representatives of the Society people lobbied to have the Covenants recognised but failed in this objective. This fact along with other compromises led them to remain outside the main Presbyterian body in Ireland (Synod of Ulster) and in Scotland, the General Assembly of the established Church of Scotland. Both of these churches accepted the Revolution settlement which involved setting aside many of the benefits of the covenanted Second Reformation.

They maintained their witness and became known as the 'Society People' or Covenanters. Having no ministers for a few years it was a matter of thanksgiving when **Rev. John McMillan** joined their ranks in 1706. At this time the membership of the United Societies was about 7,000 in Scotland with a much smaller number in Ireland. Rev. John McMillan continued faithfully until 1743 when he was joined by **Rev. Thomas Nairne**. They then constituted the Reformed Presbytery and considered themselves as the legitimate heirs of the Second Reformation Church in Scotland. There followed a time of rapid progress in both Scotland and Ireland.

In Ireland **William Martin** was ordained at the Vow, near Ballymoney in Co. Antrim, in 1757 and with the ordination of **Matthew Lynn** in 1763 the Irish Reformed Presbytery was constituted. Although their ranks were often depleted by emigration to North America (where the American Reformed Presbytery was constituted in 1774), the church in Ireland prospered in the latter end of the 18th century and the beginning of the 19th century. The man who was most instrumental in this progress was **Rev. William Stavely** who had been ordained at Conlig in 1772.

The growth of the church paved the way for the constitution of the Synod in 1811 and the organisation of the Irish Church into four Presbyteries - North, South, East and West. This volume contains the history of the congregations within these Presbyteries as they sought with God's blessing to maintain the witness for the Crown Rights of King Jesus and the Covenanted work of Reformation in Ireland.

Rev. Prof. Robert McCollum

NOTES AND ACKNOWLEDGEMENTS

The primary purpose of this history is to give glory to God, and that we the sheep of His pasture might learn to follow Him more earnestly, learning from His merciful dealings with us in past days. This book has been planned for many years. The material was in existence but required organisation and editing. We thank all those who assisted in bringing it to completion.

The primary and inerrant history of the Church is the Old and New Testaments of Scripture. Modern church histories record the continuing outworking of God's purposes and tell the story of the same fallible Church but cannot make the same claims to inerrancy, and neither do we.

While many excellent congregational histories of Reformed Presbyterian congregations have been written it is unlikely that there will ever be a complete set. In an effort to redress this, or perhaps to lay a foundation for further works, the late Dr. Adam Loughridge, who was professor of church history at our Theological College, wrote a series of articles entitled 'Where we Worship'. These were published in the church magazine, *'Covenanter Witness'*, between January 1975 and November 1977. Although Prof. Loughridge wrote a number of congregational histories, these published articles are the foundation of this book.

Over the past few years these histories have gone through a process of updating and expansion under the care of Dr. Trevor McCavery, a member of the Church History Committee. These articles were scrutinised by the respective congregations, proof read for accuracy, historically and grammatically by Prof. Robert McCollum and Miss Eileen Kerr and set into a form for printing. The Church History Committee saw that this was an opportunity to produce a definitive and complementary work to Prof. Loughridge's 'Covenanters in Ireland', published in 1984. This book also includes articles on mission work and other areas of ministry under the Irish Synod. Great effort has been made to ensure accuracy. Where facts apparently conflict in the sources a decision was made regarding the most reliable source. Where the fact is not essential it has been omitted so as not to confuse future researchers.

The format of the chapters into presbyteries follows the common usage of North, South, East, West. Within each chapter congregations are arranged alphabetically, but where they are linked historically or geographically they appear together. For example, Fairview and Tullyvallen appear consecutively and the Belfast congregations are grouped. Congregations no longer in existence are included as are recently formed congregations.

The division that affected the Reformed Presbyterian Church in Ireland, Scotland and North America in the 19th Century is reflected in the congregational histories. This is important for continuity as some of the congregations which left the Irish R P Synod to form the Eastern Reformed Presbyterian Synod in 1842 later returned. Other congregations joined the General Assembly. During the separation some ceased to exist and a few have since been absorbed into other congregations. This book has sought to record the extent of the Eastern Reformed Synod. We hope that the manner of arrangement is logical and that you will be able to navigate this book.

An important feature of this publication is the inclusion of the 'Fasti, Part 1 and 2', as was originally envisaged by Prof. Loughridge in 1970. The Fasti lists all ministers who have completed their earthly service and includes brief biographical sketches. We are grateful to Rev. Norman McCune and Mr. Trevor Magee who have revised and updated the Irish Fasti. Also published is the Fasti of Irish born men who have served in the American and Scottish R.P. churches. To complete the work the Fasti of the Eastern Reformed Synod is included. These brief sketches should prove a useful resource for both the casual reader and serious researcher.

Gratitude is expressed to those who supplied photographs, especially those who supplied rare pictures. Mr. Stephen Steele and associates who agreed that we could use pictures from their photographic record of Irish R.P. Church buildings. Most photographs here have been digitally enhanced to improve presentation and while some ephemeral objects have been removed the integrity of the subject has been maintained. The maps which accompanied Grittith's valuation of Ireland in the mid nineteenth century are used to illustrate the sites of former buildings. They are available at PRONI.

We thank all who contributed articles. The guidance of the conveners of the Church History and Publications Committees, Prof. Robert McCollum and Dr. William Roulston and all who have contributed to this book is acknowledged. We also express thanks to the printer Mr. Ted Trimble of Trimprint, Armagh and Mr. Mark Thompson for the cover design.

We pray that God will make this book a blessing to everyone who reads it as they reflect upon His gracious dealings with this branch of His church over the centuries. In His sovereign will and purpose He has maintained a witness to the attainments of the Scottish Covenanted Second Reformation in Ireland. As the Irish Reformed Presbyterian Church will, God-willing celebrate the bi-centenary of the Synod in 2011, we look forward humbly to continuing our testimony to the saving and finished work of Christ and declaring His Kingship over all things, waiting and working until His return.

> *"According to the grace of God which was given to me, as a wise master builder I have laid the foundation, and another builds on it. But let each one take heed how he builds on it. For no other foundation can anyone lay than that which is laid, which is Jesus Christ."* 1 Corinthians 3:10-11

Rev. Geoffrey Allen
Compiler on behalf of the Publications Committee

Rev. Prof. Dr. Adam Loughridge

NORTHERN PRESBYTERY

Ballyclabber Meeting House

BALLYCLABBER

In 1642 the Scottish Parliament sent an army to Ulster to defend those who had migrated from Scotland to Ulster during the Plantation. These colonists, better known as the Ulster Scots, had come under attack from the native, Gaelic Irish of Ulster who had rebelled against the English Crown the year before. The Scottish army was accompanied by chaplains who adhered to the National Covenant. The soldiers and ministers were based in Carrickfergus from where the influence of Presbyterianism, in its early covenanted form, spread in all directions. It came north to Coleraine which became one of the garrison towns of the occupying Scottish army.

In the spring of 1644 the Solemn League and Covenant was administered in the area. A record of the proceedings states that it was the soldiers who first gave their pledge. They were followed by the people of the surrounding area who solemnly acknowledged the Covenant by lifting up their hands to God. On the first day, very few of the townsmen entered into the Covenant but, in the following week, the Mayor set an example and then

many of the townsmen supported him. The Covenant was also sworn at Billy and Dunluce.
So, from an early date the Covenanting cause was established in the Coleraine district.

Hogsherd Memorial Stone at Ballyrashane Presbyterian Meeting House

Robert Hogsherd, from Glasgow was ordained in nearby Ballyrashane Parish in October
1657, but was deposed for non-conformity and his adherence to the Covenant in 1661, a
stone above the door of the present Presbyterian meeting house marks this event. It was
difficult to maintain this cause after 1660. Only occasionally were Covenanting principles
set forth and that mainly by David Houston at Derrykeighan in the 1690s and by John
Cameron, a Scottish probationer who preached in Dunluce Presbyterian Church. James
McKinney had the supervision of the society at Ballyrashane when he was the minister of
Dervock and Kilraughts from 1783 to 1793.

The regular history of Ballyclabber begins in 1805. On 10 April the society of
Ballyrashane was separated from the congregation of 'Lower Antrim' (which was
comprised of Dervock and Kilraughts and Ballymoney) and became linked with Dunboe
(or Ringrash). Dunboe may have been previously connected with the congregation of
'Bannside' (which comprised Ballylaggan, Limavady, Drimbolg and Magherafelt). The
congregation, formed from this merger, met in a thatched building on the Ballyrashane
Road. On 10 December 1805, Mr. David Graham, a Burgher Seceder until less than a year
before, preached trial sermons before the Reformed Presbytery. The trials were sustained
and he was ordained the next day. The settlement was not to last. After only two years,

he left the congregation, which met at 'Clabor Meeting House', and emigrated to America where he became a prominent lawyer in New York. However, during this short period, the congregation received some encouragement when a third society, at Bushtown, left Ballylaggan and joined the new congregation.

After a vacancy of eight years, the congregation, then known as 'Coleraine', was further strengthened in 1811 by the accession of twenty-four families from the Burgher Seceders. Consequently, the congregation issued a call to Robert Gamble Orr, a member of the congregation at Grange, Co. Tyrone. He was ordained on 30 August 1815 at Clabor Meeting House. Not a popular preacher, and therefore soon suffering from arrears of stipend, his relations with the people were never happy and he was released from the pastoral tie by the Presbytery at his own request after a ministry of five years. For some years he acted as stated supply in Limavady and the Western Presbytery before emigrating to America about 1833.

In 1816 we find the first reference to the name 'Ballyclabber', and in 1826 'Ringrash' is used in preference to the older name 'Dunboe'. If the early history of Ballyclabber was marked by short pastorates and long vacancies, a new era began on 12 September 1827 for there have been only five ministers since then.

Samuel Carlisle, a member of Creevagh and a licentiate of the Southern Presbytery, served the congregation faithfully from 1827 until his death in 1856, aged 67. He was known as a diligent, punctual, humble and unobtrusive pastor. His daughter, Leticia, married William McCollum of Inchmearn and his influence remains in the congregation through the McCollum family. The Smyths of Drimbolg are descended from his younger daughter, Martha.

During the vacancy which followed, in 1858, the Dunboe/Ringrash part of the congregation separated from the Ballyrashane/Clabor part. The desire for separation was mutual. Meanwhile, in Ballyclabber, James Dick Houston, son of Rev. Thomas Houston of Knockbracken, was ordained and installed pastor to the congregation on 15 October 1862. At this time there were 9 societies, comprising 70 families, 155 communicants, 28 adherents and 106 children. A man of outstanding gifts, and nobility of character, Rev. J.

D. Houston served the congregation and the whole Church with great distinction until his death, aged 75, on 27 April 1910. He held the offices of Clerk of Presbytery, Clerk of Synod and Professor of Church History.

On 25 April 1911, Rev. James Renwick Wright was installed minister of the congregation. Brought up in Cullybackey, he had served as minister in Creevagh for seven years. A humble and devoted man of God, he brought to all his work a sense of commitment and a spirit of faithfulness. To mark the centenary of the building of the meeting house, in 1947, Rev. Alexander Wright, minister of Ballylaggan, gave an historical sketch of the congregation which was subsequently published. During the century covered by this account, the congregation had halved in size, due to the formation of the Ringrash congregation, nineteenth century emigration and twentieth century migration, to 34 families and 87 communicants. Rev. J. R. Wright retired from active duty on 27 September 1955 and died on 1 January 1964. He is still remembered with affection in the congregation, and his family served the Church with distinction: Mrs. Norman Holmes in Ballymoney, Rev. Hugh Wright and Rev. Renwick Wright.

Rev. Thomas Donnelly, minister of Faughan, was installed on 17 May 1956. Giving himself to a diligent study of God's Word, he was an able preacher, a gifted editor of the Church's magazine and a faithful pastor of this people; he maintained the high traditions of the Gospel ministry in Ballyclabber. A happy relationship existed between pastor and people for forty-two years. Mr. Donnelly retired from the active duties of the ministry on 17 May 1998 and died on 13 December 2001.

On 9 October 2001, Warren Peel, a member of Trinity congregation and a licentiate of the Eastern Presbytery, educated at Oxford University and the Reformed Theological College, was ordained and installed as minister of Ballyclabber.

The following men have served the congregation as ruling elders: William Anderson, Andrew Auld, Andrew Calderwood, John Clark, Joseph McDonald, Neal McIntyre, Thomas Nevin, Samuel Pollock, Thomas McCandless, James Warnock, Edward Anderson,

Robert McCaughan, David Thompson, James Wilson, John Morrell, John Brown, James McFall, John Kennedy, William McCollum, James Nevin, Archibald McDonald, James Carlisle, Hugh Cheyne, Robert Nevin, William Ramsey, William Williamson, John McWilliams, James McWilliams, Alexander Higgins, William John Nevin, John McClements, Robert J. Macafee, William Maxwell, John McDowell, Robert Fleming, William Brewster, David Nevin, David J. McCollum, Robert McCaughan, James R. McKee, James Kennedy, Thomas Carson, Joseph Dale McEwen, Samuel McCollum, James McCollum, David H. McCollum, Robert James McCaughan, Robert Carson, Ian McMaster, Robert Morrison, John McCaughan (Ballyversal), William McCollum (Ballycairn), David McCollum (Blagh), Carlisle McCollum (Inchmearn) and Morrell McCollum (Boghill).

The present meeting house was built in 1847, replacing the original thatched one erected in 1804. Through the years the congregation has kept the property in an excellent state of repair. In 1890 the meeting house was renovated at a cost of £900. In 1965 the erection of a hall proved an attractive and useful addition to the facilities of the congrega-

tion. In 1975 a plot of ground was purchased from Mr. Colvin, adjacent to the car park, for a burying ground. The prime mover in this project was Mr. Thomas Carson and, in fact, it was his remains that were the first to enter the new burying ground after his death on 26 December 1976. A major addition to the congregation's property was the erection of a new hall which was opened on 22 February 1997. In association with this event a fortnight of special evangelistic services were arranged. The preachers were two sons of the congregation – Rev. Professor Robert McCollum (Lisburn) and Rev. Dr. Renwick Wright (Beaver Falls, USA).

Mr. Carlisle lived on a farm at Lisnarick, and a manse was erected near the church on the Ballyrashane Road for his successor in 1867 at a cost of £700. Mr. and Mrs. Donnelly, purchased a house in Coleraine in 1992. Four years later the committee decided to sell the manse. The congregation has provided the following men as students for the ministry: William Anderson, Samuel Carlisle, David McFall, Thomas McFall, John Ramsey, Hugh Wright, James Renwick Wright, Robert McCollum, Philip McCollum and Robert McCollum. To these we might add Robert John Morrell from Ringrash and William John Nevin, an elder in the congregation, who later became a minister in America.

Those who have worshipped in Ballyclabber have been uplifted by the quality of the praise. Through the years, several precentors, or choir leaders, have served in this capacity. Their names are: David Ramsey, Matthew Creelman, James McWilliams, John McClements, Thomas Simpson, Robert Freeman, Lisabel Cunningham, Margaretta Macafee, Thomas McFall, Thomas Carson, John McCaughan, Alison McCollum, Richard McCaughan, Robert McCollum and Stephen Wilson.

As a congregation Ballyclabber is looking in three directions. First, upwards - to worship Almighty God, Father, Son and Holy Spirit, in everything to set Him at the centre of their lives, as individuals, families and as a church. Secondly, inwards - to love and care for each other, building up each other in faith, equipping one another to walk better in God's ways. Thirdly, outwards - to reach out to the world with the Good News of salvation and so make disciples of all nations, beginning in their own community.

Synod held at Ballyclabber, 1979

The Meeting House is situated at 35 Ballyrashane Road, Coleraine, BT52 2NL.

Ballylaggan Meeting House

BALLYLAGGAN

The early history of Ballylaggan is closely linked with that of Drimbolg and Limavady. Many in north County Londonderry adhered to the Covenants from 1644 and between 1680 and 1696 and were familiar with the ministry of David Houston. On 2 July 1757, at the Vow, Mr. William Martin, a native of Co. Londonderry, was ordained to the Gospel Ministry. He was the first Reformed Presbyterian Minister ordained in Ireland and he must have preached at times to the Ballylaggan Society. In 1760 the Societies were divided into two Congregations separated by the Bann. Mr. Martin chose Antrim and Down for his field of labour, and resided at Kells.

In 1763 a third Congregation was organised along the Bannside, over which Mr. Matthew Lynn was ordained on 21 August. The congregation increased in number and in strength during Matthew Lynn's ministry from 1763 to 1773. He laboured for ten years in his native land, and then left for America in 1773. He died there on 21 April 1800.

A similar pattern of healthy society meetings and regular open-air preaching was followed by Samuel Aiken who was ordained about 1776, and ministered to the Bannside Congregation with its dependents, Dervock and Limavady, after the emigration of Mr. Lynn to America. Mr. Aiken's ministry in connection with Bannside must have been very brief. When the Irish Reformed Presbytery became extinct in 1780 (owing to Mr. Stavely being the only active minister) he does not seem to have been engaged in the duties of the ministry. Later on in 1790 he was installed in Ballylane, with charge of Ballybay and Rathfriland. He died on 25 December 1798.

The next name associated with Ballylaggan is Rev. James McKinney. He was ordained and installed minister of the congregation of Kirkhills or Dervock on 4 October 1783. His charge was very extensive, embracing the northwest portion of Co. Antrim, and a large part of Co. Londonderry, including the oversight of Ballylaggan. He was supposed to have been associated with the United Irishmen, and in 1793 he had to leave for America. A man of great learning, patriotic fervour, burning eloquence, and indefatigable exertions (see May 1831 Covenanter), he died in South Carolina on 16 September 1802, having organised many Reformed Presbyterian congregations in America.

Joseph Orr, from St. Johnston in Donegal, was ordained at Caw Wood near Garvagh in April 1798. By this time, the Covenanters of Ballylaggan worshipped in a meeting house on the Curragh Road, Aghadowey, 5 miles south of Coleraine, on the main route from Coleraine to Kilrea. It is interesting to note that the Ballylaggan Minutes of Session date back to Mr. Orr's ministry. The first Minute of Session recorded is that of a meeting of 'the Session of Ballylaggan Correspondent and part of Maghera Congregation of Presbyterian Covenanters', held on 13th June 1803. The members of Session present were : Rev. Joseph Orr, Moderator; Messrs David Smyth, James Smyth and John Oliver. As Mr. Orr lived at Drumlamph, near Castledawson, the strain of ministering to such a large scattered congregation was very great indeed and, on a total stipend of £52, he had a struggle to make ends meet. In 1805 Mr .Orr was relieved of the care of Limavady and in the following year the large society of Bushtown was transferred from Ballylaggan to Dunboe (Ringrash). Between 1805 and 1816 he had responsibility for the reduced congregation in Ballylaggan, Garvagh and Drimbolg.

In 1816 Mr. Orr resigned the pastorate of Ballylaggan and his other responsibilities, but retained that of Drimbolg. When he died in 1825 the congregation was in a position for the first time to call a minister of their own. Their choice was Simon Cameron and he was ordained on 10 September 1817. The year 1840 witnessed the commencement of one of the most important events of Mr. Cameron's ministry, the erection of the present Meeting House. There is much obscurity regarding the old building. According to tradition, the services were originally held in the open air. The first building was certainly in existence in 1804. It does not seem to have been a very imposing edifice. The roof was thatched, and must have been very low, as the horses were able to help themselves to the thatch during the service. The floor was earthen, and covered with rushes. In bad weather the water on the floor was often inches deep, and consequently the seating accommodation was anything but stationary. Notwithstanding these adverse conditions, the members attended most regularly and faithfully. Mr. Cameron ministered faithfully for 36 years. The bond that accompanied his call is a very unusual one:

We, the members of Ballylaggan congregation, promise to pay Rev. Simon Cameron, ordained our pastor, the sum of £40 annually for three-fourths of the time, and 11 shillings and 4½ pence for each day that he shall preach in the congregation more than the said time. This sum to be paid regularly in such divisions and at such times as may be thought most prudent.

Date Stone on Ballylaggan Meeting House

Mr. Cameron lived at Drumsteeple. He retired from the active duties of the ministry in 1853.   Until his death in 1855 he received a retiring allowance of £12 a year from the Ironmongers Company of London. He passed away on 11 March 1855, at the age of 73, his remains being interred in the Ballylaggan burying ground. In the Minutes of Synod, 14 July 1856, the following appears, "Mr. Cameron, an honoured servant of God, in the Ministry of His Son Jesus Christ, during the period of 38 years, was distinguished for humility, simplicity and the love of truth and peace. He was an example to all his brethren of regularity and punctuality in his attendance on the meetings of Church-Courts, and in his observance of all other public duties, as well as of strict conscientiousness and brotherly kindness in the visitation of the sick, and attention to all other private pastoral duties. He possessed the esteem and respect of all with whom he was conversant. "The memory of the just is blessed."

Mr. Cameron's wife was Esther Stavely, daughter of the famous William Stavely.

During Mr. Cameron's ministry the following young people, brought up in the congregation were ordained to the Gospel Ministry:
- On 15 October 1818 William Anderson, was licensed and later ordained in Loanhead in the autumn of 1820.
- On 26 June 1827, Mr. James Smyth, was ordained in Drimbolg.
- On 18 May 1843, Mr. James Kennedy was ordained in Broadlane, Newton-Limavady.
- On 30 May 1849, Mr. Alexander Savage was ordained in Ballenon.

The congregation of Garvagh separated from Ballylaggan in 1855 and Joseph Hamilton, a licentiate of the Northern Presbytery, ministered there from 1867 until 1872 and James Littlejohn from Lorne in Argyllshire served from 1876 until 1893.

The next minister of Ballylaggan was John Hart. He was brought up in the Rathfriland congregation, and was ordained in Ballylaggan on 10 October 1854. There were then 9 Societies in the congregation, comprising 70 families and 160 members. One of the important incidents in Mr. Hart's ministry was an act of Covenant renovation engaged in on Monday, 26 May 1856. Mr. Hart was assisted by Rev. James Smyth of Drimbolg, and Rev. James Kennedy of Broadlane. In the earliest list of collectors were names that maintained a long connection with the congregation such as Misses McConnell, Kennedy, McQuillan, Smyth, Savage, Hogan, Barr, Love, Moodie, Cathcart; Mrs. Rodgers; Messrs MacMillan, W. Kennedy and W. Dunlop. In 1863 the congregation had 260 members and paid £80 in stipend. Mr. Hart laboured for 28 years until his death on 18 April 1883 and was buried in Ballylaggan.

During Mr. Hart's period of office several young men connected with the congregation were ordained to the Gospel Ministry:

- On 20 October 1858, Mr. J. A. Moody was ordained in Convoy and in 1860 he went to Cullybackey.

- On 15 February 1865, Mr. Robert Dunlop was licensed and on 2 May of the same year he was called to Convoy and eventually went to Paisley, where he laboured all his days. For many years he was the Editor of the Reformed Presbyterian Witness.

- On 20 May 1875, Mr. M. A. Gault was ordained by the Iowa Presbytery of the American R. P. Church. His parents, John and Martha Gault, were members of Ballylaggan. They emigrated to America when he was two years old.

A son of the congregation, Rev. John Lynd, born at Knockaduff, within the bounds of the Ballylaggan congregation, and educated at Magee College between 1867 and 1871, where he graduated with First Class Honours in Mental and Moral Science, had begun his ministry in the United States and was licensed by the New York Presbytery on 20 May 1873 and later ordained and installed at Baltimore and Belle Center. In 1877 he was appointed Professor of English Literature and Greek at Beacer College, Ohio. After twelve years service in America, he returned and on 5 June 1885, he was installed in Ballylaggan serving from 1885 to 1889. He left to become the first minister of Dublin Road congregation, Belfast and was Professor of Hebrew in the Theological Hall from 1895 to 1921. He died in 1926 and was buried in Ballylaggan.

On 1 May 1889, Mr. Samuel Guiler Kennedy, one of the Ballylaggan young people, was licensed to preach the Gospel. He was ordained in Wishaw in November, 1889, and installed in Grosvenor Road, Belfast, on 5 February 1896. He became a Professor in the Theological Hall in 1910.

There followed three short ministries in the next fifteen years. Andrew Cross Gregg from Convoy began his ministry in Ballylaggan in 1890 and after seven promising years he spent more than forty years in a distinguished ministry in Scotland at Loanhead and Greenock. For many years he was the gifted editor of the Scottish Reformed Presbyterian Witness.

During Mr. Gregg's ministry, Mr. Robert Blair, son of one of the elders, went to America, and was later ordained to the Gospel ministry. He was sent as a Missionary to China, where he contracted eye trouble, which ultimately resulted in blindness.

Andrew Melville Thompson, a licentiate of the American Church, was minister from 16 August 1898 to 31 January 1901. He went on to serve in Geelong, Australia, for five years and in Stranorlar for three years before returning to America.

Thomas Alexander McIlfatrick, brought up in Drimbolg, had a four-year ministry from 2 August 1901 to 1905 before entering the Free Church of Scotland and later serving the Irish Presbyterian Church at Belturbet, Broughshane and Sligo.

The ministry of William McCullough in the years 1906 to 1917 was still remembered by the older people in the 1970s for its unique and distinctive character. He ministered with great faithfulness in Drimbolg until his death in 1957.

His successor, Rev. Robert Nevin Lyons, came to Ballylaggan from Ballenon in 1920. With his gift for friendship and his warm evangelical spirit, he served with devotion for five years before accepting a call to Grosvenor Road, Belfast, where his life's work was effectively accomplished.

Following a testing nine-year vacancy, Alexander Reid Wright from Cullybackey was ordained in October, 1934. There followed a long, busy and very effective ministry of 37 years. In 1943 the Original Secession congregation at nearby Dromore, became vacant and with their difficulty in getting supplies during the war, Rev. Wright conducted a service each Sabbath until 1956 when the Scottish Secession churches were united with the Church of Scotland, and Dromore was received into the General Assembly. In addition to the work in Ballylaggan he continued to be in charge of the congregation in Garvagh until its closure in 1970. In 1961 at the request of the Board of Evangelism and Church Extension he was the minister in charge of a new work in Castleroe, a residential area on the outskirts of Coleraine. The work began in October, 1961 and continued for 26 years the final meeting taking place in October 1987. The wooden hall that was used in Castleroe was transported to Tullyvallen where it served as a centre for youth work in the congregation. Mr. Wright had contributed for many years to a children's page in the 'Covenanter' magazine, extracts from these pages were later published into one volume. Sadly failing health brought about his early retirement in December, 1971. He is remembered as one who maintained his own high standard in an unforgotten pulpit and pastoral ministry.

The ministry of his successor, Rev. Joseph Alexander Cresswell Blair, began in May, 1973 amid high hopes and fervent prayers. In two short years his work was done and God called him to higher service in April 1975. He leaves behind him a fragrant memory and 'being dead yet speaketh'.

After a short vacancy, Robert McCollum, a member of Ballyclabber congregation, a licentiate of the Northern Presbytery, educated at Queen's University and Theological Hall, was ordained and installed minister of the congregation on 13 October 1976. During his ministry a six-month exchange took place in 1980 with Rev. Robert McFarland, Quinter R.P. church, Kansas, USA. On 14 December 1981 Mr McCollum accepted the call of the Eastern Presbytery and was commissioned on 23 January 1982 to serve as organising pastor to the Society of Covenanters meeting in Lisburn. The congregation appreciated the fine work which he had done in his pastorate of over five years.

The congregation called another licentiate from the Northern Presbytery, David McKay, a member of Glenmanus congregation, educated at the University of Ulster, London University, and the Theological College in Belfast. He was ordained and installed minister of the congregation on 6 April 1984. Having served the congregation for eleven years, the congregation was saddened when Dr. McKay accepted a call to Cregagh Road congregation on 24 April 1995.

Another chapter in the congregation's long history began with the ordination and installation of Nigel Agnew on 21 November 1997. Mr. Agnew, a member of the Ballylane congregation and a licentiate of the Southern Presbytery, was educated at Queen's University and the Reformed Theological College. He accepted a call from the Creevagh congregation and was installed there on 8 September 2006.

The congregation has been served by the following ruling elders: John Oliver, James Archibald, James Ross, William Kennedy, James Jamison, James Smyth, Robert Archibald, John Barr, Robert McConnell, Samuel McMillan, Samuel Lamont, William James Adams, William McFall, John McFall, John Kelly, John Torrens, Tom Warnock, Andy Barr, Robert McCahon, Ian McMaster, George Dunlop, Hugh Creelman, Lyons Wright, Norman McIlfatrick, Harry Forgrave, Robert James Creelman. At time of writing, the present members of Session are Hugh B. Barr, James McNeill, Samuel Pollock, Thomas Pollock, Richard Pollock, Samuel Quigley, Robbie Quigg, James Edward Salmon and Hugh Wright.

The congregation provided the following men to the work of the Gospel ministry: Samuel Brown Wylie, Samuel Wylie, William Anderson, James Alexander Smyth, William Henry, James Neill, James Kennedy, George Savage, Alexander Savage, Joseph Archibald Moody, Robert Dunlop, James Kennedy, Samuel Guiler Kennedy, John Lynd, John McFall, Wallace McCollum, Andrew Quigley and Stephen Wright.

The meeting house at Ballylaggan was built about 1800 and the present building dates back to 1841. For many years the stones out of which the new meeting house was built, lay in a heap near its present site, and it was a common observation of the people on the Sabbath morn, "We'll go to the cairn o'stanes the day." The present building was opened on 3 September 1841; Dr. Symington preached from Haggai 2; 7 and Dr. Stavely from Psalm 24; 7. The collection taken up amounted to £32. The total cost was £372. During the ministry of Rev A. C. Gregg very extensive alterations and repairs to the meeting house were carried out. The total cost was about £400.

The congregation responded to the leadership of Rev. Alexander Reid Wright in building a new manse in 1951 and a new Church Hall in 1970. In 1993 the congregation carried out extensive renovations to their church hall, which included a new roof, the former kitchen converted into a storage area and a new kitchen.

Currently without their own minister since 2006, it is the congregation's prayer that, in the Lord's time, they will have a minister of their own that they may go forward with the knowledge that He will lead them in their witness and vision for the future.

The Meeting House is situated at 81 Curragh Road, Ballylaggan, Coleraine BT51 4BS.

The 'Wee Green Hall'.

CASTLEROE

In 1960, each Presbytery was asked by Synod to investigate the possibilities of new work within its area. A small committee, consisting of Revs. Hugh Blair, Isaac Cole, Adam Loughridge and A. R. Wright, with Synod's evangelist Mr Harry Tadley, met on 21 March 1961 and discussed the situation. After thinking of several areas and factors, they decided that the Castleroe area, Coleraine, should be further considered. This was reported to Synod which considered the reports from the various Presbyteries and decided that work should be commenced in Castleroe. A number of factors influenced this decision. There were some R.P. members and former members living in the immediate area and others quite near. There was no place of worship in the area, the nearest church of any denomination being about two miles distant.

The local council had announced plans to double the number of houses in the immediate area. Most important, a number of praying Christians, who were concerned about the spiritual situation in the area, were anxious that we should work there with their support. A site was purchased, the ground was levelled and a sectional wooden hall erected and furnished, for the opening prayer meeting on Saturday, 14 October 1961, and the opening service the next evening.

Special services were conducted by Rev. Sinclair Horne, Loanhead, for two weeks, with a children's meeting every evening before the main meeting. At this time eleven children professed conversion, though most of them later moved out of the Castleroe area.

Arrangements were made for the work to continue with a children's meeting and a fellowship meeting each Friday, Sabbath School each Sabbath afternoon and a worship service each Sabbath evening. At first, Mr Harry Tadley was responsible for visiting in the area and conducting the two meetings each Friday except when he was engaged in evangelistic work elsewhere. Rev. A. R. Wright, Ballylaggan, was appointed to supervise the work and to conduct the Sabbath School and services. When Mr Tadley became a student for the ministry, the responsibility for all meetings and visiting was undertaken by Mr Wright, until he retired at the end of 1971.

During this period, there was a good response from people in the area. Records show that the children's meetings were attended by 45-55 children, and in these Mr Wright was ably supported by his wife. The Sabbath School too had a good number of pupils and teachers, some of the teachers being from the area. The fellowship meetings and services were also well attended, and greatly appreciated.

After Rev. A. R. Wright retired, the ministers of the Northern Presbytery became responsible for the work, conducting most of the Sabbath evening services. The Sabbath School continued until the middle of 1986, with varying numbers. Once there were 50 children, and ten teachers. Latterly, half of the children were from Ballylaggan congregation, coming for extra Bible study in addition to their own Sabbath School, and the other half were children who had lived in the area but had moved away and were being transported by the teachers. This period was really enjoyed by teachers and pupils, but it was not serving the original purpose of the work, and in 1986 it was agreed that the Sabbath School should be suspended.

Over the years, circumstances in Castleroe changed greatly. Most of the original local supporters died or left the area. There were still some local people who attended latterly, but they were few in number. The population of the area decreased and the promised houses were built in another area.

The oversight of the Castleroe work from 1972 was the responsibility of a committee of the Northern Presbytery and a local committee, who met jointly every quarter. After considering the situation over a long period, the joint committees recommended to Presbytery that the work should be discontinued. Presbytery appreciated all that had been done since 1961, but agreed with the committees, and on 2 September 1987 asked the members to make arrangements to discontinue the work. At the same meeting Presbytery appointed a committee to consider other possibilities of outreach within its bounds.

Looking back over the 26 years, the seed of the Word had been faithfully sown, and there clearly was fruit, souls having been saved, and believers having been built up in the faith. Many gained experience in teaching and in leading fellowship meetings. Some ministers took their first meetings or services in 'the wee green hall,' as it was known locally.

When the decision was taken that the work should be discontinued the committee offered the hall to the congregations of Fairview and Tullyvallen who had quite a number of children and young people, and had considered the provision of a hall, but owing to extension work at the manse they had postponed such a project. The committees therefore offered the hall and contents to these congregations, if they would be responsible for its removal and re-erection. This offer was gratefully accepted.

On Sabbath evening, 18 October 1987, the closing service was held in the Castleroe hall. The service was conducted by Rev. David McKay, Ballylaggan, Moderator of Presbytery and a member of the Presbytery's Castleroe committee. The address was given by Rev. Wallace McCollum, Cullybackey, who also spoke of his association with the work since his childhood, through his student days when he taught in the Sabbath School and later preached in the hall, and latterly as convener of the Presbytery's committee responsible for the work. The hall was transported to South Armagh where it was re-erected beside the manse, and became a central place of work for Fairview and Tullyvallen congregations.

Ballymoney Meeting House

BALLYMONEY

There was a Covenanting presence in the Ballymoney area prior to 1757 when the Covenanting stalwart, Rev. William Martin, formed the first Covenanter church at the Vow, and was also given the charge of Ballymoney. The 'Society People', as they were known in those days, formed cottage societies throughout the district in places such as Eden, Claughy, Ballygan, Ballycraigy, Ballyboggie, Milltown, Ballyboyland, Culduff and Ballymoney. The Covenanters in the Ballymoney district worshipped either in Kilraughts or Dervock.

In 1830, a meeting house, very similar to the present building, was erected in the town of Ballymoney in an area once known as Brewery Lane, now called Charlotte Street. At a meeting of the Northern Presbytery on 20 October 1830 a request was made 'for ministerial assistance, as a new house of worship in Ballymoney required additional ministerial aid'. Presbytery took action by dividing the existing congregation, worshipping in three places, into two congregations. The Covenanters in Kilraughts continued as one congregation while those from Dervock and Ballymoney made up a second, separate   congregation, though still meeting in the two locations of Ballymoney and Dervock. (The meeting house for those in the Dervock area was at Carnaff which was erected about 1800.) Rev. William John Stavely, who had been ordained as minister of the original large congregation in 1804, remained as minister of the new Dervock/Ballymoney congregation at a stipend of £70 a year, each portion of the congregation to pay £35.   There was a joint Session in the early years, but each congregation had a separate committee. In 1832 the congregation in Ballymoney was served by Benjamin Thompson, Malcolm Cameron, Thomas Ramsey, John Picken, Samuel Smith, James Warnock, James Lyons and John Gregg.

The new congregation was disturbed for ten years by the controversy that affected the Church regarding the power of the Civil Magistrate in spiritual affairs. This led to the withdrawal of the Eastern Presbytery from Synod and the forming, in 1842, of a separate Synod. A number of members associated with the dissentients and formed a congregation that met in the Old Town Hall. They had only one minister, Dr. John Paul Marcus, a gifted scholar who conducted a classical school in the town and ran a farm at Moneygobbin in addition to his pastoral duties. On his death in 1876 the congregation ceased to exist.

The harmonious relationship between Ballymoney and Dervock continued under the ministry of Rev. Dr. W. J. Stavely until his retirement in 1860.

Dr. Stavely's successor was James Brown of Rathfriland, a licentiate of the Southern Presbytery. He was ordained at Dervock on 25 July 1860. The joint congregations of Ballymoney and Dervock made rapid progress under his leadership and gifted ministry; Ballymoney grew to 200 members. Petitions were presented at the Northern Presbytery in November 1877 asking that the Ballymoney part of the congregation be separated. This request was granted and the minute of Presbytery states, 'Mr Brown, having signified acceptance of the Ballymoney part of the congregation, the relation existing between him and it was confirmed, and, at the same time, the relation between him and the Dervock end was dissolved.' James Brown continued his ministry in Ballymoney until his death on 28 July 1883. The growth of the congregation under Mr. Brown necessitated, in 1866, the addition of a gallery in the church to seat an additional 100 persons.

A new era for the congregation began with the ordination on 7 December 1886 of John Ramsay, a member of Ballyclabber and a licentiate of the Northern Presbytery. This gifted scholar, writer, educationalist, athlete and social reformer served the congregation, and the Church as a whole, with great distinction for more than half a century until his retirement in June 1940. He died on 26 November 1954. His gifts were evident in his work as Editor of The Covenanter and Professor of Hebrew and Biblical Criticism at the Theological Hall.

On Professor Ramsay's retirement, the congregation again called a member of Ballyclabber and a licentiate of the Northern Presbytery - James Renwick Wright. He was ordained on 7 January 1941. After an able and zealous ministry of twelve years, Rev. J. Renwick Wright accepted a call to Dromara on 3 December 1952.

His successor, Rev. Hugh Jamison Blair, son of Rev. James Blair, was brought up in the manses of Milford and Kilraughts. He graduated with honours in Philosophy from Trinity College, Dublin in 1939 and, having completed his training at the Theological Hall, was minister of the Loanhead congregation in Scotland between 1942 and 1953. He was installed in Ballymoney on 11 June 1953. He brought to all his work outstanding ability and great devotion and, in addition to his excellent pulpit and pastoral work, was appointed to the Chair of Old Testament Language and Literature in the Theological Hall in 1960. A Boys' Brigade Company (2nd Ballymoney) was formed in 1968 and a Girls' Brigade Company (273rd N.I.) was formed in 1976. Having completed 40 years as minister of Ballymoney, Rev. Dr. Hugh J. Blair retired on 21 June 1993.

Rev. H. Ian. G. Morrison, minister of Creevagh Congregation, was installed as minister on 10 June 1994. He resigned as minister on 4 November 1999.

Rev. Edward McCollum, minister of Knockbracken congregation, was installed on 14 January 2005.

During the period of its separate existence, the Ballymoney congregation has elected the following to serve as ruling elders: Hugh Hamill, Joseph Lamont, Samuel Lyons, John McIlroy, James Warnock, Robert Holmes, J. S. Brown, Andrew Wilson, James F. Taylor,

James C. Foster, William J. Pinkerton, James Pinkerton, William Warnock, Samuel L. Lyons, William John Lyons, John Calderwood, J. A. Lyons, Harold B. Holmes, John C. Calderwood, John Brewster, William James Brewster, James L. McAfee, Henry M. Wilson, James C. Carson, William A. McKeeman, James A. Simpson, James R.W. Calderwood, James R. Dymond, Robert Hart, R. Paul Hawkins, J. Martin Wilson, Thomas J. Brewster, R. G. Neville Dawson, Ian McC. Forgrave, Frank M. Stewart, Hugh McClug-gage, James B. Pinkerton and H. Raymond Wilson.

Students for the ministry who were raised in the congregation have been Alexander McLeod Stavely Lyons, William Warnock, Robert Biggart Lyons and William Norris Semple Wilson.

In 1957 a well equipped lecture hall, erected in memory of Mr. and Mrs. Robert Holmes and Mrs. Maureen Algeo by their respective families, has proved a great asset to the congregation and to the community. In 1968 the Manse at Enagh, purchased for Professor Ramsay in 1886, was sold and a house in Charles Street provided a new manse in a more convenient location. A new extension to the church building consisting of a minor hall, session room and kitchen was opened on 7 April 1978 by Mrs. Brewster, widow of elder John Brewster. An extension to the Holmes Memorial Hall, consisting of ancillary rooms and a new kitchen was opened on 29 October 1980 by Mrs. Marie Holmes and Mrs. Molly J. Holmes, O.B.E., J.P. In April 2002 work commenced on the replacement of the Church roof. The work lasted for longer than anticipated and involved the replacement of defective internal timbers, internal and external painting, improvement to external drainage systems, lowering of external paths to meet health and safety regulations and a new internal lighting system. The work was completed in 2003. The adjacent former Court House was added to the complex.

The congregation, having given Mr. McCollum the opportunity to purchase his own house, rented out the manse on Charles Street. In the second half of 2006, the church building has undergone extensive repairs because of a dry rot problem. The pews were removed, a new floor laid, interior and exterior render was removed and replaced after the walls had been treated for dry rot. Pews were reinstalled and a new sound system was put in.

Provision has also been made for wheelchair access and a disabled toilet, etc., in line with current legislation.

The congregation has a witness to many outside its bounds through the work of the Boys' Brigade and the Girls' Brigade. Their prayer is that the Word of God would have free course and be glorified.

The Meeting House is situated at 75 Charlotte Street, Ballymoney, Co. Antrim, BT53 6AZ.

Bushmills Meeting House

BUSHMILLS

A Society of Covenanters was meeting in Bushmills from an early date and was part of the original Antrim Congregation. John Cameron, a Scottish probationer was ordained at Dunluce in 1752 and served for three years. In 1840 the Bushmills Society of Covenanters, which was connected to Dervock, was taken under the care of the Mission Board as a Mission Station. Regular preaching was maintained and a meeting house was built following the 99 year lease of a property from the MacNaughton estate in 1836. The congregation was never strong enough to call a minister and was served by the minister of Dervock. Regular services were held latterly by Rev. R. J. McIlmoyle, but discontinued in 1922 and the occasional meetings finally ceased in the 1930s after a century of witness. The former meeting house at 81a Main Street is located in the car park between Main Street and the River Bush, on what was formally known as Meeting House Lane. It fell into disrepair but has recently been converted into a workshop.

Cloughmills old and new Meeting House

CLOUGHMILLS

The village of Cloughmills in County Antrim is approximately twelve miles from Ballymena and eight miles from Ballymoney. When the congregation of Cullybackey was organised in 1765, Cloughmills was one of the societies under its care. By 1800 a second society had been created, and both were organised into a congregation united with Cullybackey. In 1805, due to the commitment of two members of Kilraughts, John Baird and James Loughridge, together with support from the Cullybackey congregation, the

Reformed Presbyterian meeting house was built at Cloughmills on the Drumbare Road on the edge of the village. This came to be affectionately known to local people as the 'Old Meeting House'. Covenanters in the Cullybackey/Cloughmills congregation shared the ministry of Rev. William Stavely with Kellswater until 1813 when advancing years led him to relinquish the northern part of this widespread charge.

In 1818 the Cullybackey and Cloughmills congregation was transferred by Synod to the Eastern Presbytery. In 1841 when Cullybackey withdrew from the R.P. Synod to become, for 65 years, a congregation of the Eastern R.P. Synod, Cloughmills adhered to the parent body and, with the Kilraughts congregation taking increasing responsibility for it, the congregation returned to the Northern Presbytery.

From 1840 onwards, Presbytery met regularly at Cloughmills. In 1845 Cloughmills and Portglenone were united as a joint charge. The link was dissolved in 1856, circumstances, particularly the depopulation that followed the disastrous Great Famine, having prevented the settlement of a minister. From that time Portglenone became associated with Drimbolg, and around 1858 Cloughmills began once again a happy association with Kilraughts that continued for over 140 years. In 1856 a licentiate was appointed to work in Cloughmills and it was reported to Synod that his work had succeeded in reviving an interest in the cause of the Covenanted Reformation in the community. But the experiment was not continued and, while support for the work remained steady and encouraging, the congregation was unable to retain its standing, due to rural depopulation following the First World War and was reduced to the status of a Preaching Station in 1934.

Until the early 1990s no new initiatives were undertaken although evening services took place twice a month, and weeks of mission were carried on occasionally, whilst the building was refurbished in 1971. The responsibility for the proclamation of the Gospel on a bimonthly basis in Cloughmills was, for the most part, with the minister of Kilraughts: Rev. James Blair until 1966, Rev. Prof. F. S. Leahy 1966-1988 and Rev. Harry Coulter 1989-2000. Members of Kilraughts and other congregations gave their support to the work and a witness was maintained in this historic setting.

In 1992 Kilraughts Session, led by Rev. Harry Coulter, embarked upon a three-year review of the work in Cloughmills. As a result of much prayer, diligent presentation of the Gospel and heartfelt concern for the spiritual wellbeing of the local people, the Session was persuaded that God was guiding them to take appropriate steps to provide weekly morning and evening worship services. A small nucleus of core families from Kilraughts and other congregations in the Presbytery assembled on Sabbath 3 December 1995 to begin weekly morning and evening services, a Sabbath School and a prayer meeting. So began the process of implanting new life into an old and much loved witness in Cloughmills. An Interim Session was appointed in February 1997 consisting of Rev. Harry Coulter, Jim Calderwood, William Hanna and David Loughridge.

On 28 April 2000 the Northern Presbytery met in Cloughmills and formally granted the wish of the Fellowship to become a Congregation. The new congregation consisted of 19 adults, 17 baptised Covenant youth and 2 adherents. Jim Calderwood and David Loughridge were installed as Elders on 4 June 2000 and Andrew Aicken and Thomas Loughridge were ordained and installed as Deacons on 26 November 2000. Rev. Peter Jemphrey, Belfast, received as a minister from the Presbyterian Church of Ireland in 1999, accepted the call of the congregation and was installed on 9 December 2000. At the Sabbath evening service on 30 September 2007, Andrew Aiken and Andrew Lytle were ordained and installed as elders.

Cloughmills has given two men to the ministry. In 1842 Robert Johnston, a member of the congregation, was ordained to the gospel ministry for work in Manchester. In 2008 Andrew Lytle was taken under care of the Northern Presbytery as a student in the Reformed Theological College with a view to mission work in France.

Cloughmills Meeting House in the 1870s

The original meeting house, built in 1805, was fairly primitive with few amenities. It had a mud floor and uncomfortable box pews. The first major renovation was in 1904 when a new roof, wooden floor, stove and long forms were installed. Further renovations took place in 1933. The pulpit and pews from the old Garvagh Reformed Presbyterian Meeting House were gifted in 1970 but, despite the extensive renovations to the original building in 1971, which seated 120-140, it was felt that more was needed. The minister's room, entrance porch, and toilets were fitted into a space of only 30 feet long by 12 feet wide. Consequently, a new building erected for worship, beside the existing property, was started in the summer of 2004 and opened on 5 May 2006. This incorporated a 'meet and greet area', which also serves as an informal meeting area, together with a room for small groups, a kitchen and toilets. The old church building is now profitably employed as a facility for children, youth and other outreach work.

Cloughmills Meeting House 1971

The congregation ably hosted the meeting of Synod in 2009 which was a time of great blessing.

The present witness of the congregation involves weekly ministry to members, adherents and occasional visitors, with 'Christianity Explained' courses organised for those wanting to find out more. The congregation's vision is to see the Gospel made known to the village of Cloughmills and beyond, so that the way of salvation will be proclaimed to many who at present do not take heed to it.

The Meeting House is situated in the village of Cloughmills at 2 Drumbare Road, Cloughmills, Co. Antrim, BT44 9LA.

Cullybackey new Meeting House opened 2009

CULLYBACKEY

The strength of the Covenanting Church in the 17th and 18th centuries was the Society Meeting. This regular meeting for fellowship and Bible study was led by the elder for the district. Long before meeting houses were erected, Covenanters maintained their fellowship and their witness by this means, with the various Societies drawn together for occasional Conventicles and other meetings for public worship.

This was especially true in Co. Antrim, where the ministry of Rev. William Martin in the years that followed his ordination in 1757 strengthened the Societies considerably. One of the most vigorous of these Societies met at Laymore, to the east of the town of Ballymena. The weekly meetings were held in the homes of the people and regular open-air meetings for worship were held in a remarkable natural amphitheatre known as 'The Round Hole', which remains as it was, at time of writing. This witness in due course led to the formation of a congregation in Cullybackey, a village, three miles northwest of Ballymena.

The Round Hole, Laymore conventicle site near Ballymena.

The links between Kellswater and Cullybackey have always been close and at various times in the past they have been united as a single charge and known as the 'Antrim Congregation'. Rev. William Martin of Kellswater supervised the Societies in the Cullybackey area until 1765. In that year Daniel McClellan, an American of Irish parentage, educated and licensed in Scotland, was ordained at Laymore, near Ballymena. He was assigned work at Cullybackey. Cullybackey has been a regularly organised Covenanting congregation since that time. Mr. McClellan emigrated to America in 1769.

He was succeeded by Robert Young, born in 1732 in Kelso in Roxburghshire and a licentiate of the Associate Presbytery of Scotland. Mr. Young attached himself to the Reformed Presbytery of Scotland and was ordained and commissioned for work in America. On his way there, he was shipwrecked off Glenarm. Making his way to the Cullybackey area, he was befriended by the Wright family of Craigs. He stayed with them for a time and, being called by the congregation, he served them from 1776 until 1779 when he accepted a call to Ramelton in County Donegal.

William Gibson, a native of Knockbracken, County Down, was ordained as minister of Cullybackey and Kellswater on 17 April 1787. He graduated from Glasgow University in 1775 and completed his theological training in Edinburgh. Although not brought up as a Covenanter, he was introduced to Covenanting principles by William Gamble of Ballykelly, a fellow student at Glasgow University. On 17 April 1787 he was ordained as minister of Cullybackey and Kellswater, then known as the Antrim congregation. Two years later, the Cullybackey congregation built a meeting house on its present site and the session, consisting of the minister and ten ruling elders held its first meeting in the new church on 8 March 1791. Mr. Gibson was suspected of involvement in the United Irish Society. During 1796 he preached in the open air, reportedly often drawing crowds of thousands, and impressed upon his hearers that the covenant-breaking powers of this age would soon be replaced by the powers of the coming age. This was considered by the authorities, in the context of the times, as inflammatory. When two of his congregation were asked to take the Oath of Allegiance to the Crown, they remarked that they would be censured by their minister. The magistrate then insisted that Mr. Gibson take it or face execution. He escaped arrest and emigrated to the United States of America in October 1797. William Gibson, James McKinney, minister in Dervock between 1783 and 1793, and some elders joined to constitute the first Reformed Presbytery of the United States of America at Philadelphia in 1798. Mr Gibson was the first Moderator of the U.S. Synod in 1809.

In spite of the intense pressure on Covenanters during the 1798 rebellion, the congregation made fine progress. In 1800, William Stavely, minister of Newtownards and Knockbracken, accepted the call to the congregations of Cullbackey and Kellswater. 1 May 1811 was a historical day when the first Synod of the Reformed Presbyterian Church of Ireland was held in the meetinghouse with the minister, Rev. William Stavely, as the first Moderator and his son in the office of Clerk.

The congregation became independent again in 1813 as the membership had grown to almost 350. Unfortunately, in attempting to elect a minister, the congregation was divided over three candidates. Rev. William John Stavely had presided at the election and in the first count Clark Houston had a majority. Instead of asking the minorities to concur, Mr Stavely insisted that the congregation either elect Mr. Houston or delay the decision. The majority in favour of Mr. Houston wanted his nomination approved and the minorities appealed to Presbytery. Time helped to solve the problem and, in 1818, Mr. Houston was eventually installed, having served in Limavady between 1814 and 1816. But Synod was dissatisfied with the manner in which the Northern Presbytery had handled the matter and directed that Cullybackey be placed under the care of the Eastern Presbytery.

Mr. Houston was highly respected for his character and faithfulness. The effectiveness of his ministry may be gauged by the statistics for 1824. The congregation consisted of 182 families, 410 communicants and a total of 1120. In the course of that year alone, 48 were admitted to membership and 28 were baptised. During this period the numbers attending communion services were so great that the congregation often met outside in the graveyard.

REFORMED PRESBYTERIAN CHURCH. CULLYBACKEY, IRELAND
Rev J G McVICKER, Pastor

Cullybackey Meeting House 1858

Mr. Houston served as Clerk of Synod from 1827 to 1840. But the 1830s were years of tension in the Reformed Presbyterian Church. A controversy had arisen over the power of the civil magistrate in spiritual affairs. Rev. Clark Houston sided with Rev. Dr. John Paul in his debate with Rev. Dr. Thomas Houston. When the Eastern Presbytery seceded in 1840 to form the Eastern Reformed Synod, Clark Houston and the congregation joined them and the strength and influence of Cullybackey were lost to the Irish R.P. Synod until 1905, when it was happily reunited with the parent Church.

There were three ministers during these 65 years; John Galway McVicker, 1853-1860. Mr. McVicker was very active in the Revival Movement of 1859. However, in 1860 he confessed before Presbytery his change of views on Covenant Baptism and was therefore released from his charge. He formed Hill Street Baptist Church in Ballymena and later a Brethren Assembly. Joseph Archibald Moody, 1860-1898 who was one of the most gifted preachers of his day and Andrew Fallon, 1899-1902.

By the end of the nineteenth century the Eastern Reformed Synod was finding it difficult to maintain a separate existence. Rev. Andrew Fallon wanted to join the congregation with the General Assembly as did some other Eastern R.P. congregations. But the Session was unanimously committed to the Covenanting cause. Attempts at reconciliation between minister and Session proved unsuccessful and Mr. Fallon resigned in 1902 when the Eastern Reformed Synod ceased to function. On 22 August 1905 Cullybackey returned once again to the care of the Northern Presbytery.

Cullybackey old Meeting House prior to demolition in 2007

The congregation, then comprising 70 families, was quick to make a call. On 5 October a call was issued to James Alexander Lyons, a licentiate of the Southern Presbytery. He was the eldest son of Rev. A. S. Lyons, minister of the Riverside congregation, Newry. Educated at Newry Intermediate School, Queen's College Galway and the R.P. Theological Hall in Belfast, he was ordained on 9 January 1906. He brought a gracious dignity to his pulpit ministry and, with evangelical fervour and wise pastoral care, the congregation grew. Mr. Lyons accepted a call to Dublin Road, Belfast in November 1923 and was installed there in January 1924.

His successor was Rev. Samuel Wallace Lynas, minister of Hall Lane, Liverpool, since December 1923. He was installed on 20 January 1926 and ministered with great ability and devotion for almost twenty years. Mr. Lynas was installed in Milford on 3 October 1945.

Rev. William James Gilmour was installed on 15 May 1946. He brought 14 years of experience, having been ordained and installed as minister of Loanhead in 1932 and having served in Nicholson Street, Glasgow since 1941. The Word, faithfully and lovingly preached, bore fruit in many hearts and lives. After a most acceptable and influential ministry, he retired from active duties on 4 December 1974. During his ministry in 1961 the congregation welcomed the Synod for the third time, when, after an interval of fifty years, Rev. R. J. McIlmoyle, who had presided at the centenary Synod of 1911 in Cullybackey, was in the chair for a second term to constitute the Synod once again.

Richard Wallace McCollum, licentiate of the Northern Presbytery and member of Ballylaggan, was ordained and installed minister of Cullybackey on 8 September 1978. Mr. McCollum's ministry in Cullybackey was marked with a love for Christ and a love for His people which was exceptional and extended through, and beyond the congregation, to the village of Cullybackey. His gifts were recognised when the Northern Presbytery found other avenues of pastoral work for Mr. McCollum upon his retirement on the grounds of poor health on 12 January 2001.

In June 2008, the congregation issued a call to Philip Moffett, a member of Trinity congregation and a licentiate of the Eastern Presbytery. He accepted this call on 25 July and was ordained and installed on 10 October 2008.

In 1989 the congregation celebrated 200 years of worship and witness in the present building. To commemorate this anniversary a history of the congregation was written by Rev. Professor Adam Loughridge and launched at a bicentennial service on 20 May 1989.

The following have served as ruling elders: James Atcheson, James Campbell, Francis Cherry, John Chesney, James Girvan, James Henderson, William Loughridge, Robert Sloan, Matthew Smyth, Robert Walker, James Wright, Hugh Hall, Robert Johnston,

Matthew Johnston, Patrick Knowles, Adam Linn, William Logan, Hugh McQueston, James Mann, Charles McClellan, James Kinnear, John McCracken, John McKee, Patrick Close, John Wright, William Wright, John Knowles, James Austin, Robert Aicken, Alexander Bryson, Adam Knowles, John McKelvey, James A Evans, James Knowles Samuel McKay, Robert McKelvey, William Boyd McKelvey, John Moffett, John Wallace, Hugh Wright, John A Bryson, Joseph Gardner, William Shaw, James Kenny, John McKelvey, Hugh W. Reid, James Hilton, William J. Kennedy, James A. McCarroll, Hugh McCracken, Thomas Hugh Wright, William McCluney, Robert McKelvey, Robert McKelvey (Jun.), John McKelvey, William Burnside, John Gardner, Thomas Lowry, Samuel McIlroy, Samuel A McEwen, Dr. John K. McKelvey, Thomas Nicholl, George Simpson, Daniel Wright, Ian McCluggage, Ivor McMullan, Dr. John Turner, Maurice Knowles, Trevor McIlroy, Dr. David McKelvey.

The Cullybackey congregation has an excellent record of providing men for the work of the Gospel Ministry. Twenty students have, after training, served the Church in different parts of the world: Samuel Aiken, John Black, Samuel Brown Wylie, Samuel Wylie, Thomas Cathcart, Elijah Aicken, Alexander Wright, Thomas Houston, Robert Johnston, William Close, Hugh Austin, Alexander Wright, Samuel Moffett, James Renwick Wright, James McKelvey, David Calderwood, James William Calderwood, James Campbell, Alexander Reid Wright and Samuel Lynas Reid. The following from the congregation have given lengthy missionary service overseas: Jeanie Gardner, Jack, James, Rachel, Elizabeth and Martha Selfridge and Margaret McMullan.

The meeting house was built on its existing site in 1789 on the Main Street in Cullybackey. It was a simple rectangular structure with a gallery at each end to which access was provided by a stairway on the outside of the two gables. Because it was first located beside the village pound, an enclosure where stray cattle were kept until claimed by their owners, it was locally known as 'The Pound Meeting-house'. This field is now the church's graveyard. A hall known as a School Room was built in 1869. In 1887 the meeting house was renovated and enlarged with the removal of galleries and the addition of the 'transcept' bay and the entrance porches. A new church hall known as the 'Lecture Hall' was erected in 1929, replacing the single storey school room. On 15 June 2007, Rev. Wallace McCollum preached at the final service held in the meeting house before its demolition. A new meeting house and hall were built and the keys of the new premises were handed over on 4 December 2008. The first worship service was conducted on Sabbath 7 December 2008. An Open Day on Saturday 17 January attracted between 400 and 500 visitors. The official opening on Friday 6 February 2009 was followed by thanksgiving services from Monday to Wednesday of the following week

The first three ministers of the congregation had provided their own homes. One of these was at Knockanure, where Ballymena Academy is now sited. In 1854 the congregation built a manse in the Main Street for the sum of £313. It was thoroughly renovated, just over fifty years later, at the start of Mr. Lyons's ministry. The congregation sold this property in 2004.

The Meeting House is situated in the village at 2 Main Street, Cullybackey, BT42 1BN.

Dervock Meeting House

DERVOCK

The first Presbytery in Ireland was established in 1642 and by the end of the 1650s it met in five different areas to deal with the business of each locality. One of these was the 'Route Meeting'. The earliest covenanting influence here came from David Houston, a native of Paisley in Scotland who came to Ulster at this time. He was appointed stated supply to the congregations in this 'Route Meeting'. He ministered, amongst other places, in the Ballymoney, Derrykeighan and Armoy areas. The turbulent Scotsman made his colleagues so uncomfortable, by his attachment to the Scottish Covenants, that he was suspended by the 'Route Meeting' in 1672. After some years in Scotland, during which he fought at Bothwell Brig in 1679, he returned to Ireland and was recommended to the Covenanting Societies by Alexander Peden. From 1689 he itinerated in various parts of Ulster, which included Armoy and, in this North Antrim area, he worked for four years until his death in 1696 establishing a Covenanting cause.

When the Scottish Reformed Presbytery was formed in 1743, local Covenanters received a number of preaching appointments from men such as John Cameron, who had settled in

Dunluce, and John Fairley who preached regularly at the Vow, near Ballymoney. William Martin's ministry covered the whole of Country Antrim from 1757.

It was not until the ministry of James McKinney (1783-1793) that the foundations were laid of the congregation that was eventually formed at Dervock. Born in Kilrea about 1750, and brought up in Drimbolg, James McKinney received his education at Glasgow University and the Scottish Divinity Hall. He was ordained on 1 July 1783 at Kirkhills, between Ballymoney and Stranocum, to serve an extensive congregation of which that was the centre. In 1783 the Dervock congregation was organized jointly with Kilraughts. Mr. McKinney was a forthright preacher and it is not surprising that in the tense atmosphere that prevailed in the last decade of the eighteenth century he should put himself at some risk for his outspoken criticism of an ailing monarchy and a corrupt government. In 1793 he preached a sermon entitled 'The Rights of God', when he declared that sovereignty did not lie with any king but with God alone. The authorities interpreted this as treason and took steps to arrest and try him. Suspecting that he would not get a fair trial, he emigrated to America in 1793. There he helped organize the American Reformed Presbytery in 1798.

The old meeting house of Kirkhills, that had been so central in the early days, rapidly fell into disuse after the year 1800. The meeting house for worship at Carnaff, Dervock, was erected in 1804. It is situated one mile from the village on the Bushmills road. Even after the extensive renovation the building retains much of the distinctive character of the original low ceiling house.

In the vacancy that followed, the congregation was not idle and William John Stavely was ordained on 6 September 1804 to serve the congregation, known by then as Kilraughts and Dervock. It comprised 228 members in full communion, drawn from a wide area. Dr. Stavely had grown up in the Knockbracken congregation, of which his father, William Stavely, was the minister. He was educated at Glasgow University and the Reformed Presbyterian Divinity Hall in Paisley.

Because the congregation grew to more than 500, he recommended that a new congregation be organized to take in only the Dervock and Ballymoney part of his original charge. In 1832, it was arranged that two calls be presented to him through Presbytery: one from Kilraughts and the other from Dervock and Ballymoney. Dr. Stavely resigned Kilraughts and accepted the call from what he referred to as the 'weaker of the two'.

In 1840 the Bushmills Society of Covenanters, connected to Dervock, was taken under the care of the Mission Board as a Mission Station until the work ceased in the 1930s. In 1847 a Juvenile Missionary Association was formed.

In 1853 Dervock was chosen as the venue for the first act of Covenant Renewal by the denomination, partly out of respect for Dr. Stavely, by then one of the most venerable ministers of the Church. In 1854, at a service in Dervock, the congregation marked Dr. Stavely's 50th year as their minister. Despite heavy emigration to the United States of America, the congregation of Dervock and Ballymoney stood at 300 by 1854. Dr. Stavely retired in 1860.

Stavely's successor was James Brown of Rathfriland, a licentiate of the Southern Presby-  tery. He was ordained at Dervock on 25 July 1860. The joint congregation made such rapid progress under his leadership and gifted ministry that petitions were presented at the Northern Presbytery in November 1877 asking that the congregation be separated from Ballymoney. This request was granted and the minute of Presbytery states, "Mr Brown, having signified acceptance of the Ballymoney part of the congregation, the relation existing between him and it was confirmed, and, at the same time, the relation between him and the Dervock end was dissolved". When this separation took place Dervock was a congregation of some 140 members.

Dervock's first minister as a separate and distinct congregation was Ezekiel Teaz. A member of the Londonderry congregation and licentiate of the Western Presbytery, he was ordained and installed on 10 December 1886. Mr. Teaz's only son, Homer, was later to die in the First World War. In 1895 Mr. Teaz resigned, having accepted a call to Liverpool.

The next minister was Rev. James Alexander Smyth Stewart, originally from Drimbolg, who had served eight years in Limavady. He was the first minister to come with pastoral experience. However, his promising ministry ended with his sudden death on 6 June, 1902, aged 36. He left a widow and four children. The congregation immediately set up a fund to help them and soon £200 was gathered.

After a two-year vacancy the congregation called Rev. Robert John McImoyle, a native of Limavady, who had been minister in Ballyclare for four years. He was installed on 31 August 1904. Mr. McIlmoyle was a preacher of unusual ability and as a pastor he shared the joys and sorrows of his people with equal facility. Shortly after his arrival, Mr. McIlmoyle received the gift of a cow, followed some years later by the gift of a new rubber-tyred driving trap complete with driving rug! Both were put to good use! Farming, especially the breeding and showing of pedigree Border Leicester Sheep, was a consuming interest. As a public speaker and courageous representative of the farming community, helping to found the Ulster Farmers' Union, awarded the M.B.E., he was probably better known than any other Covenanting minister in the 20th century. Under his ministry the young people of the Sabbath School were among the first to enter the annual examination set by the Committee of the Instruction of the Young. Dervock was also one of the first C.Y.P. Societies to be formed and helped organize the first C.Y.P.U. Conference in Portrush. In 1950 the congregation, in observing the Lord's Supper, used for the first time an individual Communion Service. Mr. McIlmoyle ministered until his retirement on 18 May 1964. This achievement put the name of Dervock in the record books in that it, in only 181 years of existence, had two 60-year ministries. Mr. McIlmoyle died exactly one year after his retirement, on 18 May 1965.

Two short ministries followed. The first was that of Robert Harold Creane, member of Fairview and licentiate of the Southern Presbytery, from 1964-1967. Mr. Creane was deposed from the office of minister on 2 October 1967.

Edward Donnelly, member of Grosvenor Road and licentiate of the Eastern Presbytery, was ordained and installed on 3 October 1968 and exercised a very fruitful ministry which was long remembered for his excellent preaching and pastoral gifts. On 6 September 1972

Mr. Donnelly resigned, having accepted a call, from the Board of Foreign Missions of the R.P. Church of North America, to serve as a missionary in Cyprus.

On 1 February 1973 Rev. William Young was installed as minister. Mr. Young brought with him the experience of almost 40 years faithful service, having served the congregations of Wishaw, Stranraer and Grosvenor Road, Belfast. After a period of seven faithful and fruitful years, in which he had endeared himself to the congregation and had given unequalled pastoral care to his people, Mr. Young retired on 29 April 1980.

Trevor McCauley, member of Rathfriland and licentiate of the Southern Presbytery, was ordained and installed on 1 January 1981. He wrote an excellent history of the congregation which was published in 1983 to mark the 200th anniversary of the congregation (along with Kilraughts). Synod was held in Dervock that year. On 3 July 1984 Mr. McCauley accepted a call from the Irish Mission Board to undertake mission work in Galway.

On 25 June 1986 Rev. Norris Wilson, minister of Knockbracken and Ballymacashon, was installed. In 1990 a memorable act of covenant renewal was undertaken in the congregation. Mr. Wilson accepted a call to the Drimbolg congregation and was installed there on 1 September 2004. At a special meeting held on 27 June in the Holmes Memorial Hall in Ballymoney, to say farewell, speakers spoke warmly of Professor Wilson's gifts and contribution, through faithful preaching and pastoral care, to the work in Dervock.

Rev. John Hawthorne, minister of Dromara, was called to the congregation and was installed on 9 June 2006.

When Dervock became a separate congregation in 1877 the session consisted of Robert Carson, Robert Clarke, Samuel Chestnutt, Francis Kane, Hugh McCaw, Daniel Neill and John Nevin. The elders ordained under Mr McIlmoyle's ministry were: Alexander Carson, Daniel L. Carson, Daniel Carson, Robert Clarke (Jim), W. G. Finlay, James Lyons (who served as clerk for 38 years), John McFall, Robert McFall, David Taggart, R. J. Campbell, Robert J. Carson, Neill Fleming, Robert Patterson, James Simpson, Robert Bleakly, James Kerr, Norman McConaghie and David Millar. In 1975 two new elders were ordained,

George Hunter and Daniel McKeeman and in 1988 five more elders were ordained: Alan Kerr, Ivan McConaghie Samuel McConaghie, Archie McKeeman, David C. Millar. Mervyn McConaghie was ordained and installed on 8 Jan 2006. On 27 January 2008, Samuel Bleakly and David McKeeman were ordained and installed as ruling elders.

Students for the ministry brought up in Dervock were: John Renwick, John Nevin, James Nevin, Robert Nevin, Andrew Fallon, John Crawford and Matthew Neil. Joseph Kerr served with the Irish Mission (1964-1974).

In 1888 the congregation purchased a manse and farm for their minister. Five different ministers were to reside in the manse in Church Street over a period of 84 years. The congregation also undertook an extensive renovation of the meeting house at this time. In 1955 the congregation undertook an extensive renovation scheme, involving a new ceiling and windows and installing electric light and heat. A new manse on the Knock Road in Dervock was purchased in 1972 with Mr. and Mrs. Young as its first occupants.

A new suite of rooms was added to the meeting house, comprising a minor hall, session room, kitchen and toilet. Between March and December 1992, the congregation worshipped in Derrykeighan Orange Hall while a major renovation of the meeting house took place in which the whole building was completely redesigned and refurbished. The pulpit was re-positioned to the northwest side of the church and two small rooms were added to the other end. The hall entrance was enlarged and now serves as an entrance to the church. In 1995 the congregation decided to sell the manse and assist the minister to buy his own house. In 2004 special services were held to commemorate the 200th anniversary of the building of the meetinghouse at Carnaff, Dervock. In 2006 the congregation purchased a plot of land adjoining the meeting house for future development.

Building on what has been accomplished in the past, the Dervock congregation continues to have as its priorities the faithful preaching of God's Word for the spiritual growth and equipping of its members, the development of a church fellowship marked by love and support for one another and, by every legitimate means, the proclamation of the Gospel of salvation through faith in Jesus Christ to its immediate community and beyond.

The Meeting House is situated at 210 Castlecat Road, Dervock, Ballymoney, Co. Antrim, BT53 8AT.

Drimbolg Meeting House

DRIMBOLG

There was an early witness for the Covenanting cause west of the Bann; many from the area may have signed the Solemn League and Covenant at Coleraine in 1644 and an attachment to Covenanting principles was maintained during the next century in spite of the fact that there was no regular ministry. Encouragement came to the Covenanters in the middle of the 18th century with the itinerant ministry of William Martin, who though settled at Kellswater, preached frequently in Counties Londonderry and Donegal.

In 1761 Matthew Lynn was licensed by the Scottish Reformed Presbytery and set apart for work in Ireland. As a licentiate he preached for two years in various centres, the most frequently listed being Maghera, Drummond and Cumber. In 1763 he was ordained by the Scottish Presbytery and given the oversight of the Bannside congregation. As a result of his preaching and pastoral care the present congregations of Drimbolg, Ballylaggan and Limavady developed. These congregations may rightly claim him as their first minister. An early result of Mr. Lynn's ministry was the formation of a number of Covenanting

Societies in the Drimbolg district. The first of these was established at James Johnston's of Ballynahone in 1764. (Denis Johnston, the distinguished Irish author, is a descendant.) Later, Societies were formed at Magherafelt and Ballymacilcur in 1768, and at Killyberry, near Bellaghy, in 1770. The congregation had no meeting house during Mr. Lynn's ministry and the services were held in private houses, in barns and in the open air. Mr. Lynn's ministry ended in 1773 when he emigrated to America.. This was the result of a charge (later proved to be false), that he had officiated at an irregular wedding at Dungiven. Along with Alexander Dobbin and John Cuthbertson, he was instrumental in organising the first Reformed Presbyterian Presbytery in North America in 1774.

The second man to minister to the Covenanters of the Drimbolg area was Samuel Aiken. A native of Clough, Co. Antrim, he was ordained for the Bannside congregation in 1776 and ministered for 14 years before moving to Co. Monaghan. Despite his rather frail health, the Societies in the Drimbolg district were greatly strengthened under his leadership and new Societies were formed at Ballymacpeake, Kilrea and Moyagoney. In the ensuing vacancy of some eight years the congregation was cared for by James McKinney of Dervock and Kilraughts, and by William Gibson of Kellswater.

The third minister to the Drimbolg Covenanters was Joseph Orr. He was ordained in the open air at Caw Wood near Garvagh in April 1798. This was a year of great difficulty for Covenanters in Ireland. A spirit of unrest and bitterness prevailed and the United Irishmen prepared for open insurrection to pave the way of Irish independence. Covenanters had always been outspoken critics of the British Government and, since they refused to take an unqualified Oath of Allegiance to the Crown on the grounds of rejected Covenants, they were looked on as rebels against authority and it was assumed that they would support a Rising. Joseph Orr was arrested soon after his ordination, but there was no evidence against him and he was soon released.

At the end of the century the leadership in the Societies was in the hands of Messrs. Taylor, Dunn, Lyttle, Glasgow, Joseph Caskey, John McCaw, Samuel McKeown and John Houston. The Session met frequently at Mr. Orr's house at Drumlamph and the congregation worshipped in the Secession meeting house at Knockloughrim. This arrangement continued until 1813 when a site at Drimbolg was purchased from a Mr. Rowe and a meeting house was erected and opened for worship in 1816. It is situated at Drimbolg Crossroads, approximately half a mile from the village of Tamlaght O'Crilly, heading towards Innisrush and about 4 miles from the towns of Portglenone, Kilrea and Maghera. Until 1820 the services were held on alternate Sabbaths at Knockloughrim and Drimbolg; after that the services were held at Drimbolg. Mr. Orr died in 1825 and was buried at Bellaghy.

Date stone 1836

His successor was James Alexander Smyth. Brought up in Ballylaggan, Mr. Smyth was ordained and installed pastor of Drimbolg in June 1827. Mr. Smyth retired in 1872 after a faithful and fruitful ministry of forty-five years. He died in 1873 and was buried at Drimbolg.

His successor, Isaac Thompson of Ballenon, was ordained on 28 May, 1872. A brilliant scholar, a gifted barrister and noted preacher, Dr. Thompson was minister for 21 years. He was unmarried and resided with the Warwick family at Innisrush.

He was succeeded in 1895 by Hugh Kennedy Mack. During the ministry of Mr. Mack the meeting house was renovated and re-seated and the present manse and farm were added to the property. After 14 years in Drimbolg, Mr. Mack volunteered for work in Geelong, Australia and he served there with great faithfulness until his retirement in 1946. He was remembered in Drimbolg for his quiet manner and scholarly dignity.

The next minister was Alexander Gilmour, a native of Rathfriland. His short but effective ministry was from 1911 to 1917 when he accepted a call to Trinity Street, Belfast. In 1911 the society in Magherafelt was asked if they desired to remain under the oversight of Drimbolg and if not the Presbytery would seek to provide a supply. The six families associated with this society desired to remain and there continued a regular monthly Sabbath meeting in Magherafelt, latterly in the Christian Workers' Union Hall. The work continued through Rev. McCullough's and Rev. Cole's ministry until it closed in the early 1970's largely due to the 'Troubles'.

Rev. William McCullough from Clare, Co. Armagh, after a ministry of 11 years in Ballylaggan, was installed in Drimbolg in April, 1917. For 40 years he was a well-loved friend and pastor. His preaching gifts were unique and his characteristics distinctive. He left his mark on the congregation both on the material and spiritual level.

In March 1958 Rev. Isaac Cole, who was brought up in Ballenon and had ministered in Trinity Street for 13 years, was installed as minister of Drimbolg. He proved to be a devoted pastor and an able leader. Mr. Cole's ministry continued for just over 31 years until his retirement in April 1989.

A period of vacancy followed Mr. Cole's ministry lasting 7½ years and during that time a number of unsuccessful calls were issued. In September 1996 Vincent McDonnell, a licentiate of the Eastern Presbytery and a member of the Trinity congregation, accepted the congregation's unanimous call and he was ordained and installed as pastor on 20 December 1996. Mr. McDonnell's time as minister was relatively short. After a period of ill health he resigned the charge in June 2001.

Rev. Professor Norris Wilson, minister of Dervock, was installed on 1 September 2004.

Drimbolg's contribution to the ministry in the Church is worthy of note. James McKinney, Clarke Houston, Arthur Fullerton, Alexander Clarke, Gordon Ewing, Thomas James Orr, John Gamble, Thomas McConnell, John W. McKeown, Torrens Boyd, William McKnight, George Gilmour Warwick, John M McIlwrath, James Alexander Smyth Stewart, Thomas A. McIlfatrick, John Knox Dickey, William Lytle and Philip Murphy, all became students for the Reformed Presbyterian ministry. In addition James Stewart and James Anderson have served with the Irish Mission.

The following men have served the congregation from 1870 as ruling elders: Robert Boyd, Samuel Boggs, Andrew Warwick, William Wilson, Robert Gordon, Neal Quinn, James Ross, Robert Stewart, George Smyth, James Orr, Charles Scott, Samuel Dickey, William Smyth, John Adams, William Workman, Robert Gordon, Samuel Lytle, Andrew McIlwrath, Samuel Fullerton, James A. Smyth, R. A. Houston, Robert McElfatrick, Dr. J. B. Kelso, Samuel Adams, John Holmes, George Stewart, James Stewart, John Houston, Thomas Lytle, William Mayberry, J. Kyle Houston, William M. Aiken, Robert Aiken, David Maxwell, Stanley Lytle, Philip Murphy , Wilmor Kelso and Leslie McClean.

In 1837 a new larger building was erected on the same site at a cost of £559-6s-8½d. The new meeting house was badly damaged on the night of the 'Big Wind' on 7 January 1839, but repairs at a nominal cost were carried out by hard-working loyal people. The meeting house was thoroughly renovated and tastefully decorated in 1937. However, the 'Boxing Day' storm of December 1998 caused major structural damage which resulted in the building losing half of its roof. The link building between the church and hall was damaged too. For a period of 15 months services were held in the church hall while repairs

were carried out. The repair work involved the complete refurbishment of the meeting house including a new floor and the rebuilding of the link between the church hall and the meeting house. The cost of the complete refurbishment amounted to approximately £240,000. On Sabbath 26 March 2000 the reopening of the meeting house was marked by a special Thanksgiving Service and a week of special meetings.

Through Rev. Isaac Cole's inspiration and encouragement, a fine new church hall was opened on 1 January 1969 and it proved to be a great asset to the congregation. Prior to Rev. Vincent McDonnell's installation in 1996 extensive renovations were carried out to the manse property, costing in the region of £60,000.

For more than two centuries, the Drimbolg congregation has maintained the highest traditions and best interests of the Covenanting cause. Like many congregations that are situated in a rural setting and depending heavily on the farming community for the bulk of its membership, changes are inevitable as the congregation looks to the future. The congregation's prayer is that God will guide and equip the membership to maintain and extend the Covenanting cause in the Drimbolg district for many years to come.

The Meeting House is situated at Drimbolg Road, Upperlands, Maghera, Co. Londonderry.

The former Garvagh Meeting House

GARVAGH

In 1763 it is recorded that the Garvagh Covenanter Society formed part of the Bannside congregation and the Reformed Presbytery meeting at the Vow on the banks of the river Bann, ordained and installed Matthew Lynn from Carncastle to the oversight of the societies under the name Bannside. He laboured throughout county Londonderry, helping to form congregations at Ballylaggan, Drimbolg, Bready, Faughan, Ramelton and Garvagh. He was later appointed to accompany Rev. Alexander Dobbin as missionary to America.

Because of the troubled times in 1798 Joseph Orr was ordained in Caw Wood, a lonely spot above Garvagh, to serve as minister of Ballylaggan, Drimbolg and Limavady. As Mr. Orr lived at Drumlamph, near Castledawson, the strain of ministering to such a large scattered congregation was very great indeed and, on a total stipend of £52, he had a struggle to make ends meet. In 1805 Mr. Orr was relieved of the care of Limavady and in the following year the large society of Bushtown was transferred from Ballylaggan to Dunboe (Ringrash). Between 1805 and 1816 he had responsibility for the reduced congregation in Ballylaggan, Garvagh and Drimbolg. In 1816 Mr. Orr resigned the pastorate of Ballylaggan and his other responsibilities, but retained those of Drimbolg. He died in 1825. The Reformed Presbytery met nine times at Garvagh between 1803 and

1806 no doubt because of its geographical centrality, and it was here in 1803 that John Paul, later of Loughmourne, was licensed. In 1817 Simon Cameron was ordained and installed as minister of Ballylaggan and Garvagh on 10 September 1817. Mr. Cameron lived at Drumsteeple, near Ballylaggan. He retired from the active duties of the ministry in 1853. Until his death in 1855 he received a retiring allowance of £12 a year from the Ironmongers Company of London.

Garvagh separated from Ballylaggan in 1855 and Joseph Hamilton, born at Belraugh , Garvagh, a licentiate of the Northern Presbytery, ministered from 7th November 1867 until 1872, when he emigrated to the U.S.A.. James Littlejohn from Kilwinning in Ayrshire served from 15 July 1876. When the United Original Secession congregation in Garvagh joined the General Assembly in 1863 this occasioned a split where those against the union joined the Reformed Presbyterians.

During repairs to the roof in 1881, a great storm stripped much of the roof and so great was the damage that local people raised the greater part of the cost of repairs by public subscription. Thereafter the storm was referred to in the area as 'Littlejohn's storm'. Mr. Littlejohn retired 14 February 1893, and died in 1898. He was Garvagh's last minister as a sole charge. The congregation was supplied by the Northern Presbytery and for many years the minister of Ballylaggan conducted a united evening service at intervals of three weeks. The congregation was reduced to the status of a preaching station in 1968 and the meeting house was sold to the Free Presbyterian Church in 1970. The pews and the pulpit were given to Cloughmills Church.

Those associated with the Garvagh congregation who have served in the ministry are: Arthur Fullerton, minister in Limavady, who later joined the General Assembly, Joseph Hamilton who was born near Garvagh and later emigrated to the U.S.A. And John Martin Littlejohn, the son of Rev. James Littlejohn who ministered in Creevagh and later in the U.S.A.. He took a great interest in the developing field of osteopathy and was among the founders of this technique in the U.S.A. and the U.K..

The old Meeting House was situated on the site of the present Garvagh Veterinary Clinic, 5 Kilrea Road, Killyvally, Garvagh BT51 5LP.

Glenmanus Meeting House, Portrush

GLENMANUS (PORTRUSH)

Towards the end of the 19th century the few Covenanters in the fishing village of Portrush worshipped in Ballyclabber. A notable exception was Mr. Samuel Patton, farmer and mill owner at Glenmanus and merchant in Portrush. Mr. Patton was born in Macosquin in 1820. He did not become a Covenanter until his marriage to Miss Nevin of Dervock. He then drove his pony and phaeton the twelve miles to Dervock to worship in the congregation in which his wife had grown up. He was the subject of interesting stories regarding his attempts to enforce total abstinence from tobacco and alcohol on the Sessions of the Northern Presbytery.

Mr. Patton had known both good and bad times in business but, when success and prosperity finally began to consistently attend his efforts, he resolved to build a Covenanting Church in Portrush despite the fact that there were only a few members residing there. But he was a man of vision and determination. Failing to secure a site in the town from its owner, the Earl of Antrim, he proceeded to erect, on his own land at Glenmanus, a fine church, lecture hall, manse and caretaker's residence. These, with an endowment of £2,000 (yielding a valuable £60 per annum), he handed over, free of rent, to the Northern Presbytery.

Glenmanus Meeting House, 1900

Glenmanus Reformed Presbyterian church is unique in that the church building was erected before the congregation was organised. In the 21st Century, Glenmanus church buildings are located at a busy junction on the Portstewart Road in Portrush. But, when it was first built, there were few members, there were no houses nearer than the railway station and the prospects for extension were very gloomy. The population of Portrush was less than 1,800. The gift was almost an embarrassment to the Presbytery and some even feared that its existence might harm Ballyclabber and Dervock. However, the project received support from Rev. H. K. Mack of Drimbolg and Rev. John Ramsey of Ballymoney. The church was opened for worship in June 1899 and, with attendances holding up at between 50 and 100 between the summer of 1899 and the early months of 1900, it was decided by Presbytery in 1900 to move the work from the status of a preaching station to that of a congregation, with effect from Tuesday 3 July 1900. However, on Thursday 6 September, Mr. Patton died without making a will and the property had not yet been transferred from his personal estate. His estate was in Chancery until 1908. So Glenmanus has had the further unique distinction of having its future provided for by a Trust prepared by the Presbytery and approved by the High Court.

The first interim Session consisted of the following elders: William Ramsey (Ballyclabber), William Williamson (Ballyclabber), Samuel Chestnutt (Dervock), Robert Clark (Dervock), John F. Taylor (Ballymoney) and Joseph Lamont (Ballymoney). The first interim moderator was Rev. J. A. S. Stewart of Dervock. Several unsuccessful attempts were made to secure the services of a minister. For more than 30 years the ministers of Ballyclabber, Ballymoney and Dervock conducted the services in turn at 4.00pm on winter Sabbaths, while ministers on holiday took the services in the summer months. The congregation tended to consist of retired people and the first baptism did not take place until 1924. The numbers who came to the Lord's Table were often small. In 1914 there were only 19 communicants and in the 1920s the number of communicants often dipped to 9. However, a building programme in the vicinity of the church in the early 1930s improved the prospects of the congregation so that in April 1932 there were 30 communicants.

In October 1933, 9 members and 11 adherents called Rev. W. G. M. Martin from Liverpool. George Martin had been brought up in the Dublin Road congregation, was a graduate of Queen's University Belfast and had been ordained in Liverpool in 1931. He accepted the challenge – a call from 9 members – and his vision was rewarded when the adherents and others joined the congregation so that 50 attended the Spring Communion in 1936. During the restrictions of the war years, Mr. Martin made a virtue out of necessity. Instead of 'blacking out' the church in the winter months, the service in Glenmanus was moved back to 3.00 p.m. In addition, a service was held in Portstewart Town Hall at 4.00 p.m. and, with 140 attending, became a feature of the congregation's outreach. The students at Stranmillis Teacher Training College had been moved out of Belfast to Fawcett's Hotel in Portrush and, after weekly Bible Studies were conducted there, many students attended the worship service in Glenmanus. Many were converted in what has been called 'The Stranmillis Revival'. He laboured with conspicuous success until May 1944 when he resigned on his admission to the General Assembly as the minister of Berry Street Presbyterian Church.

His successor, Rev. J. T. Moffett Blair, was installed on 17 October 1944. Mr. Blair was the son of Rev. James Blair and was educated at Coleraine Academical Institution, Magee University College, Trinity College Dublin and the R.P. Theological Hall. He had been ordained in September 1932 in Stranraer. He was an able and well-loved minister for five years. In August 1949 he accepted a call to Airdrie, in Scotland.

Rev. Adam Loughridge, minister of Newtownards congregation, accepted a call from Glenmanus on 7 March 1950. He was installed as pastor of the congregation on 30 March 1950. During his ministry the good work done by his predecessors was consolidated. His decision to accept calls from Cregagh Road, Belfast and Ballymacashon was received with regret on 5 November 1969, after a pastorate of almost 20 years. When Professor Loughridge retired from the ministry, he and his wife became members and he subsequently was elected a ruling elder in the congregation.

George Martin McEwen from Newtownards was ordained and installed on 17 February 1972. He was a licentiate of the Eastern Presbytery and the first licentiate to be called by the congregation. He maintained the tradition of expository preaching in Glenmanus and his gifts, displayed in careful pulpit preparation and pastoral visitation, were appreciated by the congregation and by a wide circle of holiday visitors. Mr. McEwen resigned in 1979 in order to be the stated supply in McKinnon, Australia, where he served for a period of five years.

The next minister was George Ball who was pastor between 1981 and 1986. Mr. Ball, a native of Dromara and a licentiate of the Eastern Presbytery, was ordained and installed on 4 December 1981. Mr. Ball faithfully preached the Word, promoted warm fellowship and was committed to outreach in the community. He accepted a call to Fairview and Tullyvallen and was installed as minister of these congregations on 2 September 1986. The congregation in Glenmanus expressed their appreciation of the fine ministry he had exercised in Portrush at a social meeting on 28 August.

Rev. Edward Donnelly, minister of the Trinity congregation, accepted the call of the congregation and was installed on 20 March 1987. Although his ministry lasted only three years, his expository preaching and loving pastoral care had brought much blessing to the congregation. His call to return to Trinity in April 1990 was accepted with resignation by the Glenmanus members..

Andrew Stewart was ordained and installed on 5 October 1990. A member of Trinity, he was educated at Queen's University Belfast, the Reformed Theological College and the Reformed Presbyterian Seminary in Pittsburg. In March 1998 Mr. Stewart resigned as minister having accepted a call to the Geelong congregation in Australia. He had been a faithful preacher of the whole Word of God and a good assessor of the needs and gifts of the congregation. His wise guidance in Session and pastoral care of both young and old alike were missed by the congregation.

In March 2004 the Glenmanus congregation issued a call to Rev. Samuel McCollum. He accepted the call and the pastoral tie with the Bready congregation was dissolved. He was installed on 27 August 2004.

Glenmanus has provided one student for the ministry- David McKay.

Glenmanus is probably the best known of all Reformed Presbyterian congregations. Year after year holiday visitors from all parts of the world worship in the church and, for many of them, it is their first introduction to a covenanting service. For almost half a century the youth of the Church identified with the congregation in the summer holiday camps and, on numerous occasions, representatives from missionary conferences have attended public worship. The congregation is to be commended for the ready manner in which it has welcomed these visitors through the years.

A small but faithful band of elders has served the congregation. In the early years the interim Session gave valuable service. It was not until 1907 that the first local elders were appointed: Hugh Kennedy and Hugh McConaghy were installed, having been members in other congregations and William J. Young was ordained and installed. William Kerr and William Kennedy were installed in 1913. Other interim elders were appointed as need arose. The work done by one of them, John McDowell from Ballyclabber, deserves special notice. From 1921, at great personal cost in time and effort, Mr. McDowell "kept the flag flying" in days when there was no regular minister. He cycled from Coleraine to

Ballyclabber for the 11.00 a.m. Sabbath School and noon service and then cycled to Glenmanus for the 3.00 p.m. Sabbath School and afternoon worship service. For many years he took his son, Wilson, on the back of his bicycle to Glenmanus. The names of other elders are John L. Caldwell, John Maconaghie, Robert Miller, Samuel H. Kennedy, David Nevin, John Elliott, David McCandless, Joseph Creelman, John A. Gordon, William McDonald, Wilson McDowell, William Wright, Ross Carson, Joseph Gilmour, Thomas A. Warnock, Thomas J. Barr, Rev. Adam Loughridge, William McKay, Stanley W. Dean, Norman McCollum, Oliver Throne and Thomas Carson.

During Professor Loughridge's ministry, extensive renovations to the church property were carried out. In 1957 a new heating system was installed in the church and in 1963 the church was renovated and a new kitchen added. During Professor Donnelly's ministry the church and church hall were linked together by the erection of a classroom and toilet block. In the late 1990s there were significant works of renovation which included the renewing of the hall roof, some major decorating of the hall and church buildings and furnishing of the manse. A new car park was added in 2000.

The congregation continues to have an active witness in Portrush. Several times a year an evangelistic flyer, The Anchor, is distributed to homes in the town. Each year a Go Team comes to assist the congregation with its Holiday Bible Club and with literature distribution. In addition to the week-long Bible Club in the summer, the congregation has started holding a children's club for four Saturdays in March and again in October each year. Summer Bible Readings are held annually and these attract many visitors. It is the congregation's desire to see many more local people joining the Fellowship – and younger families would be especially welcome!

The Meeting House is situated at 23-25 Portstewart Road, Portrush, Co. Antrim, BT56 8EH.

Kellswater Meeting House

KELLSWATER

Kellswater has the distinction of being the oldest congregation in the Irish Reformed Presbyterian Church. Professor Adam Loughridge expressed what must be the opinion of many others when he said that the congregation has the added distinction of having its meeting house in a setting that is unrivalled for beauty in the Reformed Presbyterian Church. The meeting house is situated on the banks of the Kellswater River, on Grove Road, near the villages of Kells and Connor, about 4 miles south of Ballymena.

The earliest Covenanting witness in the area takes us back to the 17th century when Alexander Peden, the 'Prophet of the Covenanters', when seeking refuge from the 'Killing Times' in Scotland, was a frequent visitor to the district around Mistyburn, Glenwherry, where a memorial has been erected by the Reformed Presbyterian Church.

The foundations that Alexander Peden laid for the truths of the Reformation were built on by David Houston who exercised a vigorous ministry in the Kells district at various times between 1686 and 1696. His uncompromising commitment to the Covenanting cause left its mark wherever he preached, and it may be reckoned a mark of honour that, when he died in 1696 and was buried at Connor, his resting place was the object of desecration by the enemies of the Blue Banner of the Covenant.

Alexander Peden's memorial Mistyburn

For the next fifty years, the Covenanters in mid-Antrim were confronted with many difficulties. They depended for the ministry of the Word on commissioned preachers from Scotland, who, arriving at Larne or Donaghadee, passed through the district en route for Londonderry and Donegal. In each itinerary, ten or twelve places are mentioned and the name Carnaughts, the townland in which Kellswater is located, occurs in the list with regularity.

In 1757 William Martin was ordained at the Vow to minister to the Antrim Congregation of Covenanters. Services were held at Ballyrashane, Kirkhills, Laymore, Kellswater, Donegore and Roughfort. In 1760 Mr. Martin elected to make Kellswater the main centre of his work and a meeting house was built on the site of the present church where formerly a corn mill had stood. The congregation met for forty-six years in this simple meeting house beside the river.

There are no records of the congregation for this period in its history but we know that one of its main strengths lay in the regular meetings of the Societies. There was probably one in each townland with an attendance of from ten to twelve members. The meeting was run under the supervision of an elder who put the question for discussion and led the meeting in a manner not unlike a home group meeting today.

Mr. Martin emigrated to America in the spring of 1773. He gave notice of his intention in the Belfast News Letter of 27 December 1772 and invited like-minded people to accompany him. Quite a number of his congregation settled with him in South Carolina.

His successor in Kellswater was William Gibson, a native of Knockbracken. Although not brought up as a Covenanter, he was introduced to Covenanting principles by William Gamble of Ballykelly, a fellow student at Glasgow University. On 17 April 1787 he was ordained as minister of Cullybackey and Kellswater, then known as the Antrim congregation. He was suspected of involvement in the United Irish Society, something which he denied. During 1796 he preached in the open air, reportedly often drawing crowds of thousands, and impressed upon his hearers that the Covenant-breaking powers of that age would soon be replaced by the powers of the coming age. This was considered by the authorities, in the context of the times, as inflammatory. When two of his congregation were asked to take the Oath of Allegiance to the Crown, they remarked that they would be censured by their minister. The magistrate then insisted that Mr Gibson take it or face execution. He escaped arrest and emigrated to the United States of America in October 1797, where he became one of the six ministers of the Reformed Presbytery in December 1798 and was elected as Moderator of the first Synod in 1809.

In 1800, Rev. William Stavely, the most outstanding of all the Irish Covenanting ministers was called from Knockbracken and became the pastor of Kellswater, the congregation within whose bounds he had been brought up. He had been born at Ferniskey in 1743, ordained at Conlig in 1772, and was imprisoned on suspicion of supporting the United Irishmen in the 1798 rebellion even though the charges were never proved. He enjoyed a ministry of 25 years, during which he resigned his pastorate of the Cullybackey part of his charge, and, when he died on 7 May 1825, he was interred beside the meetinghouse. The present house of worship was erected, during his ministry, in 1806.

The longest of the pastorates that the congregation has had followed when James Dick, a licentiate of the Western Presbytery and a native of Strabane, was ordained on 17 May 1826. Some of the members joined the new work in Ballyclare which was being established in the 1830s.

The controversy which split the Reformed Presbyterian Church over the power of the Civil Magistrate affected Kellswater. Some of the Societies formed a separate congregation at Eskylane and joined the Eastern Reformed Synod, which was dissolved in 1902 with the congregation joining the General Assembly a year later.

Kellswater Meeting House in the 1890s, from Ferguson's Sketches

Meanwhile, the Kellswater congregation, despite losses to Ballyclare and Eskylane, was greatly blessed by Mr. Dick who laboured until his retirement after 53 years in the ministry. He was the first Professor of Theology at the Theological Hall which opened in 1854. He belonged to the family that has served the Church so faithfully at Kellswater and later in Trinity Street and Cregagh Road. The records of the 1859 Revival show that the four young men who had been meeting for prayer at Connor were much encouraged when a Kellswater member, a young man called Wasson, joined with them in their meetings.

There were 270 members of the Kellswater congregation in 1859-1860 and the numbers held at 235 a decade later.

The next minister was John McClelland Cromie, a native of Loughbrickland and a licentiate of the Southern Presbytery. Ordained on 22 November 1882, he ministered for sixteen years before moving to Kilraughts on 18 May 1898.

There was a vacancy of five years before Rev. Archibald Holmes, a native of Kilraughts, was called from Paisley and installed pastor in 1903. He was a diligent pastor and an acceptable preacher whose carefully prepared sermons were much appreciated. His ministry, in contrast to the political context of the period, was marked by stability and tranquillity. He transferred to Ballyclare in June 1921 but, after his death on 27 September 1932, was buried in Kellswater.

He was succeeded by Rev. John McIlmoyle who was minister in Creevagh. He was installed on 3 October 1923. Although his ministry was short, the congregation's property underwent extensive repairs which necessitated the congregation worshipping in the Hall between August 1925 and April 1927. He accepted a call to Faughan in October, 1929. On being called to Dublin Road Mr. McIlmoyle had then served in all four Presbyteries.

On 16 December 1932, Samuel McKay Calderwood, a native of Glasgow but of Irish parentage, was ordained to the Gospel ministry and installed pastor of the congregation. He had been educated at Glasgow University and the Original Secession and Reformed Presbyterian Halls. Mr. Calderwood pastored a congregation whose numbers remained stable at about 50 families and 96 communicants. His faithful ministry of 41 years, for which nature and grace had fitted him for shepherding the congregation, ended with his sudden death on 23 October 1973.

On 12 June 1974, Rev. James Alexander Ritchie, a native of the Broughshane district, after serving in Brannockstown, Limerick, Gateshead, Knockbracken and Bailiesmills, became the ninth minister of this historic congregation, which at this time had a membership of about one hundred. At its visitation of November 1978, the Northern Presbytery commended the pastor for his pulpit preparation. Mr. Ritchie retired from the active duties of the ministry on 13 March 1986. He later came out of retirement and was installed minister in Ballenon and Ballylane where he served until his final retirement.

On 20 December 1987 a unanimous call was issued to Rev. Robert Hanna, minister of Dromara. He became the congregation's next pastor on 18 March 1988. He retired from the active duties of the ministry in January 2000. His service was marked by his experience, diligent pastoring and faithful preaching. Like his predecessor Rev. John McIlmoyle, Mr. Hanna was one of the few ministers of the Reformed Presbyterian Church to serve congregations in all four Presbyteries- Milford, Newry, Dromara and then Kellswater.

Rev. William Stavely's grave, Kellswater

The following members of the congregation were called to the ministry: William Stavely and his son, William John Stavely, Thomas Houston, John Paul, James Dick and his sons Thomas Houston Dick and William Dick, Thomas Carlisle and Robert Barnet Cupples.

The present meeting house was built in 1806 on the site of a corn mill. During Professor McIlmoyle's ministry, in the mid 1920s, repairs were undertaken to the manse and the sexton's house. But the major work involved a new roof and a new ceiling in 1924 for the meeting house, the most extensive repairs since the church had been built more than a century earlier.   The total cost was £600 which was a heavy burden for a small congregation at that time. The church became a listed building in 1988.

During Mr. Cromie's ministry, on 4 June 1885, the congregation purchased over 15 acres at Lisnawhiggle and this was used to build a manse. During the vacancy following Mr. Ritchie, in 1986-1987 an extensive renovation was carried out on the manse at a cost of £40,000.

An extension to the Houston Memorial church hall was commenced in 1982 which cost £27,000. At a service to commemorate 225 years of history in the Kellswater area, it was officially opened on 9 March 1985.

1989 was a notable year in the history of the congregation. The W.M.A. celebrated its centenary. Also, in June of that year, a history of the congregation was published, which had been written by Robert Buchanan, a Superintendent in the R.U.C., who was murdered by terrorists on 20 March.

The elders who participated in the Covenant renovation of 1854 were John Duncan, Samuel Darragh, William Clugston and John Hyndman. These were succeeded by Robert Anderson, James Wasson, Newton Armstrong, William Armstrong, John Duncan and W.J. Aiken. On 10 October 1888 four more elders were ordained: Newton Thompson, John Duncan, James Warwick and James F. Taylor. During Mr. McIlmoyle's ministry in the 1920s the elders were Matthew Rock, Robert Moffat, Henry Adair, Samuel Wasson, Samuel Rock and Samuel Moffett.   In 1934 Samuel Carmichael and Alexander Wilson were ordained. In 1947 Robert Wallace, David Rock and John Gordon were ordained. These were succeeded in the 1950s by James Warwick, Frank Templeton, James Kenny and followed by Samuel Owens. In 1979 Malcom Smith, John O'Neill, Joseph Spence were ordained and James Simpson installed. To these men Robert McMullan was later added.

After a period of decline, membership has stabilised, at time of writing. Working in close cooperation with the Northern Presbytery, the congregation has been seeking to strengthen its fellowship and to reach out to the surrounding community and undertake the establishment of a new work in the nearby town of Antrim. On Friday 18th September, Mr. John Coates, a licentiate of the Eastern Presbytery, was ordained and installed as the eleventh minister of the Kellswater congregation. Having been without their own pastor for over nine years, the congregation has been ably cared for by the interim moderator, Rev. Wallace McCollum, but now look forward to the development and growth of the work of the Covenanted Reformation first established here in 1760.

The Meeting House is situated at 23 Grove Road, Kells, Ballymena, Co. Antrim,
BT42 3LR.

Eskylane Meeting House

ESKYLANE

The congregation of Eskylane near Kells in County Antrim came into being as a result of the controversy within the Reformed Presbyterian Church on the question of the authority of the Civil Magistrate. Several members of the Reformed Presbyterian congregation at Kellswater withdrew and formed their own congregation. They were received into the Eastern Reformed Presbyterian Synod in 1849 and remained members of that Synod until 1903 when both minister and congregation joined the Irish Presbyterian Church.

The first three ministers did not stay long in the congregation. Rev. Hugh Austin of Cullybackey died in 1853 only four years after being appointed. Rev. George Stewart of Letterkenny was minister from 1856 to 1859 when he left to join the General Assembly. Rev. William Close of Loughmourne, was stated supply of Eskylane 1864-1873. He was succeeded by Rev. Samuel Moffett who continued as pastor until 1917. In 1903 both minister and people were accepted into the General Assembly. Mr. Moffett died on 8 Oct. 1918. When Mr. Moffett retired the congregation consisted of only 26 families and it was agreed that it be united with Kells Presbyterian congregation.

The Meeting House is situated on Steeple Road, Kells, Co. Antrim.

Kilraughts Meeting House

KILRAUGHTS

The first Presbytery in Ireland was established in 1642 and by the end of the 1650s it met in five different areas to deal with the business of each locality. One of these was the 'Route Meeting'. The earliest Covenanting influence here came from David Houston, a native of Paisley in Scotland who came to Ulster at this time. He was appointed stated supply to the congregations in this 'Route Meeting'. He ministered, amongst other places, in the Ballymoney, Derrykeighan and Armoy areas. The turbulent Scotsman proved such an embarrassment to his colleagues, by his attachment to the Scottish Covenants, that he was suspended by the 'Route Meeting' in 1672. After some years in Scotland, during which he fought at Bothwell Brig in 1679, he returned to Ireland and was recommended to the Covenanting Societies by Alexander Peden. From 1689 he itinerated in various parts of Ulster, which included Armoy, and in this North Antrim area, Mr. Houston worked for four years until his death in 1696, establishing a Covenanting cause.

However, in the next century, Covenanters had few privileges and many discouragements. When the Scottish Reformed Presbytery was formed in 1743, local Covenanters received a number of preaching appointments from men such as John Cameron, who had settled in Dunluce, and John Fairley who preached regularly at the Vow, near Ballymoney. William Martin's ministry covered the whole of Co. Antrim from 1757.

It was not until the ministry of James McKinney (1783-1793) that the foundations were laid of the congregations that were eventually formed at Kilraughts, Dervock and

Ballymoney. Born in Kilrea about 1750, and brought up in Drimbolg, James McKinney

received his education at Glasgow University and the Scottish Divinity Hall. He was ordained on 1 July 1783 at Kirkhills, between Ballymoney and Stranocum, to serve an extensive congregation of which that was the centre. The meeting house was on the farm owned by Hugh Ramsey. Mr. McKinney was a forthright preacher and it is not surprising that, in the tense atmosphere that prevailed in the last decade of the eighteenth century, he should put himself at some risk for his outspoken criticism of an ailing monarchy and a corrupt government. In 1793 he preached a sermon entitled 'The Rights of God', when he declared that sovereignty did not lie with any king but with God alone. The authorities interpreted this as treason and took steps to arrest and try him. Suspecting that he would not get a fair trial, he emigrated to America in 1793. There he helped to organise the American Reformed Presbytery in 1798.

In the vacancy that followed, the congregation was not idle and William John Stavely was ordained on 6 September 1804 to serve the congregation, known by then as Kilraughts and Dervock. It comprised 228 members in full communion, drawn from a wide area. Dr. Stavely had grown up in the Knockbracken congregation, of which his father, William Stavely, was the minister. He was educated at Glasgow University and the Reformed Presbyterian Divinity Hall in Paisley. Dr. Stavely was almost immediately able to conduct his ministry in a fine new meeting house on the site of the present building, opened in 1805. These church buildings lie to the east of Ballymoney town, approximately five miles along the Kilraughts Road on an elevated site which affords an impressive view in every direction over the surrounding countryside. For this reason it has sometimes been called 'the mountain church'.

Because the congregation grew to more than 500, Dr. Stavely recommended that a new congregation be organized to take in the Dervock and Ballymoney part of his original charge. In 1832, it was arranged that two calls be presented to him through Presbytery, one from Kilraughts and the other from Dervock and Ballymoney. Dr. Stavely resigned Kilraughts and accepted the call from what he referred to as the 'weaker of the two'.

His successor in Kilraughts, William Toland, was brought up in connection with the original Belfast congregation in Linenhall Street. He was educated at St. Andrews and Edinburgh Universities and the Hall in Paisley. The commissioners at the Presbytery in 1832 asking for moderation were two brothers, Samuel and James Loughridge (the latter being Professor Adam Loughridge's great-grandfather). They presented bonds from twelve Societies pledging support for a minister. The names of the societies in 1832 and of those who signed the bonds were: Armoy: John Henry and John Dunlop; Ballyknock: James Loughridge and James Cochrane; Ballyportery: William King; Ballinaloob: Joseph McCollum and John Henry; Killymurris: John Caldwell and William Simpson; Calhame: Matthew Cathcart and Alexander Kerr; Greenshields: Hugh Stirling and Hugh Tweed; Topp: John Moore and William Kirkpatrick; Kilraughts: William Knox and William Simpson; Magheraboy: Archibald McFadden and John McNeill; Lavin: James Houston, and Samuel Creelman; Tirrygoogin: Samuel Loughridge and John Guthrie. Magheraboy: Archibald McFadden and John McNeill; Lavin: James Houston and Samuel Creelman; Tirrygoogin: Samuel Loughridge and John Guthrie. Many of these families are still represented in the congregation.

Mr. Toland was ordained and installed on 1 August 1832 and had a long ministry of 44 years, retiring in 1876 and dying in November, 1878. Mr. Toland was an excellent preacher and gave all the help he could to the 1859 Revival. Consequently, the congregation grew to 170 during these years. He was also a gifted writer and regularly contributed to the Church's magazine, *The Covenanter*. In addition he served on the Committee of Superintendence of the Theological Hall and helped to guide it, with wisdom and discretion, in its early years after its establishment in 1854.

The next ministry was a short one. Robert John Morrell, a member of Ringrash, educated at Queen's College Belfast, was ordained on 19 November 1879. Correspondence with one of the elders shows that he never settled happily. At that time, there was disagreement in both Session and the congregation over the controversial Irish policies of the British

Prime Minister William Gladstone. Session was divided in its opinion about the minister's convictions, so he moved to Knockbracken on 11 October 1883; he joined the General Assembly in December 1886.

The next minister was Rev. James Dick, son of Professor James Dick of Kellswater. Educated at Belfast Academical Institution, Queen's College Belfast and the R.P. Hall, he had ministered for 14 years in Wishaw before coming to Kilraughts. He was installed on 11 March 1884 and promised a stipend of £140 per annum, at the time, one of the largest in the Synod. He was a fine athlete and cricketer, but it was as a scholar and preacher that he excelled. He was successively Professor of Hebrew, Biblical Criticism and Church History, and Systematic Theology from 1887. Professor Dick became the first minister of the newly formed Trinity Street congregation in 1896.

Kilraughts Meeting House before 1879

Rev. John McClelland Cromie, originally a member of Loughbrickland, had served 16 years in Kellswater when he was installed in Kilraughts on 18 May, 1898. He ministered faithfully for 30 years. He succeeded Professor Dick in the chair of Systematic Theology in 1917. The congregation was greatly blessed by his thoughtful and earnest preaching and his watchful and sympathetic pastoral care. His sudden death, little more than an hour after his departure from the 1928 Synod, was a great shock.

The long and faithful ministry of Rev. James Blair from 1929 to 1966 was long remembered with affection by the congregation. Brought up in Limavady, educated at Magee College, Londonderry and the Theological Hall, he was installed on 12 March 1929. He came to Kilraughts after serving in Ballyclare and Milford. In addition to his warm-hearted preaching, he demonstrated devoted pastoral care and evangelistic and missionary zeal. He died on 30 April 1966.

The vacancy was quickly filled by Rev. Frederick Stratford Leahy called from 13 years' service in Cregagh Road and Ballymacashon. He was the third minister of Kilraughts to occupy the Chair of Systematic Theology in the Theological Hall. Professor Leahy retired in May 1988. The congregation appreciated the devoted service he gave, expressed in his teaching ministry and pastoral care. His sound scholarship and warm evangelical spirit was expressed in a number of books which he published and have a wide readership.

Mr. Harry Coulter was the ninth minister of the congregation and was ordained and installed on 22 September 1989. A native of Co. Fermanagh, he had been a member of the Trinity congregation for the previous eight years. He proved himself a worthy successor in a line of dedicated ministers. His vision and desire for the extension of Christ's Kingdom was evident in his contribution to the establishment of a congregation in Cloughmills and to the revitalisation of the Church in the Home Section of the Mission Committee. This was further in evidence when Mr. Coulter was called to be Organising Pastor of the Carrickfergus Reformed Presbyterian Fellowship. The Service of Commissioning was held in the Trinity Church building on 4 February 2004.

Rev. David Fallows of the Wishaw congregation in Scotland received a call from the congregation on 18 February 2005 and was installed on 2 September 2005.

Kilraughts has made a notable contribution to the life of the Church as a whole. In the missionary sphere the congregation has had a long representation on the mission field for more than 80 years by Dr. Samuel Kennedy (1895-1938), Dr. Archibald Guthrie (1934 -1946) and Miss Henrietta Gardner (1938-1978).

A great number of young men responded to a call to the ministry and entered training at the Theological Hall. Their names are: William White (licensed in 1791 but too ill to be ordained to the ministry), Hutchinson McFadden (1780-1812), Hutchinson McFadden (1812-1875), Adam McFadden, Alexander MacLeod Stavely, Robert Fulton (who emigrated to America), Charles Kirk Toland (who left the R.P. Church for the General Assembly after 20 years ministry in Bready), Joseph Gardner (who died in his second year of studies), James Kerr (who died shortly after his licensure for work in Australia), James Kerr (who spent his entire ministry in the service of the R.P. Church in Scotland), Henry Stewart (licensed in 1847 but entered the General Assembly in 1850), Archibald Holmes, John Carson Loughridge (who after completing his studies for the ministry turned to the medical profession), Samuel Hanna Kennedy, Samuel Hanna (who left the R.P. Church for the Free Church of Scotland after 3 years ministry in Larne), Thomas Hanna, Alexander Gardner (who died in a road accident after completing his studies), Samuel Wallace Lynas, Archibald Guthrie, Alexander Barkley, Adam Loughridge, Hugh Jamison Blair, Matthew Young and Robert Hanna.

The list of ruling elders in a congregation that originated in the late eighteenth century will of course be long. The following served in this office: Matthew Cathcart, John Craig, John Guthrie, John Picken, Thomas Mitchell, Archibald McFadden, James Clark, George Henry, Samuel Jackson, John Clark, Samuel Loughridge, Samuel Stewart, James Finlay, Andrew Wilson, Alexander Calderwood, Joseph Mulholland, James Kennedy, Thomas H Loughridge, George Stewart, William Hanna, John Chambers, James Gardner, John Holmes, Thomas Loughridge. In the late nineteenth century, the elders were Alexander Gardner, David Guthrie, Joseph Henry, Robert Kerr, William Kerr, William Millar, David Wilson and Robert Wilson. The congregation suffered heavily from emigration after World War I but the work was well maintained and supervised by the elders whose names were William Finlay, James Gardner, Thomas Hill, John Holmes, James Loughridge, William McMillan, Robert Patterson, and later, Hugh Barkley, John Henry, Thomas Loughridge, William John Pinkerton and Robert Robinson. During Mr Blair's ministry, the following elders were elected: Robert H. Barkley, Robert J. Pinkerton, Joseph McQueston, David Robinson, James Loughridge and Thomas H. Loughridge. New elders in 1970 were Arnold Barkley, William B. Hanna, Charles Knox, William James

Loughridge and Robert E. Robinson. In 1984 those ordained were Alan Kennedy, David Loughridge, Roy Pinkerton, Elliott Robinson and William Simpson.

For the first twenty years of its existence the congregation shared a meeting house with the Dervock congregation at Kirkhills, between Stranocum and Ballymoney. In 1805 the congregation built its own meeting house at Kilraughts. This building has undergone two major renovations during its lifetime. The first was in 1879 when box pews and barrel type stoves were installed. The second renovation took place in 1933. Mr. Blair had led each of his congregations in turn in a thorough programme of renovation of their church

buildings, the work in Kilraughts being done in the summer of 1933. A new roof, seating and heating system were installed and a kitchen and Session room were erected at the west end of the building. In 1994 a new  church hall was added to the existing suite of buildings. In 2005 the congregation celebrated the 200th anniversary of its existence in the church building.

Mr. Stavely had lived first at Ballyboyland House and then at Lavin House. Mr. Toland's manse was Brookville House and then Ballyboyland. Prof. Dick lived in Osmond House, Ballymoney. At the beginning of Mr Cromie's ministry, in 1900 the manse at Pine Hill was purchased. In December 2001 the manse at Pine Hill was sold and a new one was built at 8 Beckett Avenue, Ballymoney.

Kilraughts serves an area within a triangle formed by Ballymoney, Cloughmills and Armoy. The congregation is currently seeking to strengthen its body life in order to be more honouring to the Lord, more prayerful and more welcoming. Their hope is that others will join with them as a result of the natural witness of individual members and through organised forms of outreach.

The Meeting House is situated at 175 Kilraughts Road, Ballymoney, BT53 8NL.

Ringrash former Meeting House

RINGRASH

The congregation of Ringrash was originally a Covenanting society which formed part of the 'Bannside' congregation. Bannside covered the greater part of County Londonderry and included the eventual congregations of Ballylaggan, Drimbolg and Limavady. From 1805 to 1858 the Ringrash society, or Dunboe, as it was first called, was joined with Ballyclabber in the Coleraine congregation. The Covenanting cause had been established early in the Coleraine locality. In the spring of 1644 the Solemn League and Covenant was administered in Coleraine. It was difficult to maintain this cause after 1660. Only occasionally were Covenanting principles set forth and that mainly by David Houston at Derrykeighan in the 1690s and by John Cameron, a Scottish probationer who preached in Dunluce Presbyerian Church. Encouragement came to the Covenanters in the middle of the 18th century with the itinerant ministry of William Martin, who though settled at Kellswater, preached frequently in Co. Londonderry.

Matthew Lynn, a native of Larne and a licentiate of the Scottish Presbytery, was ordained the first minister of the Bannside congregation on 15 August, 1763. Mr. Lynn's ministry ended in 1773 when he emigrated to America. He was succeeded by Samuel Aiken, a native of Clough, Co. Antrim, who ministered from 1776 to 1790 before going to Creevagh.

Joseph Orr, was ordained at Garvagh in 1798 as the third minister of Bannside. As Mr. Orr lived at Drumlamph, near Castledawson, the strain of ministering to such a large  scattered congregation was very great indeed and, on a total stipend of £52, he had a struggle to make ends meet. Gradually the Bannside congregation was broken up. In 1805 Mr. Orr was relieved of the care of Limavady and it became a separate congregation. Ballylaggan became a separate congregation in 1816. Rationalisaton was taking place elsewhere. On 10 April 1805 the society of Ballyrashane was separated from the congregation of 'Lower Antrim' (which was comprised of Dervock and Kilraughts and Ballymoney) and became linked with Dunboe. This new congregation, later called Ballyclabber, formed from the merger, met in a thatched building called the 'Clabor Meeting House' on the Ballyrashane Road.

On 10 December 1805, Mr. David Graham, a Burgher Seceder until less than a year before, preached trial sermons before the Reformed Presbytery. The trials were sustained and he was ordained the next day. The settlement was not to last. After only two years, he left the congregation and emigrated to America where he became a prominent lawyer in New York.

The congregation received some encouragement when in 1806 a large society at Bushtown left Ballylaggan and joined Dunboe. The congregation was thus made up of three societies, - Dunboe, Bushtown and Ballyrashane. It was known as 'Coleraine' and met at Ballyclabber. After a vacancy of eight years the congregation was further strengthened in 1811 by the accession of twenty-four families from the Burgher Seceders.

The congregation issued a call to Robert Gamble Orr, a member of the congregation at Grange, Co. Tyrone. He was ordained on 30 August 1815 at Clabor Meeting House. Not a popular preacher, and therefore soon suffering from arrears of stipend, his relations with the people were never happy and he was released from the pastoral tie by the Presbytery at his own request after a ministry of five years. For some years he acted as stated supply in Limavady and the Western Presbytery before emigrating to America about 1833.

In 1816 we find the first reference to the name 'Ballyclabber',and in 1826 'Ringrash' is used in preference to the older name 'Dunboe'. Samuel Carlisle, a member of Creevagh and a licentiate of the Southern Presbytery, served the congregation faithfully from 1827 until his death in 1856, aged 67. During the vacancy which followed, in 1858, the Dunboe/Ringrash part of the congregation separated from the Ballyrashane/Clabor part. The desire for separation was mutual. Ringrash in 1861, was composed of 3 societies, comprising 21 families, 45 communicants, 14 adherents and 41 children. It was supplied by Presbytery for 11 years and then the congregation made a call to Rev. Torrens Boyd of Penpont in Scotland which he accepted and was installed on February 1873. But on 13 January 1875 he accepted a call to Dromara.

Torrens Boyd was Ringrash's sole minister and in 1891 the congregation was placed under the care of the minister of Ballyclabber. In 1941 it was designated a preaching station. The elders in Ringrash were Thomas Jack, Abraham McCandless, William McAleese and John Curry. Despite its short history, Ringrash provided one candidate for the ministry, R. J. Morrell, minister of Kilraughts between 1879 and 1882. William John Nevin, an elder in the congregation, later became a minister in the General Synod of the R. P. Church of North America.

The Meeting House is in a poor state of repair but is interesting in that it retains many original exterior features. It is situated near the corner of the Ringrash Road on the Windyhill Road, Macosquin, Coleraine.

SOUTHERN PRESBYTERY

Ballenon Meeting House

BALLENON

One of the places that William Stavely visited frequently in south Armagh was Sleath's Fort and the fruits of this witness laid the foundations of the Ballenon congregation. Support for the small number of Covenanters in the Ballenon area came from an unexpected quarter. In 1809, after years rejecting the Regium Donum that had been paid to the ministers of the Synod of Ulster, the local Secession Church succumbed to temptation and negotiated a grant from the Government on terms similar to those governing the grants to the Synod of Ulster. This involved taking the Oath of Allegiance to the Crown. The acceptance of this bounty by the Seceders led to the transfer of a considerable number of their members to the ranks of the Covenanters. In Tyrone Ditches Secession church, the minister, Rev.William King, was one of those who agreed with this new departure and, as a result, 23 families left that congregation and started to build their own meeting house in Ballenon. In January 1820, the Southern Presbytery of the Reformed Presbyterian Church agreed to their request for supply of preaching. On 5 May 1820, these families, separated from Tyrone's Ditches, joined with the local Covenanters to form the congregation of Ballenon. The first meeting of Session was held on 16 June 1820 in the home of John Henry of Crieve. The Moderator was Rev. Hans Boggs, minister of Ballylane. Traditionally referred to as "The Bog Edge Meetin", Ballenon meeting house and hall are situated on Corrinare Road, approximately three miles from Poyntzpass and five miles from Markethill, Co. Armagh.

Their first minister, John Hawthorn, a native of Kilkinamurry in Co. Down, was called on 5 November 1821 and was ordained on 7 May 1822. There were 381 persons in the congregation at that time. He relinquished the office in 1845. He left Liverpool for Canada but died on 2 June 1847, aged 54, on board ship as it lay off the Quarantine Station on Gross Isle in the St. Lawrence River. His eighteenth month old son, Hutchinson Hawthorn, died two days later. Mr. Hawthorn's fine work in difficult years laid a good foundation.

Alexander Savage, a member of Ballylaggan, was ordained on 30 May 1849. He built well on this good foundation and, under his faithful leadership, the work prospered in a long ministry of forty years. He was a hard working pastor and a learned expositor. He died, aged 79, after a brief illness, on 10 December 1889.

Ballenon was one of the first congregations in the Church to organise a Sabbath School. Sabbath Schools came into existence following the Synod of 1841. While there was no Synodical Committee to supervise the work, each congregation had its own programme. It is of interest to note the high standard set by Ballenon as early as 1865:

> The annual examination of the above flourishing Sabbath School took place on 3 July, being conducted by the pastor, Rev. A. Savage, Mr. I. Thompson, student, and the members of Session, in the presence of the teachers and the members of Ballenon and adjoining congregations. All present expressed their admiration and astonishment at the invaluable and accurate amount of catechetical knowledge acquired and indelibly imprinted on the tablet of memory. The scale of tasks for the past year was as follows:

First Class: To repeat the first 100 questions in the Larger Catechism together with 25 Psalms, from the 20th to the 45th inclusive;

Second Class: To repeat from the 300th question of Brown's Catechism to the end, with 20 Psalms from the 15th to the 35th;

Third class: To repeat the Shorter Catechism, 300 questions from the Brown's Catechism, and 15 Psalms from the 15th to the 30th;

Fourth class: The Shorter Catechism and ten Psalms.

Mr. Savage was succeeded by William Russell. A son of the Ballyclare Manse, he was ordained on 29 October 1890. He gave himself to the work of the congregation and was highly respected in the community. He accepted a call to Paisley in 1905.

Wilson Moreland Kennedy from Ballyclare was ordained on 8 August 1906 and served for less than a year. He resigned in May 1907 and entered the ministry of the Irish Presbyterian Church.

There followed a lengthy vacancy. Following the death of Rev. William McKnight, the minister of Ballylane, on 10 April 1911, representatives of the two congregations discussed the possibility of the congregations uniting in a call. After further meetings, on 22 January 1912, at a meeting at Ballenon, it was unanimously and heartily agreed that the congregations should unite their means and resources in order to be in a position to obtain a minister, with each congregation preserving its own identity and having separate sessions and services. It was reported that a spirit of goodwill prevailed.

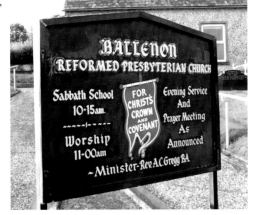

The following have served as ruling elders in the congregation: John Henry, Hugh Hawthorn, Robert Porter, Isaac Porter, Aaron Hunter, Hugh Stewart, James Brown,

Alexander Thompson, William Wylie, Thomas Stott, John McClure, John Gordon, Clark Rafferty, Hugh Stuart, Richard Hale, Thomas McCullough, John Paul, David Qua, Sandy Small, William Stewart, Alexander Stewart and John Qua, Benjamin Thompson, James McCelland Qua, James Barber, Alexander S. Stewart, Joseph James Irvine, David Cromie and David Porter. After the uniting of the congregations, the following were elected to the Session in Ballenon: Thomas J. Hale, Robert A. McEwen, James Cole, George H. McCartney, David Porter, Lowry Cole, Robert Herron, James Minish and Andrew Herron.

Ballenon has supplied five students for the ministry of the Reformed Presbyterian Church: John Stott, William Thompson, Gawn Douglas, Isaac Thompson and Isaac Cole. The following, brought up in Ballenon, served as ministers in other denominations: S. Wilson, Hugh A. Irvine and Robert Shields.

The meeting house was for many years whitewashed and had a door in each gable and a pulpit in the centre of the east wall, next to the road. Originally the floor was sanded and there was no ceiling. In 1902 the pulpit was changed to the north wall and new seating of pitch pine was installed and a vestibule erected on the south side of the building. During the ministry of Nevin Lyons (1913-1920), a heating system was installed in the meeting house. In 1962 the building was pebble-dashed and re-roofed, electricity was installed and a water supply was connected.

In the early days of the congregation there were stables and a boiler house at the roadside with two rooms above, one of which was used as a session room. In 1929 a church hall was constructed by taking in the rooms above the stables. In the mid 1970s a kitchen and toilets were constructed downstairs where the old stables had been. In November 1897 Session decided to acquire a manse and building, commenced in August 1898. Central heating was installed in the late 1970s.

With further refurbishment to the meeting house, church hall and manse in 1998, the congregation is well equipped with a comfortable meeting house and hall and a fine manse.

The Meeting House is situated on 62 Corrinare Road, Poyntzpass, Newry, Co. Down, BT35 6RY.

Ballylane Meeting House

BALLYLANE

Ballylane was one of several congregations that came into existence through the indefatigable work of Rev. William Stavely. From the time of his ordination in 1772 he was more than a settled pastor in a congregation; he was rather an itinerant evangelist for the Church as a whole. His route took him almost always into southwest Ulster and on his preaching tours he regularly visited Rathfriland, Sleath's Fort, Drumillar, Muckney and Ballybay. The congregation at Ballylane as well as those of Knockbracken, Newtownards, Dromore, Rathfriland, Fairview and Creevagh are the result of his labours.

The societies in the Ballylane district were organised into a regular congregation in 1790. They found a beautiful site for their meeting house in a glen a short distance south of the village of Mowhan, three miles from Markethill, County Armagh.

The Irish Reformed Presbytery installed Rev. Samuel Aiken as the first minister in 1790. A native of Clough, Co. Antrim, he had given fine service in the Bannside congregation from 1774 – a congregation now represented by Drimbolg, Limavady and Ballylaggan. His new congregation, like his previous one, was widely scattered and embraced the present charges of Rathfriland and Creevagh. When he died on 25 December 1798 he was interred in Creevagh. Before Mr. Aiken's death it had been intended that Creevagh become disannexed from Ballylane and linked with Fairview under his ministry based in Creevagh. These changes were brought about during the vacancy that followed his death.

In 1802, Hans Boggs, a native of Creevy, near Loughbrickland, born in 1776, was ordained and given the oversight of Ballylane and Rathfriland. In 1811 Rathfriland

became a separate congregation and Mr. Boggs remained the minister of Ballylane until his death at Dierlet on 31 October 1837. He was buried at Ballylane, together with his wife, Eleanor, who had died on 27 August 1814, aged 31; she was the first adult to be buried there. It is of interest to note that John McEwen, the father of Rev. Joseph McEwen, minister of Bready and Fairview, was associated with Ballylane for the first 25 years of his life and walked 11 miles in each direction to attend public worship every Sabbath. He later identified with Loughbrickland when it was formed and later still with Dromore. His great-great grandson, Rev. Timothy McEwen, was installed as the minister of the Ballylane congregation in 2008.

The next minister, William Sweeney, a member of Bready and a licentiate of the Western Presbytery, was ordained on 11 September 1839. At the end of one year he left the congregation and later became Presbyterian minister of Killeshandra in Co. Cavan.

His successor, Hutchinson McFadden, a member of Kilraughts, was ordained on 6 June 1853. During his ministry of 32 years, the congregation survived the rigours of the Great

Famine and the accompanying tide of emigration. The congregation reached its peak of some 120 members just after the 1859 Revival. Mr. McFadden died on 28 April 1875 and was buried at Ballylane.

William McKnight, a native of Castledawson, Co. Londonderry and a member of Drimbolg succeeded him. Ordained on 15 March 1876, he served the congregation with great faithfulness until his death on 10 April 1911. Emigration once again hit the congregation during these years and membership fell from 90 in 1876 to 50 in 1910. Mr. McKnight was the last minister of an independent Ballylane. There followed the continuing union with neighbouring Ballenon.

The following have been elected as ruling elders in Ballylane: David Alexander, William Harrison, Robert Crookshanks, Hugh Stewart, Robert Porter, John Hooks, Thomas Johnston, Hugh Thompson, Robert Woods, James Thompson, Thomas Scott, William Stewart and Thomas Holmes. Since the uniting of the congregations of Ballenon and Ballylane in 1912 the elders appointed by Ballylane have been David S. Stewart, Thomas W. Johnston, David Draffin, John Johnston, Hugh Riddall, George Douglas, John W. Hill, D. Shannon Stewart, William Johnston, William G. Armstrong and Ian Douglas.

Ballylane has provided two students for the ministry of the Reformed Presbyterian Church. Hugh Stewart served the Ann Street congregation of the Eastern Reformed Presbyterian Church in Newtownards from 1855 until 1887. Nigel Agnew was ordained and installed in Ballylaggan on 21 November 1997 and installed as minister of Creevagh on 8 September 2006. In addition the Church has been faithfully served by another member, Hugh William Stewart, well known for his devoted and effective work in the Irish Mission from 1926 until his retirement in 1963.

The meeting house underwent extensive renovations in 1983 and a new hall was opened on 24 April 1998.

The Meeting House is situated at 4 Lough Road, Mowhan, Markethill, Co. Armagh, BT60 2LH.

BALLENON AND BALLYLANE

Following the lengthy vacancy in Ballenon from 1906 and the death of Rev. William McKnight, the minister of Ballylane, on 10 April 1911, representatives of the two congregations discussed the possibility of the congregations uniting in a call. After further meetings, on 22 January 1912, at a meeting at Ballenon, it was unanimously and heartily agreed that the congregations should unite their means and resources in order to be in a position to obtain a minister, with each congregation preserving its own identity and having separate sessions and services. It was reported that a spirit of goodwill prevailed.

The first minister of the joint charge was Robert Nevin Lyons, a son of the Newry Manse. He was ordained at Ballenon on 24 September 1913. Mr. Lyons had a strong burden for evangelism and organised a monthly evangelistic service in the old schoolhouse at Ballygorman and, for a time during World War One, he was absent from the congregation, working for the Y.M.C.A with soldiers on the Western Front. Mr. Lyons moved to Ballylaggan in 1920.

William Dodds, a licentiate of the Eastern Presbytery, but brought up in Faiview, was

ordained on 20 August 1924. He was educated at The Queen's University, Belfast and the R.P. Theological Hall. He served the congregations with great devotion for forty-one years. He did not spare himself for the congregation and faithfully preached the Gospel and visited the homes in the congregation; it was said he was at his best in times of trouble or bereavement. Many individuals were indebted to him for the private tuition he offered as a preparation for admission to further and higher education. In March 1965 Mr. Dodds took suddenly ill and died on 17 March.

Andrew Cross Gregg, a member of Convoy congregation, was ordained and installed in the joint charge on 2 September 1966. Mr. Gregg had a valuable ministry towards the young people of the area. He resigned the charge on 5 February 1974 so as to devote his gifts to the work of the Irish Mission in Cork.

The tradition of faithful preaching continued with the settlement of Rev. Harry Tadley, Synod's Evangelist since 1959 and minister of Dublin Road since 1971 as minister of the two congregations on 7 October 1976. His short but fruitful ministry was characterised by commitment to evangelism, praise and visitation of the sick and elderly. It was brought to an end with his death on 28 June 1981 aged 59 years.

After seven years without a resident minister, James A. Ritchie was appointed as Minister in Charge from 1 June 1988. This arrangement continued until Mr. Ritchie was called by the congregations and was installed on 2 May 1990. He was a faithful minister and diligent pastor, earnestly displaying the heart of a true evangelist. His useful ministry ended with his retirement on 27 May 1996. Mr. Ritchie died in Scotland on 9 April 2006.

Rev. Andrew Gregg was installed (for the second time) in the joint congregations on 11 February 1998. He retired from the ministry on 30 September 2006. The Presbytery appointed Mr. Gregg Interim Moderator of the congregation.

Timothy McEwen, a member of Bailiesmills and a licentiate of the Eastern Presbytery, was ordained and installed on 5 September 2008. The congregations jointly organised a outreach event in Markethill in 2009, looking at the long history of the Covenanters, and especially the continuing relevance of their presence and the message of the Gospel in this area. Rev. McEwen resigned 11 March 2010.

Clare Meeting House

CLARE

The congregation worships in a meeting house at the crossroads in the village of Clare, about three miles from Tandragee in Co. Armagh. It became a congregation in the Southern Presbytery of the Reformed Presbyterian Church in 1919.

The congregation was originally within the Presbyterian Synod of Ulster. However, in 1812, the Presbyterian minister at Clare was in difficulties with some members of his congregation. The section of the congregation that opposed him sought, and was granted, pulpit supply by the Armagh Presbytery of the Burgher Seceders in 1813. They called Robert Hawthorne, a licentiate from Tyrone, and he was ordained on 25 August, 1818. He lived at Marlacoo, near Tandragee. He was opposed to the union of the Synod of Ulster and the Secession Synod that formed the Presbyterian General Assembly in 1840 and remained a Seceder until his death in 1873. For the next forty years the congregation courageously maintained its existence and its connection with the Original Secession Synod in Scotland, but the small denomination to which it adhered had difficulty in meeting the demands for supplies in their few widely scattered congregations in Ireland. Consequently, from 1874 Clare was united with Tyrone's Ditches under the ministry of Rev. Joseph C. Stuart.

When Tyrone's Ditches entered the General Assembly in 1919, Clare made application to the Southern Presbytery of the Reformed Presbyterian Church of Ireland and was received into membership on 22 July 1919. It was placed under the pastoral care of Rev. R. Nevin Lyons of Ballenon. In the Report to Synod in 1920, the Presbytery 'was pleased to witness the independent and enthusiastic manner in which the congregation had decided to become associated with the Covenanter Church and also to see that the temporal and spiritual interests of the congregation were in a healthy and promising condition'.

In 1922 Mr. Pollock, the minister of Loughbrickland, began his long association with Clare. When he resigned from Loughbrickland in 1941, he remained stated supply of Clare until his retirement on 1 February, 1955. He died on 28 February 1956. During his ministry he was faithfully and ably supported by two elders, William Ferguson and James McMahon.

Charles Presho, a member of Dublin Road and a licentiate of the Eastern Presbytery, had a short but promising pastorate of two years. He resigned on accepting a call to Glasgow on 21 January, 1947. Dr. Presho later became the Secretary of the British and Foreign Bible Society for Ireland.

He was succeeded in Loughbrickland by Rev. Robert Barnett Cupples. Mr. Cupples, minister of Cregagh Road since 1947 was installed at Loughbrickland on 5 April 1951. On 1 February 1955 he accepted the additional responsibility of Clare after Mr. Pollock's retirement and served the two congregations until he retired from the active duties of the ministry on 3 September 1974. His tenderhearted and compassionate disposition touched the lives of a wide circle of people.

Robert Blair McFarland, a member of Faughan and a licentiate of the Western Presbytery, was ordained and installed by the Southern Presbytery on 17 March 1977 as minister of the joint charge of Clare and Loughbrickland. The linkage of Clare and Loughbrickland was formalised prior to Mr. McFarland's ordination. During his ministry in 1984, outreach meetings began in the neighbouring town of Tandragee. The work revolved around Sabbath evening services and continued for some years. Mr. McFarland resigned when he accepted a call from the Foreign Mission Board to serve as a missionary in France at a meeting of the Southern Presbytery on 6 May 1986.

On 15 September 1988 David Silversides, from Gateshead, licentiate of the Eastern Presbytery, was ordained and installed as minister of the joint charge of Clare and Loughbrickland.

On 30 March 1999, the Southern Presbytery granted the request of Mr. Silversides to resign pastoral responsibility for the Clare congregation. Although there was reluctance on the part of the Clare congregation to agree to the separation, it was appreciated that a substantial majority of the Loughbrickland congregation supported the application; Loughbrickland had become fully self-supporting and needed a full-time minister. Loughbrickland was accordingly separated from Clare and recognised as a separate charge.

Having assured the Clare congregation of its full support, Presbytery appointed Rev. Stewart McMahon (minister of Newry), Interim Moderator of the Clare congregation. Mr. McMahon, retired to Donegal in 2006, fulfilled his responsibilities faithfully until 4 September 2007 when Rev. D. J. Magee was appointed Interim Moderator until the end of September 2008 and was succeeded by Rev. Drew Gregg.

The congregation extensively renovated their church building and it was reopened for worship on 20 April 2001. Having suffered from damp for several years the building had been closed for 6 months during which time services were conducted in the hall. The inside of the building was completely refurbished and contained a blend of the old pulpit and pews with new walls, floor and ceiling. Although the project cost £30,000, the meeting house was re-opened debt free.

The congregation has given one student to the ministry: William McCullough from Clare served the church in Ballylaggan and Drimbolg.

The Meeting House is situated at Clare Crossroads, Cloghoge Road, Clare, Tandragee, Co. Armagh.

Creevagh Meeting House

CREEVAGH

In the Plantation of Ulster, it is recorded that a number of the Scottish settlers in Co. Monaghan had an attachment to the Covenants. Societies maintained the Covenanting witness in days when supplies of preaching were hard to obtain and there was a ready welcome for preachers like William Stavely. Ballybay marked the most westerly point in his itinerary and from 1772 there was a nucleus of a congregation to receive him. The congregation gathered in Creevagh, just outside Ballybay, seven miles from the town of Monaghan.

The exact date of the congregation's formal organisation is not known, but it was around 1780. The first minister, Rev. Samuel Aiken, had served the Bannside congregation in Co. Londonderry from 1776. He was installed in 1790 and given the oversight of Creevagh, in addition to Ballylane and Rathfriland. His ministry was blessed in the formative years of the congregation's history and it is a measure of his attachment to Creevagh that he accepted the congregation's request to undertake the pastoral oversight of Creevagh and Fairview. This was about to be implemented when he died on 25 December 1798, at the early age of 52 and was buried in Creevagh churchyard.

His successor was Thomas Cathcart, a native of Ahoghill, Co. Antrim who was brought up in the Cullybackey congregation. After completing his education at Glasgow University and the Scottish R.P. Theological Hall, he was ordained on 10 September 1806. The congregation by this time had separated from Rathfriland and Ballylane and linked with Fairview. For 51 years he exercised a faithful and fruitful ministry and the congregations made steady progress, with a membership of about 120 at the time of his death in 1857.

Gawn Douglas, who was born at Ballenon in 1832, was the next minister. A graduate of Queen's College and a licentiate of the Southern Presbytery, he was ordained on 3 March 1863. He served the congregation with devotion and ability for twenty years until his resignation in May 1883. Mr. Douglas was installed in Loughbrickland in May 1884. The congregation reached its peak with a membership of 200 at the end of his ministry.

He was succeeded by John Martin Littlejohn, son of Rev. James Littlejohn, minister of Garvagh. He was ordained on 7 September 1886 but resigned after two years. He embarked on an intense period of study at the University of Glasgow graduating with an M.A.(1889), B.D.(1890) and LL.B.(1892) and emigrated to America to become President of Amity College in College Springs, Iowa. He took a great interest in the developing field of osteopathy and was among the founders of this technique in the U.S.A. and the U.K..

After a vacancy of five years, Rev. Archibald Holmes, a member of a distinguished Kilraughts family, who had served the Church for six years in Bready, was installed on 2 April 1893. His ministry of seven years in Creevagh was interrupted by his visit to Geelong, Australia (1897-1898). He resigned in 1900 and moved to Paisley in Scotland.

The sixth minister of the congregation was James Renwick Wright. A member of Cullybackey and a licentiate of the Eastern Presbytery, Mr Wright was ordained on 26

January 1904. His fine preaching and pastoral concern were a great blessing to the congregation for over seven years until he moved to Ballyclabber in April 1911.

John McIlmoyle began his ministry in Creevagh on 16 September 1913. A brilliant student and a gifted minister, he rendered valuable service in Creevagh during the difficult years of the First World War and the dangerous years of the Anglo-Irish War and the partition of Ireland. In 1923 he moved to Kellswater. He was Professor of Systematic Theology from 1941 to 1966 in the Theological Hall.

With the exception of Rev. Thomas Cathcart, all the ministries in Creevagh were comparatively short, but a series of longer pastorates began with that of Samuel Reid Archer, whose able ministry extended from 1928 to 1945. A member of Dromara and a licentiate of the Eastern Presbytery, he was ordained on 28 November 1928, and served the congregation with great acceptance until he moved to Rathfriland on 25 February 1945.

Cresswell Blair was ordained on 8 November, 1945. For fourteen years he brought all his gifts to bear on the work of the congregation. It was with sorrow that the congregation parted with him when he moved to Newtownards in 1959.

Joseph Robinson Patterson, was ordained on 18 February 1960. An able New Testament scholar, he was appointed Professor of New Testament Language and Literature in the Theological Hall in 1966. He resigned 25 June 1979 but remained on the roll of the Southern Presbytery as Minister without charge.

Thomas Gavin Reid, a member of Trinity Street and a licentiate of the Eastern Presbytery, was ordained and installed on 28 August 1980. He resigned 13 January 1983 and went to North America where he became a minister of the R.P.C.N.A.

Ian Morrison, from Dromara and a licentiate of the Eastern Presbytery, was ordained and installed on 7 November 1985. After several years of ministry, which was characterised by faithfulness, integrity and pastoral work among all sections of the congregation, Mr. Morrison accepted a call to Ballymoney in May 1994.

After a lengthy vacancy of 12 years, Rev. Nigel Agnew, minister of Ballylaggan, accepted the call of the congregation and was installed on 8 September 2006.

The following ruling elders have served the congregation: Joseph McElroy, Hugh Boyd, John Brownlee, William Carson, John Carson, George Graham, Thomas Henry, John C. Carlisle, William Perry, James Cobine, George Graham and Thomas Scott, Joseph Moffett, Thomas Moffett, Thomas Joseph Moffett, Graham Crawford, Thomas Taylor, S. J. Moffett, James Renwick Carson, Graham Moffett, W. Stanley Moffett, William E Carson, Adam Moffett, David Moffett, Alex Moffett and Eric Moffett.

The congregation has given ten of its members to the Church's ministry: John Reilly, J. W. Stewart, George Scott, Andrew Stevenson, Josiah Dodds, William Graham, Samuel Carlisle, William Scott, William James Moffett and James Robert Moffett.

The manse was extensively renovated in 1980. A new hall was erected in a period of 7 months during 1988 and opened on 26 November.

Creevagh Meeting House, in the 1890s, from Ferguson's Sketches

The Meeting House is situated at Creevagh, Ballybay, Co. Monaghan.

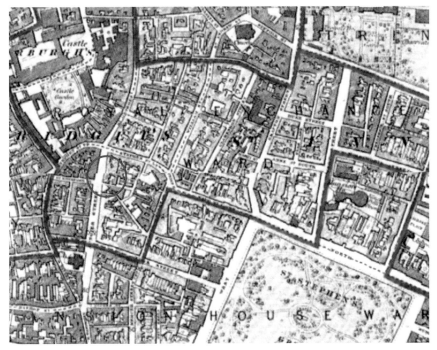

19th Century map of the area of Dublin surrounding the Meeting House in Aungier Street

DUBLIN

In 1834 a fellowship meeting in Dublin asked Synod for the 'dispensation of public ordinances'. The Missionary Board of the Church arranged for a succession of ministers to serve this meeting in Dublin and by the following year the Board was able to report to Synod that 'A Society of Covenanters in Dublin continues, zealous and steadfastly attached to our Testimony.' After 1837 the Society rented its own premises, having previously used those of another denomination. The Scottish Church also assisted with supplies of preaching and it would appear that a number of the Society were of Scottish extraction.

In 1855 Robert Allen, brought up in the Grange congregation, was ordained for missionary and evangelistic work by the Southern Presbytery for missionary work in the city of Dublin. A report of the Irish Mission in 1857 stated that Mr. Allen's diligence and perseverance were commended as he devoted a considerable portion of his time working in the streets and lanes of the city, visiting many homes of Roman Catholics and others.

The members desired a more comfortable meeting house and property, located at 11 Aungier Street was purchased and renovated at the expense of the Dublin congregation. In 1858 the Society asked Synod 'to continue their missionary in the city and also to strengthen his hands by appointing a catechist or Scripture reader to co-operate with him'. Synod directed the Southern Presbytery to explore this, organise the Society into a congregation and have elders ordained. The Society was organised as a congregation by the Southern Presbytery in 1859 and elders were ordained. In June of that year there were 15 communicants at the Lord's Table.

Rev. Robert Allen

A report to Synod considered the new situation in Dublin. It was now constituted as a congregation but still recognised as an Irish Mission station, with Mr. Allen labouring in both capacities. Mr. Allen in October 1859 offered his resignation from the specific missionary work under the Irish Mission. However, he continued as the minister from 1859 until his settlement in Newtownards in 1867.

Various attempts were made by the Synod to secure a successor to Mr. Allen but without success as there was a scarcity of students for the ministry at that time. The Synod of 1875 received an encouraging report from the Southern Presbytery regarding their steadfast adherence to the principles of the Church. By 1857 the communicant membership stood at twenty. However, over the next few years, the numbers of members and adherents declined. The Synod of 1870 decided that Dublin should be the main centre of its missionary work in Ireland, but during that period from 1872-1879 the work of the Irish Mission was in abeyance as a minister could not be settled in Dublin. The Southern Presbytery continued to provide the small and dwindling congregation in Dublin with Gospel ordinances, but no definite mission work was undertaken. The members of the congregation were anxious that this should be done, but they held that could only be carried out by a missionary who was permanently placed in Dublin.

No. 11 Aungier Street in 1986 after the fire which destroyed the building

A report for 1879 stated that over the previous year the congregation in Dublin had preaching on only 8 Sabbaths and that the Church had no funds to further endeavours in the city. In 1879 Synod regretfully decided not to maintain the work and the building in Aungier Street was sold.

No.s 8, 9 & 10 Aungier Street in 2010, the brick gable marks the site of No. 11

Attempts were made by Irish Mission workers to revive the regularity of Sabbath worship in the city and in December 1907, after a lapse of almost 30 years, the Lord's Supper was observed by Covenanters in Dublin. This was continued generally once a year until 1920. The Reformed Presbyterian witness continued to be present in the city through the faithfulness and perseverance of Irish Mission workers, most notable being the faithful service from 1929 until 1974 of Mr. Tom Beck, from Dromara, who for 45 years was a diligent colporteur, evangelist and preacher. From his retirement in September 1974 there has been no permanent Reformed Presbyterian witness in Dublin.

The old Meeting House was situated at 11 Aungier Street, Dublin. The gable of which is seen in this illustration of No.12, the birthplace of Thomas Moore.

Fairview new Meeting House

FAIRVIEW

The early records of preaching appointments allocated to ministers from Scotland after 1750, and to Rev. William Stavely from 1772, contain the name 'Mucknom', 'Muckney' or 'Muckna'. It was an area where there had been a substantial Scottish settlement. Muckna is the name of a lake in north Monaghan near Castleblayney, visible from the first meeting house in Fairview. Since the word 'muckna' means 'pig' in Irish, understandably, the name was changed to 'Fairview', with reference to the fine views of Co. Monaghan visible from the meeting house. The congregation of Fairview was formed as a result of services held in 1790.

Rev. Samuel Aiken was minister of Creevagh from 1790 to 1798 and had the oversight of Fairview in its earliest days. This relationship between Creevagh and Fairview was maintained for over fifty years during the ministry of Rev. Thomas Cathcart from 1806 to 1857. Since the congregation at this period had a membership of about sixty, permission was granted by the Southern Presbytery to call a minister of their own, at a stipend of £50 per annum. Their choice was George Lillie, a licentiate of the Eastern Presbytery who had given some years of service in the London City Mission and had shown great patience and faithfulness in supplying vacant pulpits for a period of thirteen years. He was ordained on 30 April 1861 and rendered devoted service in Fairview, and as Clerk of the Southern Presbytery, until his death on 30 September 1881. A manse and farm were acquired by the congregation during his ministry.

After a vacancy of seven years, Robert Hawthorne Davidson, a member of Grange congregation and a licentiate of the Southern Presbytery, was ordained on 16 October 1888. He resigned in 1894 on accepting a call from Londonderry.

After a vacancy of thirteen years, James Edgar, a licentiate of the Eastern Presbytery was ordained on 1 March 1907. He resigned on 5 May 1908 and became a minister of the Irish Presbyterian Church.

The next minister was Rev. Joseph McEwen, who, after a ministry of twelve years in Bready, was installed on 22 July 1909. The congregation, which had been depleted in numbers by the long vacancy at the beginning of the century, revived under Mr. McEwen's preaching and pastoral care and, when he retired in 1927, the membership at Fairview had risen to what it was at the close of Mr. Lillie's ministry.

A significant development at the close of Mr. McEwen's ministry was the connection with the congregation at Tullyvallen. For the previous eight years Mr. McEwen had accepted the invitation to act as Stated Supply of the Original Secession congregation at Tullyvallen.

When the Southern Presbytery received Tullyvallen into its membership on 7 December 1927, Mr. McEwen's fine work reached a fitting climax.

During a seven-year vacancy Rev. S. R. Archer of Creevagh gave outstanding help to the two congregations.

Fairview and Tullyvallen congregations became a joint charge in 1934 when Rev. R. B. Cupples was installed as minister of both congregations.

The original meeting house in Fairview was erected on the present site in the early 1800s. In 1985 the Fairview congregation added a new kitchen and toilet to the existing meeting house. However, in the late 1990s, the 150 year-old building was becoming structurally unsound and the decision was made to replace it. On 18 March 2006 the congregation was able to gather to give thanks to God for the provision of a new meeting house.

Four students from Fairview have trained for the Gospel ministry at the Theological Hall: William Dodds, William Reid McEwen, Samuel Robert Armstrong and Robert Harold Creane.

Fairview old Meeting House

During his ministry Mr. Lillie was supported in Session by Francis Scott, John Henry, Thomas Henry and John Armstrong. Fairview congregation is drawn from north of Castleblaney to Altnamackin. Elders in Fairview in the twentieth century have been Adam Armstrong, Robert Boyd, John Henry, George Armstrong, Wallace Creane, James Harrison, William Hughes, Robert Armstrong and James T. Creane.

The Meeting House is situated at Fairview near Oram, Castleblayney, Co. Monaghan.

Tullyvallen Meeting House

TULLYVALLEN

When Clarkesbridge Secession congregation, which belonged to the Burgher Presbytery of Monaghan, joined the General Assembly of the Presbyterian Church in 1843, a considerable minority was displeased, as the congregation had not been informed of the procedure. Some refused to go with their minister, Rev. William McAlister, and formed Tullyvallen Original Secession Church. After some years, in which the possession of the meeting house was in dispute, the minority worshipped in a barn and in a building at Milltown, Cortamlet. Eventually the "Bog Meeting House" was built in 1851. The first ministers of Tullyvallen Original Secession Church were George McMahon, 1851-1875 and Alexander Mackenzie, 1876-1884. From 1890 to 1894, Mr. Davidson of Fairview Reformed Presbyterian Church was stated supply and arrangements were in hand for the congregation to join the Reformed Presbyterian Synod. This did not materialise, however, as Mr. McMahon returned from Belfast in 1894 and continued his ministry in Tullyvallen until his death in 1912. When his successor, Mr. Laverty died in 1919, the Secession Church was unable to provide supplies.

Consequently, Rev. Joseph McEwen, of Fairview had accepted the invitation to act as

Stated Supply of the Original Secession congregation at Tullyvallen, and for these eight years the way was open for Mr. McEwen to preach and to guide the congregation towards the Reformed Presbyterian Church. When the Southern Presbytery received Tullyvallen into its membership on 7 December 1927, Mr. McEwen's fine work reached a fitting climax. During a seven-year vacancy Rev. S. R. Archer of Creevagh gave outstanding help to the two congregations of Fairview and Tullyvallen.

Tullyvallen and Farview congregations became a joint charge in 1934 when Rev. R. B. Cupples was installed as minister of both congregations.

The Tullyvallen meeting house was re-roofed, new windows were fitted, a new ceiling, asphalt floor and heating system were installed and the building was re-opened with a special service on Sabbath 26 September 1986. On 28 May 2006 a new church hall was opened by the Moderator of Synod, Rev. S. McMahon.

Tullyvallen congregation is made up of families from north of the County Armagh border in the Newtownhamilton and Keady areas.

In Tullyvallen, the following men have served as ruling elders: William Nicholson, James McKee, Robert Cornett, David Draffin, John T. Shanks, Robert Nicholson, Samuel James Warnock, William Kemps, Ivan Bingham, Douglas Hughes and George Hughes.

The Meeting House is situated at Tullyneil Road, Newtownhamilton, Co. Armagh.

FAIRVIEW AND TULLYVALLEN

Fairview and Tullyvallen congregations became a joint charge in 1934 when Rev. R. B. Cupples was installed as minister of both congregations. He was ordained in April 1934. Robert Barnett Cupples was a member of Kellswater and a licentiate of the Northern Presbytery. Despite the experiences of World War II, both congregations showed considerable increase during his ministry. This ended in 1947 when he accepted a call to Cregagh Road, Belfast.

Fairview new Meeting House

The good progress was maintained in the fourteen years of David J. Magee's ministry. A member of Stranorlar and a licentiate of the Western Presbytery, he was ordained and set apart as minister of the united charge on 3 January 1951. Early in Mr. Magee's ministry, as the result of his wise leadership and the generous response from both congregations, a new manse was erected at Altnamackin.

When Mr. Magee resigned in 1965 on accepting a call from Larne, the congregations had another lengthy vacancy. This ended on 31 August, 1971 when John Alexander Hawthorne, a member of Faughan, and a licentiate of the Western Presbytery, was ordained. Mr. Hawthorne devoted his excellent preaching and pastoral gifts to the service of the congregations and of the whole community in a difficult, and at times dangerous, situation when South Armagh, in particular, was ravaged by the forces of terrorism.

When Rev. John Hawthorne accepted a call to Limavady in 1977, the congregations had another long vacancy. This ended on Tuesday 2 September 1986, when Rev. George Ball, minister of Portrush, was installed as minister of the congregation. Mr. Ball led the congregation for the next eleven years at a time when terrorism continued. The windows of the manse were broken on two occasions by terrorist bombs exploding nearby. Mr. Ball was not deterred by these attacks but was faithful in the spread of the Gospel in this needy area. In November 1997 Mr. Ball accepted a call to Narre Warren, an eastern suburb of Melbourne, to develop a new work with the Presbyterian Church of Eastern Australia and was installed there on 13 February 1998.

Tullyvallen Meeting House

On 15 July 2002, Philip Murphy, an elder in the Drimbolg congregation, and a licentiate of the Northern Presbytery, accepted unanimous calls to the joint charge of Fairview and Tullyvallen and on 20 September 2002 was ordained and installed as minister of both congregations in the Tullyvallen meeting house.

The congregations are thankful to God for the blessings they have enjoyed in recent years. Due to an increase in membership and improved giving, these congregations are no longer dependent on Congregational Aid.

The former Grange Meeting House, now demolished

GRANGE

Grange, near Cookstown, Co. Tyrone, was a constituent congregation of the Irish Reformed Presbytery when it was reorganised in 1792. In 1810 it was placed under the care of the newly formed Southern Presbytery. John Stewart, a member of Bready, was minister from 1807 until 1812. There was a long vacancy until Rev. Gordon Ewing served for a year from 1840 till 1841, when he returned to America.

There followed the long ministry of William Stavely Ferguson, 1844 until 1894. W. S. Ferguson was a grandson of William Stavely of Knockbracken and Kellswater. William Stavely's eldest daughter, Nancy, had married a member of the Grange congregation, Andrew Ferguson. The couple named their son William Stavely Ferguson and growing up in the congregation, he became its minister. (He was the father of Rev. Samuel Ferguson, minister of

Rev. W. S. Ferguson Faughan from 1881 until 1928.) He preached extensively in Galway and Connaught as part of the work of the Irish Mission in the late 1850's.

For a small congregation Grange had the distinction of providing the Church with seven ministers: Armour McFarland and James Blackwood who served in America; Robert Gamble Orr, Limavady and U.S.A.; Robert Allen, Dublin and Newtownards; and Robert Hawthorne Davidson, who, after service in Fairview, Londonderry and Stranorlar, was the last minister to conduct services regularly in Grange, from his retirement in 1931 until his death in 1940. The work then ceased and the building was demolished in 1944. Descendants of former members are buried in the graveyard.

In November 2007 Professor Robert McCollum representing the Reformed Presbyterian Church, met Mrs. Mary K. Reany, the great-granddaughter of Rev. W. S. Ferguson and was presented with several artefacts which were from the Grange congregation: two pewter communion jugs, a silver jug, two long-handled collection pans, W. S. Ferguson's family Bible and two marriage registry books dating back to 1866.

The site of Grange Meeting House today

The site of the old Meeting House and existing graveyard is situated at Grange Road, Cookstown, Co. Tyrone.

Loughbrickland Meeting House

LOUGHBRICKLAND

The meeting house of Loughbrickland Reformed Presbyterian Church was built in 1817 and stands in the centre of the village, which is two miles south of Banbridge. Originally a Secession congregation, it was received into the Church of the Covenants, after uniting with the Covenanter congregation meeting at Drumillar, near Scarva. The years from 1830 to 1840 were difficult for the Reformed Presbyterian Church. Controversy raged on the question of the power of the Civil Magistrate and the Church as a whole was in turmoil on the issue of political dissent that led to the withdrawal of the Eastern Presbytery and the formation of the Eastern R.P. Synod in 1842. Controversy is normally barren soil for producing church extension, but it is comforting to note that during those years Loughbrickland was one of four new congregations that came into existence during this time, the others being Ballymoney, Grosvenor Road and Ballyclare.

The first minister, Samuel Simms, was ordained on 5 May 1839. Born at Ballykeel, Holywood, Co. Down in 1812 and educated at the R.P. Hall in Paisley, he served the congregation with great devotion until his retirement for health reasons on 1 November

1870. His Catechism on the distinctive teaching of the Church was widely and profitably used for many years.

His successor, Joseph Livingstone Frazer Hurst, was born at Portglenone in 1844. A graduate of The Queen's University of Belfast and a licentiate of the Eastern Presbytery, he was ordained on 19 December 1871. His gifted ministry ended in 1882 when he resigned and emigrated to New Zealand. His wife was a daughter of Rev. James A. Smyth of Drimbolg.

Rev. Gawn Douglas, was the next minister. He had just completed twenty years at Creevagh when he was installed on 6th May 1884. Widely known and highly respected for his work, he had served the Church for fifty-two years when he died on 15 November 1915.

After a short vacancy, Rev. William Henry Pollock, minister of Larne for twelve years, was installed on 23 October 1918. In 1922 Mr. Pollock began his long association with Clare. His devoted ministry, long remembered with affection, ended with his retirement from the Loughbrickland congregation on 3 June 1941. He remained stated supply of Clare until his retirement on 1 February 1955. He died on 28 February 1956.

Charles Presho, a member of Dublin Road and a licentiate of the Eastern Presbytery, had a short promising pastorate of two years, which he resigned on accepting a call to Glasgow on 21 January 1947. Dr. Presho later became Secretary of the British and Foreign Bible Society for Ireland.

He was succeeded in Loughbrickland by Rev. Robert Barnett Cupples. Mr. Cupples, had served the Church in Fairview and Tullyvallen and Cregagh Road between 1934 and 1951 before his installation at Loughbrickland on 5 April, 1951. On 1 February 1955 he accepted the additional responsibility of Clare after Mr. Pollock's retirement and served the two congregations with diligence and faithfulness until he retired from the active duties of the ministry on 3 September 1974. His tender-hearted and compassionate disposition touched the lives of a wide circle of people.

Robert Blair McFarland a member of Faughan and a licentiate of the Western Presbytery, was ordained and installed by the Southern Presbytery on 17 March 1977. He resigned on May 6 1986, when he accepted a call from the Foreign Mission Board to serve as a missionary in France.

On 15 September 1988 David Silversides, from Gateshead, licentiate of the Eastern Presbytery, was ordained and installed as minister of the joint charge of Clare and Loughbrickland. On 30 March 1999, the Southern Presbytery granted the request of Mr. Silversides to resign pastoral responsibility for the Clare congregation. A substantial majority of the Loughbrickland congregation supported the application as the congregation had become fully self-supporting and needed a full-time minister. Loughbrickland was accordingly separated from Clare and recognised as a separate charge.

Loughbrickland has given one student to the ministry of the Church: John McClelland Cromie who was minister in Kellswater and Kilraughts and Professor of Theology in the Theological Hall.

Loughbrickland Manse in 2010

The elders who served in the first two ministries were Robert McBride, Robert Potter, George F. Long, Joseph Barr, Joseph Murray, David Cromie, James Gray, William Niblock and William Morrow. During the long period from 1884, four elders rendered distinguished service in the congregation. They were Richard and Alexander Copeland,

John McIlroy and Andrew Thompson. During Mr. Pollock's ministry he was faithfully and ably supported by two elders, William Ferguson and James McMahon. To these were added Isaac McKee, Thomas Cromie, John Gilmore, followed by John S. Reid and Hugh Draffin and David Calvin. The last two named continue to serve on the present Session and were joined on 9 March 2008 by David Dunlop and Jim Murdoch. The congregation has a diaconate, currently consisting of Mervyn Flynn, Stephen Finch and Stephen Hughes.

The meeting house at Loughbrickland is of particular architectural interest. Built in 1817, it is a listed building as far as its exterior is concerned. The fact that it remains one of the best preserved buildings of its type in Ireland is a great credit to the congregation, for the nature of its structure has called for careful maintenance. It was closed for six months in 1980 so that dry rot could be eradicated and windows replaced. It was extensively renovated in 1999-2000 and again in 2003-2004. A new hall was opened in 1994. The nearby manse, having undergone extensive renovation in the mid 1970s, has been a convenient asset to the congregation's amenities.

The congregation has seen some signs of the Lord's blessing and seeks to make known the Gospel of Christ by means of open-air preaching, literature work and visiting round homes in the district. A congregational website (www.loughbrickland.org) is proving very valuable and also audio sermons are regularly made available on the Internet and listened to by individuals in other countries as well as our own.

The Meeting House is situated at Dublin Road, Loughbrickland, Co. Down.

Rathfriland Meeting House

RATHFRILAND

Reformed Presbyterianism in South Down was centred mainly at Rathfriland. Men of straightforward faith and devotion to the cause of Christ met for fellowship in Society meetings that were led, in the absence of a minister, by an elder or by the head of the house. The Psalms were sung, the Word was read and applied on a 'question-and-answer' basis and prayer was offered for the blessing of God upon his people.

The early Covenanting Societies in the Rathfriland area were located at The Course, Aughnavallog, Tieragory, Gransha and Tierfergus. The Rathfriland Covenanters welcomed the ministry of the Word, when Scottish Reformed Presbyterian ministers visited Ulster after 1743 and later William Stavely began his fruitful itinerant ministry after his ordination in North Down in 1772. Born in Co. Antrim of Yorkshire stock, his people had known the pressures of persecution and he had inherited the courage and the vision to be a pioneer minister of the Covenant.

In 1777 the members of these societies, encouraged in particular by Mr. Stavely, built their meeting house on a foundation of rock at the highest point of the hill on which Rathfriland stands, and it is known as 'The Rock'.

Mr. Stavely supervised the work here until 1790, when he was succeeded by another Co. Antrim man, Samuel Aiken from Clough. Since 1776 Mr. Aiken had ministered to the Bannside congregation – the district now served by Drimbolg, Ballylaggan and Limavady. Mr. Aiken's ministry of eight years spanned the difficult period of strife and rebellion from 1790 to 1798. He lived at Gransha and, from that centre, he exercised a ministry of great physical effort as well as the spiritual commitment to his work. He had charge of all the Societies from Rathfriland to Ballybay and was the only minister in the area now covered by the whole Southern Presbytery. He had planned to settle at Creevagh, but his untimely death on 25 December 1798 came before the plan was implemented.

He was succeeded by Hans Boggs, the first of two ministers brought up within the congregation. The son of an elder, he was born at Creevy, near Loughbrickland and, after receiving his education in Scotland, was ordained on 27 June 1802 as minister to the united congregations of Ballylane and Rathfriland. After ten years the congregation was divided and Mr. Boggs retained Ballylane. He also frequently preached at Drumillar, between Banbridge and Scarva.

Rathfriland became united with Dromore, and John Stewart, a member of Bready, was installed on 25 May 1812. He served both with distinction and devotion until his death on 30 April 1837. During his ministry an active Temperance Society was organised under the leadership of Alexander Keown. It is indicative of the local contemporary spiritual climate that Rev. Thomas Houston of Knockbracken preached, at the invitation of the Rathfriland Sabbath School Union, on Sabbath 26 July 1829, in the open air to an audience of 5,000.

Thomas Carlisle, a member of Kellswater and a licentiate of the Northern Presbytery, was the next minister and he was ordained and installed on 30 July 1839. In the short vacancy that had preceded Mr Carlisle's installation, Dromore was separated from Rathfriland. In spite of tension in the Church at that time that led to the withdrawal from Synod of the

Eastern Presbytery in 1840, and the disastrous years of The Great Famine that greatly reduced the population in rural areas, the congregation flourished under Mr. Carlisle's ministry. In 1854 when Synod first kept statistical records of congregations, Rathfriland was the largest in Ireland. With a membership of 285 communicants from 104 families, the work was supervised in fourteen societies by six elders. No less than eight students offered for the ministry during the seventeen years of Mr. Carlisle's pastorate. He died, greatly lamented, on 6 February 1856 at the age of 47.

Thomas Hart, a son of the congregation, succeeded him. One of three brothers who trained for the ministry, he was born at Tierfergus in 1824. Ordained on 10 March 1857, he served for twenty years until his early death at the age of 53 on 7 September 1877.

Two brief ministries followed: John Martin, a licentiate from Scotland, was ordained on 4 December 1879. He returned to Scotland as the minister of Wishaw on 3 April 1884. His successor, Alexander Patterson Gillespie ministered for a little over two years from 19 September 1884 until 19 February 1887 when he moved to the congregation at Loanhead, near Edinburgh.

In 1887, Joseph Thomas Potts, a member of College Street South, Belfast (later called Grosvenor Road), was ordained on 27 November. A man of fine scholastic gifts and genial disposition he led the congregation with distinction for 19 years until he moved to Glasgow in 1906.

James Buchanan, a member of Bready, who had trained at the Original Secession Hall in Glasgow and the Theological Hall in Belfast and was a licentiate of the Western

Presbytery, was ordained on 27 November 1906. Mr. Buchanan taught Psalm tunes to the Sabbath school children, took an elocution class, organised a Mutual Improvement Society and held Band of Hope meetings to encourage temperance. Midweek prayer meetings were held in the homes of members and midweek lectures were often organised. Mr Buchanan found time in the midst of all this work to take the degrees of B.D. and M.A. from the University of Indiana in 1918 and 1920. His early death on 15 December 1920 was deeply mourned by his people and by the community that loved and respected him.

Rev. Samuel Kennedy was at the peak of his powers and experience, with thirty years service in Stranorlar and Limavady, when he was installed on 22 August 1924. In addition to his careful pulpit preparation and pastoral duties which he performed with diligence, he was Clerk of Synod and Convener of the Congregational Aid Fund Committee. He had completed fifty years in a ministry of great devotion and distinction when he retired on 3 August 1944. He died on 17 December 1948.

Rev. Samuel Reid Archer, after 17 years in Creevagh, was installed on 22 February 1945. With characteristic devotion as a pastor and a gifted preacher, he served the congregation for 27 years, longer than any other minister in the 200 years under review. He guided the affairs of the congregation thoughtfully and wisely. He retired from active duty on 22 February 1972.

In August 1973 Rev. David Magee was installed as minister of the congregation. He was brought up in the Stranorlar congregation, and was ordained to the ministry on 3 January 1951. He added a wide experience to his native gifts by his pastorates in Fairview, Tullyvallen and Larne. He gave capable leadership in Rathfriland until his retirement in February 1991.

Rev. Barry Galbraith, minister of Wishaw since November 1985, accepted a call to the congregation and was installed on 26 September 1991.

Rathfriland has provided more students for the ministry than any other congregation in the Church. The long list of names is as follows: James Kennedy, Hans Boggs, John Hawthorne, William Somerville, Hugh Hawthorne, William Clokey, Thomas Johnston,

John Crory, Thomas Whiteside, James Reid Lawson, John Little, James Little, William Hanna, Thomas Hart, John Hart, James Hart, James Brown, Joseph Cromie, George Benaugh, James Little, S. R. McNeilly, Samuel Edgar, Francis Moore, Alexander Moore, Alexander Gilmour, William James Gilmour, William Russell Kennedy, Samuel Kennedy Cromie and Trevor McCauley. Outstanding service was given to the Irish Mission in Dublin and Cork by Thomas James McKee.

The following have served the congregation as ruling elders: Thomas Clyde, John Martin, James Little, James Moffett, Thomas Johnston, John McKee, Thomas Woods, Samuel Patterson, Samuel Benaugh, William J. Campbell, David Adams, James Lawson, Robert Lutton, Thomas Campbell, Thomas Cromie, John Gilmour, James Campbell, Robert James Cromie, Samuel K. Cromie, Robert Harbinson, Alexander Cromie, William Moore, Adam McNeilly, James S. Moffett, Alexander McCauley, William Irvine, David McKee, William Johnstone, Thomas W. Martin, Robert Long, Ray Morrison and Thomas Cromie (Junior).

The philanthropy of the Adams brothers, members of this congregation, was well known. The church hall bears their names. The Bible House in Howard Street, Belfast, Headquarters of the British and Foreign Bible Society, bears the honoured inscription, 'The D. and J. Adams Memorial'.

The original meeting house was stone-built and, unusually, had a slate rather than a thatch roof. During the ministry of Mr. Hart, in 1861, the meeting house was rebuilt on the same site at a cost of £700. This meeting house was again thoroughly and beautifully renovated from June 1970. It involved re-roofing, new side windows and ceiling and a minister's room. Re-opening services were held on Sabbath 16 May 1971. A Lecture Hall was erected in 1934 at a cost of £600 and a kitchen added in 1950. The congregation has worshipped on the same site since 1777.

The manse on Dromore Street was built in 1885 for £750 on a site purchased for £32.

The congregation vision is to reach out to the local community. In addition to the weekly Sabbath morning and evening services and prayer meeting, the congregation maintains a witness through fortnightly Bible Studies, meetings of the W.M.A., a Youth Club and Bookstall organised each December. By such means, each Christian in the congregation, especially younger members, are encouraged to reach out to those around them.

The Meeting House is situated at Castle Lane, Rathfriland, Co. Down.

Riverside Meeting House

RIVERSIDE, NEWRY

The story of the Newry Congregation should give encouragement and incentive to smaller groups of Covenanters in the way that early difficulties were faced and overcome. The story begins on 11 February 1834 when a request for a supply of preaching was submitted to Presbytery from a Society that had been recently organised at Corinshego near Newry. Rev. John Stewart of Rathfriland was appointed to preach on the second Sabbath of March. This Society renewed the request in May and again in November, when it was arranged that Rev. John Hawthorn of Ballenon would preach on 9 November in the Sessions House, Margaret Square, Newry at 11.30 a.m. and 7.00 p.m. The supply of preaching was maintained at regular intervals for the next two years, but a decline in membership, due to death and emigration, to just four families, comprising eight communicants, led to its discontinuance until 1844. In 1844 a forward step was taken when some members of Ballenon, led by John Gordon, an elder in Ballenon congregation, purchased for £125, the old meeting house, session house and sexton's house in Church Street that had been vacated by the Presbyterian congregation lately moved to Downshire Road. In July 1844, John Gordon, supported by Hugh Stewart and John Shaw, presented a memorial to the Synod at Londonderry giving reasons for their purchase of the meeting house and asking for recognition. Synod approved the purchase and directed the Southern Presbytery to make preaching appointments and to give assistance towards meeting the cost. Accordingly the meeting house was opened for public worship in connection with the Reformed Presbyterian Church on 30 August 1844 by Rev. Thomas Houston of Knockbracken. On 1 November 1844, about ten persons were admitted into membership. Numbers increased to between thirty and forty and the group became a congregation on 17 June 1845.

Ruins, now removed, of former Meeting House on Church Street

In December 1844, at a special meeting of Synod, Robert Wallace, from Letterkenny, Co. Donegal, licensed just a few days earlier by the Western Presbytery, was appointed to preach and to visit the families for the next few Sabbaths from 1 February 1845. He commended himself so favourably to the people that a call was issued and he was ordained and installed on 14 January 1846. Under Mr. Wallace's able preaching and gifted leadership, the congregation made rapid progress and within two years trebled its membership to about 120 communicants, despite a number of deaths and emigrations.

During this time of considerable growth, Mr. Wallace was conducting a summer Sabbath School and an adult class in which he expounded the Confession of Faith with each section being minutely explained, and a further examination of the same material conducted the following Sabbath. His ministry in Newry lasted eighteen years and his departure to Glasgow in February 1864 was greatly regretted.

His successor, Thomas Conn Britton, a member of Bready, was ordained on 21 June 1865. This happy and promising settlement ended by his untimely death on 10 March, 1869, at the early age of 33 years.

On 12 June1872 Alexander McLeod Stavely Lyons, a member of Ballymoney and a licentiate of the Northern Presbytery, was ordained. His ministry, attended with great blessing, was specially marked by the removal of the congregation from the Old Meeting House to the Riverside site. On 30 December, 1883 Rev. Lyons preached the last sermon in the old meeting house on Church Street and on 6 January 1884 opening services were conducted in Riverside by Rev. Prof. J. A. Chancellor of Belfast and Rev. John McDonald, Loanhead. Evening worship, attended by very large congregations, was held in Sandy's Street and Downshire Road Presbyterian Churches. The congregation was now well equipped for its work. Mr Lyons's outstanding ministry, characterised as winsome, simple and earnest, of 36 years ended tragically on 7 September 1908, when, in the full maturity of his gifts and powers, he was killed instantaneously by a train at Goraghwood on his way to visit a family at Jerrettspass. His passing cast a shadow over the whole community, and the Church as a whole mourned the death of a minister who had given notable service as Clerk of the Southern Presbytery for 26 years and as the founder and first convener of the Ministers' Widows' and Orphans' Fund.

The congregation found the ideal successor to Mr. Lyons in the person of Thomas Barnwell McFarland. From the Newtownstewart area, and brought up in the Mulvin congregation, he had served the Scottish Church in Glasgow for three years when he was installed in Riverside on 28 April 1909. Mr. McFarlane, an outstanding preacher and pastor, served the Church as a whole with great distinction as Professor of Church History and Pastoral Theology from 1928 to 1957 and as Clerk of the Southern Presbytery and Convener of the Irish Mission Committee for many years. He retired on 29 August 1961 and died on 20 January 1963.

The next minister, Rev. Robert Hanna, then pastor at Milford, was installed in Riverside on 16 May 1962. Mr Hanna exercised a faithful and promising ministry in Newry and his gifts brought him in due course to the attention of the Dromara congregation and when called by that congregation he moved to Dromara on 16 July 1969.

He was succeeded by his friend and fellow-student, Rev. Samuel Lynas Reid, who, having served the Scottish Church faithfully in Stranraer for twelve years, was installed on 17 December 1969. His whole ministry in Riverside was exercised with great courage and devotion in an area that was repeatedly ravaged by acts of terrorism by which the church property was severely damaged on several occasions. Mr. Reid departed from a congregation that was deeply appreciative of his faithful service when he accepted a call to Ballyclare and was installed there on 31 March 1988.

Rev. Stewart McMahon, minister of Bailiesmills, accepted a call to the Riverside congregation and was installed on 16 December 1988. Owing to the 'Troubles', which were particularly felt in this border town, the years that Mr. McMahon served as pastor brought certain difficulties. The congregation was unable to meet in its own church building because of bomb attacks on the adjacent courthouse. Tensions in the community made evangelistic work difficult but under Mr. McMahon's ministry and leadership a dedicated core of believers worked to maintain a Reformed witness in the area. In 2004 Mr. McMahon applied to the Southern Presbytery to retire from the active duties of the ministry through incapacity. This was granted on 21 September 2004 and the pastoral tie was dissolved.

On 24 June 2008, Simon Sweeney, a member of Trinity congregation and a licentiate of the Eastern Presbytery, accepted a call from the congregation and was ordained and installed on 26 September 2008.

The Newry congregation has been blessed through the years with a band of godly elders. Their names are: James Shaw, John Gordon, William McGladdery, Archibald Murphy, James Brown, Samuel Adams, Hugh Stewart, Robert Gass, Robert McGladdery, William Niblock, Isaac Barr, James McGladdery, David Frazer, Robert Sturgeon, Robert Long, John McGladdery, James McGladdery, Robert Adams, Hugh Alexander Savage, William Jamieson, James Trimble, William J. Savage, Thomas Adams, Henry C Lyons, Hugh W. Stewart, William Davis, Alex S. Lyons, S. Henry McGladdery, Samuel Murphy and Rodney Murphy.

Four members of the congregation, James Alexander Lyons, Robert Nevin Lyons, Joseph Henry McGladdery and David McCullough, entered the ministry of the Church, and Thomas Adams and Hugh W. Stewart were for many years devoted workers in the Irish Mission.

The Meeting House reflected in the old Canal Basin

The Riverside Meeting House is located in Basin Walk, on the north side of the town and not far from the Town Hall. Behind the Court House, it is easily identified by its tall red brick tower beside the Clanrye River. It had been erected by a minority of the Sandys Street congregation of the Presbyterian Church of Ireland who were recognised as 3rd Newry in 1863. Their fine church building was opened for worship in 1866. The architect of Riverside was Mr. William J. Barre, born in Newry and is remembered as the designer of the Albert Memorial Clock in Belfast. On the resignation of their minister in 1883, the congregation was dissolved. Mr. Lyons encouraged the Reformed Presbyterian congregation people to purchase Riverside Church in December 1883 and after some delay, through legal technicalities, the purchase was confirmed in 1885 by the Master of the Rolls for the sum of £600. In 1883 and 1889, Rev. Alex Lyons went to the United States to raise funds to help clear the debts on the church and manse. These trips proved successful and not only were all liabilities met, but the head rent of the church was purchased and £520 invested in the purchase of five houses in Ashbourne Street in Belfast, which the congregation owned until 1979 when the properties were vested by the Housing Executive for £1850.

A heating system was installed in the church in 1908 and the building underwent further repairs in 1945, 1965 and 1997.

In 1907 the ladies of the congregation began raising funds for the building of a Lecture Hall which cost £600 and was formally opened in 24 November 1915 and named the Lyons Memorial Hall in honour of the pastor who had served the congregation between 1872 and 1908. During the summer of 2006 extensive repairs and renovations to the hall were carried out. The kitchen was replaced and a hatch into the hall added, the downstairs toilet was upgraded for disabled use, and a toilet added upstairs. A new emergency door was made out of the hall into the congregation's car park to better utilise this space. The doors and windows were replaced on the street side, and the brickwork re-pointed. Along with the painting of the outside of the building for the first time, this has greatly improved the appearance of the building to the hundreds of people who look at it everyday.

Rockview Manse had been purchased in 1856 for £350 and Mr. Lyons moved in during November 1879. An extensive building scheme was undertaken in 1891, costing about £280. Upon the retirement of Professor McFarlane in 1961, Newry Urban District Council offered to buy Rockview and the congregation agreed to the sale for the sum of £1600. A new Manse was purchased for £3,000 from Miss Leonie Adams at Ardmore on the Belfast Road. This manse was sold in 2008 and in 2009 the congregation purchased the property at 26 Castleowen, Newry for their new minister.

In recent years the Newry congregation has hosted GO teams of ten or more members drawn not only from the denomination but from Wales and USA. The congregation has been greatly encouraged by the support of the denomination in this, and many lives have been touched by this work, especially among the children who have attended the 5-day clubs ran by the teams. With a view to building relationships within the congregation and providing a warm welcome to visitors, Riverside is looking forward to the future in the confidence of Christ's blessing and encouragement.

The Meeting House is situated at 8 Basin Walk, Newry, Co. Down, BT35 6HU.

EASTERN PRESBYTERY

Bailiesmills New Meeting House opened 1994

BAILIESMILLS

In 1772 William Stavely was ordained in the village of Conlig, between Newtownards and Bangor, to minister to a large number of Covenanting Societies that existed between Dromore and Donaghadee, in Co. Down. In the years following his ordination he built up several congregations, one of which was Knockbracken. The Societies of Carr, Creevy and Bailiesmills were under the supervision of Knockbracken Session and enjoyed the ministry of Mr. Stavely for about thirty years.

Towards the end of this period some families from Boardmills, who attended the local Seceder church, became dissatisfied that their Synod had entered into negotiations with the government to receive grants from the Regium Donum on terms similar to those paid to the ministers of the Synod of Ulster. These families joined with the local Covenanting Societies and in 1807 these Societies were organised by the Irish Reformed Presbytery to form a separate congregation in Bailiesmills, located midway between the towns of Lisburn and Ballynahinch, on the Drennan Road, in Co. Down. Consequently, when the Eastern Presbytery was formed in 1810, Bailiesmills was one of its constituent congregations. It was some years, however, before the new congregation had its own minister. As the minister of Knockbracken, Rev. Josias Alexander, had the oversight of the new congregation in Linenhall Street in Belfast, Bailiesmills was placed under the care of Rev. William Henry of Newtownards.

The first minister of Bailiesmills was John Wright Graham, who was ordained in 1826. A native of Drumbo, and a member of Knockbracken, he was educated at the Royal Belfast Institution and the R.P. Theological Hall, Paisley. During the early part of his ministry, the Synod was troubled by the controversy between Rev. Dr. Thomas Houston and Rev. Dr. John Paul concerning the powers of the civil magistrate; this eventually led to the secession of the Eastern Reformed Presbytery. Mr. Graham and his congregation took their stand with Dr. Houston against Dr. Paul, and in 1839 Synod granted their request to be transferred to the care of the Southern Presbytery. This arrangement lasted until 1870. Mr. Graham served the congregation with great devotion and distinction until his death in 1862.

The congregation called Rev. Thomas Houston Dick, eldest son of Rev. James Dick of Kellswater. He had been ordained in Ballymacashon in 1860 and having accepted a call to Bailliesmills, resigned and was installed in Bailiesmills in July 1863. In 1864 he married a daughter of John Graham of Hillhead, Lisburn, who was one of the first elders to serve in Bailiesmills. Under Mr. Dick's gifted pastorate the membership grew to about 140. His ministry was cut short in his fiftieth year by his early and lamented death in 1882.

He was succeeded by Samuel Rea McNeilly. Born at Bannfield, Rathfriland, and brought up in the congregation there, he was educated at Queen's College, Belfast and the Theological Hall. He was ordained on 22 June 1887 and served the congregation, and the Church as a whole, with great faithfulness until his retirement in August 1926. He died two years later.

In 1927 after 120 years of independence, the Bailiesmills and Knockbracken congregations came together again and John Watters was ordained as the first minister of the two congregations. A member of Milford and a licentiate of the Western Presbytery, he was ordained and installed to the pastorate at Bailiesmills on 26 October 1927, serving the congregation for more than 40 years. He retired from active duties on 7 May 1968 and died suddenly on 12 December 1970.

The working arrangement between the two congregations continued when Rev. James A. Ritchie, who was ordained at Knockbracken on 27 November 1969, was installed in Bailiesmills on 3 December 1969. A native of Broughshane, he had gained wide experience in ministry both in England and Ireland before being admitted to the R.P. Church by the Synod in June 1968. During his ministry his practical gifts were instrumental in the erection of a wooden hall, mainly for the benefit of the young people. After a very promising ministry Mr. Ritchie was installed the pastor of Kellswater on 7 June 1974.

In January 1978, Professor Adam Loughridge the minister of Cregagh Road and Ballymacashon tendered his resignation of this charge in order to facilitate a regrouping of congregations within the Presbytery that might be to advantage in a future settlement for Ballymacashon, Bailiesmills and Knockbracken. Ballymacashon renewed its association with Knockbracken, and Bailliesmills received leave to call as a single charge.

On 13 September 1978, Stewart McMahon, a native of Milford, Co. Donegal, was ordained and installed in Bailiesmills, becoming the second native of Donegal to become minister of Bailiesmills. Mr. McMahon was a faithful pastor and expounder of the Word. He and his wife and young family greatly enjoyed the tranquil, rural setting of the old manse, built in the late nineteenth century as a beautifully sited and well-appointed house on the Old Ballynahinch Road. During this period two Interim Elders, Mr. Gordon McDonald of Knockbracken and Mr. John Somerville of Lisburn, served in Bailiesmills. On 21 September 1988 Mr. McMahon received a call from Newry which he accepted on 4 November.

On Friday 19 January 1990, Rev. George McEwen was installed as Minister of Bailiesmills. Mr. McEwen had previously served in Portrush, McKinnon, Australia and in Tasmania. The congregation found Mr. McEwen to be a most caring and attentive pastor, sowing the seed of the Gospel in the young, through Bible clubs and youth groups as well as bringing comfort to the bereaved and sustaining the faith of the elderly, presenting Jesus Christ as Saviour and Lord both in the pulpit and every facet of life. He retired from the full-time pastorate at a meeting of the Eastern Presbytery on 11 September 2008. During Mr. McEwen's ministry the congregation entered a period of radical change in terms of its property. The manse had been built in the 1880s. In 1980 a solid fuel heating system and modern fitted kitchen were installed. Damp proofing, timber treatment and rewiring brought the bill to £16,000 which was soon met by the congregation. Ten years later, after much heart-searching, the old manse was sold, and the new minister purchased a house in Annahilt. Eventually, the old meeting house, which dated from the early 19th century, was demolished, and a new building was erected. During the construction period the congregation met for worship in Ballymacbrennan Old Schoolhouse. The new meeting house was opened on 12 March 1994 by Mrs. Heather McEwen, wife of the minister.

Bailiesmills old Meeting House

The Bailiesmills congregation celebrated its 200th anniversary at special thanksgiving services on Sabbath 25th October 2009. The morning preacher was Rev. Timothy McEwen, a son of Rev. George McEwen and minister of Ballenon and Ballylane, and the evening preacher was Rev David McCullough, Moderator of the Synod. These services were well attended and were a cause for thanksgiving. God's blessing was sought for the work of Christ's kingdom in this place for the years to come.

The following have served the congregation as ruling elders: John Graham, James Malcomson, John McEwen, John Hawthorne, William Harvey, James Thompson, William J. Galway, Thomas Galway, James Martin, William Martin, Thomas Graham, Samuel Graham, Thomas Smyth and William J. Anderson, James A. Hanna, Samuel Halliday, William Pharis Campbell, James G. Hanna, Hector B. Hanna, Martin Campbell, William John Martin, James McAreavy, Thomas W. Martin, Francis Milligan, John Morrison, Alan Silversides and Derek Malcolmson.

Four students for the ministry were brought up in the congregation; Hugh Hawthorne, who emigrated to the U.S.A, Rea McNeilly Campbell, who was unable to undertake a pastorate owing to ill health, William Gerald Milligan and Timothy Edward McEwen.

The Meeting House is situated on Drennan Road, Lisburn, Co. Down.

Ballyclare Meeting House

BALLYCLARE

In the summer of 1831 a few individuals in Ballyclare and its vicinity asked Rev. John Paul, the Reformed Presbyterian minister of Loughmorne and Carnmoney, to preach in the town. Mr. Paul preached in Andrew McCullough's backhouse loft to a crowded audience and, later in the year, to another large gathering in the same place. Encouraged by such good attendances, Rev. James Dick of Kellswater was invited to preach. On Sabbath 21 July he addressed a large congregation in the open air in a green field, very near where the meeting house was afterwards built. Rev. Thomas Houston of Knockbracken preached on Sabbath 27 November. On 21 March 1832 a group met in the local Methodist church and passed the following resolutions:

> 1.   That we will encourage the preaching of the Gospel in the town of Ballyclare by ministers or probationers of the Reformed Presbyterian Synod;
>
> 2.   That we will enter into a quarterly subscription to defray expenses attending the same amounting to six shillings [possibly per member].

On the same day another meeting was held, when, after prayer, a committee of Management was chosen, namely, John McMurtray, John Mackey, William Montgomery,

David Coghran, William Gardener, James Adrain, with William McCelland, Treasurer, and Samuel Hunter, Secretary. At a future meeting, the following persons were added to the Committee: Robert Owens, Hugh Buchanan, John Gamble, Andrew Robinson, Andrew McCullough, Samuel McConkey, Joseph Carlisle, David Carlisle, Evans Stewart, David Blair, James Stevenson and Charles McCelland.

The Committee asked the Eastern Presbytery that met in Belfast on 23 April 1832 to supply them with preaching, and also to the Northern Presbytery which met in Portglenone on the second Wednesday in May. About this time, application was made to the managers of the Methodist Chapel for use of their house when their own worship was concluded; the request was granted very cordially.

In the meantime, in the middle of April 1832, a large crowd assembled in a backyard in Ballyclare, belonging to Archibald McMurtrey of Belfast, to hear Rev. James Dick preach. A few went into an old barn loft and, just before the preacher commenced, a part of the loft broke down with a crash. A few ladies were a little bruised and very much frightened but no serious injury was sustained. The enemies of religion thought they had obtained a triumph and rejoiced at the disaster, but their victory was short-lived, as the new work was not in the least retarded by the event.

On 16 June 1832, the Committee determined that they would attempt to build a meeting house. A petition to Synod requested further supplies of preaching and at the Synod in July 1832, Ballyclare was designated a missionary station. During 1832 the following preaching in Ballyclare was arranged: Revs. Paul, Dick, Alexander, Houston, and probationers Messrs. Gibson, Nevin and Toland.

On 24 July the Committee agreed with Mr. John Park of Ballynure to rent a plot of ground on the Ballycorr Road in Ballyclare, near the town square. On 30 July the Committee agreed with William McCelland to supply material and build the walls of the house for 4 shillings and 6 pence per perch to be finished on 12 October. He employed Thomas Millen as mason. On 13 August the Committee again agreed with John McMurtray to find timber and do all the carpenter work of the house ready for slating, also glass and glaze the windows, for the sum of £60. On 6 August, the Committee met on the ground and the first stone of the meeting house was laid by Rev. John Alexander, the minister of the Botanic Avenue congregation in Belfast. He then delivered a very moving and solemn address to a large audience. The new meeting house was opened in March 1833 and according to the *Northern Whig*, an 'eloquent and impressive sermon' was preached by Rev. William John Stavely of Ballymoney. Notwithstanding the severity of the weather a large and respectable audience attended.

In 1835, the Ballyclare Missionary Station, strengthened by the transfer of members from the neighbouring congregations of Kellswater and Loughmourne, was organised into a congregation with fifty communicants and its own eldership.

The congregation's first minister was ordained on 9 July 1840. He was William Russell, born at Ballymagee, Bangor in 1801. Having taken an interest in helping poor families in the town, he came to the notice of Lord Bangor, who made him a tutor to the orphaned children of his deceased brother. William Russell continued his education from 1826 at the Belfast College (later called Royal Belfast Academical Institution). He turned his back on a teaching career and went to the R.P. Hall in Paisley where he completed the three-year course in two years. He then proceeded to Edinburgh University. In 1838 he applied to the Eastern Presbytery to be licensed to preach. In 1840 he was ordained by a Committee of the Missionary Board and installed as the first minister of the Ballyclare Reformed Presbyterian congregation.

The Eastern Presbytery was at this time in the throes of a controversy that eventually led to the withdrawal of the Presbytery from the Synod, so the newly formed congregation was placed under the care of the Board of Missions, a Committee of the Synod and remained in that unusual position until the Presbytery was reconstituted in 1845.

Mr. Russell gave his whole ministry to Ballyclare. A Sabbath School was commenced in 1841 and soon had an attendance of 100 in the summer and 60 in the winter months. In the first twenty years of the congregation, societies played a significant part. The number of societies increased from two to eight with a total membership of 116 in 1850. His ministerial colleague, Rev. Josias Chancellor, said that as a preacher, Mr. Russell was 'clear, judicious and especially edifying'. As a pastor he was 'sensitive, dignified and unobtrusive'. On the Sabbath Day he preached for several hours and, in the evening, he spent two additional hours conducting a home Bible class. He was known to walk seven or eight miles, conduct the class and walk home again. Mr Russell's family life was characterised by sorrow. His wife and three of his children died at an early age and he was left to bring up his surviving child himself. That child, also called William, became one of the most brilliant students of his day and was minister of Ballenon, Paisley and Trinity Street and Professor of Theology in the Church's Theological Hall in Belfast. When Mr. Russell died on 7 April 1884, he left a thriving congregation of 92 members.

His successor was Rev. Alexander McLeod Stavely. Born in 1816, the son of Rev. Dr. William John Stavely, he had been educated at the Belfast Academy, Belfast College, the University of Edinburgh and the R.P. Hall in Paisley. In 1841 he had been ordained at Kilraughts for the Colonial Mission and served the congregation of St. John's, New Brunswick, for 38 years, from 1841 to 1879. He was installed in Ballyclare on 10 December 1884, aged 68. He ministered faithfully to Ballyclare and Larne for 14 years, walking the 11 miles each way every Sabbath afternoon, until his retirement, at the age of 82, in November 1898. His ministerial colleague, Rev. Dr. Lynd described him as 'a kindly Christian gentleman, whose friendly disposition and genial humour and readiness to the service of others won for him friends wherever he met.'

Robert John McIlmoyle, then one of the most widely known of Covenanting ministers, who later served the congregation of Dervock for 60 years, began his ministry in Ballyclare on 6 September 1900. He was born in 1875 in Limavady and was educated at Magee College and the R.P. Hall. He was licensed to preach by the Western Presbytery in 1900 and was ordained and installed in Ballyclare on 6 September of that year. His able preaching made an immediate impact and the congregation showed an increase of twenty-six in membership in the short space of four years. During his pastorate, a six-strong Board of Deacons was established on 9 November 1903. In 1904 Mr. McIlmoyle accepted a call to Dervock and was installed there on 31 August 1904.

He was succeeded by James Blair, born 23 September 1880, who was also a member of Limavady. Mr. Blair graduated from Magee College in 1903 and the Reformed Theological Hall in 1905 and was a licentiate of the Western Presbytery. He was ordained and installed in the congregation on 7 December 1905. A Women's Missionary Association was formed in 1914. Mr. Blair's ministry here, as elsewhere, bore the marks of great devotion, both in the pulpit and in his pastoral care and there was much regret among the people when he moved to Milford in December 1916.

There was a vacancy of five years before Rev. Archibald Holmes was installed on 16 June 1921. He had previously ministered in Bready, Creevagh, Paisley and Kellswater, and he brought ripe experience and excellent pulpit gifts to his work at Ballyclare. As documented below, extensive renovations to the meeting house occurred in 1923. The Deacon Board was strengthened by four new members in 1929. For eleven years, he 'went out and in amongst us discharging the duties of his high calling with dignity, faithfulness and earnestness' (Minute in the Session and Deacon Book). It was said of Mr. Holmes, 'He was a man endowed with intellectual gifts of a high order. He was an able preacher, his matter and manner being both interesting and compelling. After a sudden illness of just a few days, Mr. Holmes died on 27 September 1932, aged 70.

His successor was Joseph Henry McGladdery, a member of Newry and a licentiate of the Southern Presbytery. He was ordained on 22 June 1933, and for 33 years until his retirement on 18 May 1966, he guided the affairs of the congregation with thoroughness and deep pastoral concern. He died on 3 June 1967.

Charles Knox Hyndman, a member of the Trinity Street congregation, a licentiate of the Eastern Presbytery, educated at Queen's University and the Theological Hall, was the sixth licentiate to be called by the congregation. He was ordained on 8 May 1969. His work was characterised by a deep concern for the spiritual welfare of the people. His preaching and pastoral gifts, combined with a graciousness and freshness of approach, led to much blessing in the life of the congregation. During his ministry, renovation works to the Church Hall were carried out. Rev. K. Hyndman accepted a call to the Newtownards congregation where he was installed as pastor on 3 October 1985.

Following a vacancy of two and a half years Rev. Samuel Lynas Reid, minister of Riverside, Newry accepted a call to Ballyclare and was installed on 31 March 1988. Mr. Reid served the congregation faithfully as a caring pastor. In 1990 a special service celebrating the 150th anniversary of the installation of Rev. William Russell as the first minister in Ballyclare in 1840 took place. Mr. Reid resigned from the charge and retired for health reasons on 30 September 1997.

David Sutherland, a native of Scotland, member of Lisburn congregation and licentiate of the Eastern Presbytery, was ordained and installed as minister in Ballyclare on Friday 10 September 1999. Mr. Sutherland brought to the congregation exceptional gifts in preaching and built up the work of the church especially among young people.

The congregation has down the years been well served by a faithful band of elders. From the records the following can be named: Charles McClelland, William Moore, William Gordon, Hugh Gault, Robert Cameron, Robert Witherhead, Dr. W. A. Clugston, Hugh Blair, William Kennedy, Samuel Kennedy, Robert Blair (Sen.), David Warwick, Robert Blair (Jun.), James Moore, William Byers, Thomas W. Kennedy, James Kennedy, Nat Montgomery, Robert J. Blair, Robert T. Blair, Thomas W. Kennedy (Jun.), John Armour, Bertie Blair, John Ivor Blair, James McKeown, Thomas Ferguson, Joseph P. Kennedy, George F. Wright, Steven Bell, Dr. Trevor Maze.

The meeting house was started in 1833 and it was not until 1843 that it was finished. Further renovations were undertaken in the 1860s and during Mr. Stavely's ministry. A sexton's house and a session room were built in 1850. In 1923 the roof and windows were raised 4 feet and new pews, pulpit, choir stall, pitch pine ceiling, choir room, Session room, boiler house and heating system, electric light installation and a school room were added.

Mr. Russell resided at Whitepark, Ballyclare until a manse was built in 1880 at Ballyeaston Road. The manse was enlarged and improved during Mr Stavely's occupancy. Having been in need of considerable renovation, it was sold and a new property purchased at Park Avenue in 1988, prior to the Reid family moving to Ballyclare. The manse at Park Avenue was later sold and a new town house at Mill Road purchased jointly by the minister and the congregation. On the marriage of the minister in August 2004 the congregation and minister entered in a similar arrangement to purchase a house in

Gateside Manor which was a new development in the town. During 2004 the car park was extended and tarmacadamed and extensive renovations were carried out in the church hall with the installation of new kitchen units.

The congregation has provided three students for the ministry: William Russell, Samuel Kennedy and Wilson Moreland Kennedy.

It is with thankfulness to God that the congregation in Ballyclare celebrated, in 2007, the 175th anniversary of the foundation of the meeting house. To mark this, the Annual Spring Weekend Conference was addressed by Rev. Knox Hyndman, a former minister, whose theme was 'Looking to the future' and a history of the congregation was published.

The congregation rejoices in having, in recent years, a number of new members and adherents, including several new couples. For many years, there were no young children and now there are several Covenant children, with prospects of more to come. The congregation, in God's grace, acknowledges the blessings of the past and looks forward with confidence to providing a growing witness for Christ's Crown and Covenant in Ballyclare.

The Meeting House is situated at 18 Ballycorr Road, Ballyclare, Co. Antrim BT39 9DD.

Ballymacashon Meeting House

BALLYMACASHON

On 8 April 1828, Thomas Houston was ordained in Knockbracken. Later in the year John Patterson, a farmer, and Alexander Martin, a schoolmaster, both from the townland of Ballymacashon, near Killinchy, Co. Down, applied to the Knockbracken Session asking that their minister might be allowed to conduct weeknight meetings in their district. The request was granted and the first meeting was held in Mr. Patterson's house. In December 1828, a meeting was held in Ballymacashon School and during the following years Mr. Houston conducted cottage meetings in the home of Robert Long of Thornyhill, Ballymacreely. Early members were Hugh Hewitt, Alexander Reid, Samuel Heslett, John Patterson, Robert Martin, James Carse, Alexander Martin and Robert Long. Their membership was listed in Knockbracken and many of them walked the ten or twelve miles to attend worship on Sabbath and Communion services.

From 1835, several attempts were made to obtain a site for a meeting house, but it was not until December 1846, that a site, between Balloo and Saintfield, was purchased from

Joseph Minnis for £19. The meeting house was built under the direction of William Magowan. The church was opened for public worship on 1 October 1848. The special preachers were Rev. James M. Wilson from Philadelphia, U.S.A. and Rev. Thomas Houston of Knockbracken. The first Communion service was held in June 1849. Following a recommendation of Synod in 1855 the congregation was linked to Newtownards with an arrangement that Newtownards was to have three services per month and Ballymacashon one.

This arrangement ended on 22 February 1859 after an application to Presbytery by the Newtownards congregation. On 18 July 1860 Thomas Houston Dick, a son of Rev. James Dick of Kellswater, was ordained and installed. There was much promise in this early ministry, but he resigned in 1863 on accepting a call to Bailiesmills.

A vacancy of eleven years ended when Matthew Hodge, a native of Glasgow, whose father had been brought up in Limavady, was ordained and installed on 20 October 1874. Mr. Hodge exercised a faithful and fruitful ministry until 1897 when ill health compelled him to retire from the active duties of the ministry. He died on 24 June 1915 and was buried at Ballymacashon.

William Warnock succeeded him. A member of Ballymoney and a licentiate of the Northern Presbytery, he was ordained on 1 October 1905. He was the first minister to occupy the excellent manse that had been built by the generosity of the Misses Martin, daughters of Alexander Martin who had been a founder member of the congregation. Mr. Warnock's ministry was very short as he moved to Dromara on 1 March 1908. His family of three sons and two daughters served the Church faithfully in Ireland and Australia.

In a long vacancy of 16 years the congregation owed a great debt to the help and leadership of Rev. Torrens Boyd of Newtownards.

In 1925 a long and profitable ministry began when Rev. Alexander Gilmour, minister of Dromara, was appointed minister-in-charge. Though never formally installed, he carried out all the duties with devotion and distinction for 38 years until 1963 (he continued minister-in- charge on transferring to Newtownards and then for a few years into retirement) and his memory was cherished for a long time afterwards in the whole area.

At a congregational meeting on 20 October 1963, a decision was taken to establish a link with Cregagh Road with a view to sharing the services of a minister. Rev. Frederick S. Leahy, minister of Cregagh Road, accepted a call to the congregation in these circumstances and was installed on 6 March 1964. For over two years, until he moved to Kilraughts, a very suitable working arrangement with Cregagh Road was established. His ministry was a great blessing to the congregation.

During the vacancy from 1966 to 1969, Ballymacashon and Cregagh Road agreed to maintain their association. Joint calls were addressed to Rev. Professor Adam Loughridge, minister of Portrush, in October 1969. The calls were accepted and on 12 December a very happy relationship between pastor and people began  and continued for nine years. In January 1978, Professor Loughridge discussed with the Session and with the congregation the advisability of his tendering his resignation in order to facilitate a regrouping of congregations within the Presbytery that might be to advantage in a future settlement for Ballymacashon, Bailiesmills and Knockbracken. Presbytery appointed a Commission to investigate the matter and, after prayerful and careful consideration, the congregation agreed to renew its association with Knockbracken in the calling of a minister. Professor Loughridge's resignation was accepted by Presbytery on 4 April 1978 when he was appointed Interim Moderator of Session and stated supply of the pulpit until the settlement of a pastor. The congregation was commended for the gracious spirit of co-operation manifested in this important step.

Norris Wilson, member of Ballymoney, licentiate of the Northern Presbytery, educated at Queen's University, Theological Hall and Westminster Theological College, Philadelphia, was ordained and installed on 25 September 1979. He served the two congregations of Ballymacashon and Knockbracken until he accepted a call from the Dervock congregation where he was installed on 25 June 1986.

Edward McCollum, member of the Limavady congregation, licentiate of the Western Presbytery, educated at University of Ulster and Theological Hall was ordained and installed on 14 November 1986. He resigned from the congregation on 22 March 1999 but continued as minister of the Knockbracken part of the charge. A recent illness had confirmed his opinion that he could not undertake to meet the needs of both congregations, especially as Knockbracken was situated on the edge of a major housing development and was in a position to support a minister. The congregation in Ballymacashon was thankful for the leadership and ministry of the Word which Mr. McCollum had faithfully given.

Following the resignation of Mr. McCollum from the pastorate of Ballymacashon in 1999, the oversight of the congregation was undertaken, after an initial few months, by the Session of Newtownards. This continued for two years with reviews each September. During this period Mr. Stephen Wright supplied the pulpit for four months in early 2001. In September 2001 Presbytery appointed Rev. George McEwen, minister of Bailiesmills, as Interim Moderator, and undertook to keep the needs of Ballymacashon under review.

The following men have served on the eldership: Thomas Patterson, John Hewitt, Isaac Moorhead, Thomas Cleland, William Donaldson, William McEwen, James Fulton, James Cleland, John Moorhead, Samuel Morrow, William McConnell, James McEwen, Joseph Finlay, Hugh J. Hewitt, H.L. Brown, Robert William Campbell, Isaac Moorhead, Martin Mateer, William John Finlay, Boyd McConnell, John McConnell and McEwen Finlay.

Students for the ministry were James Martin, the church's pioneer missionary in Syria, and Thomas Cleland, minister of Limavady from 1871 to 1873.

From 2000 the Eastern Presbytery began a review of the future prospects of the congregation. This review led to Presbytery's decision on 3 February 2004 that the congregation of Ballymacashon be formally disorganised. It was designated a Preaching Station with monthly services. At a meeting of Presbytery on 3 May 2005 it was decided to discontinue the services in Ballymacashon to take effect from December 2005. Rev. Harry Coulter, Moderator of the Eastern Presbytery conducted the concluding service of worship on Sabbath afternoon 4 December 2005, bringing to a close 127 years of Covenanter witness in Ballymacashon and over 150 years of witness in the locality.

Presbytery placed on record its appreciation of the faithful and fruitful service of ministers, elders and members over these years.

The former Meeting House is situated at the junction of the Saintfield Road and Ballymacashon Road, Killinchy, Co. Down.

Ballymacashon Datestone 1847

BELFAST

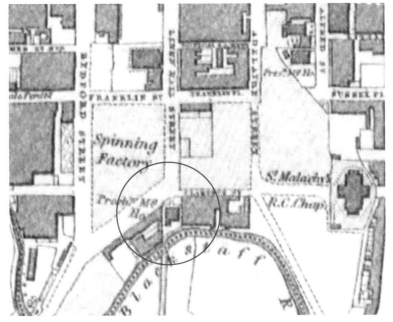

Victorian map of Belfast showing site of old Meeting House

LINENHALL STREET, LATER, BOTANIC AVENUE, BELFAST

Knockbracken is the mother church of the congregations in Belfast. From 1776, Covenanters residing in the comparatively small city were organised in Societies under the supervision of the minister and session at Knockbracken. The leading city Society was in Ballymacarrett.

In 1808 Knockbracken issued a call to Josias Alexander, minister of Bready. In the first year of his ministry a meeting house was built in Linenhall Street, Belfast on the site of the present B.B.C. building. Members of the Belfast societies were permitted to worship there on condition that they did not withdraw their support from Knockbracken. In 1822 Mr. Alexander resigned from Knockbracken to become minister of Linenhall Street, but on 10 November 1823 he died of a fever, aged forty-one.

Former Meeting House, Botanic Avenue

His successor was his elder brother John, who had been minister of Faughan from 1803. He was installed in 1826. However, a minority had voted for Rev. James Dick of Kellswater and left the congregation to form College Street South.

In 1840, John Alexander and his supporters in the congregation joined the breakaway Eastern Reformed Synod. He died in 1852. He was followed by Rev. Robert H. Henry. In 1863 Rev. John Bole was appointed to the pastoral care of the congregation and after a faithful ministry was succeeded by Rev. J. B. Stevenson in 1875.

Rev. John Bole

Due to reconstruction work in the Ormeau Avenue area in 1875, the congregation moved to Botanic Avenue. The older members of the congregation ensured that the remains of Rev. Josias Alexander, which were buried fifty-two years earlier, in a plot beside the Linenhall Street church, were reinterred in the City cemetery. The church cost £8,000 to build and was expensive to maintain. The pastor after Mr. Stevenson was John Robert Bartley who ministered between 1899 and 1902.

When the Eastern R.P. Synod ceased to function in 1902, the congregation, then much depleted, returned to the parent Synod in 1905. Membership stood at about 40. The congregation had only one other minister, James Patterson, who came from Thurso in Scotland in 1910 and returned there in 1911. Numbers fell to about 20 by 1920 and the congregation was dissolved in 1936. Although there was some thought of converting the building into a Synod Hall, the building was sold to the Irish Evangelical Church, which became the Evangelical Presbyterian Church of Ireland and this congregation subsequently moved to Stranmillis Road.

The building is still is good order but very sadly now used as a nightclub.

The old Meeting House is situated at 42 Botanic Avenue, Belfast, BT7 1JQ.

Old College Street South Meeting House. Used by permission of the Deputy Keeper of Records PRONI

COLLEGE STREET SOUTH

later

GROSVENOR ROAD

Knockbracken is the mother church of the congregations in Belfast. From 1776, Covenanters residing in the comparatively small town of Belfast were organised in Societies under the supervision of the minister and session at Knockbracken. These Belfast families enjoyed the ministry of William Stavely at Knockbracken.

In 1808 Knockbracken issued a call to Rev. Josias Alexander, minister of Bready. Mr. Alexander set about developing the work in Belfast. In the first year of his ministry at Knockbracken a meeting house was built in Linenhall Street, Belfast on the site of the present B.B.C building. Members of the Belfast societies were permitted to worship there on condition that they did not withdraw their support from Knockbracken.

Mr. Alexander resigned from Knockbracken in 1822 to become minister of Linenhall Street, but on 10 November 1823 he died of a fever, aged forty-one. His funeral sermon was preached by Rev. William Henry of Newtownards on the evening of 23 November 1822 and his text was 'All Judah and Jerusalem mourned for Josiah.' Referring to Mr. Alexander, Mr Henry said, 'By urbanity of manners, eminent and extensive usefulness, he had conciliated the affections of those whom he esteemed and commanded the respect even of enemies.'

His successor was his elder brother, Rev. John Alexander, who had been minister of Faughan from 1803. He was installed in 1825. However, a minority had voted for Rev. James Dick of Kellswater. In 1840, John Alexander and his supporters in the congregation joined the Eastern Reformed Synod. In 1875 this congregation moved to Botanic Avenue. When the Eastern R.P. Synod ceased to function in 1902, the congregation, then much depleted, returned to the parent Synod. When the congregation was dissolved in 1936, the building was sold to the Irish Evangelical Church.

The minority in Linenhall Street that had voted for Rev. James Dick of Kellswater in 1825 now withdrew from the congregation and, after worshipping for a time in Knockbracken, met as a Society in Curtis Street in the York Street area of the city. In 1832 they were organised into the "Second Reformed Presbyterian Congregation of Belfast" by the Northern Presbytery (to which Knockbracken at that time belonged). Their first minister was Thomas Boyd, a licentiate of the Southern Presbytery. The ordination took place in Donegall Street Congregational Church on 19 June 1833. Two years later, a new meeting house was opened for public worship in College Street South (renamed Grosvenor Road in 1916 by Belfast Corporation). The congregation was known as College Street South. Mr. Boyd left the R.P. Church in 1838 and became minister of the Synod of Ulster congregation at Castleblayney where he remained until his death in 1863.

Robert John Watt, born near Coleraine and brought up in Ballyclabber, was ordained on 3 July 1839. His ministry was of short duration because, for family reasons, he moved to Stranraer Original Secession Church in May 1842. The Free Church of Scotland afterwards attracted him and he was appointed to the charge of Elgin where he served until his death in 1862. His departure was sincerely regretted for he had been much liked as a man and as a preacher and under his ministry the congregation had enjoyed a period of steady growth. A man of noble character and great ability, Mr. Watt, both scholarly and popular, built up a strong and loyal congregation.

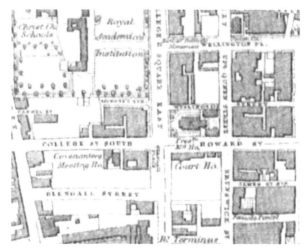

Victorian map of Belfast showing the site of College Street South

During the three years of vacancy which followed, the congregation was united with Newtownards and the congregation had supply on the first, second and fourth Sabbath and Newtownards on the third Sabbath.

College Street South Meeting House

William McCarroll was ordained on 4 June 1845 and appointed to the pastoral charge of both congregations. He was a native of Randalstown and brought up in Kellswater. He encouraged the formation of the Juvenile Missionary Association in 1846. At the meeting of Synod in 1847 it was agreed to separate College Street South and Newtownards. When the Theological Hall was established in 1854 Mr. McCarroll took a deep interest in its work and was the first Convener of the Committee of Superintendence. The Hall began a long association with the congregation that lasted more than a century. In 1859 the congregation secured a lease for ever of the site of the church on College Street South. The church buildings were enlarged, galleries were erected and a manse built. The congregation became self-supporting in 1861. Mr. McCarroll died on 4 November 1863 in his 53rd year. His death was a great loss to the whole Church for he was not only an able preacher and devoted pastor but also a gifted administrator. As his wife had died two years earlier, a family of seven children, all of tender years, were orphaned. They were provided for by a special fund raised by a committee of members of the congregation and friends, including the Mayor of Belfast and representatives of the General Assembly.

On 9 February 1865, Rev. Josias Alexander Chancellor, who had grown up in the College Street congregation and was minister of Bready for the last 18 years, was installed. He was named after the minister in Linenhall Street, Josias Alexander. The congregation grew rapidly under his preaching and, in the first ten years, 447 persons were admitted to membership. The times of services had been at the unusual hours of 11.30 a.m. to 1.00 p.m. and 1.30 p.m. to 3.00 p.m., but in 1875 they were fixed at 11.30 a.m. and 7.00 p.m. Some notable features of Mr. Chancellor's ministry were the ordination of Deacons to administer the finances and 'take an active interest in providing for the wants and in promoting the comfort of the poorer members of the congregation'. Also formed were a Band of Hope, a Young Men's Society (1877), Women's Missionary Association (1885) and, in 1875, a Sabbath School in Brownlow Street, in the Lower Shankill area, which later became the district mission of the congregation, in addition to the one held in the church. By the 1870s the two Sabbath schools had 100 pupils each with 70 members in the congregation serving as teachers. In 1879 Mr. Chancellor was appointed Professor of Systematic Theology in the Theological Hall and in 1881 the degree of Doctor of Divinity was conferred upon him by the R.P. College in Geneva, U.S.A.

In 1870-1871 and 1879 the church buildings were further extended but proved unable to accommodate everyone who wished to worship there. There were ten Societies at that time, meeting on alternate Tuesdays in the homes of members: Agnes Street, Ballymacarrett and Holywood, Brownlow Street, Carlisle Street, College Street South, Court Street, Cromac Street, Donegall Pass, Grosvenor Street and York Street. A Falls Road Society had been in existence until 1876.

In 1888 Belfast was formally recognised as a city; its population had more than doubled between 1861 and 1891. The College Street South church had difficulty in comfortably accommodating all its members and activities. It was decided that a second congregation should be formed in Belfast. In the period July 1888-April 1889 a new congregation was formed with its own minister, elders, deacons, committee, trustees and premises on Dublin Road. This might be viewed as the high point of the congregation for in 1890, even after the formation of the Dublin Road congregation, the College Street South congregation still had 400 members, 12 elders, 13 Deacons and 50 Sabbath School teachers.

In 1894 Professor Chancellor asked and obtained leave to have an assistant and successor appointed. He hoped for a younger man to help him. He was disappointed to learn that a sizeable minority in the congregation did not share his views and preferred James Dick, a man of over 50 years, who was a fellow Professor. It appears that Professor Chancellor expressed his dismay to some of the members. When it came to a congregational meeting on 12 December 1894, a majority supported the nomination of Rev. Samuel Guiler Kennedy, minister of Wishaw, but a large minority, consisting of five elders and eighty-five members dissented and objected to the fact that Professor Chancellor had canvassed actively on Mr. Kennedy's behalf. The matter came before Presbytery and Synod but no satisfactory solution emerged. The crisis appears to have affected his health and Professor Chancellor died on 26 May 1895. Meanwhile the minority group formed their own congregation, located in a former Baptist church building in Trinity Street on the north side of the city.

The effect on the College Street South congregation was devastating. The congregation was reduced to from 400 to 250 members, with 3 elders and 8 deacons remaining. The A.G.M. was postponed from January to November 1895 and the work of the congregation was described by Session as 'paralysed'. However, on 29 November 1895, a call was issued to Mr. Kennedy, which was accepted and his installation took place on 5 February 1896. Mr. Kennedy, soon to graduate LL.D. from the Royal University of Ireland, immediately won a warm place in the affections of the people and led them in the task of rebuilding the church, begun in April 1897, which was named Chancellor Memorial. The scheme, including a new mission hall at Brownlow Street, was completed at a cost of £4000. Dr. Kennedy was appointed Professor of Church History and Pastoral Theology in 1910. His heavy workload took its toll on his strength, and may have brought about his early death on 27 December 1924. A fine scholar, preacher and teacher, his able ministry made a great impact on the life of the congregation. The name of the street where the church building was located was changed from College Street South to Grosvenor Road in 1916 by the Belfast Corporation and the congregation became known as Grosvenor Road.

Sketch of The Chancellor Memorial , Grosvenor Road

Rev. Robert Nevin Lyons who had served the Church for seven years in Ballenon and Ballylane and five years in Ballylaggan was installed on 4 June 1925. His installation created an interesting situation. His older brother, James, had been installed the previous year in Dublin Road, the daughter congregation, and had acted as Interim Moderator during the vacancy at Grosvenor Road. The connection was further strengthened when the brothers lived in manses, just two doors apart in 86 and 90 Eglantine Avenue. For 30 years Rev. R. N. Lyons led the people with characteristic devotion and diligence. His preaching and pastoral work was of a high order and his retirement in 1955, followed by his death in 1961, brought sorrow to the congregation.

Rev. William Young, having served the Covenanting Church in Scotland since 1934 as minister of Wishaw and Stranraer, was installed on 4 September 1956. He exercised an earnest, sincere and warm-hearted pulpit ministry and brought total commitment to pastoral work. It was a matter of great grief to him, and to the congregation, when the church buildings were so severely damaged by a terrorist bomb in March 1972 as to render them unfit for further use. The invitation to share the facilities of Dublin Road was accepted and Mr. Young and Mr. Tadley, the minister of Dublin Road, shared the pulpit ministry. Mr. Young had shepherded the congregation in Grosvenor Road for over 16 years when he moved to Dervock on 1 February 1973.

In April 1973, Mr. Tadley took over the duties as minister to both congregations and carried the heavy burden of the two congregations until he moved to Ballenon and Ballylane on 7 October 1976.

Grosvenor Road Meeting House in the early 1970's

Even before the difficulties that resulted from the Troubles after 1968, the congregation in Grosvenor Road had seen that decline of membership that most downtown churches experienced since World War Two, a consequence of post war re-housing and population migration beyond the city boundary. The number of families had reduced by more than half between 1946 and 1966; in Dublin Road the number of families dropped from 156 to 56 in the same period. It soon became clear to both congregations that a formal amalgamation of the two congregations was the way forward. This was accomplished at a worship service organised and conducted by the Eastern Presbytery on Tuesday evening 2 May 1978. The two congregations, separated since 1888, expressed a desire to be known as Shaftesbury Square Reformed Presbyterian Church.

On 12 December 1978 Mr. Harold C. Cunningham, formerly the Baptist pastor in Carrickfergus, was ordained and installed as the first minister of the new Shaftesbury Square congregation. He retired from the active duties of the ministry on 31 December 2003.

On 30 November 2007, Rev. Professor David McKay, formerly the minister of Cregagh Road congregation, was installed as minister of the congregation.

The list of elders who have served the Linenhall Street/ College Street South/ Grosvenor Road congregation is a long and distinguished one and contains the names of faithful men: James McConkey, Robert Reynolds, Thomas Mawhinney, John Morton, Peter Reynolds, James Reynolds, John Potts, Samuel Aikin, Patrick Burns, Hugh Cheyne, Thomas Cheyne, Andrew Gray, Robert Gordon, Samuel McKeown, John Stewart, William Chancellor, William W. Houston, Nelson Cheyne, A.L. Edgar, John Graham, Thomas Hutchison, James McDowell, John Porter, James Rea, Hugh Blair, James Courtney, James Holmes, William McCoubrey, William McCullough, James Park, James Stewart, John Houston, John Allen, Samuel Flood, Nathaniel W. Gray, William C. McDowell, William Colville, T.B. Stephenson, J. O'Neill, S.H. Jamieson, Thomas Donnelly, James Burch, James McCanlis, A.F. McIlmoyle, Derek Hamilton, John Willdridge, J.D. Simpson and Robert A. McEwen.

Seven members of the congregation entered the Gospel ministry. Their names are Joseph T. Potts, Francis Moore, William Dodds, Thomas Donnelly, John Claude MacQuigg, John Marcus McCullough and Edward Donnelly.

From 1882 Miss Martha Cunningham served for ten years with Dr. James and Mrs. Martin in the R.P. mission in Syria.

Stone from the Grosvenor Road building now in Shaftesbury Square

The old Meeting House is demolished and the congregation meet in Shaftesbury Square Reformed Presbyterian Meeting House, 72 Dublin Road, Belfast BT2 7HP.

Interior of the Grosvenor Road building

Shaftesbury Square Meeting House

DUBLIN ROAD,
LATER SHAFTESBURY SQUARE, BELFAST

The formation of a second Covenanting congregation in Belfast was a consequence of the successful ministry of Dr. Josias A. Chancellor in the College Street South (later Grosvenor Road) congregation, together with the demographic facts of a rapidly growing Victorian city. The population of Belfast had more than doubled in thirty years: from 120,000 at the 1861 census to 273,000 at the 1891 census. By the late 1880s it was proving difficult to seat everyone who came to worship at College Street South, even though it could seat 600 persons. The following narrative of events demonstrates the remarkable pace at which a congregation can be established in the providence of God.

On 6 June 1888, a scheme for the organisation of a second congregation was considered and approved by the Session of College Street South congregation. On 9 July, a meeting of those wishing to join in the formation of a new congregation was held at the home of

Mr. W. W. Houston in 33 Rugby Avenue. (W. W. Houston was the son of Rev. Thomas Houston of Knockbracken.) At that meeting were present, from the College Street South Session: Robert Long, James Rea and James McDowell; from the diaconate were William G. Graham and Samuel Agnew; and Mr James A. Cunningham. A second meeting was held a week later, at which the sum of £1,500 was promised for the building of a new church and an executive committee was formed. This second meeting was supported by John Brady, Andrew McWilliams and R. B. Montgomery. The executive committee met on 19 July and decided to ask all the ministers of the denomination for the names of any of their members who had come to reside in Belfast in the last four years. By the time of their next meeting, on 27 July, the sum of £89.5 shillings was available for a stipend.

On 28 December 1888, a Commission of the Eastern Presbytery organised the new congregation as 'Second Belfast'. At this meeting five elders and three deacons were installed, and three Trustees appointed. During 1889 the Trustees secured a suitable site in Dublin Road for £800 and the tender for £2,550 for the erection of the church buildings was accepted. With the aid of two large subscriptions, £1,000 from James Rea and £250 from W. W. Houston, the total cost was met in little over a year.

In the first year the congregation had worshipped in the Central Hall, Rosemary Street but the congregation was able to meet on the first Sabbath of 1890 in their new church hall and the church, which could seat 450, was opened for public worship on 13 April 1890. By the end of 1892, the debt was cleared and membership had risen from 50 to 136. Surely few congregations could record such a speedy establishment in just four years.

Meanwhile, on 19 February 1889, a unanimous call was issued to Rev. John Lynd, minister of Ballylaggan, the congregation in which he had been brought up. The call was accepted and he was installed on 15 April 1889. In 1898 Mr. Lynd was awarded a doctorate; in 1901 he became Professor of Hebrew and Biblical Criticism in the Theological Hall. Professor Lynd's ministry was greatly blessed from the beginning. He organised the congregation into districts and made an elder responsible for each one. By 1907, there were two Sabbath Schools, 69 attending in the morning, consisting of members' children, and 107 in the afternoon drawn from outsiders. The initial membership of 50 that had withdrawn from Grosvenor Road grew to 190 communicant members by 1914. In June 1923, after a fruitful ministry of thirty-four years, Professor Lynd was compelled to retire from active duties on account of failing health.

His successor was Rev. James Alexander Lyons who had ministered in Cullybackey for eighteen years. The installation service was held on 9 January 1924. An interesting situation soon emerged. His younger brother, Nevin, was installed next year in Grosvenor Road, the parent congregation. The connection was further strengthened when the brothers lived in manses, just two doors apart in 86 and 90 Eglantine Avenue.

Mr. Lyons exercised an able and dignified ministry that was richly blessed to the congregation for twenty-two years. In spite of industrial recession and unemployment that led to mass emigration, the strength of the congregation increased and an active missionary programme was in operation. In October 1929, 153 were present at Communion. Mr. Lyons retired from the active duties on 6 August 1946 and died on 9 March 1952.

Rev. Professor John McIlmoyle was installed as the next minister on 11 June 1947. Before coming to Belfast, he had served with great diligence and acceptance in Creevagh (1913-1923), Kellswater (1923-1929) and Faughan (1929-1947). Consequently, with involvement in all four Presbyteries, he brought to his ministry in Dublin Road a wealth of experience and a total commitment to his preaching and pastoral duties. His sudden death, on the eve of his retirement on 22 June 1966, brought great sorrow to the congregation, and to the Church as a whole, as his ministry had been characterised by spiritual blessing, warmth and shared affection.

By 1966, the congregation was experiencing the difficulties that faced most downtown churches. Because of housing redevelopment and migration beyond the city boundary, the number of families had dropped from 150 to 56. In addition to this, there was, for Dublin Road, an unusually long vacancy of five years. However, the bonds between Dublin Road and Grosvenor Road were strengthened during this period.

Professor McIlmoyle's successor, brought up under his ministry in Faughan, was Harry Tadley. After serving the Church as Evangelist for ten years, he was licensed by the

Western Presbytery and ordained and installed in Dublin Road on 8 September 1971. He served the congregation with devotion and his warm-hearted and meticulous ministry and his sympathetic pastoral concern made him loved by all.

Shortly after his ministry began, in March 1972, Grosvenor Road congregation, bereft of its church buildings by terrorist activity, accepted the invitation to worship in fellowship with Dublin Road congregation. In due course, joint meetings of both Sessions and Committees took place, along with the coming together of the W.M.A.s, Sabbath Schools and CY societies. When Rev. William Young went to Dervock in February 1973, Mr. Tadley carried the heavy burden of the two congregations until he moved to Ballenon and Ballylane on 7 October 1976. The ongoing history of the Dublin Road congregation continued under the new name 'Shaftesbury Square' when an amalgamation with the Grosvenor Road congregation was completed on 2 May 1978. The Eastern Presbytery conducted a worship service during which the two congregations were amalgamated. Both congregations (separate since 1888), had expressed the desire to be formally united and chose the name of Shaftesbury Square.

On 12 December 1978 Harold G. Cunningham, formerly the Baptist pastor in Ballynahinch and Carrickfergus, was ordained and installed as the first minister of the new Shaftesbury Square congregation. The congregation received great benefit from his expository preaching, open, constructive and friendly moderation of Session meetings, visiting of the sick and elderly and his practical work on the congregation's properties. Dr. Cunningham retired from the active duties of the ministry on 31 December 2003.

On 30 November 2007, Rev. Professor David McKay, formerly the minister of Cregagh Road congregation, was installed as minister of the congregation. In December 2009, Mr. Philip McCollum a licentiate of the Northern Presbytery was called as a minister for mission work by the congregation. His ordination and installation on 5 March 2010 began a new phase of the work of Christ's Kingdom in Shaftesbury Square.

The site of the church, on the corner of Hartington Street and Dublin Road, had been purchased for the sum of £800 in 1889. Samuel Stevenson was the architect and H. & J.

Martin were awarded the building contract at a cost of £2550. The memorial stone was laid by James Rea, who had made a generous subscription of £1000. By 17 February 1892 the debt was cleared. In the German air attacks in April 1941, an incendiary bomb went through the roof of the church building and scorched some of the pews. The hole remained

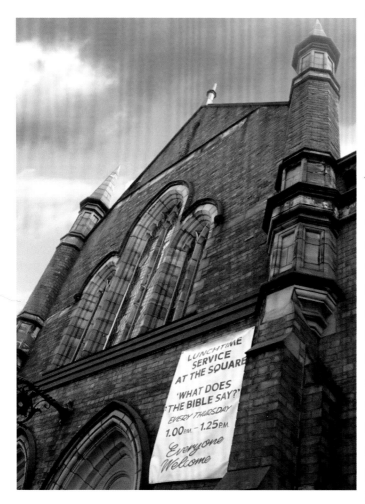

un-repaired as a reminder of God's mercy in perilous times, until the extensive repair and restoration work which began in 1955. An extensive scheme of major repair, restoration and redecoration was undertaken in the church buildings and the manse. The total cost was £1,000 but, because of the introduction of a building and repair fund envelopes a few years earlier, and a special appeal, all the work was completed debt free. Other work was undertaken in the 1960s. By 1980 the church was re-slated, rewired, and redecorated and a fire escape installed from the Lecture Hall. The committee/choir room was adapted and named the 'Chancellor Room' and contained a tablet and foundation stones from the original Grosvenor Road building. In 1984 a major building project resulted in the erection of new kitchens, cloakroom facilities and an additional room, named the Lyons Room in recognition of the service rendered to both Dublin Road and Grosvenor Road by the Lyons brothers. The roof, ceilings and windows of the church property were severely damaged by a terrorist bomb, which exploded on 24 March 1992 behind Donegall Pass R.U.C. station. For some time the congregation met in the central pews protected by overhead scaffolding under an unstable roof, with the side pews cordoned off. Later the church hall was used for services. The repair work took 14 months to complete and cost £250,000; the reopening service was held on 23 May 1993.

In 1894 the manse was erected at 86 Eglantine Avenue and served the ministers well. However, by 1967 this property required expensive renovation, and, as well, the character of the neighbourhood was changing from residential to commercial use. Consequently, the congregation purchased 11 Cranmore Gardens and Mr. Tadley was the first minister to occupy it. With Dr. Cunningham's retirement it was decided to sell the manse to give flexibility to a new minister in his choice of residence. The property which had cost £6,800 in 1968 was sold in 2006 for £530,000.

Four members of the congregation studied for the ministry: W.G.M. Martin, Charles Presho, Thomas H. Semple and Robert W. Lytle.

A young teacher from the congregation, Miss Margaret Houston, a grand-daughter of Dr. Thomas Houston, volunteered to go for three years to teach in the R.P. Mission in Alexandretta, Syria arriving in July 1922, she sadly died in August of the following year.

The following elders gave notable service to the congregations and their names are: Samuel Agnew, Nelson Cheyne, James Rea, James McDowell, Robert Long, William Houston, John Donnelly, John Porter, Robert Caldwell, William Graham, Thomas Martin, John Henry, John Kearns, Joseph Lamont, Robert Donaldson, Robert Bell, John McCullagh, John Thompson, Robert Young, David Agnew, Thomas Graham, John McCarroll, Thomas Semple, James Stewart, James Hamilton, Ian Beck Hill, Alexander Anderson, J.R.M. Blair, William Brown, Joseph McCracken, David McConaghy, Stephen McWilliams, William Aicken, Harry Morgan, T.B.Stephenson, J.R.G. McIlmoyle, Joseph O'Neill, J. Burch, S.H. Jamieson, J.D.Simpson, T.W.Kennedy, W. F.M.Wallace, W.E.Harkness, F.F.Hamilton, Tom Hamilton, S.M.Lyons, D.McCullough, James F.McIlmoyle, J.N. Simpson, J.W.Calderwood, W.J.Cromie and Dr. Hugh McCullough.

The church is the venue for regular lunchtime meetings organised in partnership with the Belfast City Mission and gatherings for students and other young people are held in the hall.

The Shaftesbury Square congregation Meeting House is situated at 72 Dublin Road, Belfast BT2 7HP.

Trinity Street Meeting House

TRINITY STREET, BELFAST,
later TRINITY, MOSSLEY, NEWTOWNABBEY

In 1894, Professor Chancellor, minister of the congregation at College Street South (later called Grosvenor Road), burdened with the weight of years, diminishing health and increasing pastoral duties, asked leave from the Presbytery to have an assistant and successor appointed. This was the procedure in many churches at that time because the provisions for retirement were very inadequate. Professor Chancellor preferred a younger minister. When he learned that a large number in the congregation preferred James Dick, a man in his fifties, he expressed his dismay to some of the members. When a congregational meeting was held on 12 December 1894, the ballot carried out in the congregation showed 162 votes for Rev. S. G. Kennedy of Wishaw and 156 for Rev. James Dick of Kilraughts. This large minority refused to accept the verdict, claiming that Professor Chancellor was canvassing on behalf of Mr. Kennedy. As the matter was not resolved at Presbytery and Synod, a third Covenanting congregation was formed in Belfast, organised by the Eastern Presbytery on 21 January 1896.

In 1896 the church building at the corner of Trinity Street and Regent Street, in the north side of the city, lately vacated by Antrim Road Baptist congregation, was purchased for the sum of £1000, and on 18 February 1896 the congregation issued their call to Mr. Dick. The call was accepted and the installation was held on 19 May 1896. The report to Synod of that year showed the strength of the congregation to be five elders and ninety-seven members.

Mr. Dick was appointed Professor of Systematic Theology in the Hall a few weeks after his installation. The congregation grew steadily under his ministry and by 1900 the membership numbered 178 with a Sabbath School enrolment of 150. Professor Dick proved to be an inspiring leader and his arresting style of preaching and his public lectures on popular themes made him widely known. It was as a result of a series of lectures that he gave on Reformation doctrines and Covenanting distinctives that the Congregation of Cregagh Road was established. Professor Dick died on 6 August 1916.

On 14 March 1917, Rev. Alexander Gilmour from Rathfriland, who had ministered for six years in Drimbolg, was installed. Though different in temperament and style from his predecessor, he exercised a most effective and profitable ministry for seven years before moving to Dromara in 1924. There were special problems for the congregation at this time as the location of the church building left the people exposed to severe rioting in the troubled years of 1920 and 1921. It was with great difficulty and much courage that the work was carried on.

The next minister was Rev. William Russell, a son-in-law of Rev. Prof. James Dick. Brought up in Ballyclare, he had ministered successively in Ballenon and Paisley before his installation on 4 January 1927. A man of great intellect and gracious personality, Mr. Russell was warmly received and much beloved by the people. He was appointed Professor of Systematic Theology at the Hall in 1928. Owing to failing health he retired from active duties on 18 July 1944 and died a few weeks later on 6 September.

He was succeeded by Isaac Cole, until then the first licentiate to be ordained in the congregation. Brought up in Ballenon and licensed by the Southern Presbytery, he was ordained on 23 January 1945. The service was held in St. Enoch's Presbyterian Church, as the Trinity Street buildings had sustained considerable damage from German Air Raids. Mr. Cole gave the congregation practical preaching, wise counsel and faithful pastoral care for 13 years until he moved to Drimbolg in 1958.

The vacancy was filled on 15 September 1959, when Rev. Hugh Wright, a son of Ballyclabber manse, who had served four years in Winnipeg and twenty-one years in Londonderry, was installed. He brought to his work in Belfast a wealth of experience and a deep sense of commitment to the gospel ministry and the work was well maintained under his leadership. His faithful ministry of fourteen years ended on 27 November 1973, when he accepted a call to Newtownards. In the later years of his pastorate the congregation was faced with great difficulties due to the location of the building in an area particularly affected by terrorism. The movement of population and civil unrest had devastated the neighbourhood and the congregation was, numerically, at a low ebb. Every effort was made to interest the people of the district and, while the meeting house was available, a fine work was done, particularly among the girls, directed by Mrs R.E. McCune.

During the vacancy that followed, this work continued, and the congregation gave earnest and prayerful thought to the possibility of relocation. After a trial period, when the evening service was held in the Barron Hall, Glengormley, it was agreed, at some sacrifice, to move completely to the Newtownabbey area, and a regular ministry on Sabbaths began in the Barron Hall on 6 April 1975. The Trinity Street building was purchased by Belfast City Council as a leisure and community centre for the district.

In this new setting (now known as Trinity) Rev. Edward Donnelly, after periods of service in Dervock and in the American R. P. Mission in Cyprus, was installed on 30 April 1975. The service took place in Ballyclare R.P. Church. He was appointed Professor of New Testament Language and Literature at the R.P. Theological Hall in 1979. Under his able pulpit ministry, pastoral care and well-organised groups for Bible study and prayer, the congregation made encouraging progress. An excellent site was secured on the Doagh Road, at the northern edge of Newtownabbey and the building was erected in 1983. It was officially opened on 17 September 1983. The congregation has been blessed with a steady growth in numbers and, by 2000, comprised about 65 families, with a good proportion of children and young people. Attendances at Sabbath worship averaged 142 in the morning and 111 in the evening. The suite of buildings was enlarged considerably in the late 1990s.

Rev. Professor Edward Donnelly accepted the call of the Glenmanus congregation and

was installed there on 20 March 1987. He and his family were held in warm affection and were honoured by the Trinity congregation at a social meeting on 12 March. However, three years later, being yet without a minister, on 7 March 1990, the congregation issued a call to Professor Donnelly and, having accepted it, he was again installed in the congregation on 8 June 1990.

The congregation has given several students for the gospel ministry: Norman McCune, Knox Hyndman, Tom Reid, Harry Coulter, Andrew Stewart, Vincent McDonnell, Peter Jemphrey, Mark Loughridge, Warren Peel, Philip Moffett, Simon Sweeney, Steven Robinson and John Coates. In addition, Billy Hamilton was called and commissioned as a worker for the Irish Section of the Mission Committee.

These first elders were A. L. Edgar, John H. Graham, Thomas Hutchinson, John Potts and John Stewart. To these were added over the years, William C. Black, William Martin, J.R. Kirkpatrick, Thomas Strahan McCune, Robert Eaton McCune, Parker Wasson, William McFerran, James Holmes, William Wasson, Walter Mill Dick, Thomas Strahan McCune, William Strahan McCune, Hugh McFerran, Thomas Strahan McCune, James Dick Russell, Robert Eaton McCune, Harold Eaton McCune, Ronald A. Loughridge, Adam Mastris,

William Stewart, W. Oswald Graham, John K. McKelvey, David H.A. Wright, Robert S. Drennan, R. Graham Moffett, Kenneth J. Nelson and R. Stanley Wilson.

The congregation's first manse, at 12 Knutsford Drive, was provided for Mr. Cole. A new manse was purchased at 103 Jordanstown Road, Newtownabbey.

A vision for planting daughter congregations was nurtured over several years, resulting in a number of members committing themselves to a new work in Carrickfergus. In 2006 this fellowship was organised as a Society under the leadership of Rev. Harry Coulter. Trinity hopes that this will not be the last daughter congregation to be produced. The congregation continues to grow in numbers, with key emphasis being the ministry of the Word and the maintaining and developing of a rich multi-faceted body life. Goals for the immediate future include the strengthening of individual and corporate prayer and a more effective outreach with the Gospel into the surrounding community.

The Meeting House is situated at 560 Doagh Road, Mossley, Newtownabbey, BT36 5BU.

Cregagh Road former Meeting House

CREGAGH ROAD, BELFAST

In the winter of 1899 Rev. Professor James Dick, minister of the Trinity Street congregation, gave a series of lectures in Cregagh Street School in East Belfast on the history and the distinctive principles of the Reformed Presbyterian Church. A number of people, influenced by these lectures, asked the Eastern Presbytery to provide a hall for missionary work in the area.

Presbytery gave favourable consideration to the request and on 22 November 1900 the Cregagh Road congregation was organised. It consisted of eleven members, seven of whom were drawn from outside the R.P. Church. Three interim elders, James Black, A. L. Edgar and William Martin, supervised the new congregation. Services were at first held in the school, but a church building was opened in 1903; it was actually situated on the Woodstock Road, just before it becomes the Cregagh Road, in East Belfast.

On 15 July 1901, the congregation issued a call to Rev. William Dick of Mulvin, a younger brother of Professor Dick. The installation took place on 6 November 1901. Mr. Dick did sterling work until his death in 1928. The membership rose to 49 and, in spite of the war years, attendances averaged 70 and a large Sabbath School was organised.

During a long vacancy which followed from 1928, however, the membership declined. Good help was given by Rev. Archibald Holmes of Ballyclare and Rev. John Watters, Knockbracken, but the membership dwindled to eleven and, but for the courage and faithfulness of Mr. W. J. Stevenson, one of the elders who led the work almost single-handedly for years, the cause would have been extinguished altogether.

Rev. John Knox Dickey accepted a call in 1937 and after a very brief ministry accepted a call from Drum Presbyterian Church, County Cavan in 1938.

Mr Alexander Barkley, member of Kilraughts and a licentiate of the American R.P. Church, was ordained on 8 March, 1939. In spite of the difficult war years, his able ministry was blessed and the membership grew steadily under his pastoral care. He resigned on 3 September 1946 in order to succeed Rev. H. K. Mack in the pastorate of Geelong R.P. Church, Australia.

Rev. Robert Barnett Cupples, after a ministry of 13 years in Fairview and Tullyvallen, was installed on 2 September 1947. He accepted a call to Loughbrickland in April 1951. His successor was Rev. Frederick Stratford Leahy, a native of County Donegal, educated at the College of the Free Church of Scotland, who had served for a number of years with the Irish Evangelical Church, later called the Evangelical Presbyterian Church. He was ordained on 23 September 1953 and began a very faithful ministry in which the membership increased and a fine work was done among the youth of the community. At a congregational meeting of Ballymacashon on 20 October 1963, a decision was taken to establish a link with Cregagh Road with a view to sharing the services of a minister. Rev. Frederick S. Leahy, accepted the call to the congregation in these circumstances and was installed on 6 March 1964. For over two years, a very suitable working arrangement with Cregagh Road was established. His ministry was a great blessing to that congregation.. Mr. Leahy accepted a call to Kilraughts and was installed there on 24 November 1966.

During his ministry, along with other members of Presbytery, he was involved with the Bangor Preaching Station where a Sabbath afternoon service was held in the Minor Hall of the King's Hall on Hamilton Road. The work began in 1930 and continued for over 30 years and those involved also included Revs. R. N. Lyons, A. Barkley, I. Cole, A. Loughridge and others.

During the vacancy from 1966 to 1969, Cregagh Road and Ballymacashon agreed to maintain their association. Joint calls were addressed to Rev. Professor Dr. Adam Loughridge, minister of Glenmanus, Portrush, in October 1969. The calls were accepted and on 10 December a very happy relationship between pastor and people began and continued for nine years. Professor Loughridge, was installed in Ballymacashon on 12 December 1969. During his ministry the membership of Cregagh Road increased to 90.

On 4 April 1978, Professor Loughridge resigned from Ballymacashon in order to facilitate a regrouping of congregations within the Presbytery that might be to advantage in a future settlement for Ballymacashon, Bailiesmills and Knockbracken. Ballymacashon renewed its association with Knockbracken. He was appointed Interim Moderator of Ballymacashon and stated supply of the pulpit until the settlement of a pastor.

Up until the mid 1970s, the congregation had been served by only two treasurers, W. J. Stevenson and F. H. Dalzell, these two men having also the distinction of leading the praise during that long period. In May 1980 Professor Loughridge retired from Cregagh Road and from the active duties of the ministry. At a social meeting to mark his retirement on Friday 25 April, the gratitude of the congregation was expressed for his ministry.

Thomas C. Donachie, Dromara, and licientiate of the Eastern Presbytery, was installed on Tuesday 2 September 1980. Mr. Donachie resigned in February 1991.

Rev. Dr. W. David J. McKay was installed as the eighth pastor of the congregation on 2 June 1995 and served the congregation until 7 November 2006. Shortly after his

installation he was appointed Professor of Systematic Theology in the Reformed   Theological College. The congregation celebrated, in the year 2000, the 100th anniversary of the commencement of the work in the area and in 2003 the congregation hosted various events to celebrate the 100th anniversary of the opening of the current building.

The following elders have served in the congregation: John Leslie Graham, Thomas Archer, James Black, Samuel McChesney, William J. Stevenson, Hugh R. McCluggage, Robert Hughes, David Archer, Frederick H. Backler, David Marshall, Robert Quinn, Robert M. Watson, W. H. Patterson, J. Rosbotham, F. Harry Dalzell, John A. Gordon, William Wilson, Herbert Yeates, Robert Armstrong, Desmond Callander, Stanley William Foreman, Stanley Alexander Foreman and Alan James Yeates.

The congregation has given two students to the Church's ministry: Barry J. Galbraith and Robert Robb.

Mr. Cupples occupied the first manse at 11 Downshire Road. In the vacancy that preceded Professor Leahy's installation, a manse was purchased at 468 Ravenhill Road but, as this proved unsuitable, a manse at 429 Cregagh Road was secured in 1959.

In the summer of 2006 difficulties surfaced within the congregation leading to an investigation by Presbytery. The majority of the members decided to join other congregations in the Presbytery and Cregagh Road was formally dissolved as a congregation in the summer of 2007. The Trustees of Cregagh Road requested that the assets of the congregation (church building and manse at 429 Cregagh Road) be administered by the Eastern Presbytery for future mission and church-planting ministry in East Belfast, seeking to re-establish a Reformed Presbyterian witness in this part of the city.

The old Meeting House is situated at 411 Woodstock Road, Belfast.

Conventicle Carrickfergus Castle 1 June 2008

CARRICKFERGUS

The Covenanting cause in Carrickfergus was marked by a Conventicle service in the open air on the green of the ancient castle on Sabbath 1 June 2008. It commemorated the administering of the Solemn League and Covenant on that spot by 1400 Scottish soldiers and 400 civilians on 4th April 1644. It had been the scene two years earlier in 1642 of the formation of the first Presbytery in Ireland.

Historically, Covenanters in Carrickfergus would have been in association with Loughmourne and ministered to by Rev. Dr. John Paul.

In the late 1990s the Home Section of the Mission Committee encouraged the planting of daughter congregations. In response to this call, some members of the Trinity congregation committed themselves to such a goal for Carrickfergus. They met weekly for prayer, fellowship and planning. In May 2003 the Eastern Presbytery granted permission to the Trinity Session to move forward with a call to an Organising Pastor for a work in Carrickfergus. In September 2003 Rev. Harry Coulter was called to be the Organising Pastor. He resigned as minister of Kilraughts in January 2004, after a ministry of 14 years and was commissioned by the Eastern Presbytery as Organising Pastor of the Carrickfergus Reformed Presbyterian Fellowship. The Service of Commissioning was held in the Trinity Church building on 4 February 2004.

The Fellowship began with a core group from Trinity of 16 members, 11 covenant children,

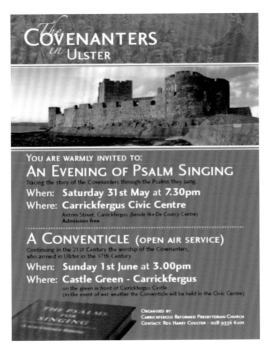

10 adherents and their children, a total of 37, including an elder from Trinity, Ronnie Loughridge. The first public worship services commenced in the Oakfield Community Development Centre in Carrickfergus on Sabbath evening of 8 February 2004 with an attendance of 57 members, adherents and friends. These were supplemented by a midweek meeting in the same venue. Between February and June Rev. Harry Coulter and Rev. Prof. Edward Donnelly shared the preaching ministry. There was an average attendance of 39 with 15 at the midweek meeting. Morning services commenced on 3 October 2004.

The Carrickfergus Fellowship was organised into a Society on 2 June 2006 with 24 people coming into membership, together with 16 covenant children and 6 adherents. Osy Graham, David Wright and Ronnie Loughridge, members of the Trinity Session were appointed as Interim Elders, with the latter serving as Interim Clerk of Session. During the first year of the Society's existence, 50-60 attended the Lord's Day Morning Worship and 25-30 in the evening. By 2009 there was an average attendance of fifty at each of the Lord's Day services.

On 15 January 2010 Mr. John George, a licentiate of the Eastern Presbytery, who had been called by the Eastern Presbytery was ordained and commissioned as a minister of the Gospel for mission work in the society.

The Society has produced one student for the ministry: Peter Loughridge.

The Society currently meets at the Oakfield Centre, Oakfield Drive, Carrickfergus, Co. Antrim BT38 7SP.

Dromara Meeting House

DROMARA

The congregation had its origin in First Dromara Presbyterian Church. When the long ministry of Rev. William Craig ended in 1871, the members had formed a warm attachment to a theological student, William Wilson. He had often preached in Mr. Craig's closing years. In the vacancy that followed Mr. Craig's death, the majority of the congregation, instead of calling a licentiate or ordained minister, was willing to wait until Mr. Wilson had completed his studies and received licence in May 1873. However, the majority of the Session and a minority of the people did not want to wait until he was ready for a call and wanted an immediate settlement with someone else. They petitioned the higher courts. The General Assembly, upon witnessing the disunity in the congregation, decided to declare Mr. Wilson ineligible for First Dromara. Although a later Commission, appointed by the Assembly, rescinded this decision, the Session, of course, adhered to the original ruling and the higher courts were willing to support what Session desired. Nevertheless, the majority in the congregation wanted to arrange a poll for Mr. Wilson but the Commission would not agree. The majority locked the church building rather than allow supplies arranged by the Commission to conduct the services. At a special meeting held on 11 February 1874 the majority party, which made up over 600 out of the 800-strong congregation, carried a series of resolutions that renounced the oversight of the General Assembly and sought affiliation with the Reformed Presbyterian Church.

Dromara Meeting House and Slieve Croob

On 16 February 1874 the Eastern Presbytery appointed Rev. Dr. Houston and Rev. Dr. Chancellor to preach at Dromara on the following two Sabbaths. There was some conflict because the General Assembly also sent supplies of preaching and a struggle ensued regarding the right to use the meeting house. On the first Sabbath, Rev. Dr. Russell, appointed by the General Assembly, arrived before Dr. Houston at the meeting house, escorted by 20 policemen but, when the congregation started to shout him down, he and 100 others adjourned to a barn to conduct the service. In subsequent weeks, the Covenanter supply arrived first and claimed the use of the building.

In due course, however, the majority, on the advice of the Eastern Presbytery, surrendered the right to the property and for the month of June 1874, worshipped in the open air. A plot of ground was temporarily secured by the Covenanters for the erection of a wooden hall. The necessary materials having been brought to the site, the work of erection of the hall was commenced on Tuesday, 30th June. It was completely finished and seated to accommodate almost 600 people and opened for public worship on Sabbath 5th July 1874. By 1876, the congregation obtained a site and the new building was opened on 25

February 1877 with 1200 persons present. A manse was also built on the Hillsborough Road on the edge of Dromara village.

The congregation, in spite of its stormy beginning, soon settled into normal work. 347 persons were admitted into membership between May and October 1874. The congregation made a call to Rev. Torrens Boyd, then minister of Ringrash. The installation took place on 24 February 1875. Mr. Boyd's evangelistic preaching and

zealous pastoral care helped to establish the work. Between the foundation of the congregation in May 1874 and May 1884 a total of 702 people had joined the congregation. A realistic revision of the roll then took place and it was reduced to over 500. Mr. Boyd, having ministered in Dromara for over 15 years, accepted a call to the Reformed Presbyterian Church in Hall Lane, Liverpool and was installed there on 2 July 1890. Rev. Torrens and Mrs. Boyd experienced much sorrow and grief through the death of their five young daughters who were stricken down with tuberculosis. Their daughters were born before their coming to Dromara and all died in the Manse at Dromara.

The second minister was Rev. John McKee. Born at Dundonald and brought up in Knockbracken, he had served in Penpont in Dumfriesshire, Scotland since 1873, before his installation in Dromara on 18 March 1891. Mr. McKee was diligent in duty and he presented the truths of the Christian faith in a simple, clear and earnest manner. With his blameless and consistent life, he endeared himself to the congregation. In a ministry of 7 years, a total of 124 persons were admitted into membership. On 17 December 1897 Mr. McKee accepted a call to Wishaw and was installed there on 27 January 1898.

In 1898 Dromore congregation was transferred to the Eastern Presbytery and placed under the care of the Dromara session. A monthly service, (bi-monthly from 1953) became the responsibility of the Dromara minister, an arrangement which continued until 1990.

On 28 March 1898 the congregation issued a unanimous call to Rev. Torrens Boyd, who since January 1893 had been minister of Knockbracken. He accepted the call, as he did to every one he received, and on 18 May 1898 Mr. Boyd returned to Dromara. In 1907 he accepted a Call to Newtownards, where he exercised his longest ministry until his death in 1925.

The next minister, Rev. William Warnock, was brought up in the Ballymoney congregation and had a short ministry of three years in Ballymacashon before he was installed in Dromara on 11 March 1908. In spite of the difficult war years and the economic depression and emigration that followed – attendances at the Lord's Table ranged between 103 and 140 - his ministry was fruitful and widely accepted. He accepted a call to Loanhead on 21 August 1923 and was installed there on 11 December.

On 18 March 1924, Rev. Alexander Gilmour began a long and outstanding ministry of 28 years. Brought up in Rathfriland, he had previously served in Drimbolg and Trinity Street. In 1925 Mr. Gilmour, was also appointed minister-in-charge of Ballymacashon and, although never formally installed, he carried out all the duties with devotion and distinction for 38 years. His ministry in Dromara was found by the congregation to be edifying and comforting and he held a high place in its esteem and affection. His special gifts as a scholar and teacher were recognised by the Synod when he was appointed Lecturer in Old Testament Language and Literature in the Theological Hall in 1945. Mr. Gilmour accepted a call to Newtownards on 27 May 1952 and was installed there on 3 July. During his ministry, the gallery was converted into a very useful Church Hall in 1926.

On 7 January 1953, Rev. James Renwick Wright, minister of Ballymoney for twelve years, was installed. Son of Rev. J. R. Wright of Ballyclabber, Mr. Wright's excellent gifts were greatly used and richly blessed in the congregation and community. On 17 December 1968 he accepted a call from the Geneva congregation, Beaver Falls, U.S.A. and was installed there the following year. Since 1969 Mr. Wright ministered with great acceptance in the Reformed Presbyterian Church of North America Church, first at Geneva, Beaver Falls then at Winchester, Kansas. He received an honorary degree of D.D. from Geneva College, U.S.A. On 19 September 1978, Dr. Wright was inaugurated as

Professor of New Testament Studies at the Reformed Presbyterian Theological Seminary, Pittsburgh. He died in Pittsburgh in October 2009.

Rev. Robert Hanna was installed on 16 July 1969. A member of Kilraughts, he came to Dromara after ministries of five and a half years in Milford and seven years in Newry. An ardent preacher of the Word and a diligent and devoted pastor of his people, he led the congregation with characteristic vigour and sincerity. In 1974 he prepared a history of the congregation entitled *The Centenary Story* in which he gave a thorough and informative record of the congregation's life. In its centenary year, the congregation acted as host to the Annual Meeting of the Synod. On 20 December 1987 a unanimous call was issued by the Kellswater congregation to Mr. Hanna. He was installed there on 18 March 1988.

Robert Robb, member of Cregagh Road and licentiate of the Eastern Presbytery, was ordained and installed on 7 September 1990. He was the first minister to be ordained in the congregation. Owing to ill health, he resigned the pastorate of Dromara on 3 September 1991.

Rev. John Hawthorne, a native of Londonderry and an elder in Ebrington Presbyterian Church before becoming a member in Faughan, was installed on 24 June 1993, having served in Fairview, Tullyvallen and Limavady congregations. After 13 years of faithful ministry, for which the congregation was appreciative, he accepted a call to Dervock and was installed on 9 June 2006.

In June 2008, the congregation made a call to Rev. Geoffrey Allen, member of Dromore and formerly a minister in the Presbyterian Church of Ireland. Mr. Allen had been taken under care of the Eastern Presbytery in September 2007 and undertook further study at the Reformed Theological College. The call was accepted and Mr. Allen was installed on 19 September 2008.

The congregation has appointed the following elders. The first session consisted of Richard Copeland, James Bryson and Robert Mack. They were joined in the next few years by Robert Bawn, William Corry, Samuel Douglas, Robert Gamble, and James Skelly. To these men were subsequently added Josiah A. Archer, George Corry, William

G. Hook, Alexander Macauley, John Fulton, W. J. Hawthorne, Samuel Mack, John Rankin, John Skelly, R. Baillie Bell, Arthur W. Davison, Samuel J. Skelly, Joseph Somerville, Alfred Wallace, Joseph Fryer, William Somerville, William F. Corry, Edward Harkness, Harry Nelson, William Campbell, Sydney Chambers, Robert Woods, William Gamble, John Somerville, Victor Draffin, John Bond, Gordon Bond, John Bell and Harold Kerr.

Seven members have offered themselves for the work of the ministry: Hugh K. Mack, Samuel R. Archer, Thomas W. Ball, Joseph Wilson, J. Malcolm Ball, Thomas C. Donachie, Ian Morrison and George D. Ball. Tom Beck served the Church's Irish Mission Board as a colporteur between 1928 and 1973. Several lady members of the congregation have also served in Mission Work. These have included Mrs Minnie Khasho (née Bell) in Syria and Lebanon with the R.P. mission, Miss Maureen Skelly in Nigeria with the Qua Iboe Mission, Mrs Myrtle McKelvey (née Skelly) in South Africa with the London Missionary Society, Mrs Lily Weir (née Bell) in Northern Ireland and the Isle of Man with Child Evangelism Fellowship and Miss Linda Corry in Romania with Child Evangelism Fellowship.

In 1950-1951 much renovation work was done to the church and manse. During 1991, the meeting house underwent extensive renovation which included a new roof, PVC windows, pine ceiling to church, vestibule and lecture hall. There was also a total refurbishment of internal plaster work, paint work, electrical systems, pews, carpets and curtains.

The Session aims to promote the following objectives in the congregation: to build up members in their faith; to present the Gospel through the Word and through the life of the congregation and community; to encourage, by grace, that the covenant youth and others are brought into a saving knowledge of the Lord Jesus Christ; to promote fellowship within the congregation so that members and adherents are bound together in Christian love.

The Meeting House is situated on the Ardtanagh Road, Dromara, Co. Down.

Dromore new Meeting House

DROMORE

Transferred from Southern Presbytery 1898.

Covenanters have been associated with Dromore for most of the denomination's existence in Ireland. One of the first Covenanting ministers ordained in Ireland was Rev. William Stavely. In 1772, the call came to him from "the Covenanted electors between the bridge in Dromore and Donaghadee in the County of Down". Although resident in Knockbracken, William Stavely exercised a ministry which extended from County Down through Armagh, Cavan and Monaghan. The Covenanters in Dromore would have benefited occasionally from his ministry.

By 1812 several Covenanting Societies existed in and around Dromore and were associating with the Rathfriland congregation. The Minutes of Synod for 1812 record that

> The Minutes of the Southern Presbytery report that the Societies
> in the vicinity of Dromore, hitherto unconnected with any
> congregation, had become attached to the congregation of

Rathfriland, which congregation had presented a call to Rev. John Stewart - that he had accepted it and was installed to the pastoral charge of the congregation of Rathfriland and Dromore on Monday 25 May 1812.

This arrangement continued until the death of Mr. Stewart in 1837.

At that time Dromore believed they had sufficient strength to call their own minister. Licentiate James Steen was ordained and installed minister of Dromore on 4 June 1839. This settlement may have been part of the motivation which led Rev. James Dick, at the Synod in July 1839, 'to give notice of motion for the formation of a fifth presbytery, comprising the congregations of Dromore, Bailiesmills, Knockbracken, 2nd Belfast (later called Grosvenor Road) and Ballyclare'. However, dissension in the Synod of 1840 and the subsequent departure of a number of congregations in the Eastern Presbytery caused Mr. Dick to withdraw the motion.

Mr. Steen's connection with the congregation was short-lived. He informed the Southern Presbytery that he thought that the congregation in Dromore was in an 'unpromising and hopeless state' and wanted to sever his ties with it. Presbytery decided to see for itself and organized a visitation of the congregation in August. We do not know if Presbytery disagreed with his assessment of the congregation, for Mr. Steen carried out his decision to resign. Within a year, he resigned from the denomination and joined the Presbyterian Church and was installed as minister of Clonduff in 1842 where he ministered for the next 39 years.

After Mr. Steen's departure, Dromore depended on pulpit supplies, sometimes on a very irregular basis. In 1845 Dromore was placed under the pastoral care of Rev. J. W. Graham, minister of Bailiesmills, this congregation having been received into the Southern Presbytery at the time of the 1840 schism. Mr. Graham conducted worship once a month; one other Sabbath service in the month was taken by licentiates and members of the Southern Presbytery. Under such circumstances, it is not surprising that, after five years, it was reported that, 'No pastoral relation, strictly speaking, has as yet been formed between him and that people,' Despite the unsatisfactory nature of these arrangements, Synod was told in 1853 that the congregation 'continued warmly and steadfastly attached to a covenanted cause and testimony and giving regular attendance on the ordinances of Divine institution'. The congregation consisted of two elders and 45 members in 14 families, meeting in 3 societies.

The mid 1850s, however, brought some setbacks. Some of the most active and influential members died and, as a result, in the words of Presbytery in 1856, 'there seems a considerable amount of deadness.' Nevertheless, the arrangement with Mr. Graham continued until his death in 1862.

In 1898 Dromore was transferred to the Eastern Presbytery and placed under the care of the Dromara Session. A monthly service, (bi-monthly from 1953) became the responsibility of the Dromara minister, an arrangement which continued until 1990. The preaching during this period was undertaken by the following Dromara ministers: Revs. Torrens Boyd, William Warnock, Alexander Gilmour, Renwick Wright and Robert Hanna.

Dromore old Meeting House after renovations in the 1950's

By the 1980s, designated as a Preaching Station, numbers were dwindling and the building was becoming increasingly derelict. Some outside observers might have considered the witness to be in terminal decline. But the Eastern Presbytery and the members themselves had a different vision.

In 1990 a Committee of Presbytery was appointed to develop the potential of the witness and, with the support of a small group of faithful attendees, a service was held every Sabbath evening. In 1991 Rev. Prof. Robert McCollum was appointed, by the Presbytery, convener of a committee to develop the R.P. witness in Dromore. In its formative stages the Lisburn and Dromara congregations gave practical and prayerful support. At least one family from each attended the Sabbath services at Dromore.

In January 1994, a morning service on the last Sabbath of the month was instituted, with an average of 26 attending. Regular Sabbath morning and evening services began on 22 May 1994. In the summer of 1995 Professor F. S. Leahy, who had retired as minister of Kilraughts in 1988, began preaching in Dromore. Within three years, a potential Society of Covenanters had emerged and, on 5 June 1998, was organized as such by the Eastern Presbytery. The Society consisted of 15 members and 5 covenant children.

Professor Leahy acted as stated supply from 1995 until 2003 and built up the Society. In January 2003 the Eastern Presbytery, on behalf of the Dromore Society, issued a call to Rev. David McCullough, minister of Faughan since 1994, which he accepted in March. On 31 May 2003, the Eastern Presbytery commissioned Mr. McCullough as organizing pastor of the Society of Covenanters in Dromore. On 14 December 2007, the Eastern Presbytery formally organized the work of Dromore into a congregation. On 27 January 2008 Dr. Raymond Steen and Mark Patterson were ordained and installed as elders. On 20 June 2008, Mr. McCullough was ordained as the minister of the congregation.

The R.P. witness in Dromore has been associated with Brewery Lane since 1825. In that year the congregation leased a property known as 'Brew House' for £80 'for the sole use and benefit of the people called Covenanters, who should assemble for the worship and service of God'. In 1881, John and Robert Harrison sold another small building on Brewery Lane to the congregation. The trustees were John Wright Hawthorne and Thomas Hawthorne of Fedney, Josiah Archer of Ballymacbrennan (farmer) and John McEwen of Dromore (tailor), many of whose descendents are active church members in several R.P. congregations. This building was given a facelift at a cost of £2,000 in 1991. But it was appreciated that more radical steps were needed. It was demolished in 1994 and the present site at the end of Brewery Lane was secured and redeveloped, at a cost of £133,000. The building was opened for worship on 19 May 1995. This is the third site in Brewery Lane to be used as an R.P. meeting house.

A manse was acquired in May 2003 at a cost of £182,000.   The Dromore congregation, then a Society consisting of 19 communicant members and 9 covenant children, with an average attendance of 28 in the morning and 32 in the evening Sabbath services, was able to make a deposit of £40,000. By 2004 all debt against both properties had been cleared.

By 2008 the Dromore congregation was comprised of 42 communicant members, 22 covenant children and approximately 20 other regular worshippers. As this growing group looks to the future, they hope to continue a third century of witness in this developing and expanding town in the heart of mid Down.

The Meeting House is situated in Brewery Lane off Meeting Street in Dromore, Co. Down.

Knockbracken Meeting House and new Hall Complex

KNOCKBRACKEN

The early history of Knockbracken is identified with the life and work of Rev. William Stavely, perhaps the most outstanding of all the Covenanting ministers in Ireland. The call addressed to Mr. Stavely in 1772 did not mention the name of any specific congregation for none at that time existed in County Down. Instead it was issued by the "Covenanted Electors between the Bridge of Dromore and Donaghadee". There were 92 signatures and these included members that later formed the congregations of Dromore, Bailiesmills, Newtownards – and Knockbracken. The ordination took place at Conlig in August 1772.

Four years later, Mr. Stavely made Knockbracken his centre in what was becoming a widely scattered area of ministry. A meeting house was built in 1806 at Knockbracken, located today about 3 miles south of the Forestside shopping complex in South Belfast. Mr. Stavely's manse was called Annsborough House in what was then the nearby village of Newtownbreda. He had a farm of about 20 acres in addition to his stipend of £50.

William Stavely is remembered for travelling widely on horseback throughout Ulster being instrumental in establishing many of the present congregations within the Eastern and Southern Presbytery.

Towards the end of the century Mr. Stavely entered a difficult period of his life when he was blacklisted by the British authorities and accused of collaboration with the United Irishmen. Covenanters generally were under suspicion at this time. They refused to take an unqualified Oath of Allegiance to the British Crown. They had given support to the Volunteer movement, a fashionable, patriotic, but armed, private militia formed to defend the country from invasion after the French Revolution of 1789. Mr. Stavely himself had been the commander of a group known as The Drumbracken Volunteers. But when the true nature of the rebellion became apparent, Presbytery urged its members in *A Seasonable and Necessary Information* not to become involved in the rebellion.

But Mr. Stavely remained under suspicion. The Church was raided during the service on Sabbath, 25 June 1797 on the pretext that arms were hidden there, and on 13 June 1798, soldiers on the evening of the Battle of Ballynahinch, plundered and burned his home at Annsborough House. Mr. Stavely was arrested and charged with preaching sedition and, though the charge was false and based largely on ignorance of the Word of God on the part of the military commander, he was detained for seven months on a prison ship in Belfast Lough. When the rebellion ended, Mr. Stavely thought it wise to accept a call to Kellswater and there from 1800 till his death in 1825 he served the Church with distinction.

By 1800 the congregation at Knockbracken had grown to about 200 members. It took in

the Societies in Belfast. As well as this, Mr. Stavely had pastoral responsibility for the Covenanters in North Down who worshipped at Conlig and, since the mid 1790s, in Newtownards. After a vacancy of five years, Hutchison McFadden, a licentiate from Kilraughts, was ordained to serve Knockbracken and Newtownards.

In 1809, however, the union between Newtownards and Knockbracken was dissolved and Mr. McFadden continued as minister of Newtownards until his death in 1812.

During this period further rationalisation occurred. In 1807 Bailiesmills was organised and became a self-supporting congregation. In 1809 the Belfast members of Knockbracken were organised into a separate congregation and they built a meeting house in Linenhall Street on a site at present occupied by the B.B.C. Josias Alexander, a licentiate from Bready, was ordained in Linenhall Street and served both Linenhall Street and Knockbracken congregations until 1822. He died in November 1823. It is interesting to note that Presbytery directed the Belfast members to pay £30 per annum to Knockbracken until they had a minister and meeting house of their own.

Knockbracken finally entered a new period of independence when Thomas Houston was minister of the congregation. He was born at Donegore on 12 October 1803. He had been brought up in Kellswater under the influence of Rev. William Stavely. At the age of 14 he was appointed a teacher in a local school. After a period of further study in Belfast Academical Institution, he was appointed as a teacher in Ballymena Academy and then Portora Royal School. In 1821, at the age of 18, he graduated M.A. from Glasgow. In December 1826 Thomas Houston was licensed as a probationer and served the Kellswater congregation for nearly two years as a licentiate. On 8 April 1828 Thomas Houston was ordained as minister of the congregation.

For fifty-four years Rev. Thomas Houston was the outstanding Covenanting minister of the Church of his day. He was the founder and Editor of the Church's magazine, *The Covenanter*, which first appeared in December 1830 and he was the first Professor of Church History and Exegetical and Pastoral Theology from 1854-1882. Professor Houston was a gifted preacher, a well-loved pastor and an able controversialist whose uncompromising adherence to the conservative viewpoint on the issue of the Civil Magistrate brought him into conflict with the Rev. Dr. John Paul of Loughmourne and led ultimately to the regrettable schism in the Synod and the formation of the Eastern Reformed Synod in 1842. Professor Houston kept a neat and informative diary that gives valuable information about his preaching and pastoral work and illustrates the tender and prayerful concern he had for his people. The congregation reached its peak strength under his ministry; in 1860 there were 260 members. He died on 27 March 1882.

Professor Houston's successor was Robert John Morrell, from Kilraughts, who ministered from 1882 to 1886 before joining the Presbyterian Church of Ireland.

He was followed by James Patterson, who had a brief ministry from 1888 to 1891 before going to Thurso in the North of Scotland, where, apart from one year in Botanic Avenue, he completed his ministry. At this time there was a large movement of population from the rural areas to the city that resulted in the formation of the congregations of Dublin Road (1888), Trinity Street (1896) and Cregagh Road (1900). In consequence the membership at Knockbracken was heavily depleted.

Rev. Torrens Boyd was the minister from 1893 to 1898, returning to Ireland from Liverpool and moving on to Dromara.

Knockbracken Meeting House, taken from Ferguson's Sketches of R. P. Ministers

When George Benaugh, a Rathfriland man, who had served in a number of the congregations of the American Church, was installed in 1898 the membership had fallen to 100. He served the congregation with faithfulness and ability till his retirement in 1913. He died in 1919. Towards the end of World War I, William Lytle, unable to proceed to Syria as a missionary, was a diligent and most acceptable stated supply from 1917 to 1919. There followed a vacancy of eight years.

Then in 1927, Bailiesmills and Knockbracken came together again after 120 years to call John Watters, a licentiate of the Western Presbytery. He ministered in his own unique and distinctive way for 41 years till his retirement in 1968. His death in December 1970 was much lamented.

The next minister in a notable succession was Rev. James Alexander Ritchie. A native of Broughshane, he had gained wide experience in ministry both in England and Ireland before being admitted to the R.P. Church by the Synod in June 1968. Installed at Knockbracken on 27 November 1969, and in Bailiesmills on 3 December 1969. He brought to his work a refreshing enthusiasm and spiritual devotion that was a blessing to many. He went to Kellswater in June 1974.

At a meeting of the Eastern Presbytery, in February 1978, Rev. Dr. Adam Loughridge, then minister of Cregagh Road and Ballymacashon, suggested that it might be of advantage to both Ballymacashon and Knockbracken if they were organised together as joint charge. To facilitate this, he offered to resign Ballymacashon. Knockbracken was happy to maintain the link with Bailiesmills, however, on learning that the latter wished to have a minister of their own, Knockbracken readily accepted Dr. Loughridge's suggestion. Dr. Loughridge resigned from Ballymacashon in April 1978 and so Knockbracken and Ballymacashon sought God's leading to make a joint call.

This was realised on 27 September 1979, when Rev. Norris Wilson who had been ordained and installed two days earlier in Ballymacashon, was installed at Knockbracken. Mr. Wilson had been brought up in the Ballymoney congregation and was a licentiate of the Northern Presbytery. He brought new vigour to the work in Knockbracken and Ballymacashon and sought to extend the witness of both congregations. On 26 May 1986 he accepted the call of the Dervock congregation. The vacancy brought about by Mr. Wilson's removal to Dervock was short. Edward McCollum, member of Limavady, licentiate of the Western Presbytery, educated at University of Ulster and Theological Hall, received the calls of both congregations in July 1986 and these were accepted by him on 17 September. He was ordained and installed on 14 November 1986 in Knockbracken. On 22 March 1999 Mr. McCollum resigned the Ballymacashon part of the charge to concentrate his attention on Knockbracken. A recent illness had confirmed his opinion that he could not undertake to meet the needs of both congregations, especially as Knockbracken was situated on the edge of a major housing development and was in a position to support a minister. The congregation in   Ballymacashon was thankful for the leadership and ministry of the Word which Mr. McCollum had given faithfully from week to week. Knockbracken was similarly thankful for such ministry, which came to an end when Mr. McCollum accepted a call from the Ballymoney congregation and the pastoral tie was dissolved on 9 November 2004.

Rev. Andrew Kerr was installed as minister of the congregation on 1 June 2007. A graduate in Medicine from The Queen's University of Belfast, he trained for the ministry at Union Theological College, was ordained and, after a two year period as an assistant minister in Carryduff Presbyterian Church, installed as minister to the triple charge of Ballygoney, Coagh and Salterlands in the Tyrone Presbytery of General Assembly. He was accepted as minister of the R.P. Church in September 2006.

Knockbracken has made a noted contribution to the ministerial ranks of the Church. The students for the ministry have been William Gibson, William John Stavely, James Paisley, John W. Graham, Josiah Chancellor, James Dick Houston, John McKee, William John Maxwell, David Musgrave and Derek Petrie.

The congregation has been served by the following ruling elders: John Musgrave, Alexander McDowell, John Beatty, Hugh Long, John McClure (Ballylenaghan), John McClure (Ballyrone), Robert Beatty, Samuel Carlisle, Ephraim Chancellor, Samuel Cheyne, John Donnelly, William John Kane, James Musgrave, John Shaw, William Smith, W. J. Milliken, William Reid, James Withers, Edward Donnelly, John Lowe, Robert McClure, George Archer, William McKibben, Gordon McDonald, Martin Smyth and Ian McCaughan.

The church building was erected in 1806 and in 1909 a renovation scheme, preserving the old walls was embarked upon; the architect was James Scott, a grandson of Rev. Dr. Thomas Houston. In 1998, in the providence of God, the congregation received a generous bequest, as well as proceeds from the sale of the manse farm, which had increased in value as a consequence of the increasing development of the area. Having appreciated the need in the area and, now having the resources to do the work set before them, a plot of ground adjacent to the church was purchased as well as a new manse in Croft Hill, off the Cairnshill Road. Plans were made for the erection of a new hall in 2002-2003 to provide facilities for the work in the community. On 21 June 2003 the new Church Hall was opened. Over 160 friends and guests gathered for a thanksgiving service.

On 4 October 2005, the Reformed Theological College, formally located on the Lisburn Road in Belfast, was opened, adjacent to the meeting house. The Convener of the College Committee, Rev. John Hawthorne, spoke of the vision that the congregation had for a modern facility to be built in their grounds for the exclusive use of the College and by their generosity they had turned that vision into a reality. At this time, the old school house, beside the meeting house, became the centre of book distribution and sales replacing the bookshop which had formerly operated from Cameron House on the Lisburn Road. At time of writing, a new Book Centre is planned.

The congregation celebrated 200 years in the church building on 17 September 2006. As well as looking back it also looks forward. The city of Belfast has expanded and will soon absorb the church into its suburbs. The congregation shows vision for outreach in the local community by door-to-door visitation, leaflet distribution and an active Youth Club of about 60 members.

The old Sabbath School room now demolished to make way for the new Covenanter Book Centre

The Meeting House is situated at 37 Knockbracken Road, Carryduff, Co. Down
BT8 6SE.

Larne Meeting House

LARNE

Many Scots ministers passed through Larne on entering Ulster from 1613 onwards and a Covenanting witness was established in the district from the earliest days. However, a considerable time elapsed before a congregation was organised. In 1803 the Covenanting Societies in southeast Antrim petitioned the Reformed Presbytery for a supply of ordinances. The request was granted and soon afterwards a minister was settled in the area when John Paul was ordained on 11 September 1805. Loughmourne was the centre of Mr. Paul's ministry, but he served the Covenanters of a wider area, which included Larne and Ballyclare. Regrettably, he withdrew from the R.P. Synod in 1840 and helped to form the Eastern R.P. Synod in 1842.

His withdrawal left only a remnant at Larne. In 1856 their number was increased by the accession of some members from First Larne Presbyterian congregation. A Mission Station was formed and supplies of preaching provided by the Eastern Presbytery. In 1861 the Presbytery reported to Synod that the Mission Station at Larne had been organised into a congregation and "By the public spirit and the great liberality of the people themselves and a grant from the Home Mission Fund they were now in a position to look for a settlement of a pastor among them." They called Mr. J.D. Houston, but he accepted Ballyclabber instead. They then called Rev. Thomas Dick of Killinchy, but he declined the call. Their membership at this time was around 20.

Ten years passed before their desire was fulfilled when James Renwick Moody, a licentiate of the Eastern Presbytery, was ordained on 19 March 1872. A ministry that was full of promise ended in just over two years when Mr. Moody had to resign on the grounds of ill health.

The congregation now had a vacancy of ten years during which the membership dwindled to 13. In the circumstances it was deemed advisable for the congregation to unite with Ballyclare and together they enjoyed the ministry of Rev. Alexander McLeod Stavely, who was installed on 10 December 1884. Although he had served the greater part of his ministry in New Brunswick, Canada, he devoted his later years to work in the two congregations. His ministry was blessed and, when he retired in November 1898, the membership had doubled under his care. Larne was now dis-annexed from Ballyclare.

In 1902 Samuel Hanna, a member of Kilraughts and a licentiate of the Northern Presbytery was ordained. His outstanding gifts as a preacher made a deep impression in the town and in the short space of three years the membership increased from 27 to 60. During his ministry the congregation moved from Main Street to Curran Road. Mr. Hanna resigned in 1905 to enter the Free Church of Scotland and later became the well-known minister of Berry Street, Belfast.

On 9 October 1906, William Henry Pollock, a member of Limavady and a licentiate of the Western Presbytery, was ordained. He exercised a quiet and gracious ministry to the 65 or so communicants for 12 years before moving to Loughbrickland in 1918. The longest ministry in the history of the congregation followed when Rev. Ezekiel Teaz was installed on 8 November 1921. He had previously served in Dervock and in Liverpool. His faithful and fruitful ministry ended with his retirement in 1942.

Rev. Thomas William Ball, a member of Dromara, who had served for a short time in Liverpool, was installed on 29 December 1942. It was regrettable that a ministry of great promise ended with his resignation on 2 May 1944 and his subsequent withdrawal from the communion of the Church, to join the Brethren movement.

His successor was Rev. James Campbell. A native of Cullybackey, he had served the Church with distinction in Convoy and Stranorlar for over 10 years when he came to Larne on 10 October 1944. A gifted scholar and a very able preacher, Mr. Campbell exercised a notable ministry until his lamented death on 29 March, 1964. His memory was cherished in the congregation for many years. Mr Campbell's knowledge of Greek and his exegetical gifts were recognised by the Synod when he was appointed Lecturer in New Testament Language and Literature at the Theological College in 1945.

The next minister, Rev. David James Magee, was installed on 25 August 1965. He had served for 14 years in Fairview and Tullyvallen. For eight years Mr. Magee led the congregation of 80 communicants with devotion, ability and deep practical wisdom until he moved to Rathfriland in August 1973.

Rev. Robert William Lytle was installed on 12 April 1974. He came, as Mr. Campbell had done, from Convoy and Stranorlar, where he had ministered faithfully for 17 years. He brought to Larne a deep sense of vocation and a wide experience. Under his wise leadership the congregation made steady progress. After a ministry of 19 years in Larne, he retired on 30 June 1993.

A long vacancy followed during which members were faithful and willing to serve. Although the fabric of the buildings was good and finances satisfactory, deaths and migration had reduced the numerical strength of the congregation. Several calls, appeals to Presbytery and attempts to achieve joint-charge status were unsuccessful. Interim Moderators, Revs. Samuel Reid, George McEwen and David Sutherland were most attentive and extended periods of service by Rev. Marcus McCullough, Mr. Stephen Robinson, a member of Trinity and a licentiate of the Eastern Presbytery and Mr. Derek Petrie were very helpful and encouraging. On 28 July 2009 a call was issued to Mr. Derek Petrie, a member of Knockbracken congregation and licentiate of the Eastern Presbytery.

This call having been accepted, Mr. Petrie was ordained and installed as minister of the congregation on 24 September 2009.

A remarkable feature has been the small number of elders who have served the congregation. Up until 1900 the Session was of an interim nature when elders from Belfast and Ballyclare gave good service and were assisted by Peter McGregor, Alexander Owens and James McFadden. Other elders have been John Boyd, Samuel Warwick, Hugh Snoddy, John McCluggage (Station Road), John Blair, James Moore, John McCluggage, James Morton, John T. Moore, Charles D. McCluggage, John Blair (Jun.), Gardiner McCluggage, Roy Moore, Rev. James Duly and Kenneth Buckley.

In the period under review although no students were forthcoming for the work of the ministry, in the earlier years, Matthew Lynn from Cairncastle, ordained at the Vow, went in 1773 to America, and William Sloane, a teacher who emigrated to the United States in 1817, was ordained to ministry there.

The Larne Covenanters met between 1861 and 1904 in Main Street. But the premises were considered inadequate. During the influential ministry of Rev. S. Hanna, which began in 1902, it was decided to move to better accommodation. Mr. Hanna built a faithful, earnest team around him: J. Blair jun. (Secretary), S. Warwick, (Treasurer), and the Building Committee composed of Alex McDowell, Alex McNeice, James Brown, Andrew Killen, Robert Gettinby, James McCluggage, Robert McCluggage, Robert McDowell, John Drummond, Thomas Beatty and J. Gordon Holmes. The ladies of the congregation were also instrumental in the collection of substantial sums towards the Building Fund.

The new church buildings were erected at a total cost of over £1,300 on the Curran Road, about half a mile from the town centre and a similar distance from the harbour area. The congregation were in the happy position of having 75% of the entire cost of the new church building subscribed before they held their opening service - a record which many a larger and richer congregation might envy. Their appeals were answered sacrificially, not only by members of the congregation, but by other congregations in the town and many friends from a distance. Mr. Hanna had not only endeared himself to the members of the congregation, but also to a wider circle of friends and well-wishers outside. The congregation was indebted to Mr. Chaine for the prominent site which he gave them. In August 1903 a memorial stone was laid in the vestibule of the new church. The preacher at the opening services in April 1904 was Rev. James Kerr of Glasgow.

On 11 April 2003, in a special service to mark the centenary an Evening of Psalm Singing, led by the Eastern Presbytery Choir was organised.   The building was filled to capacity with almost 200 people, 65% being from the local area.

Mr. Magee was the first to occupy the manse at 78 Glenarm Road. The previous two ministers had lived in the manse at Glynn Road. Prior to that, ministers had lived in homes of their own choosing. By 1994, the manse on Glenarm Road suffered from damp problems and was sold, with the proceeds invested. A new manse has been purchased in Ballygally.

The Meeting House is situated on the Curran Road, Larne, Co. Antrim.

Lisburn Meeting house, Nettlehill Road

LISBURN

In the 1970s the denomination was challenged to think of starting new centres of witness. Three members of Dromara, with a vision for Lisburn, requested the Eastern Presbytery to consider a Covenanting witness in the town. The Presbytery responded positively and the witness was established when a Bible study was held in the home of Robert Buchanan.

Perhaps it would be more accurate to say 're-established', as there is evidence of Covenanters in the area since the mid eighteenth century. When John Wesley visited Lisburn in 1756 he reported coming into contact with some 'Cameronians'. It is likely that these Covenanters were among those who, residing between Dromore and Donaghadee, had issued a call to William Stavely in 1772. The Societies of Carr, Creevy and Bailiesmills were under the supervision of Knockbracken Session and enjoyed the ministry of Mr. Stavely for about thirty years. It is recorded that there was a society at Hillhall. However, in 1807, it was in Bailiesmills, and not Lisburn, that a congregation was eventually organised. In the minutes of the Reformed Presbytery for the meeting held 7 November 1810 at Maghera, reference is made to the vacancies of Bailiesmills and also Magheragall, a townland on the western outskirts of Lisburn towards Glenavy.

The committee of Presbytery that was appointed in February 1979 to investigate the possibility of developing a Covenanting witness in Lisburn reported back on 29 March that twenty-three members of the R.P. Church, who lived in the Lisburn area, would support this work. Others, outside the denomination, also showed an interest.

The work commenced with a series of well-attended, special meetings from 2-16 September, conducted by Professor Adam Loughridge and Rev. Drew Gregg, using the theme, 'The Kingship of Christ'. Prior to these meetings, a team of young people, drawn from various congregations, had distributed 1,500 leaflets around the town. Mr. T.C. Donachie was appointed co-ordinator of the work.

Events moved very quickly. Sabbath Morning worship services, a Sabbath School and a midweek Bible study commenced immediately after the fortnight of special meetings. At a special meeting of the Eastern Presbytery in Lisburn on 22 October 1979, approval was given to the request that Lisburn be designated a Preaching Station under the care of Presbytery. The new group was known as Lisburn Covenanter Fellowship. Office bearers at this time were Robert Buchanan (Secretary) and Harry Curry (Treasurer).

By January 1981, Lisburn Covenanter Fellowship had held its first Annual Business and Social meeting and the committee of Presbytery, led by Rev. Stewart McMahon, which oversaw the work, made an appeal, through *The Covenanter Witness*, for contributions towards the purchase of a manse. 54 Parkland Avenue was purchased later that year. Following two unsuccessful calls, in November 1981 a unanimous call was made out to Rev. Robert McCollum, minister of Ballylaggan, to be the Organising Pastor. Having accepted the call on 14 December 1981, the Commissioning Service took place on 23 January 1982. At the meeting of Synod in June 1982, Mr. McCollum was appointed as Professor of Pastoral Theology and Mission at the Theological Hall.

The Reformed Presbyterian congregation was organised on 13 October 1982 at a meeting organised by the Eastern Presbytery at the Friends' Meeting House, Railway Street in the town. The congregation comprised 25 adults and 10 children, the adults having been interviewed six days earlier by the Newtownards Session, which had been appointed by Presbytery as the Interim Session. At a meeting of the congregation on 16 June 1985 the decision was made to call a minister, Professor McCollum's role as organising pastor having been fulfilled. Subsequently, a unanimous call was made to Professor McCollum and he was installed on 30 November 1985.

At a congregational meeting on 27 February 1983, Robert Buchanan and John Somerville were elected by the congregation to the eldership and installed (having been previously ordained) on 18 March 1983. The following additional elders were later appointed: Thomas Dobson, Mervyn Green (1988), David Currie, Marcus McCollum and William Simpson (1997).

On 15 May David Currie, John Frazer, Mervyn Green and Fred Milligan were elected to serve the congregation as its first deacons and were ordained and installed on 10 June 1983. The following additional deacons were subsequently appointed: Thomas Dobson, David McLernon, Samuel Ross (1987); William Buchanan, Ronnie McKee (1997); John Reid (1998); William Martin, William McCollum, Gregg Somerville, Joe Watson (2004).

Although the history of the Lisburn congregation is relatively short, it has given one of its members to the Gospel ministry, David Sutherland. He was ordained and installed in Ballyclare on 10 September 1999.

In 1991 Professor McCollum was appointed, by the Presbytery, convener of a committee to develop the R.P. witness in Dromore. In its formative stages the Lisburn congregation gave practical and prayerful support. Each Sabbath morning and evening at least one family attended Dromore. By 1998 Dromore was organised as a Society of Covenanters and on 31 May 2003, the Eastern Presbytery commissioned Rev. David McCullough as organizing pastor of the Society.

The Lisburn meeting house is situated on the Nettlehill Road on the northwest, or Antrim side, of the town. For the first three years, however, the Lisburn Covenanters met in the Orange Hall. By 1983, having paid £24,000 for the manse and having a surplus of £10,500 in their building fund, they purchased a disused Church of Ireland building on the northwest, or Antrim side, of the town for £35,000. The work of renovation, extension and furnishing, at a cost of £95,000, was completed in time for the official opening on 20 April 1985. A new manse, 27 Monaville Close, was purchased in 1988 at a cost of £48,000. A major renovation of the manse took place in 1999. A new hall was added to the rear of the meeting house in 2006 at a cost of £109,000.

The congregation celebrated its 25th anniversary on 13 October 2007. It looks back with thanksgiving for God's grace in establishing the congregation. It looks forward with hope and expectation believing that Christ will continue to build the congregation through the preaching of the Word and the life and witness of its members.

The Meeting House is situated at 49 Nettlehill Road, Ballymacash, Lisburn, Co. Antrim, BT28 3HE.

Loughmourne Meeting House

LOUGHMOURNE AND CARNMONEY

It is thought that a society of Covenanters in this district erected a meeting house about 1778 and was organised into a congregation in 1804. The first minister was Dr. John Paul. John Paul was born in 1777 in Tobernaveen, (near Antrim town), and was educated in Glasgow. Dr. Paul was installed as minister on 11th September 1805 and continued as minister until March 1848. Dr. Paul was the Church's champion of strict Confessional teaching and in 1819 he published two pamphlets attacking the Arian position and defending the principle of subscription to creeds and confessions. He was the author of 'Refutation of Arminianism' 1826, and other theological works, being described as "one of the most philosophical divines". He graduated as D.D. from Union (U.S.A.) in 1836.

However, in the 1830s, he came into conflict with his own denomination. Rev. Thomas Houston, minister of Knockbracken, had used his position as editor of *The Covenanter* to re-state the denomination's position on national covenanting and the power of the Civil Magistrate. Dr. Houston insisted that the magistrate ought to be a Christian and administer the law for the glory of God and that his authority extended to Sabbath breaking and blasphemy as well as crime such as robbery or murder. Dr. Paul challenged this, saying that it promoted persecuting principles. In 1840, when Synod did not support him, he and four other ministers and twelve ruling elders, mostly from the Eastern Presbytery, declined the authority of Synod and in 1842 established the Eastern Reformed Presbyterian Synod, organised into the Presbytery of Belfast and the Presbytery of Derry. This period has been dealt with in detail in other sources.

During his ministry much work was done in serving Covenanting societies in the district, with meetings held in Kilwaughter, Ballycraigy and Carrickfergus. In 1831 some individuals from Ballyclare and its vicinity asked Rev. John Paul to preach in the town. He continued his connection with Ballyclare in the supply of preaching until 1835 when the work was strengthened by the addition of members from Loughmourne and was organised into a congregation and enabled to call their first minister in 1840. The meeting in Larne was affected when Loughmourne withdrew from the Synod, but by 1861 the mission station had been organised into a congregation under the Eastern Presbytery.

Rev. John Paul. D.D.

There was also a meeting house erected for the benefit of Covenanters in Carnmoney in 1806 on the Ballyduff Road just a short distance from the Synod of Ulster's meeting house, and this remained in connection with Loughmourne. The building was erected by public subscription at a cost of £300. The meeting house recently demolished, served as a school for many years. Samuel Thomson (1766-1816) who sometimes attended worship there, was one of the most famous Ulster-Scots "Weaver Poets", known as the Bard of Carngranny. In 1806 he wrote a short inscription for the then new Ballyduff Reformed Presbyterian Meeting House at Carnmoney, which read as follows:

"To show the world that God respects

His covenant, full dear,

The Reformation Church erects

this Ebenezer here.
"Hitherto hath the Lord help'd us."
However a simpler inscription was used.

Carnmoney former Meeting House

It is recorded that the monthly services had from 60 to 100 in attendance, depending upon the weather. From 1830 the Covenanting congregation in Carnmoney was declining and with the death of Dr. Paul this marked the end of the cause here. The meeting house became, from 1850 the Carnmoney No.2 National School and continued in use for many years.

Dr. Paul remained in Loughmourne until his death on 16th March 1848 and was succeeded by Rev. William Close, licensed by the E.R.P. Presbytery of Belfast, who was ordained on 7 November 1848 and exceeded even his predecessor's long ministry. When negotiations for union between the Eastern Reformed Presbyterian Synod and the General Assembly broke down in 1893, the congregation asked to be received into the General Assembly and this request was granted. Mr. Close led his congregation into the General Assembly. He retired on 3rd August 1897 and died on 12 May 1903. The congregation was later greatly affected by the acquiring of 20 farms for a new reservoir to supply Belfast.

The grave of Rev John Paul D.D. Loughmourne

The Meeting House is situated on the hills above Carrickfergus on Carneal Rd, Larne, Co. Antrim.

Newtownards Meeting House with Scrabo Tower in the background

NEWTOWNARDS

North Down was one of the first places in Ulster to have a Reformed witness. The 'private' or unofficial plantation of the Scottish entrepreneurs, Hugh Montgomery and James Hamilton, began in 1606. It was a sort of pilot project for the main Plantation of Ulster, which got underway three years later. Because the small port of Donaghadee remained a major point of entry for Scottish immigrants throughout the seventeenth and eighteenth centuries, the area soon became a stronghold of Presbyterianism.

The area was blessed in the early days by effective ministers. Blair of Bangor, Hamilton of Ballywalter and Livingstone of Killinchy led revivals in their own parishes as well as the better known ones at Shotts and Six Mile Water. Driven out of Ulster by the government in the 1630s, they were to play a part in the creation of the National Covenant in Scotland (1638).

Covenanting in north Down, as in other places, received a boost with the arrival of a Scottish army and its chaplains sent in 1642 to defend the colonists. In the 1640s the

Solemn League and Covenant was administered in Comber, Newtownards and Bangor. Covenanter Societies must have been established in these areas because we know that David Houston, the outspoken Scots Covenanting minister, lived in Newtownards in 1689, and William Martin, the first Reformed Presbyterian minister to be ordained in Ireland, lived for a time in Bangor.

By 1770 Covenanting Societies, comprising almost one hundred families, across the northern half of county Down between Dromore and Donaghadee, were sufficiently strong to call a minister of their own. William Stavely accepted their call in 1772. Newtownards shared with Knockbracken the ministry of William Stavely from 1776 to 1800. Stavely, born in 1743 in Ferniskey, near Kells, educated at Glasgow University and the Reformed Theological Hall in Paisley, was licensed in 1769.

Stavely was active on many fronts. He had a hand in founding as many as twelve congregations across southern Ulster. He also engaged in public debates with the Seceders and the Governments of the day. For a time he was prominent in a fashionable pressure group, the Irish Volunteers, which was formed to defend the country from threatened invasion but which remained on standby to push the government into granting much needed political and economic reforms. With this profile, he attracted suspicion from the authorities when the revolutionary, republican United Irish movement was formed in the 1790s. Although he had publicly denounced this new organisation, the meeting houses in Newtownards and Knockbracken were raided in searches for arms by the cavalry in March and June 1797. Mr Stavely's manse was burned and plundered and he spent four months in prison until his release, without charge, in late 1798.

Relations between Stavely and the Knockbracken were strained after the 1798 Rebellion. There is evidence to suggest that some of congregation may have been active in the United Irishmen (though they withdrew before the main engagement, the Battle of Ballynahinch, because of the desecration of the Sabbath Day). Stavely believed that some of the congregation had brought trouble to him and there were others who believed that he had brought trouble to them. Consequently, in 1800, he accepted a call to Cullybackey and Kellswater.

Mr. Stavely's successor was Hutchinson McFadden. Born in 1780 at Magheraboy near Kilraughts and, like his predecessor, educated at Glasgow and Paisley, he also served the two congregations from 1805. But, in 1809, due to failing health, he was released from the oversight of Knockbracken. He remained minister of Newtownards until his death on 8 October 1812 at the early age of 31 years, leaving a wife and two daughters. He was said to have possessed 'fervent and commanding eloquence' and, even 70 years later, ministers spoke of him in terms of 'high eulogy'. As late as the 1870s, his memory was still fragrant among the older members of the congregation.

He was succeeded in 1813 by twenty-four year old William Henry, a member of Ballylaggan and a licentiate of the Northern Presbytery. Mr. Henry was active on many fronts. He started the Classical School in Newtownards, acting as its Headmaster. Mr. Henry was involved in the setting up of a Reformed Presbyterian congregation in Liverpool and his ministry in the United States of America where he was recognised when he awarded the degree of Doctor of Divinity by Indiana University. Although the congregation lost 14% of its membership between 1815 and 1827 due to emigration, it still stood at 215.

When the controversy on the Civil Magistrate divided the Church in 1840, Dr. Henry and the majority of his congregation withdrew from the parent Synod and became attached to the Eastern Reformed Synod formed in 1842. Mr Henry moved to Gortlee County Donegal, in 1843 and died in 1852. Subsequent ministers in Ann Street were Matthew Smyth, 1848-1850; J.G. McVicker, 1850-1853, and Hugh Stewart, 1855-1887. The congregation ceased to exist in 1891.

The minority, about forty, that survived the secession in Newtownards had difficulty for some years in finding a place of worship and a minister. They were associated until 1847 with Grosvenor Road (College Street South) congregation, Belfast, under the care of Rev. William McCarroll. Between 1847 and 1850 they benefited from the ministry of a licentiate, George Lillie, who served as a full-time worker on the Missionary Board of the Church. In 1854 the congregation, with a membership of fifty, acquired the Methodist meeting house on the corner of Lower Mary Street and Regent Street. Between 1856 and 1859 they were joined with Ballymacashon. Their hopes were high when William Hanna, a native of Rathfriland, who had served four years in Manchester, became their minister on 28 July 1859, but he died at the age of 36 on 12 October 1860.

Communionware used by the Ann Street congregation

However, the congregation had been blessed and strengthened by the Revival of 1859, when twenty-three joined as members in the last few months of 1859, and this was consolidated by the short, but effective, ministry of John Newell. A native of Belfast, he had served for ten years in the U.S.A., latterly as Principal of Westminster College in Pennsylvania, before his installation on 8 May, 1861. Dr. Newell accepted a call to Manchester on 10 May 1867, and in 1871 returned to the U.S.A. His memory is perpetuated in the congregation by the H. D. Cummings Memorial Bequest, left by his daughter.

He was succeeded by Robert Allen on 21 November, 1867. Mr. Allen who was from Legnacash, near Cookstown, had worked for 12 years with the Irish Mission in Dublin. He gave great, faithful service to the congregation for 39 years until his retirement in 1906. During this period he had never missed a single Sabbath due to illness. Mr. Allen's daughter, Maria, married Rev. Joseph McEwen, later minister of Bready and Fairview and Tullyvallen. When Rev. Joseph McEwen retired from the ministry, he and his wife returned to her roots in the Newtownards area in 1927 with their son John, who was elected an elder. Three of his sons, Joe, Sam and John, grandsons of Rev. and Mrs. Joseph McEwen, are in 2010, elders in the congregation of Newtownards. Another brother

George, has served the Church as minister both in Australia and Ireland, and his son Timothy was ordained and installed in Ballenon and Ballylane in 2008.

Mr. Allen's successor was Torrens Boyd. Brought up in Drimbolg he served in six congregations and accepted each call that he received. He was in his 70th year when he was installed on 4 September 1907 and it is a tribute to his amazing physique and devotion to duty that he served the congregation for almost 18 years until his death on 19 May 1925. Apart from his gifts as a pastor and preacher, he was noted for his prowess as a builder, building his own manse in 1909.

In the vacancy of over 13 years that followed, the congregation maintained its strength and witness. Apart from the loyalty of members and the diligence of the elders, this was due in no small measure to the efforts of Rev. A. Gilmour, Dromara, who preached frequently on Sabbath evenings, and to Rev. Joseph McEwen, son-in-law of Mr. Allen, and former minister of Fairview and Tullyvallen until his retirement, who acted as Interim Moderator of the Session.

On 24 August 1938, Adam Loughridge, a licentiate of the Northern Presbytery, from Kilraughts, was ordained and installed in the congregation. Though half of his ministry was shadowed by war conditions, there were encouraging signs of blessing and steady progress was made. Well-attended 'cottage' or home group midweek meetings were held during the war years and, in a sense, the congregation went back to its roots. It might be said that Mr. Loughridge's ministry was particularly influential and gave the congregation much of its distinctive ethos. He accepted a call to Portrush on 7 March 1950 and later became Professor of Church History and Pastoral Theology in the College.

He was succeeded in 1952 by Rev. Alexander Gilmour from Dromara whose gifted and profitable ministry of 7 years until his retirement in 1959 was cherished for many years afterwards.

He in turn was followed by Rev. J.A. Cresswell Blair who had served the Church in Creevagh for 14 years. He was installed on 3 September 1959 and for 14 years he gave of his best to the congregation. He was meticulous and thorough in all his work and was specially loved as a pastor and friend. He moved to Ballylaggan on 15 May 1973 and his sudden death on 28 April 1975 was a great loss to the whole Church.

The next minister, Rev. Hugh Wright, after pastorates in Winnipeg, Canada, Londonderry and Trinity Street, Belfast, was installed on 21 December 1973. His faithful preaching, pastoral leadership and gifts for organization served the congregation well. The congregation experienced considerable growth and encouragement. Mr. Wright retired from the ministry at the end of 1983, became a ruling elder in the congregation, and died on 21 January 1991.

On 3 October 1985 Rev. C. Knox Hyndman, minister of the Ballyclare congregation, was installed as pastor of the congregation.

The congregation has offered several students for the ministry: James McGarragh who ministered in America, George Martin McEwen and Dr. John Watterson. Andrew Stewart, minister of Glenmanus and Geelong, Australia, might also be regarded as a 'son' of the congregation as he grew up in Newtownards, where his father William was an elder between 1964 and 1977.

Quite a number of Belfast elders served in an interim capacity, but the names of the regular members are: Edward O'Neill, Michael Rankin, Hugh Muckle, John Simms, Thomas Dorman, Hugh Simms, Henry Montgomery, John Musgrave, William Reid, John Moore, James Young, John Simms, William Adams, John Porter, James McDowell, John Lyons, Thomas H. Brown, Rev. Joseph McEwen, William Brown, A. B. McCarroll, John H. McEwen, Andrew Thompson, James Murphy, William Stewart, J.R.M.(Mac) Blair, Joe McEwen, Thomas Warnock, James A.M. Kerr, James D. Russell, John A. McEwen, George Howson, Rev. Hugh Wright, Samuel A. McEwen, Dr. Trevor McCavery, Victor Blair and John McNeill.

The Newtownards congregation first met for worship at Conlig, a small village, a few miles outside the town, in a building that had been used by the Seceders from 1753. When the Seceders moved to Mark Street, Newtownards, to become the Second Presbyterian Congregation in 1772, the Covenanters took over their meeting house. It was probably on the site now occupied by the Gospel Hall in Conlig. By the mid 1790s the Covenanters followed the Seceders into the town and from 1800 the church was located in Ann Street. The site of the original building was occupied for many years later, during the late nineteenth and early twentieth centuries, by Lavery's Stitching Factory. In 1854 the congregation purchased the building on the corner of Regent Street and Mary Street they now occupy, from the Methodists, who had moved to a new and larger church in the same street.

Mr. Allen's manse was in 70 South Street. In 1909 Torrens Boyd built his own house at

54 Bangor Road and the congregation purchased it from his son in 1940 and used it as the congregation's manse until 1985. Extensive refurbishment took place between 1969 and 1973. In 1985 the congregation purchased a new manse in 19 Manse Park for Rev. Knox Hyndman.

In 1889 the Church was extensively renovated during which the attractive pulpit, still in use, was gifted by Alexander Martin of Killyleagh, a member of Ballymacashon congregation. The relations between Newtownards and Ballyma-cashon have always been cordial and at times they were united as a joint charge. Further renovations to the meeting house occurred in 1911, 1936,

1961-1972, 1989 and in 1993-1994, following damage by an IRA bomb which exploded nearby on 5 July 1993.

The aim of the Newtownards congregation is to bring glory to God by the preaching of His Word and the testimony of members' lives so that, by God's grace, sinners may be saved and believers built up in their faith and, as appropriate, daughter congregations formed.

The Meeting House in situated on Regent Street, Newtownards, Co. Down, BT23 4LH.

WESTERN PRESBYTERY

Bready Meeting House

BREADY

In the mid eighteenth century the Scottish Reformed Presbytery often organised preaching for the Covenanters in Ireland. In 1759 John Courtess visited the Societies in Londonderry, Donegal and Tyrone and in 1761 John Fairlie had an extended preaching tour of Ulster, visiting especially Drummond, Tirkeevney and Ramelton. Later that year he received a call from these Societies, but he decided to remain in Scotland.

The Covenanters in the North West did not have long to wait for a minister of their own. On 8 May 1765 William James was ordained in the open air near Cullion. From 1771 the Covenanters in the Bready district met for worship at their present site on the main Victoria Road in Bready, midway between Strabane and Londonderry. Mr. James was an able minister with a gift for controversial writing. He was born near Eglinton in 1741 and brought up in the fellowship of the Societies that later formed Limavady congregation. His varied gifts may be seen in the fact that, when he was a student at Glasgow University in 1761, he was not only an elder, but acted for a time as Clerk of the Scottish Reformed

Presbytery. Several of his notebooks and manuscripts have survived and give evidence of the nature of his work. After a fruitful ministry of 14 years, Mr. James died in 1779 at the early age of 38, and was buried in the nearby graveyard at Grange.

The second minister, Samuel Alexander, was a member of the congregation. Born at Tirkeevney in 1748, and educated in Scotland, he was ordained in Bready on 19 August 1783. His ministry encompassed a wide area, taking in Bready, Faughan, Londonderry and part of County Donegal. His promising ministry was ended by his early death on 17 July 1793, the result of an accident that happened when he was crossing the Foyle in a storm some years earlier. He was buried in the old churchyard at Glendermott.

Bready Meeting House from Ferguson's Sketches

Bready and Faughan then united for a time. In 1803 John Alexander was ordained at Faughan. He also ministered at Bready. In March 1809 Bready and Faughan requested to be separated. Both asked for the pastoral oversight of Mr. Alexander but he chose Faughan.

The Minutes of the Congregational Committee show that there were eight Societies - at Tamnabrine (Tamnbryan), Culmaghry (Coolmaghery), Desertone (Disertowen), Tirkeevney, Belnaboy (Ballynabwee), Ruskey, Strabane and Bready. The names of the men who represented these Societies were Samuel Gormley, Jeremiah Smith, John Keys, John Longwell, John Osburn, James McKinley, James McDougall, Samuel Mitchell, Robert Bates, John McFarland, Thomas Brown, Alexander Dick and Hugh Dennison.

The next minister was a Limavady man, Alexander Britton, a farmer's son from Myroe. He was educated at Glasgow University, the R.P. Theological Hall, Paisley and licensed by the Western Presbytery. He was ordained in Bready on 21 September 1815 and served faithfully for 31 years until his death on 31 May 1846. He was distinguished in the community for his preaching and we quote a few lines from a poem written in praise of his pulpit work by Stewart Cooke, a member of the congregation:

> *Right well the pulpit he became,*
> *'Twas there, yea there, he earned his fame.*
> *Such studied work to us he brought,*
> *That clergymen themselves he taught.*
> *He read his text, he closed the book,*
> *He on the audience cast a look;*
> *Then published tidings to the soul*
> *That must resound from pole to pole.*
> *His eager mind in rapid flight*
> *Did soar aloft in Heaven's height;*
> *And told us of redeeming love*
> *That sent the Son down from above.*

In 1843 a number of Covenanters from Bready joined the Eastern Reformed Synod, congregation in Waterside, but the journey to worship in Londonderry proved inconvenient. They decided to build their own meeting house at Cullion near Bready. Although their numbers were small, the building they erected was capable of seating 300 and became known as 'Gormley's folly' after William Gormley, an enthusiastic member of the congregation. In 1860 differences arose between the congregation and the

Rev. Samuel Patton, minister of Waterside. These were serious enough for Mr. Patton to refuse to conduct services at Cullion, confining himself to the Waterside congregation. Soon afterwards the congregation at Cullion ceased to exist and most of its members returned to Bready.

The succession of gifted ministers continued when Josias Alexander Chancellor was ordained and installed as minister on 27 July 1847. Born in Dundonald, Co. Down on 14 November 1824, he grew up and became a member of Knockbracken congregation, where his father Ephraim was an elder. He was educated at the Old College Belfast and at the Reformed Theological Hall at Paisley, and licensed by the Northern Presbytery in 1846. Rev. Josias Chancellor was one of the ablest scholars and preachers that the Church has produced. His ministry began in the lean years of the Great Famine. He saw the brighter days of the 1859 revival, in which he took an active part. Rev. John McDonald of Airdre said, 'He threw him-self heart and soul into the movement and in such a way that he was enabled by the blessing of God to prevent the follies and extrava-gances that disfig-ured it elsewhere.' During August 1859

services were conducted each evening in Second Presbyterian Church in Strabane by the congregation's minister and Mr. Chancellor. Together they agreed that only Psalms should be sung, only ministers could preach and physical prostration was discouraged. In addition to these services Mr. Chancellor met with the young men of the area between 7 and 8 a.m. each morning. He also conducted additional meetings at Bready and its mission station at Mulvin. A large number of his letters have been preserved and give us a good picture of conditions prevailing in his day. In 1865 he moved to Belfast to become the minister of College Street South (later Grosvenor Road) congregation.

Charles Kirk Toland, son of Rev. William Toland of Kilraughts, was the next minister. He served the congregation from 19 April 1866 until he was received into the General Assembly in June 1886, completing his ministry in the neighbouring town of Strabane.

 In the vacancy, Bready turned again to Kilraughts and called a licentiate, Archibald Holmes, who was ordained on 13 October 1887. He was born on 2 July 1862 near Kilraughts, grew up in that congregation and graduated from Magee College and the R.P. Theological Hall. He bore a name highly honoured in the Covenanting Church, and though his ministry was less than six years before he moved to Creevagh, and later to Paisley, Kellswater and Ballyclare, he left a marked impression on the congregation. His wife, Mary Marshall, came from one of the families in the congregation.

There followed a brief ministry from Rev. Robert Adams McFarlane, who came from Stranorlar. He was installed on 13 July 1893 and returned to Stranorlar on 28 December 1896.

His successor was Joseph McEwen, a licentiate of the Glasgow Presbytery, who was ordained on 24 August 1897. For twelve years he gave of his best in the service of the congregation. His genial disposition and gifted exposition of the Scriptures was long remembered in the congregation. His five sons, born in the Bready Manse, proved to be an ornament to the Church. Rev. Joseph McEwen later served for twenty years at Fairview and lived in retirement but giving valuable service as a ruling elder in Newtownards until his death in October 1944.

John Knox Dickey was the next minister. A member of Drimbolg, he was ordained on 26 September 1911. His ministry continued until February 1919. He later ministered at Stranraer, Londonderry, Cregagh Road and Drum, Co. Cavan and died in November 1955.

His successor, Thomas Hanna, was the third of Bready's ministers to come from Kilraughts. Ordained on 9 October 1919, he led the congregation in building a new meeting house. He saw his heart's desire completed, but a few weeks before the opening services were conducted by Rev. J. A. Lyons, Belfast and Rev. J. G. McElhinney, U.S.A.,

Mr. Hanna was called to his reward on 5 February 1924. His memory was cherished for a long time among members of the congregation.

The longest ministry in the history of the congregation began on 14 October 1924 with the ordination of James William Calderwood, a member of Cullybackey. He laboured with great ability and faithfulness for almost 50 years until his death on 18 April 1971. He will always be remembered as a preacher with gifts well above the average and as a well-loved pastor and friend of the people.

In 1977 he congregation made a joint call along with the neighbouring Clarendon Street church to Mr. Malcolm Ball, a member of Dromara congregation and licentiate of the Eastern Presbytery, educated at Queen's University and the Theological Hall. On 1 September he was ordained and installed as minister of the two congregations. After 8 years of faithful and devoted service, he accepted the call of the Foreign Mission Board on 28 November 1985 to serve as a missionary in France.

On 3 May 1989 Presbytery approved the sale of Clarendon Street church buildings in Londonderry and approved the full union of this congregation with Bready. The final worship service in Clarendon Street was 25 February 1990. On 21 October 1990 the first united communion of Bready and Clarendon Street took place with 56 communicant members. At the Annual General Meeting on 30 January 1992, held in Bready, the Clarendon Street members were received into membership in Bready and the two ruling elders, William J. Davis and W.B.C. Warnock were elected and installed in the Bready Session. A new committee was also elected and discussions took place about a new hall.

Meanwhile, on 12 October 1990, a licentiate of the Western Presbytery, Samuel McCollum, a member of the Limavady congregation and a licentiate of the Western Presbytery, educated at Queen's University and the Reformed Theological College was ordained and installed minister of the congregation. Characteristics of Mr. McCollum's ministry were his concern to spread the Gospel into the immediate community and beyond and a desire to have the congregation Biblical in its practice. During his ministry the congregation held two periods of special services, an annual Holiday Bible Club as well as other children's work. A broadsheet called *The Anvil* was distributed throughout an area stretching from Donemana to Castlederg. Seven people from outside the denomination came into membership and four elders were ordained and installed and a fifth installed. Rev. Samuel McCollum accepted a call to the Glenmanus congregation and was installed there on 27 August 2004.

On 29 December 2007, Rev. Blair McFarland, having recently returned from missionary service in France, was installed as minister of the congregation.

The roll of elders in the Bready congregation is a long and distinguished one. The earliest Session book dates from the late eighteenth century and records that there were 24 elders supervising a widely scattered congregation, twelve for Bready, seven for Faughan, and five for Londonderry. Their names are James Allen, Thomas Allen, Samuel Arthur, Jacob Alexander, John Davies, - Galbraith, John Guy, Andrew Henry, James Lawrimore, Robert McKinley, Joseph McMorris, John McNaught, Thomas Marshall, John Mathers, Robert Mathers, John Mitchell, James Richmond, Samuel Rodgers, Simon Robinson, James Salters, Moses Speers, Andrew Stevenson, Robert Stevenson, Samuel Willock. The elders in the middle of the nineteenth century were John Bates, Robert Brigham, Alexander Britton, William Cook, Alexander Dick, John Gormley, Edward Hall, Samuel Jack, Joseph Lewis, David Marshall, Robert Moorhead, Thomas Logan, John MacDougall, James Salters, William O'Neill, James Buchanan, James McIntosh, Joseph Sayers and James Gibson. Since then the following men have served the congregation as members of Session: Alexander Parkhill, James Armstrong, John O'Neill, Stephen Buchanan, John A. Buchanan and W.J. Gibson and James Throne. In recent decades the ruling elders have been Robert Stevenson, Andrew O'Neill, John H. Throne, James S. Throne, W. John Buchanan, William Davis, Carson Warnock, Alistair Buchanan, Liam O'Neill, Rodney Gamble, William Lynch, Stephen Davis, William Roulston and Oliver Throne.

The first meeting house was erected on the site of the present building in 1771. In a day when dissenters had the greatest difficulty in obtaining permission to erect buildings, it is to the credit of the landlord, the Earl of Abercorn, that he not only gave such a choice site, but also gave it free of rent. The first meeting house was hastily erected and lasted only 15 years, collapsing at the close of a Sabbath service in 1786. The church was renovated during the ministry of Mr. Dickey (1911-1919) and then rebuilt and opened in 1924.

A new hall, named the Clarendon Hall, kitchen and toilet facilities were built during 1995 and opened on 2 September 1995. This hall has enabled the Holiday Bible Club and Youth Club to take place.

The congregation has provided eleven ministers for the Covenanter Church: Samuel Alexander (Castlemellon), John Alexander (Tirkeevny), John Stewart, Josias Alexander, James Peebles Sweeney, James Dick, William Sweeney, Thomas Conn Britton, James Buchanan and James Graham Buchanan.

As with other rural congregations, the congregation has seen some decline in its numbers. However, in recent years, the local community has trebled in size and the congregation continues to witness through its Good News Club, Holiday Bible Club, Saturday night youth club, Book Fair and Psalmody festivals, praying that the Lord of the harvest will move with His Holy Spirit and will awaken many from their deadness of their sin into disciples of Christ.

The Meeting House is situated at 207 Victoria Road, Bready, Co. Tyrone, BT82 0ED.

Faughan Meeting House

FAUGHAN

The early history of Faughan is closely linked to that of Bready. The Glendermott valley was a strong centre of Scottish influence and visiting ministers from Scotland conducted services there from time to time. The earliest record of preaching by a Covenanting minister is that of Rev. John Thorburn at Cumber in 1759 and of Rev. John Fairley at Tirkeevney in 1761. Healthy and active Covenanting Societies kept the witness alive and by 1770 a congregation was established at Faughanbridge.

The first minister, Thomas Hamilton, was ordained in 1770. A native of Bovevagh, Co. Londonderry, he was a licentiate of the Derry Presbytery of the Presbyterian Synod of Ulster. After the death of Rev. William Hair, minister of First Glendermott Presbyterian Church, in 1766, the congregation was supplied by Mr. Hamilton. A minority of the congregation wanted to call him but a majority favoured another licentiate. When Presbytery ruled in favour of the majority, the minority seized the meeting house for a short period and refused to accept the ruling of Presbytery. Mr. Hamilton was deprived of his licence and applied to the Irish Reformed Presbytery and was accepted. The minority left the congregation and the Synod of Ulster and joined with the local Covenanting societies to form a new congregation. They called Mr. Hamilton and he accepted and was ordained. After a short pastorate of about three years, he resigned because of the sudden drop in Covenanting ministers from 6 to 3 and spent the next six years of his short life as an itinerant preacher for the Reformed Presbytery until his untimely death in 1779. He was buried at Derryvalley in Co. Monaghan.

Samuel Alexander was ordained as minister of Bready in 1783. His charge included Faughan. He was a local man, from Tirkeeveney, who had been educated at Glasgow University and was licensed by the Scottish Presbytery in 1781. It is likely that the Faughan Covenanters worshipped with the Bready congregation on Sabbaths. These were difficult days for Dissenters in general, and for Covenanters in particular. Oppression and poverty had driven many to seek a new life in the United States of America. For those who remained, it was well nigh impossible to get a site for a meeting house. Faughan was singularly blessed in this respect and secured in 1790 what many considered as one of the most beautiful sites in Ireland - beside the old bridge at Drumahoe on the banks of the Faughan River, some three miles from the centre of Londonderry. Originally, this was a rural setting, but by the 21st century the Faughan meeting house lies at the heart of a major residential area as the nearby city expands and engulfs the village of Drumahoe. Mr. Alexander was much loved as a meek, generous man and was known as 'the Godly Alexander'. Always of delicate health, he died in 1793, aged 45.

Robert Young, after a short ministry to Covenanters in County Donegal, came to reside in the Waterside district of Londonderry. Mr. Young was never installed, but acted as stated supply from 1787 until his death in 1794. His name is perpetuated in a local charity, the Gwyn and Young Endowment, founded by one of his sons. It appears that Faughan was still united with Bready during this period.

The next minister was John Alexander, nephew of Rev. Samuel Alexander and brother of Rev. Josias Alexander. He too was educated in Scotland, and licensed in 1803. He was ordained and installed in Faughan on 19 May 1803, the first minister to be ordained in the meeting house. He also ministered at Bready until 1809. During his ministry a congregation was organised in Londonderry and a meeting house built in Fountain Street in 1810. Mr. Alexander looked after both congregations. Faughan was strengthened by the addition of members of the Desertone society between 1811 and 1822. However, from 1821, due to the fall in food prices at the end of the Napoleonic Wars, the congregations in Londonderry and Faughan were unable to keep up the minister's stipend. Despite attempts to reach a settlement, Mr. Alexander accepted a call to Linenhall Street in Belfast in 1825.

Faughan , from Ferguson's Sketches

Following Mr. Alexander's departure, the Faughan and Londonderry congregations requested that they be separated and this was granted by Presbytery on 13 July 1826.

In May 1827 James Peebles Sweeney was ordained and served the congregation with distinction and devotion for forty-seven years. Born at Desertone in 1795, brought up in the congregation, he received his education in Scotland and was licensed by the Western Presbytery on 7 July 1824. His long ministry saw vast changes in Ulster. Although the 11 societies that made up the congregation were affected by the disastrous Great Famine in the late 1840s, yet many were greatly blessed and increased through the revival of 1859. By the late 1860s, although the number of societies had fallen to nine, the membership of the congregation reached a peak of 270 (including 96 children). In 1874, Mr. Sweeney retired due to ill health. At the time of Mr. Sweeney's death on 4 May 1877, a new generation had arisen to carry on the work.

Matthew Neill, born in 1850, brought up in the Dervock congregation and educated Queen's College Belfast and the R.P. Hall, was a licentiate of the Northern Presbytery He was ordained on 17 February 1876. Due to emigration from the area, the congregation began to decline and had difficulty in meeting its obligations to Mr. Neill. As well, he began to have objections to certain principles of the Reformed Presbyterian Church. He resigned on 3 November 1880. He later served in the Irish Presbyterian Church.

In contrast, his successor, Samuel Ferguson, had a long and fruitful ministry in the congregation. Son of Rev. W. S. Ferguson of Grange, and great-grandson of the famous Rev. William Stavely, Mr. Ferguson was ordained on 15 December 1881. Born in 1854, brought up in the manse at Grange, he was educated at Queen's College Belfast and the R.P. Hall, and licensed in May 1881. A gifted preacher, a devoted pastor and a fine historian, his long ministry left its mark upon the people and older members recalled his work with affectionate gratitude for many years afterwards. During his ministry, despite continued emigration, the numbers of the congregation remained steady at about 55 families and 150 communicants. Mr. Ferguson died on 16 December 1928.

Rev. John McIlmoyle, then minister of Kellswater, was called to the congregation. He was to serve the Church in each of the four Presbyteries and as Professor of Systematic Theology for 25 years. He was installed on 31 October 1929. He was the first minister not to come to Faughan as his first charge. A gracious, godly and intellectual gentleman, his ministry was remembered with affection for a long time after his acceptance of a call from Dublin Road in May 1947.

Thomas Donnelly, a member of Grosvenor Road congregation and a licentiate of the Eastern Presbytery, began his ministry on 1 December 1949 and showed his fine talents, enthusiasm, kindness and good humour in a pastorate of seven years before moving to Ballyclabber in May 1956.

The congregation was well served and wisely led by Rev. William Norman McCune. Brought up in Trinity Street congregation and licensed by the Eastern Presbytery, Mr. McCune spent eight years in Convoy and Stranorlar before coming to Faughan on 13 December 1956. As well as attending diligently to the spiritual oversight of the Faughan congregation, Mr. McCune played a much wider role in the Western Presbytery, as Clerk and as Interim Moderator of every congregation within its bounds at one time or another, and as the organiser or conductor of several psalmody events. He retired from the active duties of the ministry on 5 February 1992.

On 2 September 1994, David Joseph McCullough, brought up in the Newry congregation and a licentiate of the Southern Presbytery, was ordained and installed as minister of the congregation. He quickly established himself in the congregation as a gifted preacher and attentive pastor with a tremendous enthusiasm for evangelistic work. The congregation was saddened in May 2003 when Mr. McCullough accepted the call to be organising pastor of the Dromore Society of Covenanters.

In June 2008, the congregation made a call to Steven Robinson, member of the Trinity congregation and a licentiate of the Eastern Presbytery and this was presented on 5 August 2008. The call was accepted and Mr. Robinson was ordained and installed on 18 October 2008.

There were four students for the Gospel ministry between 1800 and 1816: James Steen, James Sweeney, William Sweeney and Jacob Alexander. Almost a century and a half passed before the next four students were in training. Between 1959 and 1973, Joseph

Robinson Patterson, Harry Tadley, John Hawthorne and R. Blair McFarland entered the ministry and so, in these two short periods of time, Faughan has made a significant contribution to the wider Church.

The roll of ruling elders is a long and distinguished one. The following men were ordained in the late eighteenth century: James Marshall, Thomas Allen, Simon Robinson, John Mitchell, Thomas Marshall, John Guy, Andrew Henry, John McNaught. During the ministry of John Alexander (1803-1825) the congregation was well served by the following elders: Joseph Clarke, James Glenn, James Hunter, Samuel Long, Samuel Marshall, Robert Marshall, James Orr and James Steele. They were joined in Mr. Sweeney's time (1827-1876) by Samuel Alexander, James Mitchell, Robert Boyce, George Kennedy, James Adams, James Hunter, William Long, William Steele, James Glenn, William Philips, George Sweeney, Moses Tate, Joseph Clarke (Jn), John Donaghy, Andrew Buchanan, John Mathers, Thomas Allen, Joseph Orr, James Glenn, Daniel McFarland, John Longwell, William Phillips, William Steele. Mr. Ferguson was supported by a succession of worthy elders, some of whom have descendants in the congregation today. They were James MacDonald, William Rankin, John Marshall, Joseph McEldowney, William John Mooney, David, Robert and James Longwell, Alan Phillips, John Orr, Robert McFarland, Jack Longwell and John Patterson. During Mr. McIlmoyle's ministry Hugh Adair Steele and W.S. Ferguson joined the Session. It was further strengthened in 1950 by John Longwell, Andrew Young, Harry Tadley, Robert W. McFarland and Samuel McClay. During Mr. McCune's ministry David Porter, Jack Buchanan, John J. Mitchell and J. Don McFarland were elected to serve the congregation. Other elders appointed since have been Samuel Buchanan, Robert T. Steele, James Snodgrass, Graham Fallows and Fergus Marshall.

The meeting house, built in 1790, was first renovated in the early 1830s, with a new roof, ceiling and side wall. In 1855 the session room was built, the church re-seated and the floor altered. Major renovations took place during 1898-1899. Central heating was installed, new rafters, ceiling and windows were put in place and inside and outside walls re-plastered. Electric lighting and heating was installed in 1951 and 1953.

In 1959 the old stables were converted into a Church Hall, which was extended in 1975. This Hall was demolished and a new one built in 1984 which in turn was considerably enlarged and refurbished in 2005.

The congregation first acquired a manse in 1883 - 4 Ebrington Terrace, in the Waterside, Londonderry. In 1898 Mr. Ferguson bought his own home at 'Sunnymede' on the Limavady Road. In 1930, during the ministry of Professor McIlmoyle, the manse was in Victoria Park. Another manse was obtained in Hinton Park during the ministry of Mr. Donnelly. This was sold to finance the present manse near the church at 30 Drumahoe Road of which Mr. McCullough and his family were the first occupants.

With such improvements, the congregation is well equipped to continue its witness in a lovely setting beside the River Faughan and to serve a rapidly expanding community in the immediate neighbourhood. In 2009 the congregation was composed of 42 families. It is missionary minded and actively involved in reaching out to the local community. This takes various forms: a Parents and Toddler group, a Friday Night Club and Go teams. A 'Christianity Explained' course has proved to be very beneficial. As well, a Ladies Fellowship Meeting and a C.Y., comprised of Arrows, Junior, Intermediate and Senior Groups, exists for members of the congregation.

The Meeting House is situated at 4 Fincarn Road, Ardmore, Londonderry, Co.Londonderry, BT47 3LB.

Clarendon Street former Meeting House

CLARENDON STREET, LONDONDERRY

The influence of the Covenanting testimony came early to the North West of Ulster because it was on the rota for visiting preachers from Scotland. When congregations were established at Bready in 1765 and at Faughan in 1770, interest in a Covenanting testimony was further increased and Societies were organised on the west side of the Foyle.

From 1810 Covenanters met in Fountain Street in the city of Londonderry. There was no minister for this congregation for the first twenty-one years; the work was under the supervision of the Faughan Session, the minister at that time being Rev. John Alexander. When he went to the Linenhall Street congregation in Belfast in 1825, Londonderry became a separate congregation and made several attempts to secure the services of its own minister.

In 1831 a call was addressed to Rev. Gordon Thompson Ewing. He had been born in Portglenone in 1798 and brought up in Drimbolg congregation then had emigrated to

America as a student and his first charge was Canonsburgh, Pennsylvania. He resigned this charge on account of ill health and returned home for a time. Although he never accepted the Londonderry call, valuable work was done for nine years as stated supply, before returning to the United States in 1841.

A minority withdrew from the congregation at this time and helped to form the Waterside congregation under the care of the Eastern Reformed Synod. Their meeting house, a short distance from the railway station, was for a long time distinguishable as a church, though a later use was as a shirt factory.

The majority issued a call to Robert Nevin. Born and brought up in Dervock, he was ordained on 1 February 1842. This was the beginning of a remarkable ministry of fifty-one years during which the congregation grew in strength and influence. In due course, despite losses through emigration, the congregation found it necessary to erect a new house for worship in Clarendon Street. It immediately became a centre for special meetings within the Presbytery and one of the first to be held was a conference to consider reports on the great work of Revival that reached its climax in Ulster in 1859. The Synod met regularly in Clarendon Street in the 1860s. In addition to his ministerial duties Dr. Nevin was Clerk of Synod for 30 years, editor of *The Covenanter* for 22 years and a writer of some note. Dr Nevin's main work was a large volume, *Studies in Prophecy* published in 1890. In recognition of this work, Geneva College awarded him the degree of Doctor of Divinity in 1890. Perhaps a better known work was his *Misunderstood Scriptures*.

Dr. Nevin died in 1893 and was succeeded by Rev. Robert Hawthorne Davidson. Brought up in Grange, Co. Tyrone, he had ministered in Fairview for six years when he was installed on 11 September 1894. He served the congregation well for 18 years and used his teaching gifts to help young men to prepare for entrance to university. Mr. Davidson spent the closing 19 years of his ministry in Stranorlar.

The next minister, David Calderwood, brought up in Cullybackey, was ordained in Clarendon Street on 2 November 1916. The congregation flourished under his capable ministry and in the short period of four and a half years, before he resigned on emigrating to America, thirty-three members were added to the communion roll. Mr. Calderwood remained in America and served in the R.P. Church and later in the Orthodox Presbyterian Church.

The congregation suffered by the depression in the 1920s and by the creation of the Border which cut off the valuable Donegal hinterland. A vacancy of five years was ended when Rev. John Knox Dickey, who had served eight years in Bready and seven years in Stranraer was installed on 4 February 1926. Under his leadership the work was well maintained for ten years until a regrettable tension led to his resignation on 4 November 1936. Mr. Dickey had short ministries in Cregagh Road, Belfast and in Drum Presbyterian congregation, Co. Cavan before his retirement. He died on 8 November 1955.

Rev. Hugh Wright, a son of the manse and member of Ballyclabber congregation, had served the North American R.P. Church for four years in Winnipeg, Canada, when he accepted a call to Clarendon Street, and was installed on 10 November 1938. Mr. Wright served the congregation faithfully and with great acceptance for twenty-one years until he moved to Trinity Street, Belfast on 15 September 1959. His ministry was the second longest in the history of Clarendon Street.

The congregation was vacant for eighteen years, during which they were faithfully pastored by Rev. Norman McCune, Faughan.

The congregation after having been cared for by Mr. McCune was given permission along with Bready to make out a joint call and on 1 September 1977. Mr. Malcolm Ball, a member of Dromara and licentiate of the Eastern Presbytery was ordained and installed to both charges and became the seventh minister of the congregation. He resigned when he accepted a call to serve as an R.P. missionary in France in 1986.

Situated in an area of the city that had experienced terrorism for over 20 years, the congregation in 1990 decided to sell their building in Clarendon Street and unite with Bready. At the Annual General Meeting on 30 January 1992, held in Bready, the Clarendon Street members were received into membership in Bready and the two ruling elders, W. J. Davis and W. B. C. Warnock were elected and installed in the Bready Session. Thus 180 years of Covenanting witness in the City of Londonderry were brought to an end.

Clarendon Street Meeting House and Manse 1859

The elders who served during Mr. Nevin's long ministry (1842-1893) were Robert Young, James Torrens, James McIlwaine, David Speer, Andrew McIlwaine, Edward Hall, John Anderson, James Cairns, Samuel Fleming, Samuel Stevenson, James Montgomery, David

Smyth, Thomas Mathers and Joseph Hall. The congregation continued to be well served by the following ruling elders: C. Dick, Robert Neill, W. J. Watt, James Cunningham, Andrew M. B. Watson, Robert Blair, Samuel Hyndman, Robert Thompson, Alexander B. McCarroll, Robert M. Watson and Moore Hamilton, W. B. Carson Warnock and William Davis. The office of Session Clerk has been in the hands of only three men on a period of over 132 years: James Torrens, 44 years, Thomas Mathers, 41 years and A. B. McCarroll, 47 years. This may be unique in the history of any congregation.

There have been five students for the ministry: John Teaz, James Torrens, Joseph Torrens, Ezekiel Teaz and Robert Andrew Watson.

The first meeting house in Londonderry was in Fountain Street; the inscription above the door was clearly visible: 'First Reformed Presbyterian Church built 1810'. When Clarendon Street meeting house was built in 1857, the old building in Fountain Street was sold to Samuel Fleming for £125. It later was used as a store by the builders Robert Logue and Sons and was demolished in the 1960s. The valuable Minute Book of the Building

Committee provided a most interesting account of the steps taken and the money contributed to build the church on a fine site in Clarendon Street near Queen Street. The committee consisted of the minister and John and Joseph Cooke, James Cairns, Samuel Fleming, James McClure, Samuel Hyndman, James Allen and James Torrens. The architect was Mr. Raffles Brown, whose fees were £21. The lowest tender was accepted from Mr. Robert Maxwell for £1,050. The work was completed in 1857 and, as financial support was encouraging, it was agreed to proceed with the erection of the hall and minister's room for about £350. Plans were also approved for the building of the Manse in Queen Street. This work was carried out by Mr. Alex McElwee for the sum of £474. The

church was opened for public worship at the end of October 1857.

The former Meeting House is situated at Clarendon Street, Londonderry, BT48 7ES.

Waterside Eastern Reformed Presbyterian former Meeting House, Bond's Hill, Waterside

WATERSIDE, LONDONDERRY

When the Eastern Reformed Presbyterian Synod was formed in 1843 by the withdrawal of the Eastern Presbytery congregations from the parent Synod, there were small groups in various parts of Ulster that associated themselves with them. A number of supporters of the Eastern Synod's testimony in the Waterside area of Londonderry including a minority from the Clarendon Street congregation, established a congregation and a church building was erected, on Bond's Hill, Waterside, a short distance from the Railway Station between 1857 - 58. The congregation was served by two ministers: from 1844 - 1854, Jacob

Alexander, the son of Rev. John Alexander of Faughan and Linenhall Street, Belfast, and Samuel Patton, 1859 to 1908.

Some of the Bready congregation joined the Eastern Reformed Synod, congregation in Waterside. Finding the journey to worship in Londonderry inconvenient, they decided to build their own meeting house at Cullion. In 1860 when differences arose between the congregation and the Rev. Samuel Patton, they were serious enough for Mr. Patton to refuse to conduct services at Cullion, confining himself to the Waterside congregation. Soon afterwards the congregation at Cullion ceased to exist and most of its members returned to Bready.

At a joint meeting of the Presbytery of Derry and Belfast on 20 July, 1908 the members of the Waterside congregation severed their connection with the Eastern Reformed Presbyterian Synod and joined the General Assembly. The congregation had been unable to provide financial support to Mr. Patton as the Synod's Sustentation Fund had collapsed. Mr. Patton in resigning from Waterside, had also to give up a house at Letterkenny where he had been supplying Gortlee, from which he also resigned the pastorate. He however sought to retain the status of a minister without charge under the Eastern Reformed Synod and remained in the manse at 32 Bond's Hill, Waterside. In 1911 Mr. Patton is recorded as a Presbyterian minister. The congregation was dissolved and the building was later used as a shirt factory and now stands in a derelict condition.

Largely due to the influence of Mr. James Macdonald, a local business man, a Covenanting witness was maintained in the Waterside. By his will a charitable fund was established to help to maintain this work and the sum of £200 was to be paid annually to the minister and congregation of Faughan. For more than 50 years an evening service was conducted by the minister of Faughan at 6.00 p.m. in the Victoria Hall, Spencer Road, Londonderry.

The former Meeting House is situated on Bond's Hill, Waterside, Londonderry.

Milford Meeting House

MILFORD

In the eighteenth century, the first Scottish Reformed Presbytery made out regular supplies of preaching and the two earliest places mentioned in their Minutes were Donaghmore and Ramelton where Covenanting Societies were meeting as early as 1750. So while Donegal was not neglected in the rota of supplies, it was a considerable time before there was a settled minister in the county.

In 1776 Robert Young from Kelso, in the Scottish Borders, was ordained and sent as a missionary to the scattered Covenanting families in North America. His ship was wrecked off the Antrim coast near Glenarm and, after working some time in the Cullybackey neighbourhood, in 1779 he was appointed 'to labour among the Covenanting Societies scattered about the shores of Lough Swilly'. Ramelton was the centre of a field of service that stretched from Letterkenny to Milford and became his home. He also organised a small congregation at Gortlee, then on the northern edge of Letterkenny but now, in the twenty first century, a suburb of Letterkenny. The year 1785 is shown on the Gortlee meeting house but it is uncertain if it refers to the year of the congregation's organisation or the erection of the meeting house. Mr. Young moved to Ardnabrockey, where he acted as stated supply of Faughan congregation until his death in 1794.

On 23 July 1788 William Gamble was ordained at Ballygay, between Ramelton and Milford. A meeting house was erected in Ballygay on the road just south of Lough Colmkille in 1794 at a cost of £220. It was 55 feet long and 25 feet wide and was reported to seat 400. The work prospered among the eighty families that were under his care. Mr. Gamble lived at Greenhill, near Letterkenny, and exercised a particularly fruitful ministry in a large area bounded by Milford, Convoy and Donegal Town. This included the congregation meeting at Gortlee, just north of Letterkenny. In 1802 families in the

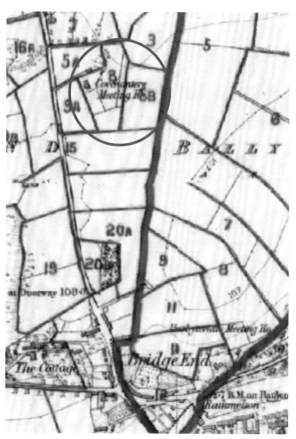

southern part of this area, around Convoy, secured a plot of land at Ballyboe, erected a meeting house and separated from Gortlee to become an independent congregation with Matthew Smyth as their first minister from 1805. Consequently, from 1802, Mr. Gamble's attention could be divided between Gortlee, Ballygay and Milford. This was still a very extensive pastoral charge.. In 1834 the number attending the two congregations of Ballygay and Ramelton was put at 874. In 1837 a house of worship was built in Milford to replace the meeting house at Ballygay.

Map showing Ramelton Meeting House which continued in use until the end of the 19th Century.

Mr. Gamble died on 6 August 1839 and was buried at Gortlee. He had been exposed to many dangers during the rebellion of 1798, but his dauntless courage and fine physique stood him in good stead. He served Gortlee and Milford for 51 years and in all these years he was absent from his pulpit on three occasions only.

Mr. Gamble's death brought changes to Milford and Gortlee. First, Milford became a self-supporting congregation and separated from Gortlee to call its own minister. Samuel Bole Stevenson from Lack, near Letterkenny, who had been brought up under the ministry of Mr. Gamble, was ordained in 1839. He lived in a house in Rosgarrow. The second change was even more far reaching in its effect for the congregation adopted the views of the majority of the Eastern Presbytery on the question of the authority of the civil magistrate and joined the Derry Presbytery of the Eastern Reformed Presbyterian Synod and was thus lost to the parent Synod for over 60 years. Mr. Stevenson was minister of Milford and of Bridge End, Ramelton,resigning from this charge in 1869 to become the minister of Linenhall Street congregation, Belfast.

The next minister at Milford was John Fritz Beck, son of Dr. Frederick Beck of Belfast. Having graduated both M.A. and M.D., he was licensed by the Belfast Presbytery of the Eastern Synod and ordained in Milford on 13 January 1870. During his ministry he lived in the manse, 'Ard Colm' in Urbalshinney which is now a private residence. When he retired in 1900 Milford sought admission to the parent Synod again and was taken under the supervision of the Western Presbytery on 9 July 1901.

Meanwhile at Gortlee, after the separation from Milford in 1839, the congregation also left the Reformed Presbyterian Synod and joined the Eastern Reformed Presbyterian Synod. In 1902, the Eastern Reformed Presbyterian Synod joined the General Assembly of the Presbyterian Church in Ireland. Whereas Milford returned to the R.P. Synod, Gortlee did not and so transferred to the General Assembly.

Milford, having resumed its links with the R. P. Church, called William James Moffett of Creevagh, a licentiate of the Southern Presbytery. He was ordained on 12 October 1905. A very gifted preacher, Mr. Moffett exercised an influential ministry for eleven years until he went to Greenock in Scotland. During his ministry a new manse was built on Church Road Milford around 1910.

His successor was his brother-in-law, Rev. James Blair. After a ministry of eleven years in Ballyclare, Mr. Blair was installed in Milford on 20 December 1916. His devoted and well-loved ministry of just over 12 years covered the difficult period of the Anglo-Irish War and subsequent partition of Ireland in 1921 that affected Donegal perhaps more than any other county. In spite of a notable fall in membership, due to migration and emigration, Mr. Blair led the congregation in an outstanding programme of renovation of the church property which cost over £1,500. He moved to Kilraughts in March 1929.

After ministries at Ballymacashon, Dromara and Loanhead, Rev. William Warnock was installed in Milford on 28 November 1929. A gifted preacher and a faithful pastor, his death, on 25 December1943, was greatly regretted though his influence in the Church continued for many years through the fine service rendered by his family in different congregations.

The tradition of fine preaching continued when Samuel Wallace Lynas was installed on 3 October 1945. Brought up in Kilraughts, he had served the Church with distinction in Liverpool and Cullybackey. His ministry was full of promise, and his untimely death on 20 April 1953 was a great blow to Milford and to the Church as a whole.

Robert Hanna, a member of Kilraughts, was ordained on 20 September 1956 and proved himself a preacher of fervency and power for over five years before moving to Newry in 1962.

Samuel Kennedy Cromie, awaiting the opportunity to open the work of the Foreign Mission in Ethiopia, acted as stated supply in 1962 and 1963.

Until William Gerald Milligan was ordained on 28 August 1974, the character and courage of the congregation was tested in a long vacancy and it is greatly to the credit of the members and of the help given by the Presbytery that the work was maintained without hindrance or loss through those years. Mr. Milligan was supported by a loyal people.

After serving faithfully for six years in Milford, Mr. Milligan accepted a call from the Stranraer congregation in Scotland.

Barry Galbraith, a member of Cregagh Road and licentiate of the Eastern Presbytery, was ordained and installed as minister of the congregation on 17 October 1981. After serving faithfully for five years in Milford, Mr. Galbraith accepted a call to Wishaw.

In 1986, Rev. Andrew Gregg, a mission worker with the Irish Mission Board in Cork, accepted the call of the congregation and was installed on 4 July. He ministered with love and compassion to the people of Milford until 1998 when he went to Ballenon and Ballylane.

In 2000 the Western Presbytery adopted a plan whereby the Milford congregation would share a minister with a developing mission work in Letterkenny and the minister would live in Letterkenny. The manse in Milford was sold and the manse for Letterkenny was purchased with part of the money from the sale of a farm left to the Western Presbytery by Mr. James Throne of Bready. The Milford congregation and the Western Presbytery issued joint calls to Mark Loughridge in October 2000 and these calls were accepted on 7 December 2000. Mr. Loughridge, a member of the Trinity congregation and a licentiate of the Eastern Presbytery, was ordained, installed and commissioned for this work on 10

February 2001. The Milford congregation has given its wholehearted backing to this endeavour and has continued to facilitate the work in Letterkenny.

However, this has not been at the expense of its witness in Milford. With renewed vision for the work in Milford and a desire to make an impact on the town, the congregation began an extensive renovation work on the 1837 meeting house. This was completed in 2006 and a service of thanksgiving was held on 14 July. Milford congregation, since the renovation of the building, has experienced a new sense of hope for the future. New people are moving to the area, and it is with anticipation that the congregation looks to the future - believing that God has placed them at the crossroads between several different towns and villages for His own purposes. They pray longingly for the day when the pews will be filled as they once were.

There has been no reference as yet to the fine work done by office-bearers during the years owing to a lack of detailed information. In 1901 the Clerk of Session was Andrew Young; the other elders were Samuel Buchanan and Richard Hemphill. The latter, who died in 1904 aged 86, had been elder for over 50 years. In 1904 Samuel Young was ordained and he was followed in 1910 by Robert McCausland, Matthew Grier, David Park, David Hay and Richard Hemphill. In 1946 George Young and Robert Ian McCausland were added to the Session. In 1956 Robert A.Starrett, William N. Hay, and James McNutt were ordained. William J McMahon and J. Kenneth McIlwaine were ordained in 1977.

The list of students who offered for the ministry recalls some of the families that have made an outstanding contribution to the life of the congregation. Their names are William McNutt, Samuel Bole Stevenson, George Stewart, Samuel Patton, Robert Wallace, John Watters, John Thomas Moffett Blair, William Young and Stewart McMahon.

The Meeting House is situated on Kilmacrennan Road, Milford, Co. Donegal.

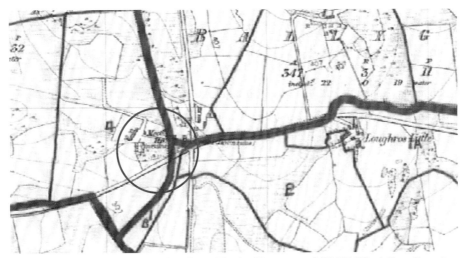

19th Century map showing the site of Ballygay Meeting House, east of R245-Milford- Ramelton rd.

Gortlee former Meeting House

LETTERKENNY, GORTLEE

The Solemn League and Covenant was administered in Letterkenny on the first week of May 1644 to a population greatly influenced by the Scottish ministers brought into the established church by the pragmatic and sympathetic oversight of Andrew Knox, Bishop of Raphoe. Presbyterians after the restoration of the monarchy in 1660 were organised into the Laggan Presbytery whose minutes give an insight into the oppression by prelacy, whereby some ministers suffered hardship and even imprisonment. Though poorly treated, Presbyterians generally rallied to the Williamite cause. However, there were those who, upon the settlement of the Anglican Church and the Regium Donum upon the Presbyterians, continued to adhere to the Covenant which had been suffered for, and then set aside. Such minority groups within a majority Roman Catholic and Anglican area organised themselves into Covenanting Societies.

In the eighteenth century, the first Scottish Reformed Presbytery made out regular supplies of preaching and the two earliest places regarding Donegal, mentioned in their

Minutes were Donaghmore and Ramelton, where Societies were meeting as early as 1750. However, it was a considerable time before there was a settled minister in the county.

The congregation of Gortlee shared the early history of the current Milford congregation. The first regular minister in the district was Robert Young from 1779 to 1787. He was appointed "to labour among the Covenanting Societies scattered about the shores of Lough Swilly". Ramelton was the centre of a field of service that stretched from Letterkenny to Milford. Mr Young also organised a small congregation at Gortlee, then on the northern edge of Letterkenny but now a suburb of Letterkenny. The year 1785 is shown on the Gortlee meeting house but it is uncertain if it refers to the year of the congregation's organisation or the erection of the building. In 1787 the centre of his work was moved to Londonderry where the Faughan meeting house was built.

Mr. William Gamble, who was born in 1763 near Ballykelly and educated at Glasgow, was licensed in 1785. On 23 July 1788 he was then ordained at Ballygay, between Ramelton and Milford. Some time later he removed his residence to Greenhill, near Letterkenny. He was married to a Miss Art from Stranorlar. Mr. Gamble's fruitful ministry, in a large area extending to Milford, Convoy and Donegal Town, included the congregation which met at Gortlee.

In 1802 the Convoy meeting separated from Gortlee to become an independent congregation. Consequently, from 1802, Mr. Gamble's attention could be divided between Gortlee, Ballygey and Milford. This was still a very extensive pastoral charge. In 1834 the numbers attending the two congregations of Ballygay and Ramelton was put at 874.

Mr. Gamble was of a striking physique, a strong man weighing 18 stone and made in proportion. Both on his travels and at home he more than held his own against robbers, raiders and plundering soldiers; several tales are told in this connection. Notably he was appointed as the Moderator to conduct the business of the first Synod of the Reformed Presbyterian Church of Ireland when it met in May 1811. Mr. Gamble died on 6 August 1839, and was buried at Gortlee, with a stone recording him as the "Minister of Gortlee, Bridge End and Ballygay. For the cause of

Christ and a Covenanted Reformation". He served Gortlee and Milford for 51 years and in all these years he was absent from his pulpit on only three occasions.

Mr. Gamble's death brought changes to Milford and Gortlee. Milford became a self-supporting congregation and separated from Gortlee to call its own minister in 1839. Samuel Bole Stevenson from Lack, near Letterkenny, who had been brought up under the ministry of Mr. Gamble, was ordained to this new charge.

On the question of the authority of the civil magistrate, the congregations of Gortlee and Milford adopted the views of the majority of the Eastern Presbytery and joined the Derry Presbytery of the Eastern Reformed Presbyterian Synod.

Gortlee's next minister was Mr. William Henry, born in 1789, son of Thomas Henry of Macosquin. He was educated at Glasgow, where he graduated in 1811. Licensed by the Northern Presbytery, in 1813 he was ordained minister in the Newtownards R.P. Church. At the split of the R.P. Synod in 1840 he took a section of that congregation into the Eastern R.P. Synod, which was formed in 1842.

Dr. Henry was called to Gortlee and he was the father of Rev. R. M. Henry, R.P. minister of Botanic Avenue, Belfast, who later joined the Baptists. Dr. Henry died 7 August 1852 and was buried at Gortlee.

Following a seven-year vacancy, during which services were supplied by the Milford minister, a call made in 1856 to a Mr. Bates of Glasgow was declined. After being a licentiate of the main R.P. Synod for a number of years, Mr. John Robinson was called to Gortlee. He was ordained 4 October 1859. A report in 1864 notes that a Classical School was conducted in Letterkenny by the Covenanting minister. The same year Mr. Robinson was reported to be seriously ill. He died 31 December 1866, and was buried at Gortlee.

Another prolonged vacancy occurred and the congregation was supplied by Dr. Beck of Milford and Rev. S. Patton of Waterside.

Mr. Joseph Moffett, the next minister, was born at Broughshane, 22 July 1844, the third son of Robert Moffett, and brought up in Cullybackey congregation within the Eastern Synod. He was educated at Galway, Belfast, Edinburgh and Philadelphia. He emigrated to the U.S.A. in 1870. Licensed there by the R.P. Presbytery of Philadelphia, he was ordained by Pittsburgh Presbytery in Darlington and New Galilee, in September 1870. The climate, however, did not suit him and he returned to Ireland in 1873, being installed in Gortlee, on 3 September 1874. He had received the D.D. degree from America. In 1876 he married Miss L. Beck of Belfast, and had three daughters and two sons, one of these being Rev. Dr. J. Moffett of Crown Court, Church of Scotland, London.

Rev. Joseph Moffett D.D

Dr. Moffett opened an Academy in Letterkenny where he educated the children of other residents along with his own up to matriculation standard. He was widely known and greatly respected by both the Protestant and Roman Catholic sections of the community. He organised evening services monthly in the schoolhouses at Ednaharnon and Ellistrin, and in a barn at Correnagh. In 1902, the Eastern Reformed Presbyterian Synod joined the General Assembly of the Presbyterian Church in Ireland. Whereas Milford returned to the R. P. Synod, Gortlee did not and so transferred to the General Assembly. The Gortlee meeting house was renovated in 1904. Dr. Moffett resigned in October 1907 and moved from his home at 142 Main Street Letterkenny, to Edinburgh, where he did pulpit supply work for the Church of Scotland. He died in 1917.

Services were maintained in Gortlee for a number of years, initially by Rev. Samuel Patton of Waterside until 1908 and later mainly by students from Magee College. At the union of Letterkenny Presbyterian congregations, negotiations were begun and finally completed for including Gortlee in the union and in 1925 Gortlee amalgamated with First and Trinity Presbyterian Churches in Letterkenny to become Trinity Presbyterian

Church, Letterkenny. The burial ground has become the principle one for Protestant church-es in Letterkenny.

The Reformed Presbyterian Church currently has a vision for work in Letterkenny. In January 2008 the new Reformed Presbyterian witness in Letterkenny, known as New Life Fellowship was established as a Society and has progressed steadily with the fellowship meeting in rented property. It is prayerfully hoped that the town once again will be the centre of a vital Reformed witness which will spread throughout Donegal.

The former Meeting House is situated at Gortlee, Letterkenny, Co. Donegal.

Day Centre, Oliver Plunkett Street

NEW LIFE FELLOWSHIP, LETTERKENNY

In 2000 the Western Presbytery adopted a plan whereby the Milford congregation would share a minister with a developing mission work in Letterkenny and the minister would live in Letterkenny. The manse in Milford was sold and the manse for Letterkenny was purchased with part of the money from the sale of a farm left to the Western Presbytery by Mr. James Throne of Bready. This project was appropriate, first, on historical grounds, as Letterkenny, as has been pointed out earlier, had been once the centre of a powerful and fruitful Covenanting witness in County Donegal led by Rev. William Gamble. Also, Letterkenny was by then Donegal's largest town. The Milford congregation and the Western Presbytery issued joint calls to Mark Loughridge in October 2000 and these calls were accepted on 7 December 2000. Mr. Loughridge, a member of the Trinity congregation and a licentiate of the Eastern Presbytery, was ordained, installed and commissioned for this work on 10 February 2001

The work in Letterkenny is known as New Life Fellowship, and has progressed steadily with the fellowship meeting in rented property. On 21 January 2008 the Fellowship was organised into a Society, consisting of eight members, six covenant children and three adherents. Like any church planting work, Letterkenny has seen a sizeable number of people passing through, yet the core at the heart of the fellowship is growing. The Society continues to reach out into the community through a variety of public meetings, leaflet distribution and personal witness.

The vision of the work in Letterkenny is to see the town once again the centre of a vital witness that spreads throughout Donegal, to the towns and villages where there is little or no witness at present.

The New Life Fellowship meets at the Day Centre, Oliver Punkett Rd, Letterkenny, Co. Donegal.

Stranorlar Meeting House

STRANORLAR

The Plantation of Ulster, which commenced in the early years of the seventeenth century brought many Scottish Presbyterian settlers to the best parts of Co. Donegal. Stranorlar is situated on the north side of the River Finn. Its twin town, Ballybofey, over the bridge, is on the south side of the river.

The congregation had its roots in the Scottish settlers who became attached to the principles and teaching of the Burgher Seceders at the beginning of the nineteenth century. On 16 May 1809, a petition was presented by a number of persons from the Stranorlar area to the Upper Presbytery of Tyrone which was in connection with the Burgher Synod. The petition asked to be accepted as a vacant congregation. A decision on the matter was deferred but, on the renewal of the application, the petition was granted in July 1809. In 1811 it was agreed that the new congregation would qualify for a share of the Regium Donum amounting to £38 per annum. Their first minister, David Fulton, a licentiate from Armagh, was ordained on 24 March 1812. After a ministry of nineteen years, he was succeeded by John McAuley, a native of Drumgooland, Co. Down. He was ordained on 30 November 1831. It is possible that he was related to Mrs Dodds, wife of Rev. William

Dodds of Ballenon. Mr. McAuley was an excellent minister and the congregation prospered under his pastoral care. When the Secession Synod and the Synod of Ulster united in 1840 to become the General Assembly of the Presbyterian Church in Ireland, the congregation was placed under the supervision of the Donegal Presbytery and listed as Second Stranorlar.

This new affiliation did not alter things very much for the congregation. Mr. McAuley was a Seceder at heart and when he died, greatly lamented by his congregation, on 3 October 1869, he left behind him not only a gracious memory but a commitment to the old ways on the part of his people. It was no great surprise when the congregation applied to be received into the membership of the Reformed Presbyterian Synod. Their application was presented to the September meeting of the Western Presbytery in 1870 in the form of a memorial representing the unanimous desire of the congregation. The Report of the Western Presbytery to the Synod of 1871 gives a full and interesting account of the proceedings:

> While Presbytery received the memorial favourably, they were not disposed to act in this important matter with undue precipitation or without further inquiry. At the same time no difficulty was felt in acceding to their wishes to send them occasional supplies of preaching.

> At the November meeting a second memorial, to the same purport as the first, was presented - this time accompanied by a copy of a formal declinature of the authority of the General Assembly. A commission with Presbyterial powers was appointed to proceed to Stranorlar on 29 November and, after the sermon, to hold a conference with the assembled congregation. Should the way seem clear as the result of this conference, the Commission was authorised to receive them into the communion of the Church.

> After the Service, the Terms of Communion were read and explained. Extracts from the Testimony were also read. The principles and position of our Church were plainly and fully stated. The names of the communicants were then called out and they were asked individually did they assent to the Terms of Communion. One member only desired some time to consider; all the remaining members distinctly

assented in answer to their name. The Commission then considered themselves justified in giving the right hand of fellowship to the Elders and a few members representing the congregation. It was left to the Session when duly constituted, with a member of Presbytery as Moderator, to admit in similar manner the members of the congregation not present on that occasion.

In due course a call was issued to Robert Adams McFarlane, a licentiate of the Western Presbytery and a member of Mulvin congregation. He was ordained on 29 November 1871. Under his gifted ministry the congregation prospered and his wise leadership and stewardship enabled the congregation to erect their fine meeting house. Mr. McFarlane served the congregation for twenty-two years until 1893.

Stranorlar enjoyed the services for two years of Samuel Kennedy, a member of Ballyclare and a licentiate of the Eastern Presbytery. He was ordained on 3 August 1894 but resigned on 5 October, 1896 on accepting a call from Limavady.

After a short pastorate in Bready, Rev. Robert McFarlane returned to Stranorlar in 1896 and continued his ministry for ten years until his death on 13 December 1906.

The third minister was Rev. Andrew Melville Thompson. Born and educated in America, he had served the Church in Ballylaggan, Denver, U.S.A. and Geelong, Australia, before coming to Stranorlar on 30 November 1909. He resigned in February 1912 and returned to America.

His successor was Rev. Robert Hawthorne Davidson, a member of Grange, Co. Tyrone. After ministries of six years in Fairview and eighteen years in Londonderry, he was installed in Stranorlar on 28 May 1912 and served the congregation until his retirement in July 1931. In addition to his pastoral work, Mr. Davidson gave valuable tuition to young men from the neighbourhood preparing for entrance to university. After Mr. Davidson's retirement, on 26 July 1932, there was a united meeting of the sessions and committees of the congregations of Stranorlar and Convoy to discuss a union and, later in the year, the congregation united with Convoy.

The congregation has provided two students for the ministry: David James Magee and Andrew Blackburn.

The congregation has been well served by a band of devoted ruling elders. In 1871 the following men were ordained and formed the first session: William Tait, John Tait, James Taylor, John Barr, James Blackburn, Adam Tait (Jr). On 11 September 1898 the following men were added to the Session: Samuel McClean, Samuel Blackburn, Samuel Tait and Robert Roulstone. Session was further strengthened on 3 November 1949 when the following men were ordained: Robert Boggs, William G. Dinsmore, John McClean and John Pollock. To the above were added, on 12 November 1971, Robert Blackburn and Richard Joseph Magee. David John Blackburn joined the Session on 27 October 1983 while ten years later, on 3 December 1993, William G. Blackburn and George A. Magee were added. More recently, on 21 November 2004, Brian W. Blackburn and Noel Blackburn became ruling elders.

From the above list of ruling elders, the following men have served the congregation as Clerks of Session: William Tait (1871-1910), Samuel Tait (November 1910-May 1917), Samuel Blackburn (May 1917- October 1923), Samuel McClean (October 1923-May 1958), John Pollock (May 1958- Nov 1974), Robert Blackburn (1974 to present).

The building was completed and opened for worship in 1877 after strenuous efforts by the people and by their pastor, Rev. Robert McFarlane, who visited the United States of America in 1875, and again in 1876, to raise money to help to meet the cost of the building. It was completely renovated in 1995, converted into a multi-functional building with chairs replacing the pews. Cloakrooms, kitchen and a new Session Room were incorporated. A gallery with double-glazing was added and has proved invaluable for parents with very young children. In addition to the regular preaching of God's Word, Bible studies, prayer meetings, C.Y and W.M.A., the Stranorlar congregation witnesses to the community in various ways by holding a Parent and Toddler group, a Friday Night Club, an annual Go Team and an annual Book Fair

The Meeting House is situated at Main Street, Stranorlar, Co. Donegal.

Convoy Meeting House

CONVOY

Convoy, one of the older congregations in the Reformed Presbyterian Church, owes its origin to the substantial settlement of Scottish Presbyterians in East Donegal. When the Scottish Reformed Presbytery was formed in 1743, supplies of preaching made out for Ireland included the Covenanting Societies at Donaghmore and Ramelton. These later became the centre of work in Donegal. Rev. Robert Young, appointed to minister to Covenanters on the shores of Lough Swilly in 1779, gave leadership for a few years, but the main contribution was made by Rev. William Gamble, ordained at Ballygay in 1788. His field of service included Milford, Convoy and Donegal Town.

In 1802 Covenanting families in the Convoy area secured a plot of land, built a meeting house and became an independent congregation. Their first minister was Matthew Smyth, a native of Rasharkin, Co. Antrim. Educated at Glasgow University and the Theological Hall, Paisley, he was ordained in 1805. His untimely death in 1818, at the age of 38, ended a fruitful and promising ministry. The congregation then suffered a long vacancy of

17 years during which several calls were issued without success, and it is to the credit of the members and of the Milford minister, Mr. Gamble, that their existence as a congregation was maintained.

On 15 July 1835, John Stott, a member of Ballenon and a licentiate of the Southern Presbytery, was ordained. His faithful and wise leadership retained the congregation for the R.P. Synod when the division of 1840 led to the secession of the Eastern Presbytery and other congregations including Milford. This ministry also spanned the difficult years of the Great Famine before he resigned on 16 October 1850 and emigrated to the United States.

After an eight years' vacancy the congregation called Joseph Alexander Moody, a member of Ballylaggan and a licentiate of the Northern Presbytery. Mr. Moody had some difficulty making up his mind regarding the call and it was withdrawn. It was presented to him again at a later date and on his acceptance he was ordained on 20 October 1858. His ministry was of short duration and ended when he accepted a call to Cullybackey in 1860.

Following a seven years' vacancy and a further anxious delay as time was taken for reflection on the call, John White McKeown, a member of Drimbolg was ordained on 27 March 1867. Mr. McKeown was an unusually gifted minister and the congregation doubled in the first eight years of his ministry from 100 to 200 members. He was also a singularly unfortunate man and was subject to a great deal of persecution and opposition. In 1875 an attempt was made on his life and he had a miraculous escape from death. He was unsettled by the incident and resigned the pastorate. Six years later he returned and was installed on 16 March 1881, but the strain was too great and he resigned again in 1883 and emigrated to Canada.

After a further vacancy of eight years the longest ministry in the life of the congregation began with the installation on 9 July 1891 of Rev. William Scott, a native of Creevagh. Mr. Scott had been ordained in Mulvin in 1877. He gave faithful service as preacher and pastor until his retirement on 31 December 1928. He died on 21 April 1931.

Three months later Rev. R. H. Davidson retired from the active duties of the ministry at Stranorlar and the necessary arrangements were made by the Presbytery to bring Convoy and Stranorlar together as a joint charge.

The congregation celebrated its bicentenary in 2002 when the Northern Presbytery choir led the special praise on Friday 8 November. On 9 April 2005 a Conventicle was held at Convoy to commemorate the 200th anniversary of the ordination of the first minister, Rev Matthew Smyth.

The congregation has been served by the following ruling elders: Alexander Storey, John Torrens, William Gregg, Alexander Smyth, William Smyth, John Eliott, William Steele, David Parks, Joseph Blair, James Galbraith, Samuel Park, James Knox, James A. Park, Alexander Blair, James A. Stuart, Adam Neely, George Blair, Joseph Blair, Rankin Stuart, Robert Tait, Mark Frizzell and Andrew Smyth.

Members from Convoy who entered the ministry are: William King, Francis Gailey, William Wilson, James McNair, Andrew Cross Gregg and Raymond Blair.

The present Church building in Convoy is situated in Ballyboe on the banks of the River Deele and was built in 1879, thus replacing the former meeting house, built in 1805. The church building and caretaker's house are maintained in good repair. The congregation, although small numerically, believe that they maintain a worthwhile witness in the area and pray for God's blessing in the years ahead.

The Meeting House is situated in Ballyboe, Convoy, Co. Donegal.

STRANORLAR AND CONVOY

James Campbell, a member of Cullybackey, was ordained to the ministry of both Stranorlar and Convoy on 4 January 1933. His able ministry of the Word left its mark on the congregation during the next eleven years until he moved to Larne in 1944. Mr. Campbell's knowledge of Greek and his exegetical gifts were recognised by the Synod when he was appointed to the teaching staff of the Theological Hall in 1945. His pastoral and teaching work ended with his untimely death on 29 March, 1964.

William Norman McCune succeeded him. A member of Trinity Street congregation, he was ordained on 10 November 1948. His devotional and practical gifts were seen in a useful and efficient ministry which ended when he accepted a call to Faughan and was installed there on 13 December 1956.

Rev. Robert William Lytle, having resigned as missionary to Lebanon, was installed pastor of Convoy and Stranorlar on 6 June 1957. With characteristic sincerity and faithfulness he ministered to the congregations for almost seventeen years until his settlement in Lame on 12 April 1974.

Rev. Samuel Kennedy Cromie, after five years with the Irish Mission and twelve years as a missionary in Ethiopia, was installed minister of the congregations on 8 October 1975. Under his experienced leadership and faithful service, the work of the congregation was maintained until his retirement from the active duties pastorate on 2 May 1990. However, Mr. Cromie did not retire from ministry. On 17 November 1990, the Western Presbytery decided to commence a Christian literature ministry in the North West, following a proposal by Mr. Cromie. The work was launched on 1 May 1991. It was, in fact the re-launch of

a previous, very successful, outreach work, which he conducted between 1983 and 1985, also called 'New Life Books'.

Rev. Tim C. Donachie, former minister of Cregagh Road, was installed on 20 June 1992. He resigned in 1996 to return to missionary and educational work in Lima, Peru with the Free Church of Scotland.

In September 1998 Rev. J. Marcus McCullough, former minister in Glasgow R.P.C., was installed as minister and served faithfully until his retirement from the active duties of the ministry on 11 September 2002. The congregation appreciated Mr. McCullough's love, hard work and dedication to the congregation.

Following a short vacancy Stephen A. Wright, member of Ballylaggan and licentiate of the Northern Presbytery, was ordained and installed as minister of the congregation on 30 November 2002. The congregation is currently active in reaching out to the whole community and the annual Go Team enables literature to be distributed and contacts made in the wider context of County Donegal.

Limavady Meeting House

LIMAVADY

In the list of supplies made out for Ireland by the Scottish Presbytery after its formation in 1743, the Limavady district is frequently mentioned. The meetings were held at Drummond, a mile or so to the east of the town. When the first Secession congregation was formed at Limavady in 1748, the Covenanting cause benefited to some extent as in the next few years five of the first eight Covenanting ministers in Ireland were from the Limavady neighbourhood - an outstanding contribution to the Covenanting cause.

The first of the five was William Martin who was born at Ballyspallen in 1731 and was the only minister in Ireland for the six years from 1757 to 1763. William Martin became minister of Antrim, centred in Cullybackey. The other four ministers from Limavady were: Andrew McClenaghan, who was ordained in Cullybackey for service in the American Church; William James, first minister of Bready, ordained in 1765; Thomas Hamilton, first minister of Faughan, ordained in 1770; William Gamble, ordained in Milford in 1778.

Matthew Lynn, a native of Larne and a licentiate of the Scottish Presbytery, was ordained minister of the Bannside congregation on 15 August, 1763. Bannside covered the greater part of County Londonderry and Mr. Lynn may be rightly regarded as the first regular minister of Limavady. For ten years he preached in barns, houses and in the open air and supervised the well-ordered Societies in which the people were instructed in the things of God. He was wrongly blamed for officiating at a wedding in Bovevagh Presbyterian Church between William Moore and Elizabeth Haslett in 1764. The Reformed Presbytery investigated the matter and found Mr. Lynn to be innocent of the charge. Years later their verdict was vindicated when a dying man at Dungiven confessed that he had been hired for the sum of six guineas to impersonate Mr. Lynn and perform the marriage secretly against the wishes of the bride's parents. Despite the verdict of the Presbytery, Mr. Lynn deemed it best to emigrate to the United States.

He was succeeded by Samuel Aiken, a native of Clough, Co. Antrim, who ministered from 1776 to 1790 before going to Creevagh. In spite of poor health he did a fine work. Towards the close of his ministry he was assisted by a licentiate called William King, a Donegal man who, in 1792, emigrated to America.

Joseph Orr, ordained at Garvagh in 1798 was the third minister. At a meeting of the Presbytery in August 1805 Mr. Orr asked to be relieved of the oversight of the Limavady portion of his congregation 'on account of the great fatigue to which it exposed him'. His request was granted and the pastoral tie dissolved at the next meeting of the Presbytery.

The congregation, undeterred by the loss of its minister, took immediate steps to establish their work and in 1806 a new meeting house was erected at Broadlane or 'Broad Land'.

In 1814 they secured the first minister they had had entirely on their own. Clarke Houston, born in Maghera in 1787, had grown up in the Drimbolg congregation and was educated at Glasgow University and the R.P. Theological Hall in Paisley. He was licensed by the Eastern Presbytery in 1811 and ordained on 6 September 1814. However, in 1816 he left the congregation because, due to the fall in food prices at the end of the Napoleonic Wars, the congregation was unable to pay him his stipend. In 1818 he became the minister of Cullybackey and remained there until his death in 1852. He was Clerk of the Synod for many years. At this time the congregation, like many others in Ulster, was affected by emigration, but in spite of that the work went on with much evidence of blessing.

Mr. Houston was succeeded by Robert Gamble Orr, a licentiate and a member of the congregation at Grange, Cookstown. He first appeared at Presbytery in 1820 and his ministry terminated with his emigration to America in 1827.

His successor, Arthur Fullerton, another member of Drimbolg, was ordained on 1 July 1828 and ministered until 1841. He resigned with the intention of emigrating, but, unable to do so, he became for a short time minister of the Presbyterian Church in Coleraine.

James Kennedy, brought up in Ballylaggan, was ordained the next minister on 18 May 1843. At the beginning of his ministry the congregation was greatly strengthened by the accession of the Derrybeg congregation of Original Seceders. The congregation, originally known as Myroe and Bolay, had been formed in 1825 and, when a division took place, the larger part, referred to as the Derrymore congregation, was received into the General Assembly of the Irish Presbyterian Church. Over the united congregation

of Broadlane and Derrybeg Mr. Kennedy ministered for twenty-seven years with great acceptance before emigrating to America. On 13 November, 1870, Mr. Kennedy was installed pastor of the Fourth New York Reformed Presbyterian congregation. Mr. Kennedy resigned the care of this congregation in 1896, and in November 1897 he moved with his daughter to St. John, New Brunswick where he died in 1898. During his ministry in Limavady in 1855 a Juvenile Missionary Association was formed in the congregation. Records give the names of eleven young people who acted as collectors. They were A. Clarke, Clarke Morrison, W. McCorkell, Thomas Gault, Misses Blair, Pollock, McDonnell, Eliza and Ellen McClenaghan, Elizabeth Millen and Susan Brown. The elders at that time were William Blair, Hugh Brittain, Alexander Eason, William McCloy, William Millen, Matthew Hodge and John Robinson. In 1868 there was a congregation of 364 with 244 of them communicants.

Following Mr. Kennedy, there were a number of comparatively short ministries. Thomas Cleland, the eighth minister was brought up in Killinchy, Co. Down. His promising ministry from 1871 to 1873 was terminated by his tragic death. He resided at Strieve Hill with the Hastings family.

William John Maxwell, a Knockbracken man, succeeded him, but after six months he resigned and went to Hall Lane, Liverpool, where he served for ten years before entering the ministry of the English Presbyterian Church.

In 1875, William Dick, son of Professor James Dick of Kellswater, was ordained. He had a fine ministry of nine years before going to Mulvin and later to Cregagh Road as its first minister in 1902.

His successor was James Alexander Smyth Stewart, the third minister of the congregation to come from Drimbolg. His ministry lasted from 1887 to 1895 when he went to Dervock. He died in 1902.

After a short pastorate in Stranorlar, Rev. Samuel Kennedy was installed in 1896 and served for twenty-eight years until his removal to Rathfriland in 1924. For a long time, the older members recalled with gratitude his fine ministry.

He was succeeded by Robert Biggart Lyons, a licentiate of the Northern Presbytery. Mr. Lyons had a distinguished university career at Magee and Trinity College, Dublin, obtaining a Senior Moderatorship in Mental and Moral Philosophy with Gold medal. Ordained on 23 October 1924, Mr. Lyons guided the affairs of the congregation with great ability for almost fifty-one years until his retirement in September 1975. He was held in high esteem in both the congregation and throughout the community through his devoted labours as a pastor and earnest evangelical preacher.

On 5 June 1977 a call was issued to the minister of Fairview and Tullyvallen, Rev. John Hawthorne. This was accepted on 4 July and Mr. Hawthorne was installed on 8 September 1977. He served the congregation until his departure to Dromara in 1993. The congregation appreciated his faithful leadership and ministry, especially in his preaching and exposition of the Word.

On 26 February 1995 a call was presented to Rev. Robert Robb, formerly a minister of the Dromara congregation. This was accepted on 11 April 1995 and Mr. Robb was installed as minister on 8 September 1995. The congregation was saddened when Mr. Robb accepted the call to be organising Pastor of the Enniskillen Society of Covenanters and was commissioned on 26 February 2009. Throughout his ministry in Limavady Mr. Robb was considered by the congregation as diligent in study, faithful in preaching, practical in application, fervent in prayer, willing to face and deal with difficult issues and continually going far beyond the call of duty in his pastoral ministry.

Limavady has done well for the Church in providing students for the ministry. Their names are William Martin, Daniel McClelland, William James, Thomas Hamilton, William Gamble, Alexander Britton, Robert John McIlmoyle, James Blair, William Henry Pollock, John McIlmoyle, Joseph Alexander Cresswell Blair, Edward McCollum, David Fallows, Samuel McCollum.

Since 1940 elections to the office of ruling elder have been held as follows:

31 October 1940: W.J .Blair, James A.S. McIlmoyle, Thomas A. McIlmoyle

6 May1949: John W. McCloy, William G. McCollum, Marcus S.F. McCollum

30 April 1967: James Blair, Ernest Fallows, Vincent McIlmoyle

21 April 1984: James Carson, Jack Williamson

30 October 1994: Neville Kerr, John McCollum

18 April 1999: Brian Dunwoody, Irwin Lockington

21 November 2004: Ian Forgrave

The first meeting house was at Broadlane or Broad land. The latter term is familiar to many and refers to the days when it stood in relative isolation. It was a thatched building and was used for eighty-two years. The present church building was opened in March 1889. A local contractor, James Wray, who built five other places of worship in the district, was the contractor. The cost of the building was £600 and the congregation was free of debt when it opened. The offering at the opening service was £80, the equivalent of £20,000 in 2007. It is situated on Greystone Road, leading into the town from the Coleraine direction and in the 21st century it is surrounded by housing development, the Recreation Centre and part of the Further Education College, reflecting the rapid growth of Limavady over the past few decades.

Encouraged by the gifted leadership of Rev. R. B. Lyons (1924-1975), the congregation again showed wonderful generosity in providing a very suitable Church Hall in 1957 and a fine new Manse. In 1994 the Session Room was built along with new toilets and an upstairs room. An impressive extension to the Church hall was completed in June 2002. During 2003-4 a new porch was added to the meeting house.

The Limavady congregation has enjoyed good growth over the past ten years, both numerically and spiritually. It continues to reach out by various means into the local community and is encouraged by the good number of regular visitors who attend the regular worship services. The Reformed, Biblical and practical preaching and the warm Christian fellowship extended and shown by the members encourage visitors to return on a regular basis. The congregation's vision for the future is to have an increasing impact for spiritual good in the town and to see more people coming to faith in Christ. The members look by faith to God to fill the building with worshippers. They are also aware of the need to maintain and, where necessary, to renovate, their present building so that it remains useful in the work of God's Kingdom.

The Meeting House is situated at 5 Greystone Road, Coolessan Drumrane, Limavady, Co.Londonderry, BT49 0ND.

Former Covenanter Meeting House Mulvin

MULVIN

Mulvin was a mission station for many years and part of the Bready congregation, the meeting house being constructed in 1837. Following the growth in attendance and an excellent spirit of loyalty and devotion which became evident, the society was organised as a congregation in 1844, under the Western Presbytery.

The ministers of Bready, Revs. J. A. Chancellor and C. K. Toland, preached at monthly intervals. In 1848, the church received its first minister, when Mr. Henry Stewart, a licentiate, was placed in charge for a year.

By 1868 there were 12 families and 38 communicants. The ruling elders were R. Watson and Thomas McFarlane. On 5 September 1871, Mulvin petitioned the Western Presbytery for a separation from Bready and independent status was granted on 7 February 1872. In 1873 the congregation's income from 30 in membership was £64.14s. Two ministers served during the next twenty-five years. The first was Rev. William Scott (a member of Creevagh) who ministered from 1877 until 1884, when he went to Convoy.

The second was Rev. William Dick from 1884 until his removal to Cregagh Road in 1902. At this point the congregation ceased to enjoy the services of a separate minister, and was later rejoined to Bready.

Since then regular supplies of preaching were provided by the Presbytery but, when the membership died out, the congregation was dissolved and the meeting house was sold in 1976 to the Free Presbyterian Church, who carried out extensive renovations and still use it as a place of worship.

Mulvin was the home congregation of Rev. Thomas Barnwell MacFarlane, who was born at Altdoghill, Newtownstewart. He was licensed in 1906 and in the same year ordained in the Glasgow North (Wallace Street) congregation of the Scottish R. P. Church. Installed in Riverside Newry in 1909, he was later also appointed by Synod to the Chair of Professor of Church History and Pastoral Theology in the Theological Hall, from 1928 to 1957.

Datestone Mulvin

The old Meeting House is situated at 292 Melmount Road, Victoria Bridge, Strabane, Co Tyrone BT82 9JG.

The Clinton Centre Enniskillen

ENNISKILLEN

Following outreach in Enniskillen for a couple of years, a fellowship with a core of three families, the Allens, Bells and Armstrongs, had been meeting regularly for worship and fellowship.

The Home Section of the Mission Committee decided early in 2008 to make a supreme effort to forward the work in Enniskillen. In August for one week a Go Team was used and Bible readings held each evening in the Ely Centre were well supported. On Sabbath 3 August weekly worship services commenced. The Mission Committee issued a call on Friday 10 October to Rev. Robert Robb, minister of the Limavady congregation, to be organising Pastor. The call was presented at a meeting in Bready on 14 November and on 3 December Mr. Robb accepted. On Thursday 26 February 2009 a Society was established under the

care of the Western Presbytery. Nearly three hundred attended this meeting in the

Enniskillen Agricultural College. Rev. Robert Robb was commissioned on this occasion and an Interim Session was appointed consisting of Graham Fallows, Neville Kerr and Rev. Stephen Wright. Public worship commenced on Sabbath 1 March 2009.

Outreach in Enniskillen

The Society meets at the Clinton Centre in Belmore Street, Enniskillen and a manse at 43 Meadow Farm, Tempo Road , Enniskillen was purchased for £200,000 through a loan from the Mission Committee.

Sabbath Meeting

COVENANT FELLOWSHIP, GALWAY

In 1848 the members of the Missionary Board of the Church were moved by the plight of the inhabitants of the west of Ireland who were suffering from the consequences of the Great Famine. In the spring of 1850 Andrew Tait, a licentiate of the Western Presbytery, was sent to Connaught to investigate the possibilities of missionary work. His report to the Synod was so positive that the Church committed itself to further outreach. There was a setback when Mr. Tait left the Church and joined the General Assembly. However, in 1855 Rev. William Russell, minister of Ballyclare, undertook to preach in Connaught for six months. Whilst there, he engaged the services of a Catechist, Mr. Patrick McTighe, a converted Roman Catholic and Irish language speaker. This was approved by Synod and Mr. Russell was asked to visit Connaught again for the month of August 1856. From 1856 to 1869 the Church was involved in mission work in Cong, twenty-five miles north of the city of Galway.

A member of Knockbracken congregation undertook to pay for the costs, for a year, of one minister, from each Presbytery, making a monthly visit to Connaught. Despite good relations with the people of Cong, the work in the West of Ireland eventually stalled and the attention of the Missionary Board became focussed along colportage lines, and directed at the more populous centres such as Dublin, Cork and Newry.

In the city of Galway itself, there was at least one Reformed Presbyterian living there because, in 1859, Rev. W. S. Ferguson of Grange visited the city and was directed to "different persons and houses known to a lady, a member of the Reformed Presbyterian Church, who resided there and carried out an extensive service of personal evangelism on her own." In the same year, Rev. James Smyth, minister of Drimbolg, preached in the city.

Mr. Smyth's great-great-grandson, was James Anderson and, in October 1966, he and his wife Eileen, after prayerful consideration, moved to Galway. Mr. Anderson had been accepted for the Irish Mission on 6 September 1963 and after training at the Bible Training Institute in Glasgow, went in 1965 to work with Tom Beck in Dublin. The Andersons laboured alone in Galway until Bob Henninger, from the Reformed Presbyterian Church of North America, joined them as a co-worker for three years in 1979. The C.Y.P.U. campaigns committee sent teams to Galway each summer from 1973.

Early outreach in Galway

By 1984 Mr. Anderson had established a Sabbath morning worship service and evening Bible study and the Irish Mission Board judged that God was opening a door for further outreach in the area. The Board called Rev. Trevor McCauley, minister of Dervock, to take on leadership of the work in Galway. Mr. McCauley accepted the call to be a mission worker and was commissioned on 14 November 1984 at Trinity R. P. Church. A house at 47 Ardaluin Road, in the Newcastle area of Galway, was purchased. This property had had an extended former garage which was adapted to a meeting place that could accommodate forty people.

In 1985 the group, which the Andersons had gathered, was called the Covenant Fellowship (Reformed Presbyterian Church) Galway. The new team saw a steady growth in numbers attending during 1985, from an average Sabbath morning attendance of 10 in January to 17 by September. The Fellowship petitioned the Western Presbytery for recognition as a Preaching Station (Covenanting Society) and this was duly granted in September.

In April 1987, after twenty years in Galway, Mr. and Mrs. Anderson indicated their wish to work with the Irish Mission board in the North in a congregational setting. Their vision, courage and dedication had laid important foundations for the Covenanting witness in Galway. On 28 August they moved to Belfast and Mr Anderson combined study at the Reformed Theological College with work with four congregations in the Eastern Presbytery. From September 1989 until his retirement in December 1999 he worked with perseverance, under the direction of the U.K. Section of the Mission Committee, in the Markets, Short Strand and Finaghy areas of Belfast.

On 27 November 1989 the Mission Committee issued a call to Raymond Blair, a member of Convoy and a licentiate of the Western Presbytery. Having accepted the call, Mr. Blair was ordained to the Gospel ministry and commissioned for work in the Republic of Ireland on 13 February 1990.

The work was further strengthened when Mr. Billy Hamilton accepted the call of the Mission Committee at a meeting on 12 June 1990 in the Trinity congregation, where he had been a member for the previous nine years. Having completed a one-year course at the Reformed Theological College, his service of commissioning took place at Trinity on 23 May 1991.

The work in Galway lost one of its most gifted and conscientious workers when Rev. Trevor McCauley died, after a short illness of several weeks, on 8 November 1991. It was most evident that his gifts and calling were to preach the Gospel and teach God's Word, but he was also remembered by those in Galway as one who took the time and interest to get to know the whole person.

Rev. Trevor McCauley

The work in Galway took an important step forward on 31 October 2004 when it was organised into a Society, with 24 adults and 10 children on the roll of membership. Robert Steele (Faughan) and Stephen Davis (Bready) were appointed Interim Elders. Synod granted permission for the Society to elect its own elders and on 22 October 2006 Frank McMurray and Billy Hamilton were ordained as ruling elders. During 2007-2008, Andrew Blackburn, a member of the Stranorlar congregation, gave valuable service in the bookshop, in door-to-door work and one-to-one Bible studies. His role in Galway was much appreciated by both the Felowship and the Irish Section of the Mission Committee.

The Covenant Fellowship meets at Galway Bridge Centre, St. Mary's Road, Galway.

9 Kenley Road Cork

CORK

In October 1931, Mr Thomas McKee, brought up in the Rathfriland congregation, was appointed to the work of the Irish Mission. After work in Newry and Dublin, Mr. McKee settled in Douglas, a suburb of Cork in 1937 and in 1940 married Dorothy, whom he met in Dublin. Mr. and Mrs. McKee gave themselves, with diligence and faithfulness, to the task of spreading the Gospel by distributing Scriptures, holding open air meetings and conducting hospital visitation.

At the 1956 Synod, Mr. McKee asked for a student to come to Cork to help with summer mission in beach and door to door work. The C.Y.P.U. Executive took up the challenge. Mr. Harold McCune drove executive members round the societies appealing for volunteers for a three week mission in July 1957 and some twenty people responded. Thereafter, Mr. Harry Tadley, the Church's evangelist, organised teams of volunteers to go to Cork for evangelistic work each summer. These continued until 1978. The retirement of Mr. and Mrs. McKee in 1977 did not end their evangelistic work, continuing to serve the Lord in the city of Cork which they had made their home.

The Covenanting witness in Cork received further impetus when Rev. Andrew Cross Gregg, minister of Ballylane and Ballenon since 1966, resigned from this joint charge on 5 February 1974 to enable him to devote his gifts to the work of the Irish Mission in Cork. His preaching, pastoral work, evangelistic endeavours helped to build up the Cork fellowship to the point when, on 13 February 1982, it was recognised as a congregation of the Western Presbytery. At a special meeting of the Western Presbytery, held in the meeting house in 9 Kenley Road, Mr. Gregg was appointed Interim Moderator, with Rev. John Hawthorne, Secretary of the Irish Mission Board and then Moderator of the Western Presbytery, and Mr. David J. Porter as Interim Elders. The first meeting of the new congregation for Sabbath worship was on the following day when there were 20 persons present and ten adults were received into membership in a moving and solemn service. On 10 March 1982, Ivan McMahon was ordained as an elder in the congregation.

Rev. Drew and Mrs. Caroline Gregg,, Jonathan, Timothy and Ruth.

During 1984-5 David Fallows took a year out of his university course and spent 8 months working in a voluntary capacity, assisting Rev. Drew Gregg. His support was greatly appreciated.

In 1986 Mr. Gregg accepted a call to Milford and was installed on 4 July. The Irish Mission Board had hoped to continue the work, believing that the nucleus of believers there formed a basis for growth.

Some of the Cork congregation 1984

However during 1987, due to the movement of members from Cork, the congregation was dissolved. After much thought and prayer, the Board decided, given these circumstances, together with the sense of isolation workers had felt in Cork, and the current lack of workers, that it would be best to withdraw from the city and sell the manse.

The Friday evening Club

THE PRESBYTERY OF NEW BRUNSWICK AND NOVA SCOTIA

The old 'Covenanter Church' Grand Pre, Nova Scotia

The Synod in 1820 decided to hear the claims of places abroad where Reformed Presbyterians had settled. In 1822 the Northern Presbytery licensed James Warnock and furnished him with credentials when he intimated his intention of emigrating to New Brunswick. His venture was of a private nature and he received no support from the Church at home. The British North American Colonies drew immigrants from Ulster and some Reformed Presbyterians settled in the Maritime Provinces of New Brunswick and Nova Scotia. Work there, under the direction of the Missionary Society of the Synod of the Irish Church, commenced in 1827. On 24 May of that year, Rev. Alexander Clarke who was born near Kilrea in 1793, was licensed and ordained in Ireland. He later sailed for St. John, New Brunswick, where he arrived on 23 August. His going was the direct result of a request from the Covenanters in New Brunswick and Nova Scotia that an ordained minister be sent to them, or that a young man be

Rev. Alexander Clarke

ordained specifically for the purpose of the mission there. After some exploration he selected Amherst, Nova Scotia, as the centre of his operations. Travelling extensively through the Maritime Provinces he established some fifteen mission stations. Three Reformed Presbyterian communities were formed by the Irish Synod in the Maritimes. They were located in the St. John River Valley of New Brunswick, the Annapolis Valley of Nova Scotia and the Chignecto Isthmus that links the 2 provinces.

Rev. William Sommerville, a member of Rathfriland, was born in Aughnavalog, near Ballyroney, County Down on 1 July 1800, educated at the University of Glasgow, and after taking his theology in Scotland under Dr. Andrew Symington, was licensed to preach in 1826. In 1831 he was sent as a missionary to New Brunswick, and in 1833, in response to urgent calls, he came to Grand Pre in Horton township, Nova Scotia. The Covenanter meeting house at Grand Pre had been built in 1804 during the ministry of Rev. George Gilmore, a Presbyterian who ministered in Ireland before coming to Grand Pre. The church was given the name 'The Covenanter' during the tenure of Mr. Sommerville who guided the congregation to follow Covenanter principles.

In 1835 he was called to the township of Cornwallis in the beautiful and fertile Cornwallis valley in Nova Scotia for part of his time, and from that date until his death in 1878, he was pastor of the Covenanter congregations of Horton and Cornwallis, living in Horton until 1845, in Woodside until 1856 and in Somerset from that time until his death in 1878.

Shortly after 1835 Mr. Clarke and he constituted the Reformed Presbytery of New Brunswick and Nova Scotia. While the Irish Synod felt that their doing so was premature, it nonetheless sustained their action.

Rev. Alexander McLeod Stavely, the son of Rev. Dr. W. J. Stavely, (Kilraughts), born in Corkey, County Antrim on 19 June 1816, studied theology for two sessions under Dr.

Thomas Chalmers, the remaining course in the Seminary of Paisley, Scotland, and was licensed by the Northern Presbytery, Ireland, 16 March 1839. In 1841 he was ordained on 12 May, as a missionary to St. John, New Brunswick. Arriving there in August of the same year, he took charge of the congregation in St. John, where a comfortable house of worship had been erected a short time previously. He laboured there and among the adjacent societies for 38 years. On 16 June, 1879, he resigned his charge and returned to his native land, where some years later he became the minister of the united congregation of Ballyclare and Larne. During his ministry in St. John the congregation had the misfortune to lose their church and manse, which were destroyed in the disastrous fire of 1877, but later a new building was erected in a more central position in the town.

Rev. A. McL. Stavely, from a portrait in his family's possession in Canada

In 1842 some differences of opinion between Mr. Clarke and Mr. Sommerville were reported over Mr. Clarke's exercise of the electoral franchise. Efforts were made to have the difficulties resolved, but without success. As a consequence, the Presbytery ceased to function for a time. The Synod having given instructions that it be resuscitated, this was done by Mr. Sommerville and Mr. Stavely, as Mr. Clarke did not accede to the terms of reunion laid down by Synod. Mr. Clarke desired the liberty and the privileges of citizenship in Nova Scotia. He and all the congregations he represented became identified with the New School branch of the Covenanter Church, and in October 1847 withdrew from the oversight of the Irish Synod. Their new association brought him fresh help in the form of men from this wider body in North America, four of whom, Henry Gordon, William Stavely Darragh, Andrew R. Gailey and Alexander Robinson, were Irish born. Approximately 20 small Covenanter congregations were established in the Chignecto isthmus, near Amherst between 1828 and 1905, mostly rural based. Congregations could be found in places like Amherst, Chapman's Settlement, Northport, River Hebert and Linden in Nova Scotia and Jolicure, Sackville and Port Elgin in New Brunswick. Rev. Alexander Clarke, was unquestionably the ruler until his death in 1874. These

Covenanters were a small group, numbering perhaps 1500. In about seventy-five years these Covenanters went from Reformed Presbyterianism to mainstream Presbyterianism by 1905. Indeed, many of those became United Churchmen in 1925.

Another missionary, Rev. James Reid Lawson, who grew up in the Rathfriland congregation, was licensed by the Southern Presbytery on 4 March 1845 and ordained on 18 September, as a missionary to the British North American provinces. He reached St. John, New Brunswick the same autumn and settled in the spring of 1846 in South Stream, New Brunswick, which later became known as Barnesville. Ten years later he received a call from the Covenanter congregation in Boston, Massachusetts and felt led to resign his charge in Barnesville. After a year's ministry in Boston he returned to Barnesville where he continued to labour until ill health caused his resignation in 1882. In 1884 Presbytery published his discourse, 'The British elective franchise, or, Why Reformed Presbyterians do not vote at political elections'.

Mr. Alexander Charles Stewart born near Londonderry into a family belonging to the Secession Church, having studied theology under Dr. Thomas McCrie in Edinburgh, came to New Brunswick in 1847 and became connected to the Covenanter Church. Recognised as a theological student he was licensed by the Presbytery of New Brunswick and Nova Scotia, and laboured in the Campbell and Millstream settlements for 3 years before moving to the United States. Mr. Robert Stewart from Ballynaloob, County Antrim, who was licensed by the Northern Presbytery in February 1847, served for a time in the Mission of Connaught in the west of Ireland, having obtained the London prize for proficiency in the Gaelic tongue. He was ordained in Ireland in 1849 as a missionary to British North America. He laboured mainly in the district of Wilmot, for over thirty years, preaching also in Margaretville and Lawrencetown. He passed away in Farmington, Annapolis County, New Brunswick in October 1899.

The work in British North America went on with varying success. The few men available did their best to supply the needs of the widely scattered localities in which they found those sympathetic to their message. But added difficulties arose. Because of the Fenian agitation it became harder to maintain the Covenanting principles. The Irish population in America had greatly increased as a result of the great famine of 1846-47. The first

Fenian organisation (an organisation for the overthrow of British rule in Ireland was formed in America in 1858). On top of the Fenian agitation came the question of Confederation, the four colonies of New Brunswick, Nova Scotia and Upper and Lower Canada being formed into the Dominion of Canada in 1867. As a result of these political changes and tax increases, emigration from British North America to the United States became much more evident than it had been. Many of the stations of the Church suffered in this way, especially the groups located in Nova Scotia.

Mr. Robert McGowan Sommerville, son of Rev. William Sommerville, was born in Grand Pre, Nova Scotia in 1837, graduated from Queen's University Belfast in 1860 and also the Theological Hall, Belfast. He was licensed by the Eastern Presbytery on 3 January 1861 and, on declining a call from the congregation of Ballyclabber, he returned to Nova Scotia. Having been ordained by the Presbytery of New Brunswick and Nova Scotia on 16 October of the same year, Mr. Sommerville was installed co-pastor with his father of the congregations of Horton and Cornwallis. He was released from Cornwallis the next year, and soon afterwards built a church at Wolfville, preaching there and in Horton for some years. In 1872 he withdrew from the pastoral oversight of Horton upon his appointment to the office of Inspector of Schools for King's County, N.S., though his people still continued for a time to enjoy the benefit of his Sabbath ministrations. The next year he accepted a call from the Cincinnati, Ohio, congregation in the United States, and later became pastor of the Second New York congregation.

Cornwallis Meeting House

On his leaving Horton, his father, who had commenced the work there many years previously as an outstation, took over the charge of the Horton congregation in addition to that of Cornwallis, though they were 24 miles apart. This was no easy task for a man who by then had been over forty years in the mission field.

It was about this time that a call went out for at least one additional labourer, as there were two most promising stations in New Brunswick - Queensville and Littleton. Each place had a comfortable house of worship. No other Presbyterian congregation of any name was in the immediate neighbourhood of either. Large congregations were present whenever the missionaries were able to visit there, but it was impossible for the missionaries to give the stations the amount of attention and service which they desired and deserved.

Giving some idea of the hardships suffered by some of the mission stations through lack of preachers, Mr. Stavely on one occasion reported that the congregation at Littleton had not been visited by a minister from the time he conducted a Communion Service in the autumn till he returned six months later. Naturally the want of public ministrations for such a lengthened period would be sadly felt by any congregation, retarding its prosperity as well as the progress of spiritual life in the hearts of the members. Littleton was 138 miles from St. John, the nearest congregation. Bearing this in mind and also the difficulties of winter travelling, the few ministers available and the calls upon them elsewhere, it is not surprising that more could not be done for Littleton. Nor, since Littleton was not alone in this respect, is it at all surprising that the Clerk of Presbytery appealed to Synod: "We are really distressed for want of help. Promising stations are slipping out of our hands because we cannot attend to them. Other denominations are likely to enter into our labours. Is it impossible for you to do anything for us? We again renew our formal and most earnest appeal for help."

Because of the fruitless calls made on the Irish Church for additional labourers and the greater strength of the Covenanter Church in the United States of America, from whom the need for men might be met, a move was originated to change the Synodical relationship of the Presbytery of New Brunswick and Nova Scotia from the Church in Ireland to that in the United States. The Commission of Synod, with whom Rev. A. M. Stavely discussed the matter, when visiting Ireland in 1872, was quite sympathetic and had no desire to hinder the change when the Presbytery itself felt that such a change should take place. Presbytery was not yet decided as to the advisability of taking such a step. The matter was kept under consideration for a number of years, but was eventually abandoned in 1877, mainly because of financial difficulties. According to the Sustentation Scheme of the American Church, each aid-receiving congregation had to contribute to the scheme an amount per member which the congregations in the Presbytery felt they could not pay.

Rev. William Sommerville was laid aside by ill health in 1871, with little prospect of his ever taking up work again, as he was now an old man. An appeal was made to the American Church for someone to come and supply his pulpit. Mr. W. J. Sproull, a licentiate, responded to the appeal and was appointed, and proved so acceptable that later on a unanimous call was made out in his favour in 1878. But before that took place, Rev. William Sommerville had passed away. He was the pioneer missionary to the British provinces; his bodily vigour and mental endowments fitted him particularly for missionary work. His abilities were those of a powerful evangelical preacher and a

resolute defender of Scriptural doctrine. He met and measured spiritual weapons with all opponents of different denominations as a gifted controversialist. For a period of 47 years he was faithful to the Church he represented, to the interests of souls, and to the Master he loved to serve.

Rev. William Sommerville's grave Cornwallis

Increasing age and fatigue in the missionary work caused anxiety among the Presbytery about the future of ministerial supplies. As a consequence of this and also in view of the fact that the Church in Ireland at this time was unable to fill its own vacancies, interest in the matter of changing the Synodical relationship of the Presbytery was revived. It was only natural that the feeling began to grow both in Ireland and in North America that, if the Church in the Colonies were to prosper, it would have to be under the care and oversight of the Synod of the American Church. The fact that the American Church was now assisting with supplies encouraged this idea still more.

Mr. T. A. H. Wylie, a licentiate of that Church, came and rendered service, mainly to the St. John congregation. This permitted Mr. Stavely, who was anxious to give place to someone else, to devote himself to carrying on negotiations with the American Synod about the transfer of the Presbytery to that Synod. The Irish Synod formally expressed to the American Synod its consent and desire that the transfer should be carried out. The brethren of the Presbytery formally memorialised the American Synod at New York, Mr. Stavely supporting the memorial by his presence. The New Brunswick and Nova Scotia Presbytery transferred to the American Synod, 2 June 1879, including all congregations in Maine, New Brunswick and Nova Scotia.

The rule about the contributions to the Sustentation Scheme of the American Synod still caused some difficulty, but the difficulty was overcome by the Commission of the Irish Synod agreeing that, in the case of a congregation or station being unable to raise the amount required, the Irish Church should, for a time at least, continue to supplement the offerings of the people so as to qualify the congregations for the aid from the American Church.

The union between the Presbytery of New Brunswick and Nova Scotia and the Synod of the Reformed Presbyterian Church of North America occurred at the meeting of the American Synod in 1879. The Presbytery was most cordially taken under the care and jurisdiction of that Synod. Immediately upon the reception of the Presbytery by the Synod there was the appointment of two licentiates to labour in the bounds of the Presbytery for the coming year. Three separate congregations, within a year or two, each obtained an ordained minister. For some years the Irish Church continued to give financial assistance and kept in sympathetic touch with the field with which it had had connections for so long.

From 1835 to 1929 the congregation at Cornwallis had only 2 ministers whose ministries lasted 93 years. The first pastor, Dr. William Sommerville, had been pastor at Grand Pre for two years when he was called to become the pastor at Cornwallis as well. From that time until his death in 1878 Dr. Sommerville preached in this church. Rev. W. J. Sproull was then given a unanimous call but he declined. In 1880, the second pastor, Dr. Thomas McFall who was born near Dervock, and was trained in the Reformed Presbyterian Seminary of Allegheny, now Pittsburgh, Pennsylvania, was called and in 1881 was ordained and installed pastor. He continued as pastor until his death in 1929.

Regarding the provision of students for the ministry, the Presbytery was not very successful. When William Sommerville was minister at the Cornwallis Covenanter community, from the 1830s to the 1870s, he joined with fellow ministers (Robert Stewart in Wilmot, Alexander Stavely in Saint John and James Reid Lawson in Barnesville) in demanding the Irish Synod to send out more missionaries. In addition, there was hope that native Nova Scotians and New Brunswickers might come forward as ministers. As Lawson wrote, "I do hope that the time will come, when the mission here will be self-sustaining, not only in money, but also in men. May the Lord hasten it in his time! "

Mr. Alexander Charles Stewart, previously mentioned, who had come to New Brunswick from Ireland in 1847, was recognised as a theological student, having studied in the Secession Church. He was licensed by the Presbytery of New Brunswick and Nova Scotia, and laboured in the Campbell and Millstream settlements for 3 years before moving to the United States.

In the 1850s, this hope of new students seemed particularly lively. No less than four young men, apparently all from King's County, Nova Scotia came forward and appeared before the Reformed Presbytery of N.B. and N.S., initially to ask to be accepted as a student. Two of whom began studies but never progressed to licensure. The other two students were John Burgess Calkin (1829-1918) and Robert McGowan Sommerville (1837-1920). Calkin appeared but twice before the Presbytery, 20 October 1851 and 8 June 1852. From other sources, it is known that, as a young man he was a pupil at Sommerville's grammar school and at the school became a Covenanter. It was later clear that he was interested in the ministry, although also interested in teaching. After studying theology with Mr. Sommerville as a mature student, he spent a winter at the Free College in Halifax, working to become a Covenanter minister. Calkin married Martha, the daughter of William Sommerville. At some point, Calkin disagreed with Covenanter principles, voting in an election. He left the Covenanter denomination, joining the Presbyterian Church. As his interest in an educational career waxed, his enthusiasm for ministry waned. Calkin taught school, then went as a teacher at the Normal School in Truro, finally named as principal. An eminent scholar and teacher, he died in Truro in 1918. Robert Sommerville appeared at Presbytery on 20 October 1851, being only 14 or 15 years of age and was accepted as a student. He had undoubtedly been a pupil in his father's grammar school. In his mid-teens, Robert was sent to Ireland, where he continued both academic and theological studies. He did not again come to the Presbytery until 13 September 1859. Two years later, on 16 October 1861, he was ordained in Cornwallis, as co-pastor and successor to his father of the joint congregation of Cornwallis and Horton. In 1865 he married Elizabeth Chipman. But after 12 years, in 1873, the couple left Canada and ministered in the R.P. congregation of Cincinnati, Ohio and later Second New York congregation, where he died in 1920.

Wolfville Reformed Presbyterian Meeting House, being moved to Main St. 1885

The Covenanter congregations of the Maritimes had either joined other denominations or had ceased to exist by the early 1960s, being supplied by summer pastorates from the

American Church. It is interesting that in August 1971 Rev. Renwick Wright of Beaver Falls, Pennsylvania and formerly of Dromara, Co. Down, took part in a commemorative service in the old Grafton meeting house, where the Cornwallis congregation had met. It is also of interest that the Irish link with the Maritime churches continued as Mr. John Teaz who was born near Londonderry in 1849, graduated in theology from the Allegheny Seminary. On being licensed by the Pittsburgh Presbytery, April 1881 with a preference for missionary work, he spent four years labouring   principally under the direction of the Central Board of Missions in the Maritime Provinces and in Western Canada.

The Presbytery under the Irish Synod included the congregations of Barnesville, Jemseg, Millstream Shemoge (Chimoquee) and St. John, New Brunswick and Amherst, Cornwallis, Goose River, Horton, River Herbert, Wilmot and Wolfville, Nova Scotia and Houlton, Maine.   There were also other mission stations accepted under the care of Presbytery. Today there are 5 Reformed Presbyterian congregations in Canada in connection with the Reformed Presbyterian Church of North America, being in the provinces of Ontario and Quebec, this area having been a mission field of the Scottish R. P. Synod.

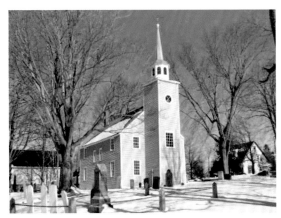

The 'Covenenter Church' Grand Pre.

Adapted and updated from, 'A Brief History of Colonial Mission Work in Canada and Australia', Rev. Hugh Wright. Published by 'The Australian Mission Board of the Irish and Scottish Reformed Presbyterian Churches', 1958

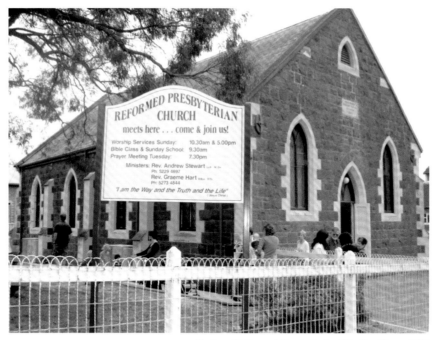

Geelong Reformed Presbyterian Meeting House 2009

THE PRESBYTERY OF AUSTRALIA

From the early 1840s the Reformed Presbyterian Church of Scotland had sent missionaries to New Zealand, which became a staging post for the well-known later work in the New Hebrides. As emigration to Australia grew apace, this included Covenanters from both the Scottish and Irish Churches. As the Irish Synod had heard requests from the Maritime Provinces, there was also a concern for the spiritual welfare in this new colony.

It was not until the year 1853 that the Irish Church decided to consider the needs in the southern hemisphere. At a special meeting of Synod at Dervock, held in connection with Covenant Renovation, Rev. J. A. Smith, minister of Drimbolg, instigated the concern for the spread of the Gospel and the promulgation of a Covenanted testimony in Australia. The matter was referred to the Missionary Board, but it was not until 1857 that Mr. Alexander McElwaine Moore, expressed his willingness to go. He was born at Ballyblack near Newtownards in November 1820. Having been a school teacher in Ulster and in Scotland, he later studied and graduated from Glasgow University in 1852. Following his graduation from the Theological Hall of the Reformed Presbyterian Church of Scotland he was licensed by the Eastern Presbytery in 1856. Mr. Moore was described in *The Covenanter* as, "an able preacher, a superior scholar, a man of manly independent mind, and one who has given evidence of extensive acquaintance with, and cordial attachment to, the principles of the Covenanted Reformation". Ordained in August 1857 in the College Street South church, Mr. Moore along with his wife sailed for Australia in September, arriving in Melbourne after a favourable voyage of 84 days.

In Melbourne they were cordially welcomed by Covenanter families. Mr. Moore quickly sought out those whose names had been given to him before leaving. He moved to the town of Geelong 50 miles from Melbourne, where he knew he would find greater support and there he was welcomed by those who had sought assistance from the Scottish Church. After his arrival in Geelong he began preaching, advertising meetings in the press. They met first, as a small congregation, at the house of Mr. John Wright and later in the Free Church meeting house. Discussions were held with interested friends as to the best means of establishing a congregation and securing a place for public worship. The use of a large classroom in the Free Church school was readily granted for this purpose and later a public hall was rented by the congregation as the average attendance at this time was from 50 to 60 worshippers. By 1858 a number of persons were admitted into membership and in June the first congregational meeting in connection with the Reformed Presbyterian Church in Australia was held. A committee was elected, elders were later chosen and on the first Sabbath of December, the sacrament of the Lord's Supper was dispensed for the first time in Geelong with 36 communicants at the Lord's Table. Mr. Moore sought to visit those Reformed Presbyterians who were engaged in farming, scattered through a vast area of the 'Bush'. Travel was difficult, with him staying at farmhouses and holding services for any who would come. These early journeys took him into many parts of rural Victoria where there were groups of Covenanters living in remote locations.

Rev. A. M. Moore

By March 1859, with a membership of 45 communicants, and Sabbath attendances from 70 to 120, the congregation took steps towards erecting a suitable meeting house of their own. The project was completed and the present building opened on 10 August 1862, the service being conducted by the noted Rev. John G. Paton, who had been sent by the Scottish Church as a missionary to the New Hebrides. The manse was completed in 1869.

Initial results were encouraging for a time. However, migration was continually taking place, office-bearers and members moving to new places and finding it difficult to keep in touch with the work in Geelong. There were opportunities for church extension but many were lost to the cause because of lack of ministers. One group at Yackandandah in the Victorian high country, built a place for worship, but it was a further two years before a minister made it to this community. The initial call from Synod had been for two workers for Australia. Rev. John Bates, who had been brought up in the Bready congregation, had been licensed by the Glasgow Presbytery of the Reformed Presbyterian Church of Scotland and he expressed his desire to serve overseas, due partly to his poor health. Arriving in Melbourne in April 1858, he served briefly at Geelong but, when in August he had travelled to Sydney to consult a doctor, he died suddenly at the railway station.

The call from Australia was as urgent as that of North America, but was largely unsuccessful. Unfortunately, Covenanter families were lost to the communion through a want of

ministerial supplies. Mr. Moore had to take up teaching, presumably to assist his financial state and by 1880 wrote expressing the burden of carrying the work alone. His plea was for "fresh labourers into this dry and parched land". The report, that came from the Colonial Mission Committee to Synod that year, made it clear that for 22 years Mr. Moore had been labouring alone and the Church had been unable to fulfil their expectations.

A theological student Mr. Kerr, who because of poor health had been advised to go to Australia, petitioned his Presbytery to license him that he might be able to assist Mr. Moore. He died before plans could come to fruition. Further offers of help did not result in the addition of new workers for various reasons.

In the autumn of 1896, it was clear that Mr. Moore's health was failing. Being laid aside from pastoral duties the faithful and lonely worker died on 18 February 1897 after 39 years of service. In addition to his missionary and pastoral work he ran a school and was strongly opposed to the moves towards secular education. He supported the Chinese Evangelisation Society, lectured and wrote extensively on matters of theological controversy. However, the closing days of his ministry would have cheered him with the news that Rev. Archibald Holmes, minister of Creevagh and Fairview, had agreed to assist him for at least one year. The news of Mr. Moore's death was received on the day that Mr. Holmes sailed from Plymouth.

Mr. Holmes ministered in Geelong and conducted a midweek service in Melbourne which was encouraged by an attendance of 15-25. Further help was acquired when Mr. Walter McCarroll, a nephew of Rev. William McCarroll of Belfast, being a graduate of Geneva College and the R.P. Theological Seminary in Allegheny, answered the pleas for help by the American Church. It was agreed that he would complete his studies at the Theological Hall in Belfast and then was ordained by the Eastern Presbytery and designated to the work in Geelong in January 1899. He and his wife arrived there in April 1900 and laboured for four years before accepting at call to the RPCNA mission work in Cyprus.

In view of Mr. McCarroll's departure, a licentiate of the Eastern Presbytery, Mr. David Musgrave, had hoped to supply Geelong but was unable to do so because of ill health. Following this Rev. Albert Melville Thompson, who had been brought up in the American Church and who had responded to an earlier call for the supply of vacant Irish pulpits, on hearing of the need in Geelong offered his services and was accepted by Synod for a period of three years. This was extended by him to 5 years. Mr. and Mrs. Thompson gave themselves devotedly to the work from March 1904 until March 1909, when they returned to Ireland and he became minister of Stranorlar, returning to America in 1912.

At a meeting of Synod in 1909, Rev. Hugh Kennedy Mack, minister of Drimbolg, volunteered to go to Geelong. Arriving in October 1909, he laboured there for 37 years, only once visiting his homeland. Like Mr. Moore he laboured alone for the first 21 years of his ministry in Australia. He was noted as a man of sound wisdom, careful in his words and exerting a great influence for righteousness far beyond the bounds of his own congregation. He continued in his ministry until September 1946 and preached his farewell sermon in January 1947 after the arrival of his successor. Mr. Mack passed away on 1 November 1951 after 56 years of ordained ministry. He was active in the publication of booklets dealing with contemporary matters upholding the Reformed faith.

Rev. Hugh Kennedy Mack

To allow Mr. Mack the opportunity to visit home, Rev. William Reid McEwen was appointed by Synod to take charge of the work during Mr. Mack's absence and afterwards to continue as a second worker in Australia. Born in 1906, the son of Rev. John McEwen, he was ordained in September 1928 and, after one year of further study at the Reformed Presbyterian Theological Seminary in Pittsburgh, he continued his journey to Australia arriving in August 1929. For the first year he was engaged mainly in Geelong, giving Mr. Mack opportunities to visit and explore outlying districts for the possibility of extending the work. This work greatly encouraged many families isolated by distance, who had few opportunities to engage in public worship.

Rev. W. R. McEwen

On his one visit home, Mr. Mack travelled with his daughter through Ireland and North America in 1931 returning to Australia in April 1932. After this Mr. McEwen was enabled to begin the task of building up a second congregation which he commenced at McKinnon, a suburb of Melbourne. Mr. McEwen continued outreach work in Melbourne and also carried on this new work. A house was rented that served as a residence and meeting place for worship and the numbers attending soon increased. A church building was opened for public worship on 24

February 1940 and the manse was completed in 1949. The congregation was formally organised in 1946 under the jurisdiction of the Reformed Presbyterian Church of Ireland. Synod's work was carried out in Australia by a standing commission of the Eastern Presbytery, which had been set up in 1944.

Owing to Mr. Mack's poor health the Colonial Mission Committee took steps to send another missionary. Rev. Alexander Barkley, minister of Cregagh Road congregation, offered his services and was appointed to succeed Mr. Mack. Mr. and Mrs. Barkley and their family reached Melbourne in December 1946. In 1955 the Irish and Scottish churches formed the Colonial Mission Board by which they would co-operate in the work in Australia; however, the primary responsibility for financing the work remained with the Irish Synod. Close contact was also maintained with what was formerly the Free Church in Australia, now officially known as the Presbyterian Church of Eastern Australia. Following contact with ministers and members of the Dutch Reformed Church who worked among immigrants to Australia, there was a desire that young men be trained for the ministry in a Reformed theological college, which was then founded. Early classes were held in the Reformed Presbyterian premises at Geelong, Mr. Barkley being on the lecturing staff, teaching Church History and Hebrew. From December 1964, his duties became full time, being principal from 1958 to 1978. He died in Geelong aged 88 on 28 August 2000. Mr. McEwen also lectured for a time in Church History at Melbourne Bible Institute and at the John Knox Theological College of the Presbyterian Church of Eastern Australia. 'WR' as he was widely known, served the congregation of McKinnon until his retirement in September 1978. He and his wife had one child, now Rev. Alastair McEwen, who has taught full time in the Reformed Theological College in Geelong since 1982. Rev. W. R. McEwen passed away on 7 April 1989.

Rev. Alexander Barkley

The Australian Presbytery was organised on 9 October 1958 as a Presbytery of the Reformed Presbyterian Church of Ireland and on 12 June 1974, independence from

Ireland having been sought and obtained, the Presbytery of the Reformed Presbyterian Church of Australia was inaugurated.

There was, however, a continuing connection with the Irish Church. Rev. George McEwen, the minister of Glenmanus and a nephew of Rev. W. R. McEwen, resigned his charge in 1979 in order to be the stated supply in McKinnon, where he served for a period of five years.

Three other ministers served in Geelong from 1966 until 1996: Arthur Palmer, 1966-1969, Lynsey Blakston, 1972-1986, Anthony Power, 1986-1996. Rev. Andrew Stewart, minister of Glenmanus, accepted a call to the Geelong congregation in March 1998. A former member of Trinity congregation he had received his theological training at the Reformed Theological College and the Reformed Presbyterian Seminary in Pittsburgh.

The prospects of the Australian Reformed Presbyterian Church have fluctuated over the years. A congregation was established in Sunbury in 1981, but closed in 2006. Extension work took place in Frankston from 1977 until 1989 and recommenced in 2004. Rev. Alastair McEwen the minister of Frankston, received permission from Presbytery to teach Old Testament at the Reformed Theological College on one day per week in 1980 and in 1982 he resigned from the congregation to teach full-time at R.T.C.

In early 2007 a group from Frankston, including some previous members and their descendants, expressed an interest in re-starting the work there. An evening service began in October 2004. The Frankston group officially became members of the McKinnon congregation in 2005.

Rev. Edwin Blackwood from R.P.C.N.A., arrived with his wife and family in January 2006. He ministered in McKinnon in the morning and Frankston in the evening. Mr. Tony McKeeman, originally from Ballymoney, who lives in the Frankston area, was installed as an elder in McKinnon/Frankston congregation in 2006 having previously been ordained in Frankston in 1985. In 2008 Frankston became a separate congregation, currently pastored by Rev. Blackwood and Rev. Alastair McEwen is Interim Moderator in McKinnon.

The Geelong congregation, currently pastored by Rev. Andrew Stewart and Rev. Graeme Hart, is still growing, with a congregation of well over 100 comprised of many different ethnic groups.

Rev. Alistair McEwen at McKinnon Meeting House

Presently the Church owns a campsite at Dixon's Creek where family camps are held. The church is also seeking to re-establish the work in Melbourne. In 2006 the Church sent out its first overseas missionary, Miss Lara Nelson, to be a teacher in Yemen.

Geelong Meeting House is situated at 10 Fenwick Street, Geelong, Victoria.
McKinnon Meeting House is situated at 261 McKinnon Rd., McKinnon Victoria.
Frankston Congregation meet at Frankston Guides Hall, Delacombe Park, Overport Rd. Frankston South, Victoria.

Adapted and updated from,
'A Brief History of Colonial Mission Work in Canada and Australia', Rev. Hugh Wright. Published by 'The Australian Mission Board of the Irish and Scottish Reformed Presbyterian Churches' 1958.
 Thanks to Rev. Alistair McEwen for additional material.

REFORMED PRESBYTERIANS IN ENGLAND

Communionware used by Hall Lane Reformed Presbyterian Congregation, Liverpool

LIVERPOOL

The congregation in Liverpool owed its origin to Covenanters from Ulster and from Scotland who went to the city on business. A society was formed on 23 September, 1823, in the home of Mr. Thomas Coulter, a native of Donegal. Services were conducted at regular intervals by ministers sent over from Ireland.

Applications were received from Covenanters in the North of England for a supply of preaching. The Synod of 1827 gave consideration to an earlier resolution that:

> *"...the state of our religious connexions in England be recommended to the particular attention of the Missionary Society of the Reformed Presbyterian Church in Ireland".*

Rev. William Henry, minister of Newtownards congregation, read to the Synod a narrative of his experiences in Liverpool in 1823 and again in 1827, and pleaded with the Synod to give every possible help and encouragement to those 'solitary and exiled brethren'. He stated that a number of people in the city of Liverpool had not only professed themselves friendly to the Reformed Presbyterian cause, but had expressed a willingness to give their support to a minister, should the Church see fit to settle one there. It was not found possible to do this immediately, but ministers visited Liverpool and preached from time to time and maintained a connection with the Society.

In 1835, John Nevin, from Ballymoney, was ordained minister of a newly formed congregation in Liverpool. The salary paid by the congregation was £50, and this was augmented by a grant of £30 from the Board of Missions. For a time things moved forward smoothly, but in 1839 a severe setback was experienced when it was reported to Synod:

> "...that Mr. Nevin had left his charge in a manner inconsistent with ordination obligations".

The report further stated:

> "...that he acted injuriously to the congregation in forsaking his flock and preaching to another congregation in the same town".

Mr. Nevin was admonished for this breach of duty, following which the pastoral tie between him and the Liverpool congregation was dissolved. He emigrated to America in 1839.

For some years the work at Liverpool did not make much progress. Misunderstandings and divisions proved a handicap, and the Irish Church turned her attention to a more promising field in Manchester. The congregation had a meeting place in Hunter Street by 1852. Part of the congregation, however, became associated with the Eastern Reformed Presbyterian Synod in Ireland and appealed to them for supplies this proving difficult owing to their weakness. The dissenting group turned to the R. P. Church of Scotland for help having been taken under the care of the Presbytery of Glasgow, Rev. Dr. John Graham from Ayr being installed in 1856. From 1857 to 1861 worship was held at Hackin's Hey in the city centre and later at Hope Hull. In 1860 a new meeting house was built on Shaw Street, Everton. Dr. Graham led the majority of the congregation into the English Presbyterian Church in 1870.

After a long vacancy, the congregation of Liverpool showed signs of reviving and the remnant turned again to Ireland for assistance. The division that had lasted from 1840 until 1875 was healed, and the work enjoyed the ministry of five Irish ministers and two students for the next 70 years.

Their names and terms of service are as follows:

William John Maxwell, 1875-1886

Torrens Boyd, 1890-1892

Ezekiel Teaz, 1895-1921

Samuel Wallace Lynas, 1923-1925

William George Moffett Martin, 1930-1933

James Fitzgerald Crawford, 1936- 1940

Thomas William Ball, 1941-1942

Thomas Hutchins Semple, 1943-1945

The congregation in Liverpool reached its peak in the early years of the 20th century when there was a membership of about 100.

War conditions had made it impossible for the congregation to carry on and when the building was damaged in an air raid, the majority of the congregation left the district. The meeting house at Hall Lane, built in 1875, was sold to the Barbican Mission to the Jews.

REFORMED PRESBYTERIAN CHURCH MANCHESTER

MANCHESTER

In the period that work began in Liverpool, a Society of Covenanters was formed in Manchester. For some years the work at Liverpool did not make much progress. Misunderstandings and divisions proved a handicap, and the Irish Church turned her attention to a more promising field in this industrial centre. At first it was a small society formed by Reformed Presbyterians from Scotland and Ulster, but in 1841 its prospects were cordially commended to the favourable attention of Synod with a view to establishing a regular congregation. This was done in 1842, and Mr. Robert Johnston, a licentiate of the Northern Presbytery, was ordained at Cloughmills, Co. Antrim, for work in Manchester, on 3 August. Services were held in Manchester's Temperance Hall.

Mr. Johnson resigned in 1849 and emigrated to America. His successor, William Hanna, a member of Rathfriland, was ordained at Manchester in September 1855.

A church, erected at New Bridge Street, Strangeways, was opened on 20 June 1856. Mr. Hanna was later installed in Newtownards in July 1859 and died in September 1860. The last minister was John Newell, a native of Belfast. After a short pastorate in America he followed William Hanna, serving in Newtownards from 1861 to 1867, before going to Manchester for a ministry of four years. He returned to America in May 1871.

In 1872 the congregation became affiliated with the majority R.P. Synod of Scotland and, when it united with the Free Church of Scotland in 1876, the congregation passed outside the supervision of the R.P. Church.

Apart from a small Society in London that received assistance from the Irish Church following the Union of the majority of the Reformed Presbyterian Church of Scotland in 1876 with the United Free Church, the R.P. Church had no other centres of influence in England. There are now no Reformed Presbyterian congregations in England.

Victorian Ireland

THE IRISH MISSION

About 1830 the Reformed Presbyterian Church of Ireland formed a missionary board for the care of isolated groups and societies of Covenanters throughout Ireland and beyond. One of the first objects of their superintendence was the supply of a Dublin Society of Covenanters, having mostly come from Scotland. A society was also formed in Drogheda 1839, continuing for only a few years. It was not until 1846 that they undertook the work of disseminating the Scriptures among Roman Catholics in Ireland during a time of great Protestant witness throughout the island seeking to relieve both physical and spiritual misery during that time of famine and distress.

A special committee was appointed to form a mission to Roman Catholics and the aims of the mission were published in 1850 by the Synod, the purposes being 'to make known the glorious Gospel to a people sitting in the shadow of death'. Areas in the south and west of the country were to be visited by the workers who would consist of ministers and licentiates of the Church, Scripture readers and teachers and, if possible, those who could converse in the Irish language.

LEINSTER & CONNAUGHT

In early 1850 Mr. Andrew Tait, a licentiate of the Western Presbytery, was sent by the Irish Mission to Connaught to discover the prospects for mission work. He laboured hard but encountered only some success in his efforts to promulgate the Gospel. However, he later joined the Presbyterian Church. Accordingly an appeal was made for young men to offer themselves for training with a view to this work, but it was not until 1855 when Mr. Robert Allen, from the congregation of Grange, was ordained and appointed to work in Dublin. Ministering to the Society of Covenanters, he was also asked to undertake evangelistic work. He received assistance and encouragement from members of the Dublin Society and was diligent in visiting the streets and homes of the city, being able to converse with them regarding salvation. In

Rev. Robert Allen

1858 a suitable place of worship was procured situated at 11 Aungier Street. Synod arranged that the Society in Dublin be organised into a congregation, have elders ordained and taken under the care of the Southern Presbytery. On the second Sabbath of June 1859, the newly organised congregation met around the Lord's Table, there being 15 communicants. A report to Synod considered the new situation in Dublin. It was now constituted as a congregation but still recognised as an Irish Mission station, with Mr. Allen labouring in both capacities. Mr. Allen, in October 1859, offered his resignation from the specific missionary work under the Irish Mission; however, he continued as the minister from 1859 until his settlement in Newtownards in 1867.

Various attempts were made by the Irish Mission to secure a successor, but without success as there was a scarcity of students for the ministry at that time. In 1875 the Southern Presbytery reported to Synod: "It is questionable if any part of our Church has more consistent and steadfast adherence to her principles and usages as has been manifested in our little congregation in Dublin." The communicant membership stood at twenty. However, over the next few years, the numbers of members and adherents declined. In 1879 Synod regretfully decided not to maintain the work and the building was sold.

In County Mayo, Mr. Patrick McTighe, who had been brought up a Roman Catholic, was directed in his youth by a Scripture reader to God's Word, was converted and became an eager student of the Bible. The secretary of the missionary board, Rev. W. Russell, minister of Ballyclare, spent some months in Connaught and on meeting Mr. McTighe engaged him as a Scripture reader and set him to work in the surrounding districts. He was very diligent in his labours, being allowed an openness to read the Scriptures in many Roman Catholic homes.

In 1857, Rev. J. A. Chancellor, then minister of Bready, found a cordial reception in Irish

Mission stations in Mayo. He reported on the suitability of Mr. McTighe in his colportage work, although some members of the Church had doubts in employing one who was not formally a member of the Reformed Presbyterian Church. However, in 1858, he clearly expressed his adherence to Reformed principles. Later on his reporting to Synod, he was thoroughly endorsed. In 1858 two Scottish landowners in County Mayo made a generous offer to support the work of a missionary in their district who would be appoint-

Rev. J. A. Chancellor ed by the Reformed Presbyterian Church and agreeable to them. The commission felt that Mr. McTighe was best qualified and that Mr. George Lillie, a licentiate, would replace him in Cong, County Mayo. Amidst the tumult between Church of Ireland missionaries and revived Roman Catholicism the animosity made both their works very difficult. Mr. Lillie felt he had to resign, later becoming minister of Fairview. Mr. McTighe was then unable to take up this generous offer of support.

A member of Knockbracken offered his support to a programme involving ministers appointed to preach each for a stated time in Connaught. Those involved were Rev. James Smith of Drimbolg and Rev. W. S. Ferguson of Grange. They in turn preached throughout the district in 1859. However, they found the work difficult during that time of political and social tension.

By 1863 there was a plea for more ministerial help and the possibility of the mission school being established was recommended. Professor J. Dick along with the secretary of the Irish Mission found more favourable circumstances in Connaught when they visited in the company of Mr. McTighe in March 1864. During this visit they had the opportunity of visiting Sir William Wylde near Cong, who was in sympathy with the commission's desire to begin a scriptural school and he placed at their disposal a school already on his property. Sabbath services were begun with a nucleus of families and children, and both a Sabbath school and daily scriptural school were established. These were to be placed under the direction of the commission and to be funded by it. By 1865 there were 27 children on the role, 4 Protestants and 23 Roman Catholics. Mr. McTighe was involved in teaching the Scriptures at a school and the work continued until August 1868 when pressure from the Roman Catholic hierarchy reduced drastically the number of pupils. Mr. McTighe continued to labour faithfully through times of great opposition and social upheaval, and his death on 4th February 1869 after 13 years of labour was a major blow to the mission work of the Reformed Presbyterian Church in this province. His appointed replacement remained for only six weeks.

DUBLIN & NEWRY

The Synod of 1870 decided that Dublin should be the main centre of its missionary work in Ireland. But during that period from 1872-1879 the work of the Irish Mission was in abeyance, and a minister could not be settled in Dublin. The Southern Presbytery continued to provide the small and dwindling congregation in Dublin with Gospel ordinances. However, no definite mission work was undertaken. The congregation was anxious that this should be done. It was found that support for the distinctive testimony in Dublin was no longer sustainable and assistance was withdrawn in 1879. The meeting house was sold.

There was a desire to renew the work of the Irish Mission in 1893, stirred by a memorial to Synod from the session in Stranorlar, to bring the Gospel to the Roman Catholic population of Ireland. Rev. R. A. McFarlane was appointed convener and they identified a colporteur already working in Connaught under the authority of the General Assembly of the Presbyterian Church, whom they could support. In 1894 Mr. Joseph Martin, a member of Dublin Road, agreed to be engaged as a colporteur under the Mission. He was appointed to work in Newry under Rev. A. S. Lyons. Later he was succeeded in 1904 by Mr. David McCullough. In June 1899, Mr. Thomas Adams of the Newry congregation began work in Dublin and continued there until July 1929. He served during times of great upheaval and violence in Irish society. For over 30 years his diligence was rewarded with opportunities to work among some of the poorest of the city. In 1907 he was joined by Mr. James Stewart of Drimbolg and during the War they availed themselves of the opportunity to minister to soldiers stationed in Dublin. Mr. Stewart retired in 1926 and was succeeded by a member of Ballylane, Mr. Hugh William Stewart, who began in Dublin and then continued in Newry for 37 years until his retirement in September 1963.

Attempts were made to revive the regularity of Sabbath worship in the city of Dublin and in December 1907, after a lapse of almost 30 years the Lord's Supper was observed by Covenanters in Dublin. This was continued generally once a year until 1920.

Mr. Thomas Beck

The faithful colportage work in Dublin continued through the appointment in October 1928, of Mr. Thomas J. Beck a member of Dromara, who commenced work the following April. Mr. Adams was removed to Belfast where even though in failing health continued to work until a few weeks before his death in 1931. Mr. Beck was, for 15 years, from 1950-1965, the superintendent of the Y.M.C.A. Hostel in Lower Rathmines Road and he carried on an effective work among the youth. In latter years many of the poor of the city were gathered by him under the sound of the Gospel in the Brunswick Hall on Pearce Street. A man of unique gifts he contacted and distributed Scripture portions and tracts to thousands during his missionary work. Mr. Thomas McKee, from the Rathfriland congregation, began working with Mr. Stewart in Newry and in July 1932 moved to Dublin, working in conjunction with Mr. Beck for 5 years, after which he began the work of mission in Cork. In 1956, Mr. Samuel K. Cromie, an elder in Rathfriland was accepted for mission work and after some study was set aside for this purpose in 1958, labouring for a time in Dublin with Mr. Beck. Mr. Cromie was greatly involved in evangelism through a bookstall in O'Connell Street on 2 evenings each week. Having worked in other southern counties, he resigned at the end of 1961, when he and his wife were appointed to the new overseas mission in Ethiopia. The Irish Mission work in Dublin was encouraged by the commissioning as a colporteur in August 1962 of Mr. Joseph Kerr, a member of Dervock. He commenced his work in the city in September. The Mission committee had made proposals regarding County Donegal, where Mr. Kerr took up an appointment in 1965, which brought him and his family into a close association with the Milford congregation. He resigned from the work of the Irish Mission in October 1974. But the Dublin work was not neglected as Mr. James Anderson, a member of Drimbolg, after 2 years of training joined Mr. Beck in August 1965. In 1967 after prayerful consideration Mr. Anderson and his wife Eileen removed to Galway to commence a new mission work there.

Mr. Beck's faithfulness had been blessed with much fruit from over 45 years of his work in Dublin, from which he retired on 30 September 1974. He passed away on 31 May 1981 after a lengthy illness. Following his retirement no permanent worker has been placed in Dublin.

CORK

Mr. Thomas McKee had settled in a suburb of Cork in 1937 and found many opportunities for mission in and around the city. However, over the years he was able to extend the circle of his work to visit most of the towns in west Cork and many in other neighbouring counties as well. The work of the Irish Mission was greatly aided by the regular assistance of teams coming to help at special times of outreach. From 1957 the Cork Campaign became an annual summer outreach throughout the city and neighbouring seaside resorts. This was ably organised by the R.P. Church Evangelist, Mr. Harry Tadley and these continued until 1978. Mr. and Mrs. McKee retired in 1977 from the Irish Mission in Cork but continued their involvement in evangelistic work in the city where they had decided to remain.

McKee family home Cork

Cork Team 1966

The Covenanting cause in Cork received further encouragement when Rev. Andrew Cross Gregg, minister of Ballylane and Ballenon since 1966, accepted the challenge in early 1974 to devote his gifts to the work of the Irish Mission in Cork. His preaching, pastoral work and evangelistic endeavours helped to build up the Cork Fellowship to the point when, on 13 February 1982, it was organised as a congregation of the Western Presbytery at a special meeting of the Western Presbytery, held in the

9 Kenley Road, Cork

meeting house in 9 Kenley Road. The new congregation met for Sabbath worship the following day, when there were 20 persons present and ten adults were received into membership. During 1984-85 Mr. David Fallows took a year out of his university course and spent 8 months working in a voluntary capacity, assisting Mr. Gregg. His support was greatly appreciated.

Mr. & Mrs Tom McKee served in Cork from 1937

In 1986 Mr. Gregg accepted a call to Milford and was installed on 4 July. The Irish Mission Board had hoped to continue the work, believing that the nucleus of believers there formed a basis for growth. Unfortunately in 1987 due to the movement of members from Cork, the congregation ceased to exist. After much thought and prayer, the Board decided, given these circumstances, together with the sense of isolation workers had felt in Cork, and the current lack of workers, that it would be best to withdraw from the city and sell the manse.

GALWAY

In October 1966, James Anderson and his wife Eileen, after prayerful consideration, moved to Galway. Mr. Anderson had been accepted for the Irish Mission on 6 September 1963 and after training at the Bible Training Institute in Glasgow, went in 1965 to work with Tom Beck in Dublin. The Andersons laboured alone in Galway until Bob Henninger, from the R.P.C.N.A., joined them as a co-worker for three years in 1979. The Covenanter Young People's Union Campaigns Committee sent teams to Galway each summer from 1973.

C.Y.P.U. Campaigns in Galway

By 1984 Mr. Anderson had established a Sabbath morning worship service and evening Bible study and the Irish Mission Board judged that God was opening a door for further outreach in the area. The Board in 1984, called Rev. Trevor McCauley, minister of Dervock, to take on leadership of the work in Galway, which he accepted. In 1985 the group of worshipers were known as the 'Covenant Fellowship (Reformed Presbyterian Church) Galway'. There was a steady growth in numbers attending during 1985, from an average Sabbath morning attendance of 10 in January to 17 by September. The Fellowship petitioned the Western Presbytery for recognition as a Preaching Station (Covenanting Society) and this was duly granted in September.

Mr. & Mrs. James Anderson and the Galway group

In April 1987, after twenty years in Galway, Mr. and Mrs. Anderson indicated their wish to work with the Irish Mission Board in the North in a congregational setting. Their vision, courage and dedication had laid important foundations for the Covenanting witness in Galway. Mr. Anderson worked with four congregations in the Eastern Presbytery, from September 1989 until his retirement in December 1999 with perseverance, under the direction of the U.K. Section of the Mission Committee, in the Markets, Short Strand and Finaghy areas of Belfast.

On 27 November 1989 the Mission Committee issued a call to Raymond Blair, a member of Convoy and a licentiate of the Western Presbytery. He was ordained to the ministry and commissioned for work in Galway on 13 February 1990. The work was further strengthened when Mr. Billy Hamilton, a member of Trinity, accepted the call of the Mission Committee in June 1990, after completing a one-year course at the Reformed Theological College. He was commissioned in May 1991. The work in Galway lost one of its most gifted and conscientious workers when Rev. Trevor McCauley died, after a short illness of several weeks, on 8 November 1991. His ministry is especially remembered in the congregation for his diligence in preaching the Word and his faithful pastoral work.

The Covenant Fellowship in Galway continues to meet at Galway Bridge Centre on St. Mary's Road. They took an important step forward on 31 October 2004 when the

congregation was organised into a Society, with 24 adults and 10 children on the roll of membership. The Galway Society continues the work of those who have laid the groundwork of a Reformed witness, in modern secular Ireland with society's ever loosening and shifting perceptions of religious belief and commitment.

Premises in Lower Abbeygate Street, occupied by Aisling Bookshop an outreach of the Galway Society

The Irish Section of the Mission Committee continue to have a vision for church planting throughout Ireland as a considerable number of provincial towns do not have a permanent evangelical witness. They give thanks for growth in Letterkenny, Galway and Enniskillen and, in learning from these works, to extend the Kingdom of Christ throughout Ireland.

Adapted and updated from, 'A Brief History of the Irish Mission of the Reformed Presbyterian Church of Ireland.', Samuel J. Archer, B.A., published by The Irish Evangelisation Board of the R.P.C.I., 1970

THE FOREIGN MISSION,
SYRIA & LEBANON

In 1839 the synod considered a request from the Secession Synod that they would corporate in establishing and conducting a foreign mission. However, the following year, the Seceders united with the Synod of Ulster and this request was not pursued.

A number of years passed before the Reformed Presbyterian Synod resumed consideration of foreign missions as opposed to those in the colonies. The Home and Foreign Missionary Society was formed, and by 1845 a series of resolutions on the subject of missions were passed by Synod, largely to educate and encourage the Church regarding the nature and need of foreign mission. From 1847 to 1855 a monthly missionary magazine was published to stimulate interest in foreign mission. However much of the effort of the Church was then involved in the home mission and colonial mission.

The American Mission buildings in Latakia

In 1856 the American Reformed Presbyterian Church established a work in the Latakia district of Syria. There was an immediate interest shown in their work by the Irish Church and correspondence took place between the two churches and with the American mission-ary to Syria, Rev. R. J. Dodds. Interest grew in the possibility of joint co-operation in this mission field. During this time Dr. Thomas Houston stressed the importance of establishing a mission to the Jews, and it was later decided that this could be best carried out by supporting the work of the Scottish Reformed Presbyterian Church among the Jews in London.

One of the American missionaries to Syria wrote to the Irish Church in 1866 asking if it could take charge of the mission station in Aleppo in Syria, but suitable personnel were not found. Mr. James Torrens a theological student volunteered in 1868 and further personnel were sought. In 1870, Mr. James Martin was accepted as a missionary candidate. He had been born in 1845 and brought up in Ballymacashon congregation and

was a licentiate of the Eastern Presbytery and at this time also a medical student. Dr.. Dodds of the American mission died in December 1870, but rather than take over the Aleppo station, at the suggestion of the American synod, Latakia promised to be a better situation for the Irish work. In 1871 Synod adopted the report of the Foreign and Jewish Mission and called Mr. James Martin to service as a foreign missionary. Mr. Torrens sadly died before his preparations for going to the mission field work were completed.

Rev. James Martin

James Martin had been greatly influenced by Rev. Thomas Houston, the minister of Knockbracken with responsibility for Ballymacashon. He had been instrumental in promoting missionary interest throughout the church and missionary associations were formed in many congregations encouraging the young people to take an interest in and be involved in this work. James Martin obtained further qualifications and training and sailed in December 1871 from Liverpool to Alexandria arriving in Syria in January 1872. From the beginning a goal of the Foreign Mission was to establish schools where Christian education could be provided to train native evangelists to reach their own people and that missionaries would preach wherever opportunities would present themselves. The work in Syria represented co-operation of the Churches in Scotland, Ireland and the United States. In 1876 they agreed to select Antioch as a station and establish a mission school and if possible to have a medical missionary also located in the city. Dr. Martin was recommended to explore and if possible establish this new work.

The country of Syria was part of the Ottoman Empire which although weakened in power was ruthless in application of its authority. Those who were not Muslims were severely treated and during the period of this mission work hundreds of thousands of ethnic Armenians were massacred wherever they were throughout the Empire. Muslims were forbidden to convert and if they did, faced execution, often by their own family. Some of the missions converts were murdered. At times hostility broke out against the missionary work from both Muslim and Orthodox groups, with the threat to life and the destruction of property. There was little redress in the courts.

Mission buildings, Antioch, Syria

The work in Antioch enjoyed an encouraging measure of success in spite of opposition and persecution of native converts by the Turkish authorities. The medical services were a means of contacting people and opening opportunities to promote the Gospel. Scriptures were circulated and Christian education established in the day school which by 1880 had an enrolment of 190. Dr. Martin was dependent on the help of his wife and a number of native workers. He regularly appealed to the home Church for assistance especially for a young lady who would work among the woman and oversee the girls' school. This request

was answered in 1882 when Miss Meta Cunningham, a member of College Street South, who then worked for 10 years in the school at Antioch. In 1895 Rev. Samuel H Kennedy from Ballymoney offered himself as the second ordained minister in the work. He served in Syria from 1895 until 1939. By 1890 the congregation in Antioch was 71, 37 of whom were communicants. Mr. Kennedy moved to Alexandretta in 1903 to open a new station and establish a school for higher education.

Rev. Samuel H. Kennedy

Mr. Martin experienced much sorrow and personal illness in his life while on the mission field. Both James and his wife Elizabeth suffered the loss of their daughter Annie who died only 3 months old in May 1876. Elizabeth then died after a short illness in Antioch on 28 July 1876 aged only 23 years. In 1879 Mr. Martin married again, to Miss Rebecca Crawford who had been with the American R.P. mission since 1868. Their five year old son died in 1887. Rebecca then died in 1896. He married again in 1904, to Emma Lienhard a Swiss school teacher who taught in Aleppo, and they had two children.

By 1900 the work of the mission in Syria was well established. The school at Idlib had 40 to 50 in attendance, the school at Alexandretta, reported 86 boys and 94 girls. By 1906 despite much official and local opposition, the building work of the missionary compound was completed. This included a dwelling house, school rooms, medical centre and a meeting place for worship. During this period Dr. Martin suffered much illness and the situation in the Turkish Empire was desperate and after the genocidal policies of the Sultan's rule, he was deposed and replaced by revolutionaries who rather hastened the policy of persecution and annihilation of opposition. The mission sought to assist and shelter Armenian refugees where possible, but along with foreign powers they were unable to prevent the massacres.

Turkey was engaged in the Balkan War in Eastern Europe and the mission work had to cease temporarily when war came in 1914. The British missionaries left for Cyprus in September 1914 and Dr. Kennedy in Alexandretta was imprisoned in Adana in Turkey for two months and then expelled, finding refuge in Alexandria in Egypt where he worked with the Y.M.C.A. among British soldiers throughout the war. The American missionaries were able to continue the work for a short time.

A theological student from Upperlands, William Lytle offered himself in 1916 for work as a missionary in Syria. He spent much time with Dr. Martin studying Arabic and equipping himself for the missionary work. He also enrolled as a medical student at Queen's University. Miss Margareta Cunningham from Stranorlar was also preparing for missionary work as a teacher.

After the liberation of Syria by the British in November 1918, Dr. Kennedy returned to Alexandretta. He visited Antioch to discover the state of the congregation and mission property which he found had been ransacked. Mr. Lytle arrived in Alexandretta in early 1920, allowing the Kennedys to have a furlough, but conditions did not yet enable the Martins and other missionaries to return until 1921. The Church had suffered. Some had died and many had emigrated and false teaching had caused much distress. A young teacher from the Dublin Road congregation, Miss Margaret Houston volunteered to go for three years to teach in Alexandretta arriving in July 1922. She sadly died in August of the following year.

Miss Margaret Houston

Dr. Martin sought to maintain the independence of the Reformed Presbyterian Church in Syria from pressure to become part of a united missionary body which would have compromised their spiritual standing and testimony. Dr. Martin retired from the work in Syria in April 1924. His labours and had a lasting effect in the cities of Latakia, Antioch, Alexandretta, Aleppo and Idlib and this extended beyond to Beirut and Mount Lebanon.

Working alongside the other missionaries he was a pioneer into many fresh fields, facing all kinds of persecutions and personal trials. He died in Belfast on 23rd January 1931 at the age of 86.

Rev. A. Guthrie

In 1924 Rev. William Lytle his wife and son moved to the mission premises in Antioch. Dr. and Mrs Kennedy continued rebuilding the work in Alexandretta. Other missionaries joined the team: Dr. Emily Lytle and Miss Muriel Russell in 1928, who later married Rev. Archibald Guthrie from Kilraughts who joined the missionary team in 1934 Miss Henrietta Gardner a teacher also from Kilraughts who went to Antioch in 1938.

In the late 1930's the tensions in Europe were threatening and part of Syria was ceded to Turkey. This included Antioch and Alexandretta. Turkish restrictions greatly impeded missionary work. Christian instruction in schools was forbidden, and many from the Church emigrated or moved to other parts of Syria. The Kennedys retired and Miss Gardner and Miss Cunningham moved temporarily to Jerusalem. The Guthries returned home in 1947, Rev. Guthrie becoming minister of Wishaw R.P. congregation in Scotland.

Miss. H. Gardner

Mr. and Mrs. Lytle moved to Idlib from Antioch and developed the work there. Miss Gardner joined them as a teacher and Miss Minnie Bell from Dromara, as a nurse, in 1946. In December 1951, when the Lytles were expelled from Syria, there were over 100 boys from all over the Arab world in the boarding department. It was decided that the Lytles should relocate to Zahleh in Lebanon where at Kub Elias, a Christian school run by the Arab Synod (Presbyterian) was considering opening a boarding department, and a disused hotel was acquired for this purpose. Rev. Robert Lytle, their son joined them from 1951-1956 and Rev. Claude MacQuigg a member of Grosvenor Road served from

1954-1957. Miss Gardner, who had taught in Idlib worked also in Zahleh before helping to establish the new work in Ethiopia in 1963.

Mr. William Lytle's ministry was much appreciated throughout the evangelical community in Lebanon. No further missionaries were sent to Lebanon as the Irish Church had begun work in Ethiopia. Mr. Lytle retired from the school and continued to live for sometime in Lebanon preaching and teaching and finally he retired from missionary work moving to Belfast in 1970. Mrs. Lytle died in 1982 and her husband passed away in 1984 at the age of 92. From the 1970's the political situations in Syria and Lebanon have been very difficult with the rise of Arab nationalism and such mission work as took place in the past has been impossible. However there has been a lasting effect in the building of the church of Christ in these lands and we are sure of the fruit that will be seen on the last day.

Miss Norma Gill & Miss Phyllis Gilmore visiting Rev. Lytle & Mr. & Mrs. George Iter, and other teachers at Kub Elias, Lebanon in 1968

Rev. William & Mrs Agnes Lytle in their retirement

Based on, James Martin, Pioneer Medical Missionary in Antioch, by Isobel Lytle B.A. Cameron Press 2003.

Foreign Mission Box

THE ETHIOPIAN MISSION 1963-1975

Makale

The foreign mission work of the Reformed Presbyterian Church of Scotland and Ireland was carried on for over ninety years in the Middle East, in Syria, Turkey and Lebanon. From 1952 onwards, Syrian Government restrictions made it impossible to continue the work in Syria and for the next ten years work was carried on in Zahleh, Lebanon, by Rev. William and Mrs. Lytle and Miss Henrietta Gardner. In 1957 Synod instructed the Foreign Mission Board to explore the possibilities of opening a new mission field. In the years that followed the Board gave careful consideration to the matter. Brazil, Equador, Tanganyika, Nigeria, Kenya and North Africa were all considered, but the Board was not led to undertake work in any of these places. In 1960 attention was directed to the needs of Eritrea and Ethiopia and a deputation consisting of Dr. Archibald Guthrie, Prof. Adam Loughridge and Miss Henrietta Gardner visited Ethiopia in 1961 and that same year the Synod decided that plans should be made to begin work in the Tigre Province of Ethiopia as soon as possible.

By 1963 the Foreign Mission Board of the Irish and Scottish Churches had committed itself to a new work in Ethiopia. Those who had been preparing for missionary work in Ethiopia soon arrived in Africa. Miss Henrietta Gardner, who had been working previously in Lebanon, arrived in October, 1963 and began language study. Rev. Samuel

Cromie from Rathfriland, who had been stated supply in Milford from 1962-1963 and his wife Mrs Phemie Cromie and their son John, arrived in November of the same year in Addis Ababa. Miss Norma Gill, from Loanhead Edinburgh, arrived in January 1964 and studied Tigrinya in Asmara, Eritrea. A property was rented in Addis Ababa and the rest of the group began a period of study in the Amharic language.

Rev. Samuel and Mrs. Phemie Cromie and family

Selecting a place for work in Ethiopia was crucial. Detailed investigations were undertaken in the Tigre Province in February 1964 and it was thought that the town of Dessa would be chosen. It was 30 miles north east of Quiha. Dessa was a central market on a camel route from the Red Sea plains to Makale the provincial capital.

Sheket 1969

Miss Phyllis Gilmore from Loughbrickland, having completed study at the Bible Training Institute in Glasgow, arrived in September of 1964. Headquarters were established in the main town of Makale and plans were laid for a library and reading room in this important town. Makale proved to be a suitable centre for missionary operations, and a bookshop was established and opened in 1965 and agricultural programmes were undertaken. Mrs

Phemie Cromie took over the running of a Nursery School at the request of Princess Aida the wife of the provincial governor Ras (Prince) Mengesha Seyouna, with opportunities for Christian teaching among children of different religious backgrounds including the majority Ethiopian Orthodox. This school was later expanded.

Miss Norma Gill the Saturday Children's Club Makale 1965

Mr. Sam & Mrs Phemie Cromie teaching

In 1965 plans for Dessa had to be abandoned because of difficulties over leasing land and the interest moved to the village of Sheket a little south of Dessa and east of Makale. The Mission went to Sheket at the invitation of the Governor General of the Tigre Province and found a real opportunity for the Gospel in this needy area. A site was granted and building began in 1965. Soon a school and clinic were built and agricultural development plans began. These practical programmes helped break down the barriers of suspicion and opened doors to the teaching of God's Word.

The work in Sheket became very much part of the community and was recognised as making a real contribution to the life of the people. It however required continual close contact with Makale. In Makale the bookshop helped foster relationships with the community. By means of Bible Studies, assisted by Christian literature, leadership training was provided for a group of young national Christians.

By 1966 the buildings in Sheket were complete and medical work began. In the early years an average of 50 patients attended a week and this was also became a base for the visitation of local villages. The medical clinic that was established saw over 4000 patients in the year 1968. This provided opportunity for personal witness and the provision of Christian books and tapes. Local villages were regularly visited to operate medical clinics. A day school and an evening school were opened and staffed by Miss Phyllis Gilmore and Miss Henrietta Gardner with an emphasis on Bible teaching. The day school concentrated on children and the night school on an adult literacy programme; these were excellent

channels for evangelism and Bible teaching. Under Miss Gilmore's supervision national teachers effectively provided teaching in the day school. The area of Sheket was excessively poor and children were part of the agricultural economy but the contact through the school children gave the opportunity of home visitation.

Miss Gardner teaching in Sheket

The clinic in Sheket was under the supervision of Miss Norma Gill and later Miss Jean Pollock from Stranorlar, who arrived to assist. Along with Ethiopian helpers, they showed the mission's concern for the welfare of local residents. Evangelistic work accompanied the medical treatment, and many local villages were visited. The Gospel was preached and Bibles and Christian literature distributed. In Makale the capital of Tigre Province, the bookshop over which Kifle, a local Christian, was set in charge, sold Scriptures in many different languages. There were regular Sabbath services and a girls' Bible class and children's meeting also took place.

Makale bookshop, Kifle on the right

Mr Ronnie Loughridge from Kilraughts, arrived in June 1966, initially allowing the Cromies to take furlough. He made a significant contribution in bringing the finishing touches to the buildings under the care of the Mission. From 1966-1967, when Mr and Mrs Cromie were away, Miss Gardner, Miss Gill and Miss Gilmore continued to witness in the school and clinic in Sheket. Mr Ronnie Loughridge staffed the bookshop business and mission in Makale, acquiring supplies for the mission and was also engaged in many construction and repair

projects. Miss Gardner continued to teach evening and day school with literacy and Bible lessons. Miss Gill continued in the clinic with an increasing amount of Danakil people attending for treatment; this provided a new opening into another tribe but brought the matter of another language to learn.

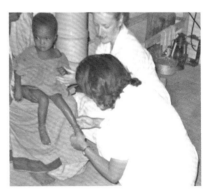

The work at the clinic in Sheket

When Miss Gill and Miss Gilmore were on furlough, Miss Helene Gregg from Convoy, covered the nursing responsibilities. In the early years of the mission two local men, Mehari Araya and Zeru, faithfully served the work before moving to a different area to serve in another missionary organisation. By 1981, Mehari Araya had become a refugee in Sudan and the Foreign Mission Board was able to send some assistance to him and his family and later they were assisted in coming to live in Ireland. In 1970 Miss Jean Pollock arrived to undertake medical work and by 1971 after language study she joined Miss

Norma Gill in Sheket. Mr Anthony (Tony) McKeeman from Ballymoney, volunteered in 1968 for a period. He was responsible for laying water pipes from supply to storage in Sheket. The plastic piping was supplied free of charge by Wavin Pipes Ltd., Dublin. He was greatly involved in demonstrating the effectiveness of the irrigation of crops. This work was particularly effective in making evangelistic contact with the young men of the village. Sabbath services were held in Sheket. It was hoped that this would encourage contact and evangelism among the nomadic Danakil tribes.

Dr. Hugh Blair with Miss Jean Pollock and Mr. Tony McKeeman and villagers during his visit in 1970

In 1970 Mr Raymond and Mrs Heather Morton of the R.P.C.N.A. congregation in Almonte, Canada offered themselves for the Ethiopian R.P. Mission and began their preparatory training. In 1971 they moved to Sheket and worked in development projects along with the vital work of Bible teaching and discipling, taking over the supervision of the day school when Miss Gilmore left in 1972. After leaving the mission, Mr Morton was ordained and installed minister of Airdrie Reformed Presbyterian congregation in Scotland in May, 1975. The work in Makale consisting of the bookshop, Sabbath afternoon meetings and a poultry unit, continued under the leadership of Rev. S. K. Cromie. Mrs. P. Cromie worked in Makale school with about 50 pupils. Each morning the whole school engaged in worship in English and Amharic. School finances were met by contributions from Princess Aida and by the fees paid by the school children. Four additional rooms were built in the Makale school.

After Sabbath Service

Miss Gilmore unfortunately suffered recurring ill-health. A tropical infection, resulted in her returning home on furlough. In October, 1972 after medical advice she had to resign from the work of foreign mission in Ethiopia. In her seven years of service in Ethiopia she made an invaluable contribution with the leadership of the day school in Sheket and visitation of homes and especially the Christian encouragement of her Ethiopian colleagues.

The Ethiopian population is extremely vulnerable to drought and famine. Such a catastrophe occurred during 1973, especially in the northern part of the country, which had a devastating effect on livestock and then on the population. Mr Cromie writing home in October, describing a journey to Addis Ababa, recorded the scene of hundreds of animal carcasses and thousands of the hungry scouring the country for food. Ironically it was a period of heavy rain but still people in Makale died of starvation. The missions were at the forefront of aid. Although comparatively small the R.P. Mission contributed to the relief work offering food and in Sheket the clinic was able to feed about 400 children a day along with a vaccination programme. In Makale help was given to clothe those in the relief centre.

Villagers at Sheket

1974 saw an increase of political turmoil. The military removed Emperor Selassie from power and there was growing oppression of any opposition. In 1975 the unsettled political situation resulted in the overthrow of Emperor Haile Selassie and his government and the intensified effort of the Eritrean Liberation Army to secure independence from Ethiopia placed missionaries in a dangerous situation. The McKeeman family returned home at the start of the year as Tony was denied a further work permit. Unfortunately they were at this time also suffering from hepatitis. Miss Gill was evacuated to Addis Ababa, and Mr Bob Hemphill, from Beaver Falls congregation in Pennsylvania, who was a short-term worker from 1973, left for home in 1975. Yet even in the trying circumstances the Lord was blessing the work with great encouragements in the interest in Bible study. The projects in Makale and Sheket were greatly inhibited. Mr. Cromie and his family returned to Ethiopia in 1975 from some months furlough in Australia. However, the situation was greatly changed. Mr Cromie was naturally deeply concerned about the safety and welfare of his wife and children owing to the unrest and military activity around Asmara. He felt with great reluctance he had to resign from the mission work in Ethiopia in July, 1975, and he and his family returned home. Tribute was paid to the Cromie family for their excellent years of work in Ethiopia. Mr Tony and Mrs Norma McKeeman returned on a temporary visa into Ethiopia to assist where possible the missionary work under such difficult conditions.

The continued unsettled nature of the country and the lack of a permanent male worker to undertake the spiritual leadership, led the Foreign Mission Board after earnest prayer and careful consideration to recommend reluctantly the withdrawal of its missionaries in 1975. This was a difficult period for many missionary organisations in Ethiopia and the new regime and civil and military unrest brought subsequent well documented periods of war and famine to this poor nation.

Miss Gilmore and some of her class, Sheket, 1967

Tribute is paid to those who went for longer periods or those volunteering for shorter terms of service. Miss Janneth Russell from Bangor was accepted by the Foreign Mission Board for nursing service in Ethiopia in 1974 but was unable to take up the position in the following year due to the uncertainties in the country. These were days of blessed opportunity where the Royal household gave support for the work of various Christian missions throughout the Kingdom. The mission work was successful in leaving both medical and educational work in the hands of trained and trusted Ethiopians along with the continuing evangelical work. A young Christian from Makale, Kashay Berhe was able to attend the Reformed Presbyterian College in Ireland in the early 1980's and later returned to his homeland where he continues to be supported in his Christian work. The interests of the Irish and Scottish church continue through the Relief Fund. In this way the church is able to assist where appropriate, through other aid providers and missions, those suffering under the strain of war and famine.

These were interesting and challenging times of great transformation in this land and the Lord held the door of opportunity open for the building of the indigenous evangelical church. Any such record of events cannot here fully express the daily contacts for Christ which were made and the overall effect that this work had on the general growth of the church in Ethiopia. Those involved in the missionary work can testify to many God given opportunities to communicate the Gospel and tell of the times when people professed saving faith in the Lord Jesus and gave evidence of the fruits of the Spirit in their membership and involvement of the local church. While a concise history of this missionary work has yet to be written, the record in glory will bring forth its blessed fruit on the last day.

Mehari and his wife Agayba

Kifle and his wife

REFORMED PRESBYTERIAN CHURCH
IN FRANCE 1986- PRESENT

When the Church's missionaries had to leave Ethiopia, it was hoped that when peace was restored, they would be able to return, but the coming to power of a strongly communist regime firmly closed that door. After a time of considering the wider issues, it was concluded that mission work in Europe was as needful as in Africa, without having the added demands of providing educational and medical facilities. During this period the French denomination, Eglises Réformées Evangéliques Indépendantes (E.R.E.I.), a member along with the R.P.C.I. at that time in the Reformed Ecumenical Synod, issued an appeal to other churches in that body to come and help in France. This led the Foreign Mission Board to send a delegation consisting of Rev. Norman McCune, moderator of Synod, Rev. Edward Donnelly, secretary of the Board, with Miss Evelyn McConaghie as translator, to visit various centres and people of influence. It was their favourable report which led the Board to call for a special meeting of Synod in November, 1977, where the proposal was warmly received.

Subsequently, in the autumn of 1979, three simultaneous calls were made out, only one of which was accepted, by Miss Margaret McMullan. This unexpected outcome opened up an extended time of uncertainty both within the Foreign Mission Board and the Synod concerning both the appropriateness of France as the field and the speed at which further progress could be made. The green light to proceed was finally given by the 1985 Synod.

This resulted in a series of successful calls to Rev. Malcolm Ball, minister of Bready and Clarendon Street (accepted in November, 1985) and to Rev. Blair McFarland, minister of Loughbrickland and Clare (accepted in April, 1986). The call to Margaret McMullan was reactivated by the Board and confirmed by her.

Miss Margaret McMullan and the Ball and McFarland families in 1989

Malcolm Ball and his wife Muriel along with Blair McFarland and his wife Clare, and their families began language study in September, 1986, at Massy in the southern suburbs of greater Paris and were joined there the following year by Margaret McMullan. In parallel they were seeking to find a location for the future missionary work. Operating within the bounds of the original recommendation that it should be in the particularly spiritually barren west of France, visits were made to various centres to discuss with those knowledgeable about the area. In terms of size of population and number of existing evangelical churches, the decision was reduced to a choice between Angoulême and Nantes. Two factors in particular led to the choice of Nantes.

1. The support and encouragement from the pastors of the three existing evangelical churches, who indicated that the north-west of the city had no Christian presence.

2. In Angoulême, another evangelical group was planning to begin work at that same time, which was felt could lead to confusion. Happily, in 1988, both the Foreign Mission Board and the Synod approved the recommendation.

THE BEGINNING OF THE WORK

To appreciate something of the radical nature of what was being undertaken it is extremely rare, in France, for first-time church planters to debark in a town or city without having received an invitation from existing contacts in that location. Most church plants are from an established work. The unannounced pioneer has usually gained experience elsewhere in France. That was not the case for our missionaries. Besides, the mission goal wasn't just to establish under God an evangelical church similar to others, but one that was distinctly Reformed in doctrine and Presbyterian in government.

In believing that gaining the confidence of people through friendship was vital to the work, the missionaries' homes were spread throughout the north-west of Nantes, allowing them to have contact with different sets of people and be involved in various activities. From the beginning, a worship service in French was held on the Lord's Day in one of the homes. The situation of the McFarland house in a large estate with lots of children lent itself to beginning a regular children's club, which still continues today, though now in the *salle,* (the current meeting place).

The publicity surrounding the film "The last temptation of Christ" in the autumn of 1988 led to the printing of the first leaflet for distribution, this literature being later used by the other evangelical churches outside the main city centre cinema. Other tracts followed, including for the bicentenary of the French Revolution in 1989, *Liberté* and *Egalité*. In 1990 a standard format for all publications was adopted, hence *Réflexions* was born. Topical events were used as a springboard for evangelistic material. For example, in that year, the completion of the ring road around Nantes with the finishing touches to a new bridge over the Loire was a major event in the local calendar, so the gospel was presented with Jesus as the 'bridge to God and heaven'. To help with the distribution, the very first GO team came at Easter 1990. As part of their activities a musical and cultural evening was organised to which were invited an increasing circle of friends. Wheaten bread, song and gospel were all on offer. With slight variations this recipe has been maintained.

The acceptance by the prefecture of the statutes, which gave a theological and practical direction to the work, meant that in 1990 the team, instead of being a number of individuals in French law, became a fully fledged association, a necessary step to opening bank accounts, renting property and doing all that a church would want to do.

The building that houses the 'Salle'

THE 'SALLE'

The various outreach methods had brought the team into contact with many people, with some of whom they were able to begin regular one-to-one Bible studies. However, increasingly they felt that a private home could never truly function as a place of public worship and so the search began to find a convenient meeting place. After many fruitless

visits, eventually all agreed that the new-ly-built ground-floor commercial proper-ty at 141 Route de Rennes, Orvault met the requirements. It was rented in March, 1991, with just time to install a minimum of furniture, welcome the second GO team, and then receive a regular small stream of visitors at the worship services. A mid-week Bible study and English

classes followed soon after. Over the years since, the *salle* has played host to a wide variety of outreach activities and conferences. A special highlight was the weekend of preaching in September, 2003 by Pastor Stuart Olyott, the well known Welsh pastor with a long interest in the French-speaking world, which also planted ideas for the future.

In addition the team was involved, along with others, in many evangelistic events, of which two stand out as a reminder of what God can do. Firstly, for all who had become used to indifference and apathy, seeing long queues forming, despite the intense cold, to visit Logos, the Operation Mobilisation ship, in December, 1995 or attend some event onboard remains an indelible memory. Again the excitement of the World Cup in 1998 enabled many encouraging international events to be held in and around Nantes.

CHANGES

Some of the first visitors in the early 1990s were young students from Cameroon, Charles and Charlotte Ekwelgen. Almost 20 years later Charlotte still attends, Charles having returned to Yaoundé, being unable to find suitable employment in Nantes. In the late 1990s, Joël Macé, a neighbour of the McFarlands, began to regularly attend worship and now he and his present wife are pillars in the church. Attendances have gone up and down over the years. In the late 1990s serious consideration was given to finding larger premises, but sadly that need is not currently pressing. Many students have spent time in the church, some of whom still remain in contact. Notably, for a period many Korean students made the church their spiritual home. The greatest change is to have seen a number coming to saving faith, taking their first steps as young believers and then becoming witnesses themselves. Alas the harsh reality of modern city life and of life in general, is that people are increasingly mobile and move on for many reasons. The result has been that the overall numbers have remained stable.

The annual GO Team continues to be a blessing and in 2000 the church welcomed an American summer team for the first time, this experience being enjoyed every second year. 2000 also saw the retirement and return to Ireland of Margaret McMullan. In 2002-2003 Miss Kate McFarland, from the Cloughmills congregation spent a year working with the church. Then in 2006, Blair and Clare McFarland also returned to Ireland. Currently Mr and Mrs Andrew Lytle, from Cloughmills, plan in God's will to join the mission team in Nantes.

THE FUTURE

God's faithfulness is unchanging as is the power of His Word and Christ's promise to build his church. These things give the assurance that seed sown, Bible studies held, sermons preached, times of prayer, moments of witness, have not been in vain. All those involved in the work over the years have been conscious of being upheld and encouraged by many faithful prayer warriors and of being assisted in their labours by scores of young and older helpers.

A public meeting for worship

The increasing secularisation and suspicion of sects in French society, together with an expanding Islamic presence, mean that France remains a most needy mission field. Obviously hopes for the church in greater Nantes are in part linked to the advance of the Gospel and of Reformed teaching all over France. The particular longing is that God would strengthen the work by sending more families, preparing men for future leadership and bringing to saving faith the young people associated with the fellowship as well as the many contacts made over the years.

The road may have been long and winding in beginning and establishing the work in France, but he who made all its twists and turns and ups and downs remains faithful.

God will bless us and all the ends of the earth will fear him. Psalm 67:7

Malcolm Ball

The Covenanter Flats, Ballymoney

THE COVENANTER HOUSING ASSOCIATION

The history of the Covenanter Flats began when, according to a minute in the Minutes of Synod, 1975, "Synod accepted sympathetically the recommendation in the Report of the Business Committee that the Church should make some provision for her elderly members particularly those who live alone, and agreed to appoint a Committee to investigate the whole matter, and report to Synod." Some of the members of the Committee which was appointed had some knowledge of the fine work being done in the Reformed Presbyterian Home in Pittsburgh, and it was felt that perhaps a small beginning might be made if a large house could be purchased and adapted as a home for a few elderly members Providentially, just at that time legislation was passed which made it possible for legally constituted Housing Associations in Northern Ireland to administer sheltered accommodation for the elderly in buildings provided by the Department of the Environment for Northern Ireland through capital grants to be repaid as long-term loans.

The Covenanter Residential Association Limited was one of the earliest housing associations in Northern Ireland to take advantage of this scheme and in 1978 the Covenanter Flats were built at a cost of approximately £250,000 and opened officially in April, 1979 by the Mayor of Ballymoney, Mrs. Mollie J. Holmes, O.B.E., J. P. The generosity of church members meant that, through the Comforts Fund, many extras not included in Government specifications, were provided for the residents' flats - cookers refrigerators, carpets, curtains, equipment for the communal kitchen, and much more Financial Reports of 1980 show that approximately £12,000 was raised for the Comforts Fund to make such extra provision, by the congregations of the church and generous friends

The Covenanter Housing Association continues to be a registered Housing Association The Reformed Presbyterian Church does not own or manage the flats but does support the work and ethos of the association giving thanks for how many of its members have found blessing in the care and friendship they have received. The ethos of the Covenanter Flats gives a clear indication as to their purpose: "to provide sheltered accommodation for retired people wishing to share in Christian fellowship and worship." Christian fellowship has been a marked feature of the Flats since they were opened. Applications are open to anyone who wishes to apply and are assessed by the point system under the Housing Executive. There has been great friendships built over the years between residents, belonging to different denominations, who share in the regular worship service in the Flats.

The Flats were extensively refurbished and some extra accommodation built and adapted to create 27 flats, 14 double and 13 single, including three to wheelchair standard. These were re-opened in September 2004 by Rev. Dr. Hugh Blair, the former (and first) Chairman of the Association.

RENWICK HOUSE

The Association also manages a singles hostel for 14 young people studying or working in Belfast, Renwick House. The origin of Renwick House goes back to the early 1980s when a number of R.P. church members had a concern for the spiritual welfare of young people leaving home for the first time and coming to Belfast to study or work. The provision of a suitable residence for young people would allow them to live in an environment which would encourage Christian fellowship and friendship.

At that time a four-storey terrace house at 42 Elmwood Avenue came on the market. While houses in the area were being purchased and developed for office use, the title deeds of No. 42 contained a clause specifying that it be used as a residence and not for commercial purposes. As this specification limited the number of potential buyers, a negotiated purchase price of £15,000 was agreed. The Department of the Environment, recognising a need for student accommodation at that time in the area, readily awarded a grant. The purchase price, along with around £90,000 for renovations, was paid in full by the Department of the Environment. Like other Voluntary Housing Associations funded by the DoE, the Covenanter Residential Association comes under the scrutiny of the DoE which ensures that the Associations are administered in an effective manner.

The choice of an appropriate name was discussed and the name of James Renwick was chosen as he was one of the youngest of the Scottish martyrs at the age of 26.

Renovations to Renwick House were completed early in 1985 and a Sub-Committee of the Covenanter Residential Association Committee was set up to manage the undertaking The first four residents in April 1985 were Raymond Blair from Stranorlar congregation as Warden, Elizabeth Barr (Ballylaggan), Andrew Aicken (Drimbolg) and Ivor Spence (Kellswater).

Renwick House is located at 42 Elmwood Avenue, near Queen's University, Belfast,

The Covenanter Flats are located at 8 Eastermeade Park, Ballymoney, County Antrim BT53 6HP.

The former Cameron House 98 Lisburn Road Belfast

CAMERON HOUSE

After assisting Rev. R. B. Lyons for a number of years in the work of the Witness Bearing Committee, Professor F. S. Leahy succeeded him as Convener. In the early sixties the Committee considered the possibility of implementing the earlier decision of Synod to open a Book Shop in the city. The search for suitable property began and eventually 98 Lisburn Road was purchased in 1963 by the Trustees of Synod and named 'Cameron House.'

A loan from the Synod's Trustees of £5000 enabled the Witness bearing Committee to purchase the property. As the Committee had no regular income this purchase was a venture of faith. At Synod in the following year a legacy was received from the estate of Mr. T. C. McConnell, late of Alberta, Canada, of £8279/19s/10d. £5000 of this legacy was applied to clear the amount shown against the Witness Bearing Committee.

Cameron House was opened officially on 17 October 1963. Initially the upper floors were rented out, the ground floor being adequate for the Covenanter Book Shop. The basement was used for a time by the Queen's University Christian Union as a meeting place, but soon it became the area for the display of Sabbath School prizes where teachers could choose their books in comfort. The original vision for the shop was seen as a witness-bearing venture, uniquely situated in the University area. The original Witness Bearing Committee was later divided into three separate committees -Cameron House; Book Shop and Publications; and Reformed Witness. The upper floors of the building accommodated the Reformed Theological College and an office for the Covenanter Residential Association Ltd. The College Library was housed in the basement.

The property was sold in 2005. With the building of the new college in Knockbracken some of the proceeds were used to fit out the new Theological College. The bookshop moved to temporary premises in the old school room in Knockbracken. The work of the Covenanter Bookshop continues as 2010 sees the erection of a purpose built book centre in the grounds of Knockbracken congregation.

The former Cameron House is located at 98 Lisburn Road, Belfast.

Front elevation of the new Covenanter Book Centre at Knockbracken

HISTORICAL BIOGRAPHIES.

THE LIFE AND MINISTRY OF
DAVID HOUSTON: 1633 -1696

David Houston was born near Paisley in Scotland in 1633. It was a time when Scots Presbyterians were suffering the erastian and ecclesiastical pressure of King Charles I. He entered Glasgow University at the age of 15 and obtained a Master's degree at 21. The years from 1654 to 1660 passed in comparative obscurity. During that time, however, he was licensed to preach the Gospel and came to Ulster and was accepted as a licentiate by the Route Presbytery in 1660. He had an itinerant ministry, preaching mainly at Armoy, Ballymoney, Derrykeighan and Macosquin. When the Covenants that were signed throughout Ulster in 1644 were rejected by Charles II on his accession to the throne in 1660, many Presbyterians grew lukewarm in their defence of them. In this situation David Houston's total commitment to them was an embarrassment to the Presbytery and he was asked either "to moderate his views or to withdraw a while out of the country". Refusing to do so, he was suspended by the Presbytery in 1672. This suspension was withdrawn in 1673 to encourage him to return to Scotland. A minute on his departure reads: "Then had the Churches rest throughout the regions of Antrim and the Route."

David Houston suffered because he acknowledged and advocated those crown rights of the Redeemer that were clearly set out in the Solemn League and Covenant of 1643 which had been subscribed to widely in the north of Ireland in 1644. This Reformation document defined the clear implications of the Gospel not only for the people and the Church, but also for the nation and its institutions.

In the 1640's and 50's the Gospel was advancing in Ulster, congregations were being formed, and covenanted Presbyterian churches were being established. The restoration of Charles II in 1660 brought about a sudden change. He hated Presbyterianism with a special hatred reserved for the Covenants and their subscribers. When the persecution became acute, many succumbed to the pressure to relinquish adherence to the Covenants. In 1670 King Charles made an offer to the covenanted Presbyterians which proposed that Presbyterianism would be tolerated and loyalty was expected in the form of a repudiation of the Covenant and its principles and aspirations. This would be rewarded with a Royal Gift, an annual governmental contribution to the stipend of ministers. A majority of the Presbyterian ministers in Ireland relented and fell in with the compromise. Nevertheless, there was a remnant, a few thousand covenanted Christians and a licentiate, David Houston that remained true to the Covenant and its perpetual obligations. Houston gave leadership to a covenanted Presbyterian church which continued in Ireland, later to become known as the Reformed Presbyterian Church.

Battle of Bothwell Bridge

David Houston took part in the Battle of Bothwell Brig on the 22 June, 1679. Following the disastrous defeat of the Covenanters, he sought refuge back in Ulster and was accompanied on his return by Alexander Peden. His presence and his preaching were warmly welcomed by the Covenanting Societies. It appears that he had been ordained in Scotland, for in 1686 he was listed as an accredited minister by the Scottish Societies and he was able to produce certificates both of his licensure and ordination.

The Scottish Covenanting Societies, at a General Meeting, 22 September, 1686, invited Houston over to confer with them. He appeared at a meeting held at Wanlockhead, 26 December, 1686. After long conference the Societies expressed themselves satisfied with him, and called him to preach among them, although not as a settled minister. At a meeting in June 1687, it was "appointed that one should go to Ireland to conduct Mr David Houston's wife and family from thence to this land; and £5 sterling was allowed for their charges."

Memorial near Cumnock to John McGeaghan who died rescuing Houston

David Houston seems to have laboured for some months among the Societies, but in January 1688 he was in Ireland, where he was apprehended. The minutes of the General Meeting of the Societies, held 7 June, 1688, record that he had been long kept in prison in Dublin and badly used, and that he was brought as a prisoner out of Ireland and was to be carried to Edinburgh, where it was feared they would take his life. Preparations were made to rescue him, but the soldiers did not come at the expected time. On the 20 June, however, he was rescued at Carbelpath, about 3 miles from Old Cumnock on the road to Muirkirk. In the scuffle several soldiers were killed, and, according to the proclamation issued June 22, 1688, "others were desperately wounded." Houston himself was badly hurt. As a prisoner, his feet had been tied and in the scuffle he fell, and his head was trailed for some time on the ground before he could be relieved. After this a contemporary records he was discovered to be "short in his naturals." There had evidently been concussion in the brain. There is a martyrs memorial on the site to John McGeaghan who was only one of those killed in the action.

After the Revolution, Houston returned to Ireland and by 1689 he was back in Ulster, living in Newtownards. In a Bond of Compliance in that year he promised Lord Mount Alexander that he would use his influence for the peaceful settlement of the country, a clear indication of his standing in the community. It is believed that he was also present at the Siege of Derry.

The last four years of his life were spent at Armoy, in north Antrim, where a meeting house was built. The strength of his support may be judged from a complaint made by the Anglican Bishop to the Lord Lieutenant in 1694 which referred to him as "A clergyman who preaches up the Solemn League and Covenant, accusing the people of Scotland of perjury, and having a congregation of five hundred resolute fellows that adhere to him". If we assume that "fellows" mean men, by counting women and children, the total may have reached a thousand over this part of north Antrim. His critics referred to him as turbulent, rash, inconvenient and irregular. His friends used the words 'zealous, uncompromising and faithful'. But we are impressed by the tributes from three very different sources;

First, we have James Renwick's view. "As for Mr. David Houston, he carried very straight. I think him both learned and zealous. He seems to have much of the spirit of our early professors. He much opposes the passing from any part of our testimony. He hath authority with him". His biographer, Classon Porter, writes: "He went forth as his failing strength permitted, on frequent excursions through the counties of Down, Antrim and Derry, confirming the churches he had built, and with undiminished boldness and un-shrinking fidelity, testifying to his devoted followers what he believed to be the Gospel of the Grace of God. For this work he had lived; in the discharge of this work he died". A critic said of him: "As a probationer, as a minister and as a man, he was brave, outspoken, honest and sincere".

David Houston's ministry was exercised in the dark and difficult days that prevailed throughout the British Isles in the latter half of the 17th century. This servant of Christ was unflinching in his adherence to the Covenanted Reformation. This stand not only caused him to be suspended from a compromising and an accommodating church, but it also resulted in him being arrested by the authorities. He would undoubtedly have ended up on the scaffold like his contemporary James Renwick had he not escaped.

He died at Kellswater on the 8 December, 1696 and was buried at St. Saviour's Church of Ireland, Connor Co. Antrim. His grave was subsequently desecrated, but the inscription on the headstone has been preserved.

It read:

"Here lies the body of Mr. David Houston,

a faithful minister of the Gospel of Christ,

who departed this present life

the 8th December 1696,

and of his age the 63rd year".

The only local memorial is at the congregation of Kellswater, their Church Hall, built by a descendant and called "The Houston Memorial Hall".

Adapted from the addresses given at the David Houston Tercentenary Conventicle, Kellswater 19 June 1996. Prof. Adam Loughridge and Prof. Robert McCollum.

JOHN MacMILLAN
OF BALMAGHIE: 1669-1753

The continued presence of Reformed Presbyterianism, under God, is largely due to the labours and influence of one man, John MacMillan. It was largely through him that the Reformed Presbyterian Church came into organized existence. For 37 years he was the only ordained minister among the Covenanter Societies in Scotland and Ireland. These Societies were made up of Presbyterians who adhered steadfastly to the Covenants and also refused to enter the Revolution Church which, at best, was lukewarm towards the Covenanted aspect of the Scottish Reformation.

MacMillan's home Barncauchlaw in 1896

MacMillan was born at Barncauchlaw, a hill farm about 4 miles from Newtownstewart in Kirkcudbrightshire, in 1669. That part of Scotland suffered great hardship and deprivation in the latter part of the 17th century because of the tyrannical measures introduced by the Stuart kings. When John was 16, a neighbouring farmer's 18 year old daughter, Margaret Wilson, was tied to the stake and drowned in the rising waters of the Solway because of her love for and loyalty to Jesus Christ and the Covenanted Reformation. Such events must have made a deep impression on John for, even though his parents were not associated with the Covenanting movement, he joined the Societies when he went to Edinburgh in 1695 to study for an Arts degree. He graduated M.A. in 1697.

MacMillan had now reached the point where he had to decide whether to remain with the Societies or join the Church established after the Williamite Revolution. He decided to break his connections with the Societies and join the Presbyterian Church of Scotland. He later felt this was a mistake and keenly regretted his decision. However, at the time, he believed it was the only course open to him. It was only in the Church of Scotland that he could obtain the necessary training and license to preach. In the Societies there was no provision for either; they were training no ministers and 'simply waiting on events'. Rev. Matthew Hutchison of the Reformed Presbyterian Church of Scotland explains the outlook of the Societies at that time:

> "The original purpose was to stand apart for the time from the corrupt part of the Church of which they still claimed to form a constituent portion, and to wait till, in the Providence of God, the way should be opened up by the removal of corruptions, for a coalescing of the partially-sundered sections. They did not dream of forming a separate and independent Church; they could not entertain the notion of more than one organized Church in the land, that would have seemed to them destructive of the unity of the Church and liable to the charge of schism."

Balmaghie Meeting House built 1794, showing the ruins of the original building

MacMillan completed his theological studies and returned to his native Galloway in 1700. He was licensed to preach in November and after receiving a unanimous call from the congregation of Balmaghie, was ordained to the Gospel ministry on 18 September 1701. Events were soon to bring MacMillan onto a collision course with his Presbytery. The Synod of Galloway directed the ministers within its bounds to explain to the people the National Covenant. MacMillan's convictions would not allow him to ignore the Solemn

League and Covenant. With the consent of his Session he explained both Covenants, and he and his people renewed them. Other matters followed which brought home to MacMillan the compromise which his church had made in 1690 by accepting the terms of the Revolution Settlement. For example, the heavy hand of the State was still all too evident in church life because the General Assembly could not meet or dissolve without royal mandate. MacMillan was charged with following divisive courses and in 1703 was deposed by the Presbytery from his congregation. His congregation, with few exceptions, supported him so strongly that they refused to allow any successor to occupy church or manse. For twenty-six years MacMillan continued to live in the manse at Balmaghie and preach in the church building when he was at home.

In the providence of God, MacMillan's difficulties in the Revolution Church led him to look again to the Societies with whom he had formerly been associated. For 16 years they had been without an ordained minister. MacMillan conferred with them and attended the General Meeting in January 1705. Step by step events moved forward until, on 10 October 1706, the Societies gave him a unanimous call to be their minister. After some consideration he accepted the Call, and on 2 December 1706, he began his ministry among the Societies when he preached at Crawfordjohn.

In this way began a new life of strenuous service for MacMillan in which he journeyed, preached, and administered baptism and the Lord's Supper over a wide area in the south and west of Scotland. He was held in the highest esteem by those to whom he ministered and subsequent historians have spoken eloquently about his gifts and faithfulness. H.M.B. Reid pays this tribute:

> "Like his covenanting forbears, he often, and for a time always, preached in the fields, or in houses and barns. For thirty-seven years he did his heavy work quite unassisted, save in those parts which an un-ordained minister (a layman, in fact) could perform. The Holy Sacraments, indeed, became specially dear when dispensed by John MacMillan."

A contemporary in the Church of Scotland, Mr Archibald Guthrie, referred to Mr MacMillan as a "faithful Gospel minister", and declared his conviction that "all the ministers in Scotland should contend as zealously as he had done for Reformation principles."

In his extensive ministry among the Society people John MacMillan was assisted by licentiate John McNeil. Over the years various discussions took place in the Societies as to how they could have men ordained in the absence of a Presbytery. So highly principled were these Covenanters that they would not countenance MacMillan ordaining anyone by himself. That would give the appearance of episcopacy.

It must have seemed to the aging MacMillan that, with his demise, the Society people would never enjoy the blessings of an ordained ministry again, especially after the licentiate John McNeil died in 1734. MacMillan continued to labour alone, to the utmost of his ability, till in the providence of God, help came from an unexpected quarter. Thomas Nairn, a minister of the Secession Church, found himself in trouble with his Presbytery because of his commitment to the Solemn League and Covenant. After application, he was received into the fellowship of the Societies and called to be their minister. On 1 August 1743, MacMillan, now aged 74, and Nairn, along with certain elders, formed themselves into a Presbytery under the name of 'The Reformed Presbytery'. This event took place at Braehead, in the parish of Dalserf, where MacMillan resided and where afterwards the Presbytery frequently met. They chose the designation 'Reformed Presbytery' because they were thoroughly Presbyterian in principle, holding strongly to the view that this form of church government was alone divinely instituted. The term 'Reformed' was prefixed, to "indicate that they claimed to stand in a specially close connection with the Presbyterians of the Second Reformation, holding fast to all its attainments in Church and State."

Soon after the Presbytery was formed, there was a stream of candidates for the ministry. It must have brought great joy to the aged MacMillan to see this development and especially to be involved in the ordination of his son John in 1750, beginning another MacMillan ministry which extended for 51 years. In 1778 his grandson John was ordained and installed as minister in Stirling Reformed Presbyterian congregation, later serving the church as Professor of Theology. A number of very able and useful ministers were trained under him. Foremost among these were the Symington brothers, Andrew and

William, whose illustrious ministries in the 19th century had a great impact on Scotland and further a field. The godly succession of MacMillans served the Covenanter Church in Scotland for 145 years.

John MacMillan began life in an obscure part of Scotland as a farm boy, but under God he was used to give leadership to the Covenanted Reformation in Scotland when it was at a very vulnerable stage. Not only did his life and ministry begin a godly succession in Scotland in the 18th century, but also Reformed Presbyterians in the 21st century look back and thank God for the steadfastness of this Galloway Covenanter and his ceaseless labours for Christ's Crown and Covenant.

MacMillan Memorial Dalserf Parish South Lanarkshire,

From an Article written by Prof. Robert McCollum which appeared in the Covenanter Witness Vol. XXXVII No. 11. December 2003

REV. WILLIAM MARTIN: 1729-1806

FIRST COVENANTER MINISTER IN IRELAND
FIRST COVENANTER MINISTER IN SOUTH CAROLINA

The old graveyard at the Vow, near Ballymoney

Rev. William Martin was born 16 May, 1729, the eldest son of David Martin of Ballyspallen, Ballykelly, Londonderry. He entered Glasgow University where he studied theology under the direction of the Rev. John McMillan, and graduated in 1753 and was licensed by the Reformed Presbytery of Scotland, 10 October, 1756.

Mr. Martin was the first Covenanter minister to be ordained in Ireland and at that time the only minister in Counties Down and Antrim. The ordination took place on 2 July, 1757, at the old graveyard of The Vow near Ballymoney on the banks of the River Bann and convenient to a crossing place. In 1760 the congregations on both sides of the Bann were divided and he resided at Kellswater retaining the oversight of Covenanting societies at Cullybackey, Laymore, Cloughmills, The Vow (Ballymoney) and Dervock. He also preached in Counties Londonderry and Donegal. Kellswater was established as a Reformed Presbyterian congregation in 1760.

Mr. Martin was passionate about the Gospel and the people of Ulster. He was fearless in his opposition to the established church and the authorities who continued to discriminate against his people. It was after a period of excessive rent and the evictions of tenants from their homesteads that while preaching at The Vow he proclaimed his opposition to these excessive demands.

Across the Atlantic, Presbyterians and Covenanters from Octoraro in Pennsylvania, Virginia, and North Carolina, who had gone to South Carolina and settled at Rocky Creek in 1750, had by 1755 formed the "Catholic" (a union of various groups of Presbyterians; Associate, Covenanter, Burgher, Anti-Burgher and Seceder) church on Rocky Mount Road, 15 miles South-East of Chester. Covenanters began holding society meetings in 1770 and wrote to Ireland for a minister. Mr. Martin replied positively to the call in 1772.

About one thousand Covenanters, Seceders, and others, including Roman Catholics, agreed to go with him. Mr. Martin led the five shiploads of emigrants which sailed in 1772. The first two sailed from Larne, the next two from Belfast, and the last one from Newry. William Martin acted as an agent for 460 families and sailed on the Lord Dunluce which left Larne on 4 October and arrived in Charleston on 20 December. The majority of those who travelled were from the vicinities of Ballymoney, Ballyrashane, Derrykeighan, Kilraughts, Ballymena, The Vow and Kellswater.

William Martin settled in the general area of Abbeville (Rocky Creek in Chester County) where he bought a tract of land one mile square and his people took up 'bounty land'. He was the first Covenanter minister who settled in the southern colonies. In 1774 the Covenanters under his leadership built their own meetinghouse separate from Catholic Presbyterian, a log building on the same road as that of the 'Catholic' congregation at Rocky Creek.

In 1777 he was dismissed on account of alleged intemperate habits. However poor judgement regarding the customs of frontier hospitality could have led to the accusations which his opponents readily brought forward. As a man of God Mr. Martin was ever ready to speak his mind and was an outspoken critic of the injustice of British government policies in the Colonies. At one point he had to answer his statements before Lord Cornwallis himself.

The British Tory troops stationed nearby at Rocky Mount burned Martin's log church building as a result of Martin's sermons in 1780. He was imprisoned for 6 months at Camden and Winnsboro, and was put on trial before Lord Cornwallis, the famous general, in 1781. It is reported that Martin stood erect before him 'gray hair uncovered, eyes on Cornwallis. His countenance was marked with frankness and benevolence.'

Cornwallis: "You are charged with preaching rebellion from the pulpit - you an old man and a minister of the gospel of peace with advocating rebellion against your lawful sovereign, King George III! What have you to say in your defence?"

Martin: "I am happy to appear before you. For many months I have been held in chains for preaching what I believe to be the truth. As to King George, I owe him nothing but good will. ..... As a king he was bound to protect his subjects in the enjoyment of their rights. Protection and allegiance go together and where the one fails the other cannot be exacted. The Declaration of Independence is but a reiteration of what our Covenanting fathers have always maintained. I am thankful you have given me liberty to speak, and will abide your pleasure, whatever it may be."

He was sentenced to death but later freed through the influence of a British officer who knew his family in Ireland.

In the spring of 1781 on account of the disturbed state of the country in the Chester District, he sought refuge in Mecklenberg County North Carolina where he established further congregations. After the surrender of Lord Cornwallis at Yorktown, in 1781, he returned to South Carolina, and resumed his charge around Rocky Creek.

In 1782 some Covenanter ministers, mostly in Pennsylvania joined with some from the Associate (Seceder) Presbyterian Church and formed the Associate Reformed Presbyterian Church to which most of the Covenanter groups in America united. However Martin refused to join. While it was true that he was not in good standing with the church at that time he still held tightly to his convictions and beliefs, and was one of the few ministers who kept the Covenanter cause alive in America .

There is speculation that after he was again dismissed for his conduct in 1785, that this charge was brought because he refused to join the Associate Reformed Church. Ever popular, he continued to preach in schoolhouses, church buildings, and homes. In 1793, he was restored to his privileges, and was made a member of the Committee of the Reformed Presbytery of Scotland, with Revs. King and McGarragh, to judicially manage the affairs of the Church in America. He continued to preach at the Jackson's Creek Church, Wolf Pen or Wolf Pit Meeting House, Winnsboro, and at private houses in all the settlements between Statesville, North Carolina, and Louisville, Georgia. Sadly his sin of intemperance continued and at meeting of the Reformed Presbytery of America, charges were brought against him and he was deposed from the ministerial office by that court, 12 March, 1801. He did not cease preaching, however, until shortly before his death.

Memorial at the grave of William Martin erected by the Daughters of The Revolution 1936

He died of a fever, brought on by an injury received by falling from his horse, 25 October, 1806, and he was buried in a small graveyard near his cabin. William Martin was man of his times. A pioneer and clear advocate of the Gospel, he fearlessly applied scriptural principles to his contemporary society. He was a proficient scholar, an eloquent preacher, and an able divine. However his career was blighted by his sinful intemperance no doubt exacerbated by the extreme hardships of life and the great trials of ministering on the frontier.

He is remembered as one of the most important founders of the cause of Christ's Crown and Covenant in the New World.

'Scottish Migration to South Carolina, 1772'. by Jean Stephenson 1971.
'Rev. William Martin', unpublished article by Linda Smetzer

Memorial stone placed at the Vow to commemorate the 250th anniversary of
William Martin's ordination in June 2007

REV. WILLIAM STAVELY: 1743 -1825

Signature of Rev. William Stavely

William Stavely was born in 1743 in Ferniskey, near Kells, in County Antrim. His great-grandfather had left Yorkshire and settled in the area in 1638 and the family were members of the Church of Ireland until William Stavely's father, Aaron, became a Covenanter by conviction. The family farm was of a reasonable size and William Stavely grew up, by the standards of the day, in comfortable circumstances. Aaron and his wife early dedicated their son to the ministry of the Reformed Presbyterian Church and were determined to give him the best education that they could afford. He was sent to the Classical School in Antrim as soon as he was able to go and then, having studied at Glasgow University, finished his training at the Reformed Presbyterian Theological Hall in Paisley, Scotland. He was licensed to preach by the Scottish Reformed Presbytery in 1769. After two years as a probationer, assisting William Martin, William James and Matthew Lynn in Antrim, Londonderry and east Donegal, he accepted the call to minister to the Covenanters in north Down.

By 1772 the Covenanters in north Down were sufficiently strong to be able to issue a call to William Stavely and he was ordained in August of that year. The call was 'from the Covenanted Electors between the Bridge of Dromore and Donaghadee in the County of Down'. Those who signed the call to Stavely were not all members of the societies in the immediate vicinity of Conlig. Many were from Societies which later became the congregations of Dromore, Bailiesmills and Knockbracken. The new minister was aged 29 when he accepted this call.

In 1776, Mr Stavely while continuing to minister in Newtownards, chose to make Knockbracken the centre of his ever-increasing ministry. He had married Miss Mary Donald of Marymount, Antrim, and settled at Annsborough House at Newtownbreda, on a farm of twenty acres. They had a family of six daughters and two sons.

A meeting-house was established at Knockbracken. However, Mr Stavely's workload increased still further when three of the Church's six ministers emigrated to America in these years. When the two other ministers died in 1779, leaving only Mr Stavely, the Reformed Presbytery was dissolved. He then had to shoulder the leadership of the entire church until more ministers were ordained in the 1780s and the Presbytery was re-formed in 1792. This was a period of immense productivity as Mr Stavely rode back and forward across southern Ulster through Down, Armagh, Monaghan and Cavan. Wherever he went, he commanded respect and attracted large crowds. In these years he organised five more new congregations; at Rathfriland, Drumillar, Ballylane, Fairview and Creevagh.

Mr Stavely had two spells in prison because of the very public stand which he had taken against the government over a range of issues. For over twenty years, he had engaged in public controversy concerned with the application of biblical standards to the issues of his day.

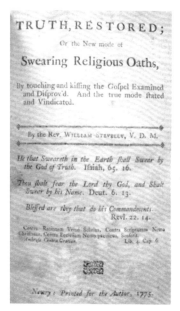

His first confrontation with the government was in 1775 when he published a pamphlet which dealt with the manner of taking oaths by kissing the Bible, many refusing to swear by this method and were fined. Mr Stavely contended that all that was necessary was the simple biblical method of swearing with an uplifted hand.

The 1780s were also a time of controversy with the Seceders, who after 1783 had accepted a share of the Regium Donum, the funds made available by the government for Irish Presbyterians. In these years, Mr Stavely led the campaign to expose the inconsistency of the Seceders' position, claiming to be the true heirs of the Scottish Covenanters while also prepared to accept help from a Government that refused to carry out its Covenant obligations. This was an attack on both the Seceders and the government.

The Volunteer movement, formed by Protestants in Ireland to defend against a threatened French invasion had become a pressure group to press for reforms from the Dublin Government. William Stavely became a captain in his local regiment, and many of his congregation in Knockbracken joined his unit, the 'Drumbracken Volunteers'. He asserted that people had the right to expect from government the security for their lives and property, the preservation of peace and impartial administration and decision-making.

In north Down the radical volunteers, the United Irishmen, were very active. It was widely believed that Covenanters were heavily involved in the organisation. William Stavely was suspected to be a United Irishman because of his active involvement in the former Volunteers and his outspoken condemnation of government, his influence across Ulster and his refusal, as a Covenanter, to take an Oath of Allegiance. His Covenanting principles would not permit him to swear allegiance to a king and government which had departed from the seventeenth century covenants.

In 1796, he published a book called *An Appeal to Light* as a direct reply to the very influential book among the radicals, *The Age of Reason* by Tom Paine, the philosopher of the French Revolution. He may have been sympathetic to some of the goals of the United Irishmen in their earliest, non-violent, phase. But, when in 1796 the movement allied itself with the Roman Catholic Defender movement and sought help from a deistical government in France, he distanced himself from it. He was most adamant that he had never actually joined the movement. In 1796, after conferring with the Reformed Presbyterian Church in Scotland, Mr Stavely was instrumental in drawing up a declaration issued by the Reformed Presbyterian Churches in the counties of Antrim and Down which condemned disorderly meetings. While not naming the United Irishmen and others, it was clearly directed at them.

However by his actions, William Stavely appeared to the authorities to show some sympathies with the United Irish movement. He accompanied William Orr, who had been found guilty of administering the United Irishman's oath, to the scaffold at Carrickfergus in October 1797. He also walked with Daniel English, another alleged United Irishman, from Ballymena to Connor to his execution singing Psalms and praying with him. However, Orr was a neighbour, and English a fellow Covenanter. In each case it was widely held that they were falsely accused and it was likely that Mr Stavely wished to show solidarity with them.

The authorities were, however, so suspicious that on 13 March 1797 a detachment of cavalry raided the Covenanters' meeting-house, in Ann Street, Newtownards, looking for arms or other incriminating evidence. Acting on information that arms were concealed at the Knockbracken meeting-house, a raid took place there too on Sabbath 25 June 1797. The service was interrupted by Colonel Barber, the Mayor of Belfast, and a troop of cavalry. William Stavely dismissed the congregation and surrendered to the soldiers. Nothing was found in the raids on the Newtownards and Knockbracken meeting-houses, nevertheless he spent two months in prison.

Finally, in the winter of 1797-8, he gave solemn warning to every Society which he inspected to avoid all links with the United Irishmen. This indicates that Mr Stavely's ministry in this period was to refocus men's eyes on the eternal and spiritual and not upon political revolution.

Rev William Stavely was again arrested a second time. On 13 June 1798 soldiers returning from the Battle of Ballynahinch, the principal engagement of the Rebellion in County Down, seized him, without any charge. He was alleged to have concealed arms at the Knockbracken Meeting-house for use by the rebels. Following his arrest, five rooms of his house were burned, along with his turf stack, carriage house and carriage. Over the next few nights, all his furniture and clothes were plundered. His books and papers were destroyed. Mr Stavely spent until the following December confined in various gaols, ending up in a prison ship in Belfast Lough. During these six months in prison, he was threatened and treated harshly. His baby son, Joseph, whom he had never seen, died. The only contact he had with his wife was when she came each morning to the shore within sight of the ship and held up a white sheet as a sign to reassure him that all was well with his family at home. He was released when no charge could be made against him.

In 1800, two years after William Stavely was released from prison, he accepted a call to Cullybackey and Kellswater and in 1811 he was appointed Moderator of the first meeting of Synod. During this time the congregation, divided into two separate charges and he chose Kellswater in 1813 where he remained until his death in 1825 at the age of eighty two. His son William John became the minister of Kilraughts and Dervock, and grandson Alexander McLeod Stavely was the notable missionary to New Brunswick.

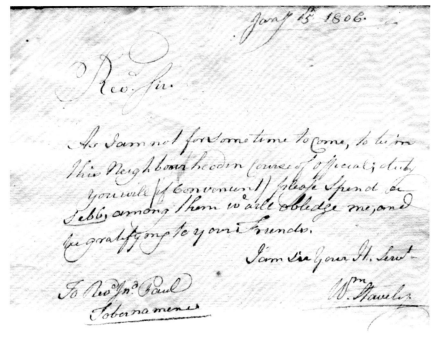

Letter from William Stavely to Rev. John Paul of Loughmourne, 15 January 1806

Rev. William Stavely was blessed with an outstanding stamina. In his early ministry he travelled extensively and was called upon to preach throughout the province and even with his months of imprisonment, in over fifty-three years of ministry he never once failed to preach on the Sabbath. William Stavely was described by J. S. Reid, the historian of Irish Presbyterianism, as the 'apostle of the Covenanting church in Ireland.' For a time he was the Church's only minister, he had been twice imprisoned and was the founder of perhaps as many as twelve congregations. He had made a mark for God in his generation. A century after his death, his name was still mentioned in many places in Ulster with respect, veneration and love. The use of the name 'Stavely' has given him a notable memorial with its attachment to many Covenanter children throughout the years. In his day, and for long afterwards, he was, in the words J.S. Reid, 'the most distinguished minister' of the Reformed Presbyterian Church.

Grave of Rev. William Stavely, Kellswater

Article adapted from;

'The Rev. William Stavely 1743-1825.' by Trevor McCavery, in Reformed Theological Journal. Volume 14; November 1998

'William Stavely, Brief Biographical Sketch', by Rev. Samuel Ferguson, 1897, Republished by The Mid-Antrim Historical Group 18; 1993.

WILLIAM STAVELY'S TABLE

William Stavely's table now in Canada, the chairs are Irish but perhaps not original to the table

The piece of furniture in question is a plain square roughly built mahogany table and it is believed that the table was a wedding gift to William Stavely and Mary Donald and dates from 1776 and was part of the furniture of their home at Annsborough, near Knockbracken. The current owner of the table who lives in Montreal Canada, is the great grandson of Rev. Alexander McLeod Stavely (William Stavely's grandson) the Irish church's missionary to St. John's New Brunswick. The table came into his possession through A. McL. Stavely's sister the present owner's father's great aunt a Mrs Ann Adams Moore (nee Stavely) who gave the table to her grand nephew.

The table is a silent witness to the stirring events where Ulster Covenanters were caught up in the events of 1798. Soldiers returning from the Battle of Ballynahinch on the night of Tuesday, 13 June, 1798, seized William Stavely at his house at Annsborough in Newtownbreda, on the grounds that he was "a general officer of the United Irishmen". It was later determined that a British spy had come to see him before the battle in order to entrap him but failed to receive any useful reply. Mr. Stavely refused to go until he had finished writing his sermon. To amuse themselves while they waited, the soldiers went about slashing the furniture with their swords.

William Stavely describes the scene:

'They set fire to the house, in four rooms and kitchen. They burned my turf-stack and car-house and car, also a variety of articles. They took away that night and three succeeding nights almost all my furniture, plate and apparel to the amount of £200 and upwards. I was very ill-used by the military on my way to Belfast, giving me the worst of language.'

In Belfast, he was thrown into prison and kept there 3 weeks...
Eight days and nights without having a bed to lie on, or even having off my clothes. Sundry times I was insulted by the military. Sundry times they threatened to hack me, to hang me, to burn me. One of them swore nine times by the Holy Ghost, he would shoot me before I left that yard.

There is no doubt that the table belonged to William Stavely, and that it escaped being burned or carried away by the soldiers is remarkable in itself. The outhouses and other rooms may have been ransacked and torched about him but his presence perhaps in the very room where the table was, may have prevented its destruction. The slashes indicate that the flaps were down. It may therefore have been pushed against the wall and thus escaped notice - or perhaps returned after his release from prison.

A sword mark on the table

Because of his principles, William Stavely, aged 55, the father of 11, was put on board a prison-ship in Belfast Lough. Eventually Stavely was released as there was no firm evidence against him. An attempt to receive compensation from the government for his losses (furniture etc., books, manuscripts, Minutes of Presbytery, plus £70) went unanswered.

Thanks to Mr. Jim Armour, Montreal, and Mr. John O'Neill, Kellswater

THOMAS HOUSTON: 1803-1882

Thomas Houston was minister of Knockbracken Reformed Presbyterian congregation, from 1828 until his death in March 1882, at the age of 78. Houston's name became a household word among Covenanters on both sides of the Atlantic.

Houston was born in 1803 at Donegore, between Antrim and Templepatrick in County Antrim. When he was about eight years old, his family moved to Cullybackey, where he sat under the ministry of Rev. William Stavely. His 'first-remembered yearnings and impressions were those of true religion'. He later wrote that as a boy of thirteen, 'the preaching of the Word and the other ordinances of the sanctuary made a deep and I trust saving impression on my mind. I was led to see the excellency of the Saviour, and the suitableness of his finished salvation to my necessities'.

In 1819 he went to study at Belfast Academical Institution and this was followed by brief periods of teaching in Ballymena Academy, Portora in Enniskillen and the Academical Institution in Belfast. However from an early period he had been led to desire the office of the ministry. In 1825 he went to study at the Theological Hall of the Reformed Presbyterian Church of Scotland at Paisley, under the instruction of the Rev. Andrew

Symington. Being licensed to preach by the Eastern Presbytery of the Reformed Presbyterian Church of Ireland on 25 December 1826, he preached in Knockbracken the following Sabbath and received a call there the next year, being ordained on 8 April 1828. During the next 54 years he had a huge influence on the Knockbracken congregation, the denomination as a whole (both at home and abroad) and the wider evangelical movement.

Houston was born at a time when the Reformed Presbyterian Church in Ireland was undergoing considerable expansion, yet the early years of Houston's ministry were ones of tension within the Reformed Presbyterian Church, eventually resulting in a division in 1840. On one side of the debate was the Rev. John Paul of Loughmourne and Carnmoney, a gifted theologian, whose writings had helped Henry Cooke and the orthodox party in the Synod of Ulster during the Arianism conflict. On the other side of the debate was a young Thomas Houston. The dispute was over the power of the civil magistrate *circa sacra* – or the extent of the civil ruler's responsibility to establish true religion. The controversy began in 1831 when Paul wrote a letter to the *News-Letter* taking issue with several statements regarding the civil magistrate in Houston's recently launched periodical, *The Covenanter* and claiming that they did not represent the views of the Reformed Presbyterian Church in either Ireland or Scotland. Houston claimed that his views were merely those of the Westminster Confession of Faith but according to Paul's reinterpretation of the church's doctrinal standard:

"The Westminster Divines, when they wrote the 20th chapter of their Confession, had not the slightest idea that the civil magistrate should punish a heretic or an idolater as well as a thief, a murderer, or a traitor – they had not the faintest conception that heresy should be suppressed by the sword of the civil magistrate."

For Paul, if a magistrate actually put the views of 'our zealous young friend' into practice, 'human blood would flow like water' and 'the globe we inhabit would become a howling wilderness'. The Synod strove for peace and its 1833 meeting seemed to have brought the matter to an amicable conclusion. Three years later though, the controversy was re-ignited by a 'memorial' from the Knockbracken congregation, which led to the Synod issuing a *Declaration on Civil Government* in 1837. This supported the view of Houston that 'authoritative restraint of the open violation of the first, second, or any other commandment of God is not persecution; for, as no man has a right to violate the Divine Law, no right is invaded'. On the penultimate day of the 1840 Synod, Paul's party, which had been threatening separation for the last two years, read out a document protesting against the decisions of the Synod regarding the civil magistrate and declining its authority. They handed in a copy of this 'Declinature and Protest' signed by five ministers of the Eastern Presbytery, along with twelve elders, and withdrew from the Synod. Three years later they constituted themselves as 'The Eastern Reformed Presbyterian Church'. In 1902 the Eastern Synod united with the Presbyterian Church in Ireland, but half of its congregations took independent action and returned to the Reformed Presbyterian Church.

 The committee set up by the church in 1842 to issue a conclusive statement on the whole affair expressed the opinion that while Houston and the other editors of *The Covenanter* should have perhaps expressed themselves more carefully, solemnly declared the Rev.. Thomas Houston, not guilty of advocating persecuting principles.

The debate with Paul however is just one example of Houston's influence on the denomination as a whole, and his commitment to her distinctive principles. He played a key role in the annual meetings of Synod right from his ordination, led campaigns for Temperance and against National Education and was responsible for large parts of the church's revised historical testimony, book of discipline and other Synodical publications. It was Houston who suggested that the denomination produce its own periodical, and then edited the *Covenanter* for over thirty years, following its launch in 1830. He wrote pamphlets against hymns and Sabbath desecration, and was appointed as one of the Irish Reformed Presbyterian Church's first two professors of theology when it established its own   theological college. He was committed to the belief in the perpetual obligation of the Covenants, National and Solemn League, and was the main driving force behind the denomination formally renewing them in 1853.

While firmly committed to the teachings of his own denomination, Thomas Houston was, however, far from a small-minded or sectarian individual. 'Never has the Covenanted Church held the doctrine of exclusive salvation', he wrote in the first article ever published in *The Covenanter*. He believed that the divisions in the church were sinful, and 'ever unfeignedly rejoice[d] that, while the points on which evangelical Christians differ are not immaterial, those on which they are agreed are numerous and fundamental'. He had a keen interest in the work of evangelical societies and played a key role in founding the Destitute Sick Society, the Belfast Juvenile Society and the Belfast Town (later City) Mission. In terms of the cultural emphases of evangelicalism, Houston was one of six people who signed the first temperance pledge in Ireland in September 1829. For Houston, 'the unsectarian character of the movement formed one of its strongest recommendations' and four years after this first pledge was signed, there were 15,000 members of temperance societies in Ulster.

The greatest outpouring of evangelical fervour in the nineteenth century however was undoubtedly the 1859 revival. Houston addressed the Synod on the subject of revival and when the Synod passed resolutions about the revival, he greeted it in *The Covenanter* greeted as 'most gratifying that the Synod has declared itself decidedly in favour of Scriptural revival – and has given every encouragement to its members and people, by every Scriptural means, to help forward the great movement'.

The greatest passion of Houston's life, though, was 'the great work of making known [Christ's] light and salvation throughout the nations'. '[I] have been trying a little to excite a missionary spirit,' Houston wrote in his journal after a year in Knockbracken. His 'missionary zeal' had been recognised at the first meeting of Synod following his ordination, and he had been appointed one of the secretaries of the Synod's Missionary Association. For the rest of his life he presented 'full, hearty and stimulating' reports of the association's work to the Synod. In 1831 he assisted in the ordination of William Sommerville as a missionary for Nova Scotia and New Brunswick. Houston had read a paper annually at Synod on the subject of foreign missions for many years before the court finally set up a Foreign Mission in 1843 and in 1859 a Jewish Mission was set up at Houston's proposal. As a Professor at the Church's Theological Hall, 'he never failed to bring the duty of missions and some view of the progress of the work before the class'. In 1871, Dr James Martin was sent as a medical missionary to Syria mainly through Houston's influence. Indeed, the Synod declared on his death that Houston had been 'the very heart of our Church-life in our action towards Syria'. Closer to home, he had a key involvement in the planting of a new Reformed Presbyterian congregation in Killinchy (Ballymacashon)..

Thomas Houston also made his influence felt through his writings. His contributions to *The Covenanter* aside, Houston was perhaps one of the most prolific authors in the history of the Reformed Presbyterian Church.. The ten books he wrote before 1876 were included in the four-volume *Works doctrinal and practical of the Rev. Thomas Houston D.D..* These included theological topics such as '*The adoption of sons*', practical works such as '*The fellowship prayer-meeting*', and historical treatments of the Covenanters John Livingstone and James Renwick. '*A practical treatise on Baptism*', included in his *Works*, was complemented by a book on *The Lord's Supper: its nature, ends, and obligation* in 1878. In a significant departure from most British Presbyterian thought, he argued for a weekly administration of communion.

THE LORD'S SUPPER:

ITS NATURE, ENDS, AND OBLIGATION;

AND

Mode of Administration.

BY

THOMAS HOUSTON, D.D.

EDINBURGH
JAMES GEMMELL, 15 GEORGE IV. BRIDGE
1878

Never one to argue for a novelty however, Houston cited the support of John Calvin, Puritans such as John Owen and Stephen Charnock, and more recent theologians such as Jonathan Edwards. Two more works followed, *The dominion and glory of the Redeemer* in 1880 and *The intercession of Christ*, published posthumously in 1882.

Houston therefore had an influence far beyond the bounds of the Reformed Presbyterian Church but closest to his heart was the congregation he pastored. He had received, according to their own testimony, a 'poor, dispirited people' but within twelve years, under his pastoral care, their condition had been 'completely reversed' and they had been increased 'into a great multitude'. The journal he kept for the first four years of his ministry reveals a pastor who cared deeply for his own people, sought for God's blessing before he preached, and applied his sermons to his own heart. 'In the pulpit', wrote a contemporary, 'he had a peculiarly earnest, impressive and affectionate manner, as one who yearned over souls ... Those who have only read him can scarcely have an idea of the impression produced by the living presence, voice, or that inexpressible something which moves and warms the inner man'. An obituary comments that 'It was when addressing communicants at the sacramental table that he was at his best. He seemed like a messenger who had come straight from the presence of his blessed Lord ... His face seemed to shine like that of Moses'. Above all, his journal reveals someone who walked closely with God

At a time when little separated the worship practices of the Presbyterian churches, his convictions were clearly seen in his commitment to the original Reformed Presbyterian

distinctives – Christ's kingship over the nation, and the perpetual obligation of the Scottish Covenants. To Houston, mainstream Presbyterianism, although claiming descent from the Covenanters, was in danger of 'compromising a faithful testimony and encouraging national apostasy by incorporating with a civil system that refuses homage to the reigning Mediator'. He deplored the divisions of the church and sought unity – which he believed could be brought about through the Covenants and the Westminster Standards. However 'the tenacity with which he held by the distinctive principles and position of the Reformed Presbyterian Church never hindered him from co-operating in any good work with evangelical men of other denominations, when he could do so without compromising himself.

Thomas Houston's grave, Knockbracken

Thomas Houston was a key figure in the Irish Church,. In his death he was mourned as 'the revered father of the Covenanting Church in Ireland'. However, Houston had an influence far beyond the bounds of the Reformed Presbyterian Church, as was demonstrated at his funeral at which all the Protestant denominations of Belfast were represented. According to his obituary in the *Belfast News-Letter*, he was 'widely known and greatly respected by every branch of the Church of Christ'. Today Houston deservedly remains one of the best known of Covenanting ministers. The fact that he could hold such firm Covenanting convictions and yet be so involved in the gospel work of the universal church of Christ is perhaps his greatest legacy.

Stephen Steele

FASTI
OF THE REFORMED PRESBYTERIAN
CHURCH OF IRELAND

Fasti

of the

Reformed Presbyterian Church
of Ireland

compiled and edited by
Rev. Prof. ADAM LOUGHRIDGE, M.A., M.LITT., D.D.

Part I

Published jointly by the Committee on Church History of the
Reformed Presbyterian Synod of Ireland and
The Presbyterian Historical Society
1970

Fasti, a Latin word, was used in ancient Rome, and subsequently elsewhere primarily to denote any record or plan of official and religiously sanctioned events.

The fasti of ministers who have completed their earthly service in the history of the Church is an invaluable source of basic biographical details which result from a large amount of research, yet serve as the source for others in the future. The fasti exist of other church bodies and the Reformed Presbyterian Church is no different. The explanation of the late Prof. Adam Loughridge in the Presbyterian Historical Society of Ireland Bullitin 1970 at the publication of Part 1, is of worthy note and sets in context the work compiled in 1970 and his plan for Part 2 which is now here published together with an updated and re-edited Part 1.

An introduction to the Fasti of the
Reformed Presbyterian Church of Ireland
by Rev. Prof. Adam Loughridge.
Part 1. 1970.

For many years the only record of the life and ministry of Reformed Presbyterian ministers was to be found in a notebook in the handwriting of the late Rev. James McConnell. The work, while bearing the stamp of Mr. McConnell's painstaking research and careful compilation, was rather incomplete and some of the notes were mere fragments. Some years ago at the suggestion of some friends in the Presbyterian Historical Society I undertook the preparation of a Fasti of Reformed Presbyterian ministers. The first part has just been published jointly by the Presbyterian Historical Society and the Committee on Church History of the Reformed Presbyterian Church.

The size of the publication, some 16 pages, makes a small contribution to historical literature, but it represents a great amount of effort. The historically minded will readily understand that genealogical research is a time consuming and sometimes frustrating occupation. The main sources of information are the obituary notices in the Press and in Church magazines. The difficulty that confronts the student of history lies in the fact that 19th century obituary notices were eulogies full of purple patches in which facts were few and far between. We turn, for instance, to a copy of the Covenanter of 1875. We note in the index that on page 160 there is an obituary of the Rev. John Smith. We are hopeful that the record will supply the facts that are looked for. We find instead that John Smith was born towards the end of the previous century of excellent parentage; that after passing through various unnamed local schools he had a fine scholastic record and graduated with academic distinction; that he was licensed to preach the gospel; that after serving the Church of his fathers for more than 50 years he passed away peacefully after a brief illness. With records like these, and there are many of this sort, the historiographer's work is like that of making bricks without straw!

Yet research of this nature gives unexpected pleasures and rewards and the writer is stimulated with the sense of satisfaction that Old Mortality must have felt on the hills and moors of Scotland, as yet another tribute in stone to a worthy saint of God was uncovered and adorned by loving hands.

The fasti's earliest subject is David Houston, the turbulent contemporary of Cameron and Renwick, who, though a thorn in the flesh of the Route Presbytery, earned the fine tribute from Renwick: "As for Mr. David, he carries himself very straight". Others of outstanding interest are William Martin, the first Irish Covenanter to be ordained, and William Staveley, "the apostle of the Covenanters", who in an effective ministry from 1772 to 1825 was responsible for founding twelve congregations.

It is hoped at a later date to complete the record by issuing a second part dealing with ministers of the Eastern Reformed Presbyterian Synod, and ministers of the R.P. Church of North America who were born in Ireland.

ADAM LOUGHRIDGE. Bulletin of Presbyterian Historical Society of Ireland, December, 1970.

List of the main abbreviations used in the fasti

appt. ....appointed

br. ....brother

d. ....daughter

ed. ....educated

grad. ....graduated

inst. ....installed

int. ....interred

lic. ....licensed

m. ....married

O.C.B. ....Old College Belfast

ord. ....ordained

res. ....resigned

ret. ....retired

s. ....son

s.s. ....stated supply

y. ....youngest

Fasti

of the
Reformed Presbyterian
Church of Ireland

Based upon the
First Edition compiled and edited by
Rev. Prof. Adam Loughridge, 1970

edited by
Rev. W. Norman McCune and Mr. Trevor Magee

Aiken, Samuel

b. near Clough, Co Antrim, c. 1746; ed. Scotland; lic. by Refd. Presbytery; ord. Bannside Congregation 1776: res. 1790; inst. Rathfriland, Ballylane and Creevagh, 1798; died 25th December, 1798; int. Creevagh; m. Miss Adams, Clough.

Alexander, John

b. near L'derry, 1773; br. of Rev. Josias Alexander; ed. Scotland; lic. 1803; ord. Faughan and L'derry; res. 1825; inst. Linenhall Street, Belfast, 1826; joined Eastern R.P. Synod, 1840; Prof. of Theology in Eastern R.P. Church, 1841-1852; ret. 1850; died 22nd August 1852; Jacob Alexander, Waterside R.P. Church, was a son; Samuel Quigley, was a son-in-law.

Alexander, Josias

b. near L'derry, 1782; brother of Rev. John Alexander, Belfast; ed. Glasgow University; grad. MA, 1803; ord. Linenhall Street, Botanic Avenue, Belfast, and Knockbracken, 1809; res. Knockbracken, 1822; teacher of mathematics in Belfast Academy; died 10th November, 1823; int. Linenhall Street, later in City Cemetery.
Cf. B.N.L. 14th November, 1823

Alexander, Samuel

b. Tyrkeeveny, L'derry, 1748; ed. Scotland; lic. Scottish Refd. Presbytery, 1781; ord. Bready R.P. 19th August, 1783 for Covenanters in N. Tyrone, N. L'derry and E. Donegal; died 17th July, 1793; int. Glendermott
Cf. Brief Biographical Sketches by S. Ferguson, Covenanter, Vol. 1 , p. 312.

Allen, Robert

b. Legnacash, Cookstown; s. of Samuel Allen; ed. R.P. Theological Hall; lic. by Southern Presbytery, 1854, ord. missionary for work in Dublin, April, 1855; inst. Newtownards, 21st November, 1867; Clerk of Eastern Presbytery, 1894-1906; ret. June, 1906; died 28th November, 1910; m. Eliza Dale, d. of Edward Dale, Cork, 1857; one d., Maria Jane, m. Rev. Joseph McEwen.
Cf. Mins. Of Synod, 1911.

Archer, Samuel Reid

b. Redhill, Dromore, 16th July, 1900; s. of Josiah A Archer and Dorothy Reid; ed. Shaftesbury House, Q.U.B., grad BA Q.U.B., 1925; R.P. Theological Hall, 1925-28; lic. by Eastern Presbytery August, 1928; ord. Creevagh 28th November, 1928; minister in charge of Fairview, 28th November 1928 to 29th March 1934; inst. Rathfriland, 22nd February, 1945; ret. 22nd February, 1972; died 7th May, 1979; int. Rathfriland; Moderator of Synod, 1935; m. Jean Crawford, d. Joseph and Mrs Crawford, Creevagh;
1 d. Elsie m. Harold McCune, Belfast; author of "A Brief History of the Irish Mission", 1970.

Ball, Thomas William

b. Mullaghdrin, Dromara, 21st May, 1916; s. of James and Martha Ball; ed. Greenmount Agric College, Q.U.B., R.P. Theological Hall, Belfast; grad. BA 1938; ord by Eastern Presbytery 13th May, 1941 for work in Liverpool R.P. congregation, installed Larne, 29th December, 1942; res. 2nd May, 1944; Brethren evangelist in Ireland, France and

Australia, emig. Australia 1965; died 6th July, 2007; m. Annie (Nan) Rice, Belfast; 3 s., David, John, Raymond, 2 d., Helene, Hazel.

Barkley, Alexander
b. Knockahollet, Kilraughts, 22nd April, 1913; s. of Hugh Barkley and Annie Thompson; ed. Knockahollett P.S., Ballymena Academy, Dalriada, Magee, T.C.D., grad BA 1935; R.P. Theological Hall, 1935-1937; R.P.T.S., Pittsburgh 1937-1938; lic by Pittsburgh Presbytery 1937; ord. Cregagh Road, 8th March, 1939; res. 3rd September, 1946; inst. Geelong, Victoria, 1st February, 1947; res. 1965 to lecture full-time Church History and Hebrew, Reformed Theological College, Geelong; Principal, 1958-1978; D.D. College of Divinity, London University; ret. 1980; died 28th August, 2000, Geelong; int. Highton Cmty. Geelong; m. Elizabeth (Elsie) Simpson, Cullybackey; 2 s. David, Lester; 2 d. Ruth, Rosemary.

Benaugh, George
b. Drumlough, Rathfriland, County Down, 12th October, 1845; s. of George Benaugh and Mary Ann Dickson; ed. Crawford's Academy Warrenpoint, Q.C.B.; Princeton and McCormack Seminaries, grad. 1869; lic. by Chicago Presbytery, 3rd April, 1871; ord. and inst. Summit Hill, 1873, Pa.; inst. Philadelpia, 1877; inst. Mifflintown, Pa., 1880; inst. Camden, N.Y., 1885; inst. Lexington and Mansfield, Ohio, 1888; inst. Knockbracken, Co. Down, 1898; ret. 13th May, 1913; died 3rd December, 1919, in Belfast; int. Rathfriland; D.D. from New Windsor College, Maryland, 10th June, 1885; m. Nettie Androbus, of New London, Iowa, 6th February, 1880; d. Mary Elizabeth, wife of Henry C. Lyons, Newry.

Blair, James
b. Aughensillagh, Limavady, 23rd September, 1880; e.s. of John Blair and Elizabeth McCloy; ed. Magee College, 1903, R.P. Theological Hall, 1902-1905; lic. by Western Presbytery, 1905, ord. Ballyclare 7th December, 1905; res. 1916; inst. Milford, 20th December, 1916; res. 1929; inst. Kilraughts, 12th March, 1929; died 30th April, 1966; m. Mary Susan Moffett, Creevagh, 30th April, 1908; 3s., Rev. John Thomas Moffett, Rev. Hugh Jamison, Dr James William McCloy; 1 d., Beth.

Blair, John Thomas Moffett
b. Milford, Co Donegal, 17th July, 1909; e.s. of Rev. James Blair and Mary Susan Moffett; ed. Milford Primary School, Coleraine Academical Institution, Magee College, T.C.D.; R.P. Theological Hall, Belfast 1929-32; grad BA (T.C.D.) 1930; lic. by Northern Presbytery, 1st June, 1932; ord. Stranraer, 5th October 1932; inst. Glenmanus, Portrush, 17th October, 1944; inst. Airdrie, 17th October 1949; inst. Stranraer, 17th June, 1970; ret. 1978; died 1st April 1994; int. Ayr; m. Kathleen Beck, daughter of J.W Beck, Belfast; 1 d. Maureen, 1 s. Brian.

Blair, Joseph Alexander Cresswell
b. Carnamuff, Carrichue, 23rd November, 1921; 4th s. of William John Blair and Sarah Moore McIlmoyle; ed. Dunbrock Primary School, Limavady Grammar School, Magee College, T.C.D.; R.P. Theological Hall, Belfast 1942-45; grad. B.A. (T.C.D.), 1943; lic. by Western Presbytery, 30th May, 1945; ord. Creevagh, 8th November, 1945; inst. Newtownards, 3rd September 1959; inst. Ballylaggan, 15th May, 1973; Moderator of Synod, 1956; Clerk of Eastern Presbytery, 1966-1973; died 28th April, 1975; int. Ballylaggan; m. Sallie Kennedy, Belfast; 2 s. Alexander and Moore.

Boggs, Hans
b. Creevy, Loughbrickland, 1774; e.s. of Hans Boggs; ed. Glasgow, 1792, R.P. Theological Hall, Scotland; lic. by Refd Presbytery; ord. Rathfriland and Ballylane, 1802; res. Rathfriland and retained Ballylane, 1812; died 31st October, 1837, Dierlet, Co. Armagh; m.; youngest d., Jane Isabella, m. 11th June 1841, Wm McCormick.
Cf. Matric Alb. of Glasgow Univ. "Northern Whig" 16th November 1837, History of Rathfriland by James Buchanan.

Boyd, Thomas
b. 1800; ed. O.C.B. and R.P. Theological Hall, Paisley; lic. by Southern Presbytery, 1831; ord. College Street South, Belfast, 19th June, 1833; res. 1837; joined Belfast Presbytery, Synod of Ulster, 1838; inst, Magherally, 27th March, 1839; res. June, 1839; inst. First Castleblayney, 21st June, 1839; died 26th November, 1863; m.1. only daughter of James McBirney, Millmount, Co. Monaghan; m.2. Miss Mossman, Castleblayney.

Boyd, Torrens
b. Lismoyle, Swatragh, Co. L'derry, 1838; ed. O.C.B., R.P. Theological Hall, Belfast; lic. Northern Presbytery, 1866; ord. Penpont, 1867; res. 1873; inst. Ringrash, Co. L'derry, 5th February, 1873, res. 1875; inst. Dromara, Co. Down, 24th February, 1875; res. 1890; inst. Liverpool, 2nd July, 1890; res. 1893; inst. Knockbracken, 11th January, 1893; res. 1898; inst. Dromara, 18th May, 1898; res. 1907; inst. Newtownards, 4th September, 1907; s.s. Killinchy (Ballymacashon); died 19th May, 1925; int. Dromara; m. Mary Simms, Tamlaght, Co L'derry, 5 d. (died in early years), 1 s., William Simms.

Britton, Alexander
b. 1786; s. of Joseph Britton; ed. Glasgow University, 1806; R.P. Theological Hall, Scotland; lic. by Western Presbytery; ord. Bready, 1815; Clerk of Western Presbytery; died 31st May, 1846; int. Grange, Bready; m.; 4 s. including Rev. Thomas Conn, Joseph.

Britton, Thomas Conn
b. Bready, 1836; 4th s. Rev. Alexander Britton; ed. Glasgow University, R.P. Theological Hall; lic. by Western Presbytery; ord. Newry, 21st June, 1865; res. 1868; died Bready, 10th March, 1869.

Brown, James
b. Ballynagappog, Rathfriland, 1835; ed. O.C.B., R.P. Theological Hall; lic. by Southern Presbytery; ord. Dervock and Ballymoney, 25th July, 1860; res. Dervock, retained Ballymoney, 1878; died 28th July, 1883; m. d. of James Stavely, Belfast; 4 s. James Stavely, William, Martin, Joseph; 5 d., Janie, Hessie, Anne, Elizabeth, Marianne;
Cf. Minutes of Synod, 1884.

Buchanan, James
b. Cullion, Co Tyrone; s. of James Buchanan; ed. Magee College; 1899-1902, R.P. Theological Hall, Belfast, Original Seceders Hall, Glasgow; grad. G.A.M.C., 1902; M.A. (Indiana) 1918 and B.D. (Central University, U.S.A.) 1920; lic. by Western Presbytery, 1906; ord. Rathfriland, 27th November, 1906; died 15th December, 1920; unm.

Calderwood, David

b. Dunnygarron, Cullybackey, 14th September, 1891; s. of William John Calderwood and Sarah Jane Lowry; ed. Magee College, T.C.D.; R.P. Theological Hall, Belfast 1913-1916; grad B.A. (T.C.D.) 1914, M.A. 1917; lic. by Northern Presbytery, May, 1916; ord. Clarendon Street, L'derry, 2nd November, 1916; 4 months in France in 1918 Y.M.C.A.; res. 6th July, 1921; inst. by Colorado Presbytery, Denver, 21st September, 1922; inst. Seattle, Washington, 1925; inst. Los Angeles, 4th January, 1929; inst. St. Pauls Presbyterian Church, Los Angeles; appt. Minister of Education, Glendale Presbyterian Church, 1943; res. 1945; appt. Sec. California Branch Nat. Assoc. Evangelicals; joined Orthodox Presbyterian Church; inst. Grace O.P. Church, Los Angeles; died 29th March, 1970; m. Annie Mary King, Seattle, Washington; 2 s. Deryk David, Noel King.

Calderwood, James William

b. Dunnygarron, Cullybackey, 2nd March, 1896, s. of William John Calderwood and Sarah Jane Lowry; ed. Ballymena Academy, Magee College; R.P. Theological Hall, Belfast, 1921-23; grad. G.A.M.C. 1921, lic. by Northern Presbytery, 7th May, 1924; ord. Bready, 14th October, 1924; Clerk of Western Presbytery, 1929-1971; Moderator of Synod, 1934, 1954; died 18th April, 1971; int. Cullybackey; m. Kathleen Moorhead; 3 d. Pauline, m. W.J.L. Rankin, Margaret, m. R.E. McCune, Wilma; 1 s. James.

Calderwood, Samuel McKay

b. Glasgow; s. of Samuel Calderwood and Elizabeth McKay; grad. M.A. Glasgow University, 1931, Theological Halls of the United Original Secession Church and Trinity College, Glasgow, 1929 -1931; lic. by Joint Presbyteries of Edinburgh and Glasgow, 8th September, 1931; ord. Kellswater, 14th December, 1932; Moderator of Synod 1966; died 23rd October, 1973; int. Kellswater; m. Jeannie McCollum; 1 d. Elizabeth m. Roy C. Moore.

Cameron, Simon

b. 1779; ed. Glasgow University, Scottish R.P. Theological Hall; lic. by Northern Presbytery; ord. Ballylaggan, 10th September, 1817; died 11th May, 1855, Drumsteeple, Aghadowey; m. d. of Rev. William Stavely, Kellswater.

Campbell, James

b. Cullybackey, 15th September 1905; s. of William Campbell and Rosetta Calderwood; ed. Ballymena Academy, Magee College, T.C.D.; grad. B.A. (T.C.D.), 1930; R.P. Theological Hall, 1929-31; R.P. Seminary, Pittsburgh, 1931-32; lic. by Iowa Presbytery, R.P.C.N.A., 11th May, 1931; ord. and inst. Stranorlar and Convoy, 4th January, 1933; inst. Larne 10th October, 1944; appt. Lecturer N.T. Language and Literature, R.P. Theological Hall, Belfast, 1945-1964; died 29th March, 1964, int. Cullybackey; m. Mary Burns Smith, Winnipeg; 2 s. Melville, William, 2 d. Joan, Sylvia.

Carlisle, Samuel

b. Ballybay 1790; s. of John Carlisle, farmer; ed. Glasgow University, R.P. Theological Hall; lic. by Refd. Presbytery; ord. Ballyclabber, 12th September, 1827; died 1856, m. Letitia Craig; 3 s. John, Samuel, James; 4d. Jane, Elizabeth, Letitia, Martha.

Carlisle, Thomas

b. Carnaughts, Co. Antrim, 1809; ed. O.C.B., R.P. Theological Hall; lic. by Northern Presbytery; ord. Rathfriland, 30th June, 1839, Clerk of Southern Presbytery, 1847-56;

died 6th February, 1856; m. 22nd April, 1841, Elizabeth Mary Martin, Tieragory, Rathfriland; 1 d., wife of Rev. John Hart, Ballylaggan.

Cathcart, Thomas
b. Ahoghill, Co. Antrim; 2 s. of Wm. Cathcart; ed. Glasgow University, R.P. Theological Hall; grad. M.A, Glasgow, 1800; lic. by Northern Presbytery; ord. Creevagh and Fairview, 10th June, 1806; died 1857; s. James Cathcart, M.D., Ballybay.

Chancellor, Josias Alexander
b. Dundonald, Co. Down, 14th November, 1824; s. Ephraim Chancellor; ed. O.C.B., R.P. Theological Hall; lic. by Northern Presbytery, 1846; grad. D.D. S.T.P., ord. Bready, 27th July, 1847; res. 1865; inst. College Street South, Belfast, 9th February, 1865; appt. Prof. of Theology, R.P. Theological Hall, 1879; died 26th May, 1895; m. 1861, d. of James Thompson, Saintfield; 2nd d. Minnie m. Dr. Nevin, 27th August, 1902.

Clarke, Alexander
b. nr. Kilrea, Co. L'derry, 16th July, 1793; s. of William Clarke and Elizabeth Craig; ed. O.C.B., grad. Glasgow University, 1819, Theological Hall, Paisley; chosen by the Irish Synod as missionary to North American British Provinces; lic. and ord., 24th May, 1827; arrived St. John, New Brunswick, 23rd August, 1827, selected Amherst, Nova Scotia; He travelled extensively; est. 15 mission stations; Clarke and all his congregations joined General Synod (New School), 14th October, 1847; contd. Amherst, N.S., and the vicinity; Hon. D.D. University of Pa, 1856; Moderator of General Synod, 1856; died, 15th March, 1874; m. Catherine McMillan, of Belfast, 22nd May, 1821.
Cf. 'The Chignecto Covenanters,' by Eldon Hay, 1996.

Cleland, Thomas
b. Crossgar, Co. Down, 1844; ed. Queen's College, Belfast, R.P. Theological Hall; grad. B.A. (R.U.I.) 1868; lic. by Eastern Presbytery, April, 1871; ord. Limavady, 1st July, 1871; died (suddenly) 8th August, 1873.

Cole, Isaac
b. Eleven Lane Ends, Co Armagh, 13th January 1919; s. of James Cole and Margaret Crothers; ed. Taniokey P.S., Newry Intermediate School, Magee College, T.C.D.; grad B.A. (T.C.D.), 1941; R.P. Theological Hall, Belfast, 1940-1943; lic. by Southern Presbytery, 1st June, 1943; ord. Trinity Street, Belfast, 23rd January 1945; inst. Drimbolg 5th March 1958; ret. 24th April 1989; clerk of Northern Presbytery, 1966 to 1988; Moderator of Synod, 1955, 1972; died 24th April 1990; int. Drimbolg; m. Anella McCandlis, Hillsborough; 3 s. Rodney, Alistair, Nigel.

Cromie, John McClelland
b. nr. Rathfriland, 1859; ed. Queen's College, Belfast, R.P. Theological Hall; grad. B.D., lic. by Southern Presbytery, 1882; ord. Kellswater, 22nd November, 1882; res. 1898; inst. Kilraughts, 18th May, 1898; appt. Prof. of Theology, R.P. Theological Hall, 1917; died 3rd July, 1928; m. Miss Mary Dinsmore, Kellswater; 1 s., David; 2 d., Sarah, Mary.

Cupples, Robert Barnett
b. 13th June 1905; s. of David Cupples and Margaret Barnett; ed. Ballymena Academy, Magee College, T.C.D.; R.P. Theological Hall, Belfast, 1930 to 1933, grad, B.A. (T.C.D.)

1930; lic. by Northern Presbytery, 9th June, 1933; ord. Fairview and Tullyvallen, 29th March, 1934; inst. Cregagh Road, 2nd September, 1947; inst. Loughbrickland, 5th April, 1951; minister in charge Clare, 1st February, 1955 to 3rd September, 1974; ret. 3rd September, 1974; Moderator of Synod, 1943; died 19th November 1995; int. Loughbrickland; m. Anna Isobel Pillow; 1 s. Brian; 1 d. Margaret.

Cuthbertson, John

b. Ayr, Ayrshire, 3rd April, 1718; ed. theology under Rev. John McMillan, lic. by Refd. Presbytery, 16th May, 1745, ord. 'sine titulo' Braehead, 18th May, 1747, for work among the scattered societies of Scotland; Moderator of the Refd. Presbytery in 1750; with Rev. Thomas Cameron missionary to societies of Covenanters in Ireland; 1751 missionary to America, arrived New Castle, Delaware, 5th August, 1751; first Covenanter minister who came to America, settled Middle Octorara, Lancaster Co., Pa; died 10th March, 1791; int. Lower Octorara; m. Sally Moore, Philadelphia, 25th February, 1756.

Davidson, Robert Hawthorne

b. Grange, Co. Tyrone, 1861; ed. Queens College, Galway; R.P. Theological Hall; lic. by Southern Presbytery, 7th August, 1888; ord. Fairview, 16th October, 1888; res. 1894; inst. L'derry, 11th September 1894; res. 1912; inst. Stranorlar. 28th May, 1912; ret. July, 1931; Clerk of Western Presbytery, 1895-1927; died 20th October, 1940; m., 1 d., Cherie.

Dick, James

b. Strabane, 7th November, 1799; s. of Alexander Dick, Merchant; ed. Glasgow University; grad. M.A. Glasgow, 1818; D.D., New York; R.P. Theological Hall, Scotland; lic. by Western Presbytery, 1822; ord. Kellswater, 17th May, 1826; appt. Prof. of Theology, R.P. Hall, 1854; ret. 1879; died 24th May, 1880 at L'derry; m. 1830, Jane, d. of Robert Wallace, Ballymena; 6 s., Alexander, Robert, Rev. Thomas Houston, Rev. James, John, Rev. William; 1 d., Frances, m. Rev Robert Wallace, Newry.
Cf. Mins. Of Synod, 1880.

Dick, James

b. Kellswater, 22nd March, 1842; s. of Rev. James Dick and Jane Wallace; ed. St. Andrew's, Q.C.B., R.P. Theological Hall; grad. M.A. (Q.U.I.) 1866; D.D. (Geneva); lic. by Northern Presbytery, February, 1869; ord. Wishaw, Scotland, 19th May, 1870; res. 1884; inst. Kilraughts, 1884; res. 1896; inst. Trinity Street, Belfast, 19th May, 1896; appt. Prof. of Hebrew, Biblical Criticism and Church History, 1887-1895; Prof. of Theology, 1895-1916; died 6th August, 1916; int. Dundonald; m. 1. Georgina Hamilton, Glasgow; 1 s., James Guthrie; 6 d., Maggie, Jeanie, Georgina, Helen, Frances, Agnes; m.2. Sarah McMullan, Ballycastle; 3 s., Walter Mill, William Gordon, John Owen; 2 d., Mary, m. Sir Francis Evans; Nan, m. Brigadier Williams.

Dick, Thomas Houston

b. Kellswater, 1832; 1st s. of Rev. James Dick and Jane Wallace; ed. Q.C.B., R.P. Theological Hall; lic. by Northern Presbytery; ord. Killinchy, 18th July, 1860; res. 1863; inst. Bailiesmills, July 1863; died 14th May, 1882; m. 1864 dau. of John Graham, Hillhead, Lisburn.

Dick, William
b. Kellswater, November, 1844; 5th s. of Rev. James Dick and Jane Wallace; ed. Q.C.B., R.B.A.I., R.P. Theological Hall; grad. MA, BA 1867, Q.U.I., 1871 (hons. classics); lic. by Northern Presbytery 6th August, 1872; ord. Limavady, 9th June, 1875; res. 1884; inst. Mulvin, 17th September, 1884; res. 1902; inst; Cregagh Road, Belfast, 5th November, 1901; ret. 18 March, 1919; died 23rd May, 1928; unm.; editor "Covenanter", 1890-1924.

Dickey, John Knox
b. Drumlamph, Castledawson; 5th May, 1877; s. of Samuel Dickey ed. Q.C., Belfast, R.P. Theological Hall Belfast; grad. B.A. R.U.I., 1908; lic. by Eastern Presbytery, 1911; ord. Bready, 28th September, 1911; res. 1919; inst. Stranraer (R.P.), 1919; res 1926; inst. Clarendon Street, L'derry, 4th February, 1926; inst. Cregagh Road, Belfast; res. 1938; joined General Assembly; inst. Drum, Co. Cavan, 13th September, 1938; died 8th November, 1955; m. 6th August, 1912, Anna Lee, Bailiesmills, 2 s., Rev. John Knox Dickey, minister in English Presbyterian Church, Newcastle Upon Tyne, Rev. Alexander Peden Dickey, minister in English Presbyterian Church, Bedlington, Northumberland; 2 d., Anna Lee, Rhoda, wife of Rev. C. G. McKnight, Ballyalbany.

Dobbin, Alexander
b. City of L'derry, 4th February, 1741(2?); s. of John Dobbin, a 'pious sailor'; ed. grad. Glasgow University, 1771. Theological lectures in Glasgow; lic. by Refd. Presbytery of Ireland, 6th July, 1772, ord. 'sine titulo' Conlig, Co. Down, 20th August, 1772, as a missionary to the Covenanters in America; sailed with Rev. Matthew Lynn, from L'derry and landed in New Castle, Delaware, 13th December, 1773; He, with Revs. John Cuthbertson and Matthew Lynn, constituted the Refd. Presbytery of America, at Paxtang, Dauphin Co. Pa., 10th March, 1774; ministered at Rock Creek (Gettysburg), Adams Co, Pa.; involved in the union forming the Associate Refd. Church, 1782. continued at Rock Creek; died Gettysburg, 1st June, 1809, int. Marsh Creek graveyard; m.1. Isabella Gamble, of Co. Down, July, 1772; m.2. Mrs. Mary (Irvin) Agnew, of Adams Co., 1801. Cf. Howe's History of Presbyterian Church in S. Carolina

Dodds, William
b. Co. Monaghan; s. of William Dodds and Miss Smyth; ed. Queen's University, Belfast, R.P. Theological Hall; grad. B.A. (Q.U.B.); lic. by Eastern Presbytery; ord. Ballenon and Ballylane, 20th August, 1924; died March, 1965; Clerk of R.P. Synod of Ireland, 1937-1950; m. May Macauley, d. of Matthew MacAuley, Croskelt, Co. Down; 1 s., William; 1 d., Vera.

Donnelly, Thomas
b. Belfast, 29th January, 1924; s. of Thomas Donnelly and Edith Smyth; ed. Methodist College; Q.U.B., grad BA 1946; R.P. Theological Hall, 1946-1948; R.P. Seminary, Pittsburgh 1948-1949; lic by Pittsburgh Presbytery, 1948; ord. and inst. Faughan; 1st December, 1949; inst. Ballyclabber 17th May, 1956; ret. 18th May, 1998; died 13th December, 2001; int Ballyclabber; m. Mary Eileen (Ivy) McPhillimy, of Newtownstewart; 2 d. Elizabeth, Mary; 1 s. Roger.

Douglas, Gawn
b. Ballenon, Co. Armagh, 1832; ed. O.C.B. and R.P. Theological Hall; lic. by Southern Presbytery; ord. Creevagh, 3rd March, 1863; res. May, 1883; inst. Loughbrickland,

6th May, 1884; died 15th March, 1915; m. 1865 daughter of Francis Scott, Drumguilla, Castleblayney.

Edgar, James
b. Belfast; ed. Q.C., Belfast and R.P. Theological Hall; grad. B.A. (R.U.I.) 1904; lic. by Eastern Presbytery; ord. Fairview, 1st March, 1907; res. 5th May, 1908; joined General Assembly; inst. Belturbet, 22nd July, 1908; res. 1912; inst. Tanderagee, 5th November, 1912; inst. Clonaneese; inst. Fannet and Rathmullan; m. 1910 d. of R. Watson, Castleblayney; 2 s., including Rev Kenneth M. Edgar, Rhodesia, 1 d.

Ewing, Gordon Thompson
b. nr. Portglenone, Co. Antrim, 17th July, 1798; s. of John Ewing and Mary Thompson (Anti-burgher Seceders); ed. under Rev John Bryce, and grad. O.C.B., 1821; emig. 1822, Philadelphia; befriended Rev Samuel Wylie, and went with him to Kaskaskia, Illinois, opened a classical school; espoused R.P. principles, studied theology under Rev Samuel Wylie; 1824, Philadelphia Seminary; lic. by Pittsburgh Presbytery, 9th May, 1825; ord. and inst. by Pittsburgh Presbytery, Canonsburgh, Washington Co., Pa., 23rd October, 1827; res. 16th May, 1830, ill-health returned to Ireland late 1830; 1831, called to L'derry; but engaged as s.s., 1831-40; inst. Grange, Co. Tyrone, 20th July, 1840; res. 9th November, 1841, returned to America, joined New School branch;. inst. 2nd Pittsburgh (Bayardstown), 9th September, 1842; Moderator of General Synod, 1847; died 21st March, 1848; m. Margaret Black, of Pittsburgh, 13th March, 1828.

Ferguson, Samuel
b. Grange, Co. Tyrone, 1854; s. of Rev. W. S. Ferguson, Grange; ed. Q.C., Belfast, R.B.A.I., R.P. Theological Hall; grad. B.A. Q.U.I., 1880; lic. by Southern Presbytery, May, 1881; ord. Faughan, 15th December, 1881; died 16th December, 1928; m. 1881 Miss Matier; 2 s., William Stavely, Jack. Author "Brief Biographical Sketches", 1897.

Ferguson, William Stavely
b. 1811; s. of Andrew Ferguson, Tevena, Cookstown; grand.s. of Rev. William Stavely; ed. O.C.B., T.C.D., and R.P Hall; lic. by Southern Presbytery, 1844; ord. Grange, Co. Tyrone, 2nd October, 1844; res 1894; died 16th October, 1905, at Tevena; m. 1850, d. Alexander Ferguson, Ardtrea, Cookstown; 3s., Samuel, William Alexander, James; 1 d.

Fullerton, Arthur
b. Garvagh; s. of Stewart Fullerton; ed. Q.C.B. and R.P. Theological Hall; lic. by Northern Presbytery; ord. Limavady, 1st July, 1828; res. 8th May; 1841, joined Coleraine Presbytery (General Assembly); inst. Killowen, 24th February, 1846; res. 28th October, 1849; died 22nd April, 1867; Rev. Stewart Fullerton, 3rd Ahoghill, was a son.

Gamble, William
b. nr. Ballykelly, 1763; s. of Robert Gamble; ed. Scotland; lic. by Refd. Presbytery, 1785; ord. Ballygay and Gortlee, Co. Donegal, 23rd July, 1788; died 6th August, 1839 at Greenhill, Letterkenny; m. Miss Art, Stranorlar; author "The Glory of Christ", N.B. "Brief Biographical Sketches", Ferguson.

Gibson, William

b. nr. Knockbracken, Co. Down, 1st July, 1753; s. of Robert Gibson and Susannah McWhirr; joined R.P. ed. grad. Glasgow University,1775, theology in Edinburgh; lic. by Refd. Presbytery of Ireland, 19th May, 1781; ord. and inst. by Refd. Presbytery congs. of Kellswater and Cullybackey, Co. Antrim, Ireland, 17th April, 1787; emig. Philadelphia, 18th October, 1797; s.s. Coldenham, New York, and in Vermont; with Rev. James McKinney and ruling elders, constituted the Refd. Presbytery of America, at Philadelphia, May, 1798; inst. Ryegate, Caledonia Co., Vermont, 10th July, 1799; inst. 13th April, 1815, Canonsburgh, Washington Co., Pa., 23rd October, 1817, res. ill-health, 27th May, 1826; s.s. Paterson, New Jersey; 1836, s.s city of New York; Moderator of first Synod, 1809, and 1816; died 15th October, 1838, New York; m. Rebecca Mitchell, of L'derry; s. Rev. John Gibson, Rev. Robert Gibson.

Gibson, William

lic. by Southern Presbytery, 1831; ord. Lisdonnan, 9th October, 1833; res. 12th November, 1839; supplied Coronary (Original Secession); Minister without charge, 1839-1842.

Gillespie, Alexander Patterson

b. Carrickfergus; s. of David Gillespie; ed. Q.C. Belfast and R.P. Hall; grad. BA, R.U.I., 1883; lic. by Eastern Presbytery, 1884; ord. Rathfriland. 19th September, 1884; res. 1887; inst. Loanhead, Scotland, 17th February, 1887; emig. to U.S.A.; joined United Presbyterian Church; m. Miss Hanna, Lisburn.

Gilmour, Alexander

b. Rathfriland, 1886; s. of John Gilmour and Elizabeth Savage; ed. Glasgow University; grad. M.A. Glasgow, 1908; O.S. Hall, Glasgow, R.P. Theological Hall, Belfast; lic. by Southern Presbytery, 6th October, 1910; ord. Drimbolg, 14th March, 1911; inst. Trinity Street, Belfast, 14th March 1917 inst. Dromara, 18th March 1924; inst. Newtownards, 3rd July 1952; ret. 3rd March, 1959; minister in charge, Ballymacashon, 1925-1963; lecturer O.T. Language and Literature, RP Theological Hall, 1945-1960; Moderator of Synod, 1924; died 15th May, 1972; int. Manchester. m. Margaret, d. Samuel Lytle, Drumlane, Upperlands, Co. L'derry; 1 s. Samuel; 1 d. Elizabeth.

Gilmour, William James

b. Rathfriland, 30th June, 1904; s. of John Gilmour and Susan Hope; ed. Drumballyroney C. of I. P.S., Shaftesbury House College, Belfast, Magee College, T.C.D.; R.P. Theological Hall, Belfast; 1929-1932; grad. BA (T.C.D.), 1930; lic. by Southern Presbytery, 20th May, 1932; ord. Loanhead, 4th October, 1932; inst. Nicholson Street, Glasgow, 11th February, 1941; inst. Cullybackey, 15th May, 1946; ret. 4th December, 1974; Moderator of Synod, 1952, 1969; died 8th September, 1991; int. Cullybackey; m. Elizabeth Mary Coulter; 2 d. Marian, Susan.

Graham, David

b. Coleraine, Co. L'derry, 8th September, 1779; s. of Thomas Graham and Mary De Witt; ed. grad. Glasgow University, 1799, Theological Hall, Paisley; lic. by Refd. Presbytery of Ireland, 9th March, 1804; ord. and inst. Magherafelt, Co. L'derry, 16th October, 1805; went to London, 1807, was deposed by Refd. Presbytery of Ireland, for abandoning his charge; emig. 8th February, 1808, city of New York; restd. by Northern Presbytery, at Milton, Northumberland Co., Pa., 12th August, 1809; 1810, called to Canonsburgh, Pa., depd. by Middle Presbytery, 20th August, 1811; identified with Seceder Church, Butler Cos., Pa.; admitted to the practice of law, 9th November, 1820; died 13th September, 1839, New York, ; m. Mary Hazleton, of L'derry, 16th March, 1807.

Graham, John Wright
b. Drumbo, Co. Down; ed. Q.C.B., R.P. Theological Hall; grad. G.C. 1822; lic. by Northern Presbytery; ord. Bailiesmills, 1826; died 1862; died 12th January, 1898; m. Hannah Bell; 1 s., William Stavely.

Gregg, Andrew Cross
b Magheranappin, Convoy, Co Donegal, 23rd July, 1866; s. of John Gregg, farmer and Mary Cross; ed. Queen's College, Galway; R.P. Theological Hall; grad, 1886; B.D. New College, Edinburgh; lic. by Eastern Presbytery, 1889; ord. Ballylaggan, 22nd May, 1890, res. 1897; inst. Loanhead, Scotland 12th February, 1897; res. 1922; inst. Greenock, 2nd November, 1921; editor "R.P. Witness", 1910-1940; died 13th September, 1949; m. 19th November, 1904, Elizabeth Anne, d. of James Guthrie, shipping agent, Troon.

Guthrie, Archibald
b. Lisnisk, Ballymena, 22nd April, 1908; ed. Magee College, T.C.D.; R.P. Theological Hall 1931-34; grad. B.A. (T.C.D.) 1932; Ph.D. (Glasgow) 1953; lic. by Northern Presbytery, 23rd May, 1934; ord. at Kilraughts, 12th September 1934, and designated missionary to Syria; res. November 1946; inst. Wishaw, 5th February 1947; Glasgow, "Editor, "The R.P. Witness", 1953-1966; "The Covenanter Witness", 1967 -1975; died 9th March 1975; int. Daldowie, Broomhouse; m. Muriel Russell, d. Rev. Prof. William Russell; 1 d. Jean; 2 s. James, Russell.

Hamilton, Joseph
b. Belraugh, Garvagh, Co. L'derry, 13th June, 1842; s. of Joseph Hamilton and Susannah Logan; ed. Belfast Academy, grad. Q.C.B.1861, Theological Hall, Belfast; lic. By Northern Presbytery, 30th January,1866; ord. and inst. by Northern Presbytery, Garvagh, Co. L'derry, 7th November, 1867; res. 6th August, 1872; emig. 1873, rec. by Rochester Presbytery, 30th May, 1873, supplied esp. Canadian vacancies; suspended by the Rochester Presbytery, 5th October, 1875.

Hamilton,Thomas
b. Bovevagh, Dungiven Co L'derry; s. of Thomas Hamilton; ed. Glasgow University; lic. by L'derry Presbytery (G.A.), 1764; joined R.P. Church, 1769; ord. Faughan, 1770; res. 1773; an itinerant preacher for Refd. Presbytery, 1773 - 1779; died 1779 in Monaghan; int. Derryvalley.

Hanna, Samuel
b. Ballybradin, Loughguile, Co. Antrim; s. of William Hanna and Matilda Jane Loughridge; ed. Intermediate School, Ballymoney, Queen's College, Belfast, R.P. Theol. Hall; grad. B.A. (R.U.I.), 1899, M.B., B.Ch., B.A.O. (Q.U.B.); lic. by Northern Presbytery, 1902; ord. Larne, September 1902; res. November, 1905; inst. Whiting Bay Free Church of Scotland, 1905; res. 1912; inst. Berry Street, Belfast, 30th May, 1912; died 29th January, 1944; m. Miss Shaw, Arran; 1 s. William; 1 d., Maureen.

Hanna, Thomas
b. Corkey, Cloughmills, Co Antrim, 1886; s. of Robert Hanna and Matilda Loughridge; ed. Ballymoney Intermediate School, Magee College, T.C.D., R.P. Theological Hall, Belfast; grad. BA (T.C.D.), 1917; lic. by Northern Presbytery, 1919; ord. Bready, 10th October, 1919; died 5th February, 1924.

Hanna, William
b. Rathfriland, 1824; ed. O.C.B. and R.P. Theological Hall; lic. by Southern Presbytery, 1855; ord. Manchester R.P. September 1855; res. 1859; inst. Newtownards, July 1859; died 12th October, 1860; int. Movilla; m. 1858; d. of Robert Alexander, Newtownards.

Hart, John
b. Tierfergus, Rathfriland, 1826; ed. O.C.B., R.P. Theological Hall, Paisley; lic. by Southern Presbytery; ord. Ballylaggan, 10th October, 1854; died 18th April, 1883; m. Elizabeth, Carlisle, d. of Rev. Thomas Carlisle, Rathfriland.

Hart, Thomas
b. Tierfergus, Rathfriland, 1824; bro. of Rev. John Hart, Ballylaggan; ed. O.C.B.. R.P. Theological Hall, Paisley; lic. by Southern Presbytery; ord, Rathfriland, 10th March, 1857; died 7th September, 1877; int. Rathfriland.

Hawthorne, John
b. Kilkinamurray, Co. Down, 7th December, 1795; s. of John Hawthorne and Mary Graham; ed. R.B.A.I., grad. Glasgow University, 1816, Theological Hall, Paisley; lic. by Southern Presbytery, 10th March, 1821; ord., and inst. Ballenon, 7th May, 1822; res. 28th October, 1845; emig. April, 1847, with his family, for Muskingum Co., Ohio; died 14th May, 1847of a fever, in quarantine at Quebec; m. Ann E. Boggs, of Ballylane, 1823.

Henry, William
b. Macosquin, 1789; e.s. of Thomas Henry; ed. Glasgow University, R.P. Theological Hall, Paisley; grad. M.A. (Glasgow), 1811, D.D., Indiana, 1835; lic. by Northern Presbytery; ord. Newtownards, 1813; withdrew with part of his congregation (Ann Street) and joined Eastern R.P. Synod in 1842; res. 1843; inst. Gortlee, 1843; died 7th August 1852; int. at Gortlee; m.; 1 s,, Rev. Robert M. Henry; 1 d., Mrs McFarland, who had 2 S., Sir John Henry McFarland, M.A., L.L.D., Chancellor of Melbourne Univ., Robert Arthur Henry McFarland, Headmaster of Campbell College, Belfast; pub. "The Warning to Sardis" 1848, pub. "The Funeral Sermon for Rev. J.A. Alexander, 1823.

Hodge, Matthew
b. Glasgow, 1839; parents from Limavady; ed. Glasgow University, R.P. Theological Hall; lic. by R.P.C.S.; ord. Killinchy, 20th October, 1874; ret. owing to ill-health, 1897; died 24th June, 1915, aged 76; int. Ballymacashon.

Holmes, Archibald
b. Kilraughts; ed. Magee College, Assembly's College, Belfast, R.P. Theological Hall, Belfast; lic. by Northern Presbytery, 1887; ord. Bready, 13th October, 1887; res. 1893; inst. Creevagh, 2nd April, 1893 (one year in Geelong, Australia, 1897-1898); res. 1900; inst. Paisley, 1900; res. 1903; inst. Kellswater, 1903; res. 1921; inst. Ballyclare, 16th June,

1921; died 27th September, 1932; Clerk of Eastern Presbytery; m. Miss Mary Marshall, Philadelphia; 1 s., Marshall; 4 d., Marina, Ethel, Gertrude, Edna.

Houston, Clarke

b. Maghera, 1787; youngest. s. of Clarke Houston, merchant; ed. Glasgow University, R.P. Theological Hall, Paisley; lic. by Eastern Presbytery, 1st November, 1811; ord. Limavady, 1814; res. 1815; inst. Cullybackey, 1818; he and congregation joined Eastern R.P. Synod in 1842; grad. D.D. (hon. caus.); died 13th November, 1852, at Newcastle-on-Tyne; 2 weeks after the death of his son, Rev John Clarke Houston, minister of Clavering Place U.P Church, 2 d.

Houston, David

b. Paisley, 1633; ed. grad. Glasgow University,1654; lic. Scotland; joined Route Presbytery (Irish Presbyterian Church), preached in Co. Antrim; suspended by Route Presbytery 27th February, 1672; continued to preach on Covenanting lines at Ballymoney, Derrykeighan and Macosquin; 1673, Route Presbytery withdrew suspension; returned to Scotland; 1675, returned to Ulster for a short period; call from Glenavy stayed; 1675-1679, in Scotland; 1679, fought at Bothwell Brig on 22nd June, 1679; returned to Ulster with Alexander Peden; introduced to Covenanting Societies; ord. in Ireland between 1680-1685; 22nd December, 1686 accepted in Scotland as an ordained minister; deposed by Route Presbytery 7th February, 1687; 1689, preaching at Newtownards; 1692-1696, preached at Armoy; died 8th December, 1696, at Kellswater; int. Connor Churchyard.

Houston, James Dick

b. Knockbracken, December, 1835; s. of Thomas Houston and Catherine Wallace; ed. Queen's College, Belfast, R.P. Theological Hall, Belfast; grad. BA (Q.U.I.) 1857; lic. by Eastern Presbytery; ord. Ballyclabber, 1862; Clerk of Northern Presbytery, 1876-1910; Asst. Clerk of Synod, 1887-1893; Clerk of Synod, 1893-1910; Prof. of Church History and Pastoral Theology in R.P. Hall, 1896-1910; died 27th April, 1910; m. d. of Rev. Wm. Anderson, Loanhead, 1866; 4 s. William Anderson, Prof. of Maths, Q.C.G., Asst. Commissioner for Intermediate Education, Thomas, Prof. of Pathology, Q.U.B., James Dick, Robert; 6 d. Polly, m. Prof. T. B. McFarlane, Cissie, m. W. M. Graham, Katie, Agnes Lamont, Annie and Grace.

Houston, Thomas

b. Donegore, 12th October, 1803 or 04; s. of Thomas Houston; ed. O.C.B., R.P. Theological Hall, Paisley; grad. G.C. 1825; lic. by Northern Presbytery 25th December, 1826; ord. Knockbracken, 8th April, 1828; Prof. of Church History and Exegetical and Pastoral Theology in R.P. Theological Hall, Belfast, 1854-1882; Editor of "Covenanter" December, 1830; died 27th March, 1882; int. Knockbracken; m. Catherine, d. of Robert Wallace, merchant, Ballymena, 13th May, 1833; 6 s. including Rev. James Dick, John Knox.

Hurst, Joseph Livingstone Fraser

b. Portglenone, 1844; ed. Queen's College, Belfast, R.P. Theological Hall, Belfast; grad. BA (Q.U.I.), 1881, lic. by Eastern Presbytery, 1870; ord. Loughbrickland, 19th December, 1871; res. 1882; emig. to New Zealand; officiated in Caversham, Dunedin, 1885-1889; returned to Ireland; joined General Assembly, 1889; inst. Fermoy, 25th November, 1890; died 29th March, 1902; m. 1871, d. of Rev. J. A. Smyth, Drimbolg.

James, William
b. nr. Eglinton, 1741; ed. Glasgow University, Scottish R.P. Tutors; lic. by Refd. Presbytery of Ireland, November, 1763; ord. Bready, 8th May, 1765; died 1779; int. Grange, Bready; m. Miss Burgess.

Johnson, Robert
b. Killygore, Cloughmills, Co. Antrim, 17th November, 1810; s. of Robert and Margaret Johnson; grad. R.B.A.I. 1836, Theological Hall, Paisley; lic. by Northern Presbytery, 17th May, 1839; ord. and inst. to mission cong. of Manchester, England, 3rd August, 1842, res. 9th April, 1849; emig. rec. by R.P. Synod, North America, 23rd May, 1849; inst. Toronto, Canada, 4th November, 1852, res. 10th April, 1859; inst. Vernon, Waukesha Co., Wisconsin, 7th November, 1859, res. 17th December, 1867; inst. Kossuth, Des Moines Co., Iowa, January 7, 1868, res. ill-health, 27th July, 1875; died 27th July, 1879, Kossuth, Iowa; unm.

Kennedy, James
b. Drumreagh, Ballymoney, Co. Antrim, 15th August, 1818; s. of George Kennedy and Mary Paul; ed. Bryce's Academy, R.B.A.I, 1840, Theological Hall, Paisley; lic. by Northern Presbytery, 10th May, 1842; ord. and inst. by Western Presbytery, Newton-limavady, 18th May, 1843; res. 2nd August, 1870; inst. 4th New York City, New York, 13th November, 1870; Moderator of Irish Synod 1846, American Synod in 1875; grad. D.D. (Geneva), 1886; appt. Prof. in R.P. Theological Seminary in 1887, declined appointment on account of age and attachment to pastoral ministry; ret. 30th October, 1894; died 26th January, 1898, at daughter's home, St. John, New Brunswick; int. Covenanter burial ground, Bronxville; m. Eliza Conn, of Coleraine, 9th May, 1848; s. Rev. George.
pub. "Tekel" (1858), "Assurance of Grace and Salvation" (1877), "Christ in the Song";

Kennedy, Samuel
b. Clement's Hill, Ballyclare, Co. Antrim, 6th August, 1871, (b of Rev. W.M. Kennedy); s. of Samuel Kennedy; ed. Queen's College, Belfast, R.P. Theological Hall, Belfast; grad. BA (R.U.I.), 1890; lic. by Eastern Presbytery; ord. Stranorlar R.P. 3rd August, 1894; res. 5th October, 1896; inst. Limavady, 6th November, 1896; res. 21st May, 1924; inst. Rathfriland, 22nd August, 1924; ret. 3rd August, 1944; Clerk of R.P. Synod, 1915-1937; died 17th December, 1948; m. d. of Thomas McKay, Cookstown; no issue; adopted family, Jean, William Russell.

Kennedy, Samuel Guiler
b. Drumreagh, Ballymoney, 1862; s. of William Kennedy and Charlotte Long; ed. Q.C.B., R.P. Theological Hail; grad. BA (R.U.I.), 1887, LLB. and LLD. (R.U.I.), 1899; lic. by Northern Presbytery, 1889; ord. Wishaw R.P., Scotland, 12th December, 1889; res. 1896; inst. College Street South, Belfast, 5th February, 1896; ret. 25th June, 1924; Prof. of Church History and Pastoral Theology in R.P. Theological Hall, 1910-1924; died 3rd January, 1925; m. 3s., 1 d.

Kennedy, Samuel Hanna
b. Garryduff, Ballymoney; s. of James Kennedy and Mary Hanna; ed. Ballymoney, Q.C.B., R.P. Theological Hall; grad. BA (R.U.I.) 1892; D.D. (Geneva), 1911; lic. by Eastern

Presbytery, 1893; ord. 30th October, 1895; appt. missionary to Syria; res. 31st October, 1939; O.B.E. 1918; died 2nd November, 1950; m. Jennie Boggs Dodds; no issue.

Kennedy, Wilson Moreland
b. Clement's Hill, Ballyclare; s. of Samuel Kennedy; ed. Magee College, R. P. Theological Hall, 1903-1906; grad. B.A. (R.U.I.), 1903; lic. by Eastern Presbytery, 1906; ord. Ballenon R.P., 8th August, 1906; res. May, 1907; joined General Assembly, Newry Presbytery; inst. Castlebar, 23rd July, 1907; res. 1912; inst. Ballylinney, 23rd May, 1912; res 1921; inst. Strand, Belfast, 31st May, 1921; inst. 1st Derry; Moderator of General Assembly 1942; d. 17th July, 1945; m.1. d. of Rev. Robert Henry, Limavady; 2 s., Robert Samuel Moreland, Frank; m. 2. Miss. Herald; 1s., John Herald.

King, William
b. Donegal, Co. Donegal, 6th January, 1747; ed. grad. Glasgow University, 1782, Theology, Stirling; lic. by Refd. Presbytery of Scotland, 16th March, 1784, preached in Coleraine, Co. L'derry, for seven years; ord. 'sine titulo' by the Refd. Presbytery of Scotland, at Wishaw, 4th June, 1792, Missionary to America; settled Chester District, South Carolina; settled at 1794 Beaver Dam S.C. congregation; invited to organize the Refd. Presbytery in Alexandria, Virginia, May, 1798, but on account of serious illness he was not able; died 24th August, 1798, at his house in Chester District, S.C.; m. Nancy Neil, of Chester, S.C., September, 1794.

Lawson, James Reid
b. Rathfriland, Co. Down, 23rd May, 1820; s. of James Lawson and Elizabeth Reid; ed. R.B.A.I. 1841, Theological Hall, Paisley; lic. by Southern Presbytery, 4th March, 1845; ord. 'sine cura' by Southern Presbytery, 18th September, 1845, a Missionary to the British North American Provinces; settled in South Stream, now Barnesville, Kings Co., New Brunswick, in the spring of 1846; res. 17th October, 1856; inst. Boston, Massachusetts, 20th November, 1856, res. 22nd October, 1857. He returned to Barnesville, N.B., res., 12th April, 1882; died 4th July, 1891, Barnesville; m. Margaret Hastings, of St. John, N.B., 1st July, 1851.

Leahy, Frederick Stratford
b. nr. Stranorlar, Co. Donegal 15th September, 1922; ed. Free Church College, Edinburgh; grad M.Th. Calvin Theological Seminary, 1977; ord. and inst. Finaghy Evangelical Ch. 15th October, 1949; res. Irish Evangelical Ch. 30th June, 1953; joined R.P. Synod; ord. and inst. Cregagh Rd. 23rd September, 1953; inst. Ballymacashon 6th March, 1964; res. 1966; inst. Kilraughts 24th November, 1966; ret. 25th May, 1988; Prof. of Systematic Theology, Apologetics and Christian Ethics 1967-1995; Principal R.P. Theological College, 1993-2002; died 4th January, 2006; m. Margaret E. Williamson; 1 d., Helen.

Lillie, George
lic. by Eastern Presbytery 4th April, 1848; agent with London City Mission prior to 1845; ord. Fairview, 30th April, 1861; Clerk of Southern Presbytery, -1871; ; s.s. Newtownards and Manchester; d. 30th September, 1881; m..

Littlejohn, James
b. Kilwinning, Ayrshire; 3rd s. of Buchan Littlejohn; ed. Glasgow University, R.P. Theological Hall; lic. by Scottish Refd. Pres; ord. Lorne R.P., Argyllshire; inst. Garvagh

R.P., 15th July, 1876; ret. 14th February, 1893; died 1898; mar; 2 s., Rev John Martin, William.

Littlejohn, John Martin

b. Glasgow, 15th February, 1865; s. of Rev. James Littlejohn (Garvagh); ed. Glasgow University, Original Seceder Hall, R.P. Theological Hall; lic. Northern Presbytery, 1886; ord. Creevagh, 7th September, 1886; res, 1888; grad, M.A. (Glasgow), 1889, B.D. (Glasgow), 1890, and LL.B. (Glasgow), 1892; emig. 1892 because of ill-health; Ph.D. Columbia University, 1893; rec. by Philadelphia Presbytery; 1895, under Kansas Presbytery, President of Amity College, College Springs, Iowa; 1889, res. ill-health; 1899, The American School of Osteopathy in Kirksville, Missouri; 1900 in Chicago, M.D.,1900; under Iowa Presbytery, develops the science, theory and practice of osteopathy; 1913 returns to U.K., Thunderley, Essex, certified under, R.P.C.S.; establishes the British School of Osteopathy; died 8th December, 1947.

Loughridge, Adam

b. Ballyveeley, Armoy, 7th March, 1915; 3rd s. of Thomas Loughridge and Annie McQuiston; ed. Ballyveeley P.S.; Knockahollett P.S., Ballymena Academy, Magee College; T.C.D.; grad M.A. 1936; R.P. Theological Hall, 1935-1938; grad. M.Litt. (T.C.D.) 1963; Hon. D.D. Geneva College, Beaver Falls, Pa; 1967; lic. by Northern Presbytery June 1938; ord. and inst. Newtownards 24th August, 1938; inst. Glenmanus, 30th March, 1950; inst. Cregagh Rd, 10th December, 1969; inst. Ballymacashon 12th December, 1969; res. Ballymacashon 4th April, 1978; ret. 16th April 1980; appt. Prof. of Homiletics, Church History and Pastoral Theology 1957-1983; principal 1973-1993; Moderator of Synod,1949, 1976, 1987; clerk of synod 1950-1975; died 8th November 2001; int. Kilraughts; m. Evelyn Kincaid, 1s Allen, 1d Margaret.

Lynas, Samuel Wallace

b. Kilraughts; s. of Samuel Lynas; ed. Ballymoney Intermediate School, Magee College, L'derry, Trinity College, Dublin, R.P. Theological Hall, Belfast; grad. B.A. (Mod.), 1921; lic. Northern Presbytery; ord. Liverpool (Hall Lane), 19th December 1923; res. 15th December, 1925; inst. Cullybackey, 20th January, 1926; res. 1945; inst. Milford, 3rd October, 1945; died 20th April, 1953; m. Mina Calderwood, L'derry; 1 s. Hugh Austin Evans; 2 d. Mary, Anne.

Lynd, John

b. Knockaduff, Aghadowey, Co. L'derry, 2nd March, 1850; s. of Andrew Lynd and Rosa Gilmore; ed. Aghadowey Classical School, Coleraine Academy, grad. Magee College, 1871. R.P. Theological Hall, Belfast; emig. April, 1873, grad. 1st Hons. Mental and Moral Sc., D.D., Geneva College Pa.; lic. by New York Presbytery, 20th May, 1873; ord. and inst. by Philadelphia Presbytery, Baltimore, Maryland, 4th December, 1873, res. 6th November, 1877; appt. Prof. of Greek and English Literature in Beaver College, Northwood, Ohio, also inst. Belle Centre, Logan Co., Ohio, 5th January, 1879; res. the chair at the removal of the College, 26th May, 1880; inst. Rushsylvania, Logan Co., Ohio, 12th August, 1880; res. 14th April, 1885; inst. Ballylaggan Co. L'derry, 5th June, 1885; res. 1889, inst. Dublin Rd., Belfast, 16th April, 1889; appt. Prof. of Hebrew and Biblical Criticism, Theological Hall, 1901-1921; ret. 26th June, 1923; Moderator of the Irish Synod of 1886; died 27th June, 1926, at Alsager, Cheshire; int. Ballylaggan; m. Isabel (Belle) Purvis, of Baltimore, Maryland, 8th April, 1875. 2 s. Tom, William, 1 d. Sally.

Lynn, Matthew

b. Corkermain, Carncastle, Co. Antrim, 10th August, 1731; s. of Matthew Lynn; 1757, ord. a ruling elder; ed. grad. Glasgow University, 1760; lic. by the Refd. Presbytery of Scotland, 16th July, 1761; ord. at the organization of the Refd. Presbytery of Ireland, at Vow, Co. Antrim, inst. to societies of Bannside, Limavady and Aghadowey, 21st August, 1763; helped to form congregations at Ballylaggan, Drimbolg and Garvagh; fruits of his ministry seen in development of Covenanting cause at Bready, 1765, Faughan 1770, and Ramelton; appt. to accompany Rev. Alexander Dobbin as Missionary to America; arrived New Castle, Delaware, 13th December, 1773; Revs. Lynn, Cuthbertson and Dobbin, organized the Refd. Presbytery of America, at Paxtang, Dauphin Co. Pa., 10th March, 1774; assigned to Paxtang, Dauphin Co., and Stoney Ridge, Cumberland Co., Pa.; joined Associate Reformed Church at its formation, 1st November, 1782; 1783, inst. A.R.P. congs. Green Castle, Chambersburg, West Conococheague and Great Cove, Franklin Co., Pa.; res. 13th March, 1798; died 21st April, 1800, Green Castle, Franklin Co., Pa.; int. graveyard at Brown's Mills; m. Jennett Fulton, of Co. Antrim (cousin of Rbt. Fulton. of steamboat fame), 1769.
Cf. Howe: "History of Pres. Ch. in S. Carolina" p. 697.

Lyons, Alexander McLeod Stavely

b. Ballygan, Ballymoney, Co Antrim; s. of James Lyons and Agnes Anne (Nancy) Lamont; ed. Queen's College, Belfast, R.P. Theological Hall; lic. by Northern Presbytery, 1871; ord. Newry, 12th June, 1872; died 7th September, 1908 (result of an accident); Clerk of Southern Presbytery, 1883-1908; m. Margaret, d. of John Nevin, Carnaff, Dervock; 3 s., James Alexander, Robert Nevin, Henry Clarke; 1 d., Lydia (Ida).

Lyons, James Alexander

b. Newry, 14th June, 1879; 1st s. of Rev. A.S. Lyons and Margaret Nevin; ed. Newry Inter-School, Queen's College, Galway, R.P. Theological Hall; grad. B.A. (R.U.I.), 1902; lic. Southern Presbytery, 1905; ord. Cullybackey, 9th January, 1906; res. 21st November, 1923; inst. Dublin Road, Belfast. 9th January, 1924; ret. 1946; died 9th March, 1952; m. 1907 Agnes Anne, d. of Thomas McKay, Cookstown; 3 d. Elizabeth (Elsie), Margaret (Rita), Mary (Mollie) m. Rev. John McCaughan, Legacurry.

Lyons, Robert Biggart

b. Ballygan, Ballymoney, 1900; s. Josiah Alexander Lyons and Annie Boyd, ed. Ballymoney Intermediate School, Magee College, L'derry, Trinity College, Dublin; R.P. Theological Hall, Belfast, 1921-1924; grad. B.A. (T.C.D.), 1921; lic. by Northern Presbytery, 7th May, 1924; ord. Limavady, 23rd October, 1924; ret. 3rd September, 1975; Editor, "The Covenanter", 1936-1966; "The Covenanter Witness", 1967-1972; Moderator of Synod, 1942, 1965; died 24th August 1976; int. Limavady; m. Jean McCollum, Boghill, Coleraine; 1 s. Robert Morrell; 3 d. Elizabeth, Jennifer, Margaret.

Lyons, Robert Nevin

b. Newry, Co Down; 2nd s. of Rev. A.S. Lyons and Margaret Nevin; ed. Newry Intermediate School, Magee College, L'derry, R.P. Theological Hall, Belfast; grad. G.A.M.C.; lic. by Southern Presbytery, 1913; ord. Ballenon, Ballylane, 24th September, 1913, and Clare 1919; res. 1920; inst. Ballylaggan, 13th October, 1920; res. 6th May, 1925; inst. Grosvenor Road, Belfast, 4 June, 1925; res. 1955; died 1st January, 1964; m.1.

Mary, d. of Mr and Mrs Hugh McCammon; 3 d., Mary, m. Rev. Harry Pinkerton, Trinity Presb. Omagh, Margaret Nevin (Vina), Ida; 1 s., Hugh Alexander; m.2. Mrs Blair.

Lytle, William
b. Drumlane, Upperlands, Co L'derry, 15th March, 1892; s. of Samuel Lytle and Hannah Mayberry; ed. Coleraine Academical Institution, Magee College, T.C.D., Q.U.B., R.P. Theological Hall, Belfast, 1913-1916; grad. BA (T.CD.), 1914; lic. by Northern Presbytery, 16th May, 1916; ord. Ballymoney, 2nd October 1917; designated missionary to Syria; s.s. Knockbracken, 1917-1920; served Antioch and Idlib, Syria; Zahleh and Kub Elias, Lebanon; ret. 8th October, 1970; died 30th April 1984; int. Knockbracken; m. Agnes, d. Josiah and Mrs Archer, Redhill, Dromore; 2 s. Samuel, killed in action, R.A.F., 12th April 1945, Rev. Robert William; 1 d. Dorothy.

Lytle, Robert William
b. Antioch, Syria, 31st October, 1925; 2nd s. of Rev William and Agnes Archer; ed. Royal Belfast Academical Inst.; Magee College; T.C.D.; R.P. Theological Hall, Belfast 1948-1951; ord. 27th June, 1951 for R.P. mission work in Idlib (Syria) and Zahleh (Lebanon) res. 5th December, 1956, inst. Convoy and Stranorlar, 6th June, 1957; inst. Larne, 12th April, 1974; ret. 4th July 1993; died 9th November, 2008; int. Knockbracken; m. Isobel Kennedy; 1d., Rosemary, 2 s., William, Andrew.

Mack, Hugh Kennedy
b. Mullaghdrin, Dromara, Co. Down; s. of Robert Mack; ed. Queen's College, Belfast; R.P. Theological Hall, Belfast; grad. BA (R.U.I.), 1893; lic. by Eastern Presbytery, 1895; ord. Drimbolg. 1895; res. 1909; inst. by Eastern Presbytery for Colonial Mission for work in Geelong, 10th August, 1909; ret. 3rd September 1946; died 1st November, 1951; m. Miss Lillie, Belfast, 1898; 1 d., Lillie; s. Robert.

Martin, James
b. nr. Killyleagh Co Down, 1846; s. of Robert Martin, merchant; ed. Queen's College, Belfast, R.P. Theological Hall, Belfast, grad. M.A. (R.U.I.) 1868; M.D. (Q.U.I.), 1871; lic. by Eastern Presbytery, 1871; ord. by Eastern Presbytery, 14th November, 1871; desig. missionary to Syria; died 23rd January, 1931; m.1. Lizzie, 9th March, 1875, d. of Robert Kerr, Ballymoney; m.2. Rebecca Crawford, d. of American missionary; m.3. Emma Lienhardt; 1 d. Margaret, 1 s., Robert.
Cf. 'James Martin, Pioneer Medical Missionary to Antioch'. by Isobel Lytle, 2003.

Martin, John
b. Laggan, Dumfriesshire; s. of Thomas Martin and Marion McMurdo, ed. Glasgow University; lic. by R.P. Presbytery of Edinburgh and Glasgow; ord. Rathfriland, 4th December, 1879; res. 3rd April, 1884; inst. Wishaw, 1884; res. 1888; inst. Stranraer, 1888; joined English Pres. Church; inst. Leeds; died Laggan, Drumfriesshire, 1900; m. Jane Lorimer; 3 s., Thomas, George and John; 3 d., Annie, Marion and Jane.

Martin, William
b. Ballyspallan, nr. Ballykelly, Co. L'derry, 16th May, 1729; 1st s. of David Martin; ed. grad. Glasgow University, 1753. Theological Hall under Rev. John McMillan; lic. by Refd. Presbytery of Scotland, 10th October, 1756; ord. at Vow nr. Rasharkin, the first Covenanter minister ord. in Ireland, inst. to societies in Cos. Antrim L'derry and N. Down,

2nd July, 1757; 1760, served Co. Antrim at Kellswater; emig. with large body of people, 1772, Rocky Creek, Chester District, South Carolina; the first Covenanter minister settled in the South. In 1774, built, Catholic, R.P., S.C.; dismissed 1777, continued preaching 1781 and resumed his charge; 1785, dismissed, 1793 restored; member of the Cmte. of the Refd. Presbytery of Scotland, for the church in America; preached widely, N.C., S.C. and Georgia; deposed 12th March, 1801; died 25th October, 1806; m. 1. Mary, died Ballymoney; 2. Jennett Cherry of Co. Antrim, d. Nancy; 3. Susanna Boggs, S. Carolina. Cf. 'Scots Irish Migration to South Carolina, 1772'. by Jean Stephenson 1971.

Martin, William George Moffett
b. Belfast, 1904; s. of Joseph Martin; ed. Shaftesbury House School, Belfast, Q.U.B.; R.P. Theological Hall, Belfast 1928-1930; United Original Secession Hall, Glasgow; grad. B.A. (Q.U.B.) 1928; lic. by Eastern Presbytery, 16th September, 1930; ord. Hall Lane, Liverpool, 26th November, 1930; inst. Glenmanus, 5th October, 1933; res. May, 1944; joined Belfast Presbytery, General Assembly; inst. Berry Street, Belfast; inst. 1st Carrickfergus, 1947; inst. 2nd Dunboe, 1968; ret. 1974; died 8th January 1998, int. Roselawn cemetery; m. Maida, d. of Rev. T.C. Stuart, Carryduff, 1 d. Margaret, 3 s. Thomas, Will, Peter.

Maxwell, William John
b Carr, Lisburn, younger s. of William Maxwell; ed. Queen's College, Belfast, R.P. Theological Hall, Belfast; grad. MA (Q.U.I.), 1872; lic. by Eastern Presbytery, 1873; ord. Limavady, 12th August, 1874; res. February, 1875; inst. Hall Lane, Liverpool, 1st July, 1875; res. November, 1886; joined English Pres. Church; inst. Wimbledon, London, 1887; died 22nd September, 1894, Rothesay.

McCarroll, William
b. Randalstown, Co Antrim, 1826; lic. by Northern Presbytery; ord. College Street South, Belfast, 1845; s.s. Newtownards; died 1863; m. 15th December, 1846, d. of John McCreery, Raffrey, Crossgar, Co Down.

McCauley, John David Trevor
b. Rathfriland, Co. Down, 20th June, 1954; s. of Alexander McCauley and Elizabeth Ervine; ed. Edendale Primary School,. Banbridge, Banbridge Academy, Q.U.B; R.P. Theological Hall, Belfast, 1979-1980; R.P. Seminary, Pittsburgh; grad. B.Sc. B.Agr. (Q.U.B.) 1977, M.Div. R.P. Seminary, Pittsburgh; lic. by Southern Presbytery, 16th September, 1980; ord. Dervock, 1st January, 1981; commissioned for Irish Mission work in Galway, 14th November, 1984; died 4th November 1991, int. Rathfriland; m. Shirley Haire; 1 d. Gillian; 3 s. Peter, Cameron, Jeremy.

McClelland, Daniel
b. Bovevagh, Co. L'derry, 1736; emig. America, returned to Ireland, where he studied theology; lic. by Refd. Presbytery of Scotland, 21st December, 1763; he preached for a time in Ireland; ord. 'sine titulo' by Refd. Presbytery of Ireland, at Laymore, nr. Ballymena, 13th July, 1765, as a Missionary to America; 1766, settled in Connecticut; joined Newcastle Presbytery, Synod of New York and Philadelphia; 1767 preached in Eastern Pa.; 1768, returned to New England; Remaining events unknown, probably drifted from the Church.

McCullough, William
b. Clare, Tandragee, 1875; s. Abraham McCullough; ed. Queen's College, Belfast, R.P. Theological Hall, Belfast; grad. B.A. (R.U.I.), 1903; lic. by Southern Presbytery, 1906; ord. Ballylaggan, 11th September, 1906; s.s. Garvagh; res. 1917; inst. Drimbolg, 18th December, 1917; died April 1957, int. Drimbolg; m. d. of Wm. Martin, Glasgow.

McEwen, Joseph
b. Dromore, Co Down, 1st January, 1866; s. of John McEwen; ed. Magee College, R.P. Theological Hall, Belfast, Original Seceder's Hall, Glasgow; lic. by Refd. Presbytery of Glasgow; ord. Bready, 24th August, 1897; res. 1909; inst. Fairview, 22nd July, 1909; s.s. Tullyvallen; res. 1927; minister without charge; Clerk of Eastern Presbytery, 1932-1944; died 9th October 1944; m. 17th November, 1897, Maria Jane, d. Rev. Robert Allen, Newtownards; 5 s. Robert Allen, John Henry, William Reid, Joseph Dale, David.

McEwen, William Reid
b. Bready, Co Tyrone, 1905; s. of Rev. Joseph McEwen and Maria J. Allen; ed. Magee College, L'derry, Trinity College, Dublin; R.P. Theological Hall, Belfast, 1925-1928, R.P. Seminary, Pittsburgh, 1928-29; grad. B.A. (T.C.D.). 1926; lic. by Southern Presbytery, 22nd May, 1928; ord. at Newry by Southern Presbytery for missionary work in Australia, 5th September, 1928; s.s. Geelong, 1930-31; organised new congregation at McKinnon, Melbourne, 1946; ret. 31st December, 1978; Secretary Bible Union of Australia; Editor, "Evangelical Action"; Moderator of R.P. Synod of Ireland, 1950; died 7th April, 1989; m. Bessie, d. Mr and Mrs McDonald, Geelong; 1 s. Alastair.

McFadden, Hutchinson
b. Magheraboy, Kilraughts, Co Antrim, 1780; 1st s. of Galbraith McFadden; ed. Glasgow University, R.P. Theological Hall, Scotland; lic. by Northern Presbytery; ord. Knockbracken and Newtownards, 1805; res. Knockbracken, 1809; died 8th October, 1812, at Magheraboy; m.; 2 d.; Jane, m. 20th July, 1830, Rev. John McAuley, Donaghadee; Roseanne, m. 29th November, 1830, James Hurst.

McFadden, Hutchinson
b. Kilraughts, Co Antrim, 1812; nephew of Rev Hutchinson McFadden; ed. O.C., Belfast, R.P. Theological Hall; lic. by Northern Presbytery; ord. Ballylane, 6th June, 1843; died 28th April, 1875; int. Ballylane.

McFarlane, Robert Adams
b. Newtownstewart, Co Tyrone; ed. Queen's College, Belfast, MA (Q.U.I.-1869); R.P. Theological Hall; grad. M.A. (Q.U.I.), 1869; lic. by Western Presbytery, 1870; ord. Stranorlar, 29th November, 1871. res. 1893; inst. Bready, 1893; res. 1896; inst. Stranorlar, 1896; died 13th December, 1906; uncle of Rev. T.B. McFarlane.

McFarlane, Thomas Barnwell
b. Altdoghill, Newtownstewart, Co Tyrone; s. of Thomas McFarlane and Eliza Mary Brown Gregg; ed. Queen's College, Belfast, R.P. Theological Hall, Belfast; grad B.A. (R.U.I.), 1903; lic. by Eastern Presbytery, 1906; ord. Glasgow North Cong. 19th September, 1906; res. 1909; inst. Riverside, Newry, 28th April, 1909; ret. 29th August 1961; Prof. Church History and Pastoral Theology in R.P. Theological Hall, 1928-1957;

Clerk of Southern Presbytery; died 20th January, 1963; int. Newry; m. Polly, d. of Rev. J.D. Houston, Ballyclabber, 1909; no issue.

McGarragh, James

b. Donaghadee, Co. Down, July, 1752; ed. grad. Glasgow University,1781; studied under Rev. William Stavely; lic. by Refd. Presbytery of Scotland, at Bready, Co. L'derry, 20th August, 1783;He preached with much acceptance to the scattered societies throughout Ulster for several years; accepted call to S. Carolina, ord. Bready, 28th August, 1789; 1791, Beaver Dam, a branch of the Rocky Creek congregation, Chester District, S. C.; suspended 24th June, 1795; deposed 5th February, 1801; school teacher; died 6th September, 1816; int. Paul's graveyard, nr Mount Prospect, Chester District, S. C.; m.1. Elizabeth Clark, of Co. Down, m.2.

McIlfatrick, Thomas Alexander

b. Drumlane, Co L'derry, 1st February, 1874; s. of Archibald McIlfatrick; ed. Queen's College, Belfast, R.P. Theological Hall, Belfast; grad. B.A. (R.U.I.), 1896; lic. by Northern Presbytery, 1901; ord. Ballylaggan, 1901; res. 7th November, 1905; inst. Cawdor Free Church of Scotland, 1906; inst. Kirkcaldy Free Church 3rd June, 1909; res. 1913; inst. Belturbet, General Assembly, 8th April, 1913; Chaplain to Forces. 1915-1917; res. 1st July, 1919; inst. 2nd Broughshane, 27th June, 1921, inst. Sligo, 15th January, 1930; ret. 15th October, 1947; died 28th July, 1950; m. 2 s. Alistair, Robert; 1 d. Shiela.

McIlmoyle, John

b. Stradreagh, Limavady, 1890; ed. Magee College, T.C.D., R.P. Theological Hall, Belfast; grad. B.A., (T.C.D.), Sen. Mod., Phil., 1911, M.A. 1917; lic. by Western Presbytery 1913; ord. Creevagh, 16th September, 1913; res. 1923; inst. Kellswater, 3rd October, 1923; res. 1929; inst. Faughan 31st October, 1929; res. 1947; inst. Dublin Road, Belfast, 11th June, 1947; Prof. of Systematic Theology and Ethics, 1941-1966; Editor of "The Covenanter"; Moderator of Synod, 1938; R.P. Dean of Residences, Q.U.B.; died 22nd June, 1966; m. Greta Gault, d. of Robert and Margaret Gault, Limavady; 1 s. John Robert Gault; 2 d. Margaret, Ann Felicity.

McIlmoyle, Robert John

b. Stradreagh, Limavady, 10th April, 1875; ed. Magee College, R.P. Theological Hall, Belfast; grad. G.A.M.C., 1897; lic. by Western Presbytery, 1900; ord. Ballyclare, 6th September, 1900; res. 1904; inst. Dervock, 31st August, 1904; ret. 1964; Clerk of Northern Presbytery 1910-1944; Moderator of Synod 1911 and 1961; awarded M.B.E.; died 18th May, 1965; int. Ballymoney cmty; m. Louise Hopkins, Limavady; 2 s. Lewis, Vincent Hopkins; 3 d. Enid, Elvina, Kathleen.

McKee, John

b. Dundonald, 1842, 2nd s. of Robert McKee; ed. Queen's College, Belfast and R.P. Theological Hall; lic. by Eastern Presbytery, 1872; ord. Penpont, Scotland, 1873; res. 1891; inst. Dromara, 18th March, 1891, res. 17th December, 1897; inst. Wishaw, 1898; ret. 1930; died 5th December 1933; m. d. of Rev. Wm. Toland, Kilraughts; 3 d.;

McGladdery, Joseph Henry
b. Sheeptown, Newry; ed. Magee College, T.C.D., R.P. Theological Hall, Belfast; grad. B.A. (T.C.D.), 1930; lic. by Southern Presbytery, 20th May, 1932; ord. Ballyclare, 22nd June, 1933; ret. 18th May, 1966; Moderator of Synod, 1945; Clerk of Eastern Presbytery, 1950-1966; died 3rd June, 1967; m. Muriel, d. of Mr and Mrs Anderson; 2 d. Lois, Muriel.

McKeown, John White
b. Drimbolg, Co. Derry; ed. Queen's College, Belfast, R.P. Theological Hall; lic. by Northern Presbytery, 1866; ord. Convoy, Co. Donegal, 27th March, 1867; res. 1875 after an attempt upon his life; again inst. Convoy, 16th March, 1881; res. 16th May, 1883; emig. Canada; m. Miss McKeown, sister of Rev James McKeown, Ballymena.

McKinney, James
b. Kilrea, Co. L'derry, 16th November, 1759; s. of Robert McKinney and Elizabeth McIntyre; ed. grad. Glasgow University 1778; full course in medicine and theology; lic. by Refd. Presbytery of Ireland, 19th May, 1783; ord. and inst. Dervock, Co. Antrim, 14th October, 1783. emig. 1793; Missionary to scattered Societies from Vermont to the Carolinas; with the Rev. William Gibson and ruling elders, constituted the Refd. Presbytery of America, at Philadelphia, May, 1798; congs. Galway and Duanesburgh, New York; res. Duanesburgh, New York, 4th April, 1802, inst. Rocky Creek, Chester District, South Carolina; died 16th September, 1802, int. Rocky Creek; m. Mary Mitchell, of Co. L'derry, 1794. author "A View of the Rights of God and Man".

McKnight, William
b. Castledawson, Co L'derry; s. of Alexander McKnight; ed. Queen's College Belfast, R.P. Theological Hall, Belfast, lic. by Northern Presbytery 1870; ord. Ballylane, 15th March, 1876; died 18th October, 1911; m. Miss King; 1 d.

McNeilly, Samuel Rea
b. Bannfield, Rathfriland, 1851; s. of Adam McNeilly; ed. Queen's College, Belfast, R.P. Theological Hall, Belfast; grad. BA (R.U.I.), 1886; ord. Bailiesmills, 22nd June, 1887; ret. 3rd August, 1926; Clerk of Eastern Presbytery, 1906-1928; died 19th May, 1928; int Rathfriland; unm.

Moffett, William James
b. Creevagh, Ballybay 1st November, 1878; s. of Thomas Moffett and Sarah Graham; ed. R.P. Theological Hall, Belfast; grad. BA (R.U.I.); lic. by Southern Presbytery, 1905; ord. Milford, Co. Donegal, 12th October, 1905; res. 1916; inst. Greenock, Scotland, 1916; res. 1921; inst. Airdrie, 1st September, 1921; ret. 24th May, 1949; died 1st January, 1952, in Glasgow; Clerk of R.P. Synod of Ireland, 1910-1916; Clerk of R.P. Synod of Scotland; m. Miss Margaret Graham Sturgeon, Liverpool; 1 d. Joyce Graham, O.B.E.; 1 s. Thomas.

Moody, James Renwick
Licentiate of the Eastern Presbytery, 1870; ord. Larne, 19th March, 1872; res. 7th May 1874, ill-health.

Moore, Alexander McIlwaine
b. Ballyblack, Co. Down, 1820; grad. Glasgow University 1852; R.P. Theological Hall, Paisley; lic. by Eastern Presbytery 1856; ord. by Eastern Presbytery in College Street

South, 18th August 1857, for work in Australia, settled in Geelong, Victoria; congregation organised 22nd June, 1858; died 18th February, 1897; m.
c.f. 'A Brief History of Colonial Mission Work in Canada and Australia', Rev. Hugh Wright.

Morrell, Robert John

b. Ballywilldrick, Articlave, Coleraine, 1856; ed. Queen's College, Belfast, R.P. Theological Hall, Belfast; lic. by Northern Presbytery, 1879; ord. Kilraughts, 19th November, 1879; res. 1882; inst. Knockbracken, 11th October, 1883; res. 1st December, 1886; joined General Assembly; inst. Killymurris, 23rd August, 1887; res. 1893; inst. Trinity, Bangor, 16th May, 1893; ret. 7th February, 1929; died 26th July, 1937; m. Miss Cheyne; 3 d., who m. Rev John Waddell, m. Rev W. N. Maxwell, m. Rev John Irwin, LL.D.

Neill, Matthew

b. Carnaff, Dervock; ed. Queen's College, Belfast, R.P. Theological Hall, Belfast; lic. by Northern Presbytery, 1875; ord. Faughan, 17th February, 1876; res. 3rd November 1880; joined L'derry Presbytery, General Assembly; inst. Urney and Sion, 11th August, 1886; ret. 1931; m. d. of Samuel Kennedy, Rossdowney, 1878; 1 s. Gilmore (minister of Hillhall); 2 d. who m. Rev. Joseph Morrison and Rev. W. J. Logan.

Nevin, John

b. Carnaff, Dervock 1805; s. of Robert Nevin and M Dunlop; lic. by Northern Presbytery; ord. Liverpool, 23rd September, 1835; emigrated 1839 to U.S.A; rec. by General Synod (New School) Reformed Presbyterian Church, inst. Shenango, Pa.; died 24th August, 1866, Hill Prairie, Marissa, Illinois.

Nevin, Robert

b. Dervock, Co Antrim; s. of James and Annie Nevin; ed. O.C.B., R.P. Theological Hall, Paisley; grad. Gen Cert 1839; D.D. (U.S.A.) 1890; lic. of Northern Presbytery, 1841, ord. Clarendon Street, 1842; Clerk, Western Presbytery, 1863-1893, R.P. Synod of Ireland, 1863-1893; Editor, "The Covenanter" 1868-1890; died February, 1893; m.1. M. Laughlin; 1 s. John; 1 d. Ellen; m.2. Kathleen, d. of Wm. Manson; 3 s., Robert, William, Alexander; 3 d., Annie, Kathleen, Jane; author, 'Misunderstood Scriptures'.

Newell, John

b. Belfast, 18th August, 1824; s. of Thomas Newell and Elizabeth Gregg; ed. grad. R.B.A.I., 1845. Theological Hall, Paisley; lic. by Eastern Presbytery, Ireland, 9th October,1849; emig. 1850; ord. and inst. by Rochester Presbytery, Syracuse, New York, 7th May, 1851; res. 26th May, 1853; 1853, Presidency of Westminster College, Allegheny City, Pa.; res. 1860, returned to Ireland; inst. Newtownards, Co. Down, Ireland, 8th May, 1861; res. 10th May, 1867; inst. Manchester, England, 14th August, 1867; returned to U.S. May, 1871, taught in Newell Institute, Pittsburgh; Moderator of the Synod of Ireland in 1862; died 20th September, 1875, Wilkinsburgh, Pennsylvania; m. Harriet Finlay, of Buffalo, New York, 20th May, 1851. 8 children.

Orr, Joseph

b. Moness, Co Donegal, 1762; ed. Glasgow Univ., R.P Divinity Hall, lic. 1791; ord. Drimbolg, 1798; arrested for alleged assoc. with United Irishmen, 1798; released soon after, had charge of Ballylaggan and Garvagh until 1816; died 14th July 1825; int. Bellaghy, Co L'derry; m., 3 s.

Orr, Robert Gamble

b. Brigh, Co. Tyrone, 8th July, 1787; 3s. of Robert (or James) Orr and Elizabeth Gamble; ed. grad. Glasgow University, 1810, Theological Hall, Stirling; lic. by Southern Presbytery 16th March, 1813; ord. and inst. by Northern Presbytery, Limavady, 31st August, 1815; res.1827; emig.1832, U.S.A.; 1833, joined New School branch; preached at Ogdensburgh, New York; died 12th June, 1835, Paterson, New Jersey; m. 2d.

Patterson, James

ord. Knockbracken, 20th February, 1888; res. 22nd April, 1891; inst. Thurso, 1891; res. 1910; inst. Botanic Avenue, Belfast, 2nd June, 1910; res. 19th September 1911; ret. to Thurso as supply; m. dau. of Hugh Scott and grands. of Rev Thomas Houston ..

Paul, John

b. Tobernaveen, Antrim, 1777; s. of John Paul; ed. Glasgow University, R.P. Theological Hall; lic. by Irish Refd. Presbytery at Garvagh, 1803; ord. Loughmourne, 11th September, 1805; grad. D.D. (Union, U.S.A.) 1836; res. from R.P. Synod of Ireland, 1840; joined (with his cong.) Eastern Refd. Synod at its formation 1842; author "Refutation of Arianism"; died 16th March, 1848; m. 1807 Rachel Smith, Ballyearl, Carnmoney; 1 d. m. Rev. D Stewart Bates, Glasgow.

Pollock, William Henry

b. Termaquin, Limavady; s. of William Pollock; ed. Foyle College, L'derry, Magee College, R.P. Theological Hall, Belfast; grad. B.A. (R.U.I), 1904; lic. by Western Presbytery, 1906; ord. Larne, 19th October, 1906; res. 1918; inst. Loughbrickland, 23rd October, 1918; res. 3rd June, 1941; s.s. Clare, -1954; ret. February, 1955; Moderator of Synod, 1922 and 1947; died 28th February, 1956.

Potts, Joseph Thomas

b. Belfast, 1862; s. of John Potts; ed. Queen's College, Belfast, R.P. Theological Hall, Belfast; grad. BA (R.U.I.), 1884; lic. Eastern Presbytery, 1887; ord. Rathfriland, 27th December, 1887; res. 28th August, 1906; inst. Nicholson Street, Glasgow, 1906; m. Miss Martha Mills, Townsend Street, Belfast; 2 s., John, Thomas; d. Sydney Josephine.

Ramsey, John

b. Barview, Coleraine, 1860; s. of William Ramsey, and Isabella Young; ed. Trinity College, Dublin, R.P. Theological Hall, Belfast; grad. B.A. Hons., L.L.B. (T.C.D.); lic. by Northern Presbytery, 1886; ord. Ballymoney, 7th December, 1886; res. 1940; ret. May, 1940; Prof. of Hebrew, Greek and Biblical Criticism, R.P. Theological Hall, Belfast, from 1922-1945; Editor of "The Covenanter", Headmaster, Ballymoney Intermediate School; died 26th November 1954; m. Miss Anne Martin, Dublin; 2 s., William, Robert; 5 d., Mina, Isabel, Eileen, Freda, Bertha.

Reid, Samuel Lynas

b. Craigs, Cullybackey, Co Antrim, 12th February, 1931; 2nd s. of Hugh Reid and Jeannie Lynas; ed. Magee College, T.C.D.; R.P. Theological Hall, Belfast, 1953-1956; lic. by Northern Presbytery 1956; ord. Stranraer 9th January, 1957; inst. Riverside, Newry, 19th

December, 1969; inst. Ballyclare, 31st March, 1988; ret. 9th September, 1997; died 28th June, 2008; int. Cullybackey; m. Dorothy McEwen, Newtownards; 1s. David, 3d. Mary, Valerie, Deborah.

Ritchie, James Alexander
b. Broughshane, 12th July, 1917; ed. Baptist College, Dublin; pastor of Brannockstown, Limerick and Gateshead Baptist Churches 1947-1967; ord. and inst. Bailiesmills, Knockbracken, 27th November, 1968; res. 11th May, 1974; inst. Kellswater, 7th June, 1974; ret. 13th March, 1986; installed Ballenon, Ballylane 2nd May, 1990; ret. 27th May, 1996; died 8th April, 2006; m. Eveline James, Belfast; 1 s., Edwin., 1 d., Maureen.

Russell, William
b. Ballymagee, Bangor, 1801; s. of William Russell; ed. Edinburgh University, R.P. Theological Hall, Paisley; ord. Ballyclare, 9th July, 1840; Clerk of Eastern Presbytery; died 7th April, 1884; m. dau. of Adam Lowry, Raffrey, 1858; 1 s., William; 1 d. Margaret Jane.

Russell, William
b. Ballyclare; s. of Rev. Wm. Russell; ed. Queen's College, Belfast, Assembly's College, Belfast, R.P. Theological Hall, Belfast; grad. M.A. (R.U.I.), 1887; lic. by Eastern Presbytery, 1887; ord. Ballenon, 29th October, 1890; res. 31st October, 1905; inst. Paisley, Scotland, November, 1905; res. 23rd November, 1926; inst. Trinity Street, Belfast, 4th January, 1927; Prof. of Systematic Theology and Christian Ethics in R.P. Theological Hall, 1929-1941; m. Margaret, d. of Rev. Prof. James Dick; 2 s. William Lowry, James Dick; 3 d., Georgina m. Rev. Andrew Prentice, Muriel m. Dr. A Guthrie, Margaret m. Mr S. Stewart.

Savage, Alexander
b. Ballylaggan, Co L'derry, 1811; ed. O.C.B., R.P. Theological Hall; lic. by Northern Presbytery; ord. Ballenon, 30th May, 1849; died 10th December, 1889; int. at Ballenon; m.; 3 d., a daughter m. Rev H. A. Irvine, Drumlee; Annie, m. Rev. James Mulligan, Poyntzpass; Sarah, m. Joseph Haire; 3 s., Hugh Alexander, William, George.

Scott, William
b. Drumgilla, Castleblayney; s. of Francis Scott; ed. Queen's College Belfast, R.P. Theological Hall, Belfast; lic. by Southern Presbytery, 1873; ord. Mulvin, 4th January, 1877; res. 1884; inst. Convoy, 9th July, 1891; ret. 1st January, 1929; died 21st April, 1931; int. Faughan.

Semple, Thomas Hutchins
b. Belfast, November 1918; s. of Thomas Hutchins Semple, ed. Methodist College, Belfast, Q.U.B.; R.P. Theological Hall, Belfast, 1940-1943; grad. BA (Q.U.B.) 1940; lic. by Eastern Presbytery, 4th May, 1943 at Dublin Road, Belfast; ord. 18th August, 1943 and appointed to Hall Lane, Liverpool; res.1945; teacher in American R.P. Mission School, Latakia, Syria, 1947-1949; teacher in England, 1958-1980; died 1977.

Simms, Samuel
b. Ballykeel, Holywood, Co Down, 1812; ed. O.C.B., R.P. Theological Hall, Paisley; grad. G. C. 1837; ord. Loughbrickland, 15th May, 1839; ret. 1st November, 1870; Moderator of Synod; died 21st March, 1881; m. 1841 d. of John Reid, Banbridge.

Smyth, James Alexander

b. Carndougan, Ballylaggan, March, 1800; s. of Alexander Smyth; ed. O.C.B., R.P. Theological Hall, Paisley; lic. by Northern Presbytery, 1824; ord. Drimbolg, 26th June, 1827; s.s. Magherafelt; ret. 1872; died 29th December 1873, Lakenew, Portglenone; m., 1 s. James Alexander; 1 d. m. Rev. J.L. Frazer-Hurst, Loughbrickland.

Smyth, Matthew

b. Rasharkin, C.1780; 4th s. of Matthew Smyth; ed. Glasgow University, R.P. Theological Hall; grad. Glasgow University, 1796; ord. Convoy, 4th December, 1805; died 12th July, 1818.

Sommerville, William

b. Ballyroney, Co. Down, 1st July, 1800; s. of William Sommerville and Jane Kirk; ed. grad. Glasgow University, 1820, Theological Hall, Paisley, Scotland; lic. by Southern Presbytery, 5th December, 1826; ord. 'sine titulo' by Southern Presbytery, 31st May, 1831, Missionary to the British North American Provinces; settled Cornwallis Valley, in Nova Scotia; minister to Presbyterians, Grand Pre, Horton Township, King's Co., 16th May, 1833; inst. add. cong. Cornwallis, Grafton, 9th May, 1835; died 28th September, 1878, Somerset, Kings Co., N. S.; m.1. Sarah B. Dickie, of Amherst, Nova Scotia, in 1832; m.2. Mrs. Jane E. (Caldwell) Woodworth, of Grand Pre, Nova Scotia, September, 1854; s. Rev. Robert McGowan Sommerville.

Stavely, Alexander McLeod

b. Corkey, Co. Antrim, 9th June 1816; 4th. s. of Rev. Dr. William John Stavely (Kilraughts) and Jane Adams; ed. O.C.B., grad. Edinburgh University, 1835, Theological Hall, Paisley, lic. by Northern Presbytery, 16th March, 1839; ord. by Northern Presbytery 'sine titulo' 12th May, 1841, Missionary to St. John, New Brunswick; res. 16th June, 1879; preached in vacancies in Ireland; inst. Ballyclare Co. Antrim, 10th December, 1884, s.s. Larne; ret. November 1898; died 9th July 1903; m. Margaret Cameron, 2nd d. of Ewen Cameron, St John's, 21st April 1851(2?), ; 3 d., Lizzie Cameron, m. Professor James McMaster, Magee College; Jane Adams, m.1. Dr Hamilton, Leeds; m .2. Rev. J. B. Armour, Ballymoney; Annie.

Stavely, William

b. Ferniskey, Kells, Co. Antrim, 1743; grandson of Rev. Patrick Vance, Ray; ed. Antrim, R.P. Theological Hall; lic. by Irish Refd. Presbytery, 1769; ord. at Conlig, Co. Down, by Irish Refd. Presbytery August, 1772; located at Knockbracken, 1776; preached in Cos. Down, Armagh, Monaghan; helped to form R.P. congregations at Newtownards, Knockbracken, Dromore, Rathfriland, Ballylane, Fairview, Creevagh; imprisoned 1797-98 on charge of sympathising with United Irishmen; listed as an officer in Drumbracken Volunteers; res. 1800; inst. Kellswater, 1800, for work in Co Antrim; died May, 1825, Marymount, Antrim; int. Kellswater; m. Mary Donald, of Irishtown, Antrim, 1776; 1 s., Rev. William John (minister of Kilraughts and Dervock); 7 d., Nancy m. Andrew Ferguson; 1 d. m. Rev. Simon Cameron, Ballylaggan; Margaret m. Francis McMullan; Mary m. William Clugston; Eliza m. John Graham; Eleanor died 18th February 1827; Jane died unmarried at Marymount.

C.f. Ferguson, "Brief Biographical Sketches".

Stavely, William John
b. Knockbracken, Co. Down, 12th October, 1780; s. of Rev. William Stavely, Knock-bracken; ed. Glasgow University, R.P. Theological Hall, Scotland; lic. by Irish Refd. Presbytery at Cullybackey, 17th November, 1802 (known as Lower Antrim); ord. Dervock and Kilraughts, 6th September, 1804; res. Kilraughts, 1832; retained Dervock and Ballymoney; grad. D.D., U.S.A.; ret. 1860; died 4th December, 1864, at Lavin House; int. Kilraughts; m. Jane, d. of John Adams, Chequer Hall, Co. Antrim; 3 s., William James, Rev. Alexander McLeod; 4 d., Mary, Elizabeth, m. Hugh Loughridge, Ballymoney; Jane, m. Hugh McFadden, Ballymoney, 11th December, 1844; Annie, m. 16th September. 1851, Quintin Moore, M.D., Lavin.

Steen, James
b. nr. City of L'derry, 1800; ed. O.C.B., R.P. Theological Hall, Belfast; grad. G.C. 1833; ord. Dromore, 4th June, 1839; res. 4th August, 1840; joined General Assembly; inst. Clonduff, 21st June, 1842; died 17th July 1896; m. 1854 d. of Patrick Doran, Ballynagappog; 2 s., Alfred, Edwin; 1 d., Ophelia.

Stewart, James Alexander Smyth
b. Castledawson, 5th November, 1865; s. of James Stewart and Margaret McLernon; ed. Queen's College, Belfast, R.P. Theological Hall, Belfast; lic. by Eastern Presbytery, 1886; ord. Limavady, 6th October, 1887; res. 1895; inst. Dervock, 21st August, 1895; died 6th June 1902; m. Miss Beck, Liverpool; 1 d.

Stewart, John
b. Castlemellon, Donemana, 1771; 2nd s. of Charles Stewart, ed. Glasgow University, R.P. Theological Hall, Scotland; lic. by Irish Refd. Presbytery, 1797; ord. Grange, Co. Tyrone, 28th April, 1807; res. 1812; inst. Rathfriland, 25th May, 1812; s.s. Dromore; died 30th April, 1837; m. wife died 3rd December, 1858; 2 s., 2 d.;

Stewart, Robert Miller
b. Ballynaloob, Co. Antrim, 5th April, 1824; s. of William Stewart and Elizabeth Beggs; ed. grad. R.B.A.I., 1843., Theological Hall, Paisley; lic. by Northern Presbytery, 3rd February, 1847; Missionary in Connaught; London prize for proficiency in Gaelic; ord. 'sine titulo' by R.P. Synod 12th July, 1849, Missionary to the North American British Provinces; 1849 mission station of Wilmot, Annapolis Co., Nova Scotia, also Margaretville and Lawrencetown for over thirty years; res. 26th May, 1881, and supplied vacancies in U.S.A.; died 29th September, 1899, Wilmot, N.S.; m. Margaret Morrison, of Melvern Square, N.S., 7th November, 1855.

Stott, John
b. nr. Cremore, Co. Armagh, 17th May, 1808; s. of Thomas Stott and Jane Hamilton; ed. grad. R.B.A.I., 1830, studied medicine; Theological Hall, Paisley; lic. by Northern Presbytery, 9th March, 1834; ord. and inst. by Western Presbytery, Convoy, Co. Donegal, 8th July, 1835; res. 16th October, 16, 1850; emig. 1851; rec. by Synod, 28th May, 1851; inst. Princeton, Gibson Co., Indiana, 13th October, 1851, suspd. 2nd June, 1868; formed independent organization, preached without ecclesiastical connection, practiced medicine, Princeton, Indiana; Moderator of Synod of 1865; m. 13th March, 1842, Eliza., d. of Wm. Black Aughigalt.

Sweeney, James Peoples
b. Desertone, Glendermott, C1800; y.s. of William Sweeney, ed. Glasgow University, R.P. Theological Hall, Scotland; grad. M.A. Glasgow, 1821; lic. Western Presbytery, 1824; ord. Faughan, 1827; ret. 1874; died 4th May 1877.

Sweeney, William
b. Desertone, 28th November, 1816; s. of George Sweeney; nephew of Rev. J.P. Sweeney; ed. Glasgow University, R.P. Theological Hall; grad. M.A. (Glasgow), 1837; lic. by Western Presbytery, 1838; ord. Ballylane, 11th September, 1839; res. 27th December, 1840; joined General Assembly, Belfast Presbytery; inst. Killeshandra, 30th March, 1841; died 17th July, 1868; m.1. d. of James Miller, L'derry; m.2. d. of William Harper, Lisadian, L'derry.

Tadley, Harry
b. L'derry, 1st August, 1921, s. of John Patton and Maltilda Mary Tadley; R.P. Theological Hall 1969-1971; commissioned as Synod's Evangelist, 9th August, 1959; lic. by Western Presbytery 27th May 1971; ord. Dublin Road, 8th September, 1971; inst. Ballenon and Ballylane, 7th October 1976; died 28th June 1981; int. Ballenon.

Teaz, Ezekiel
b. Burnfoot, L'derry, 1859; s. of Ezekiel Teaz; ed. Magee College, R.P. Theological Hall, Belfast; grad. G.A.M.C., 1883; lic. by Western Presbytery, 1886; ord. Dervock, 10th December, 1886; res. 1895; inst. Hall Lane, Liverpool, 1895; res. October, 1921; inst. Larne, 8th November 1921; m. Miss Janet Agnew Carswell, Belfast, 19th November, 1889; 1 s. Homer Nevin, M.C.; killed in action.

Thompson, Albert Melville
b. Londonderry, Ohio, 4th December, 1874; s. of Rev. James Alexander Thompson and Sarah McBride; ed. Amity College, Iowa, R.P. Seminary Pittsburgh; lic. by Kansas Presbytery, April, 1897; grad. B.A. 1894 and M.A. 1898 (Amity College); ord. Ballylaggan, 10th August, 1898; res. February, 1901 inst. Denver, 1901; res. 1904; s.s. Geelong, Australia, March, 1904; res. March 1909; inst. Stranorlar, 30th November, 1909; res. February, 1912; returned to U.S.A, June, 1912; inst, Utica, Ohio, 3rd April, 1914; res. 13th September, 1916; mission work under Kansas Presbytery, 1917, 1918; inst. Bovina, New York, 15th November, 1923; res. 1st September, 1930; inst. Hemet, California, 3rd October, 1930; ret. 31st March, 1938; died at Santa Ana, California, 18th January, 1948; m.1. Mary Luella Elliott, 29th September, 1898, at Ballylaggan; m.2. Margaret Jane Carswell, 16th September, 1926, of Santa Ana, California.

Thompson, Isaac
b. Jerretspass; s. of Isaac Thompson; ed. Queen's College, Belfast, R.P. Theological Hall, Belfast; grad. B.A. (Q.U.B.), 1867, M.A. (Q.U.B.), 1882, L.L.D. (Q.U.B.), 1878, B.L.; lic. by Southern Presbytery, 1871; ord. Drimbolg, 28th July, 1873; res. 3rd May, 1893; died 1895.

Toland, Charles Kirk
b. Kilraughts, 20th November, 1839; s. of Rev. William Toland; ed. Glasgow University, R.P. Theological Hall, Belfast; lic. by Northern Presbytery, 1865; ord. Bready, 19th April, 1866; s.s. Mulvin; res. 1886; joined General Assembly; inst. 2nd Strabane, 22nd July,

1886; united cong. with 1st Strabane, 1911; died 26th October, 1916; m.; 2 s., William died in infancy, John Thompson, died aged 9; 1 d., Elizabeth Susanne, died aged 2.

Toland, William
ed. O.C.B., St. Andrews and Edinburgh Universities, R.P. Theological Hall, Paisley; lic. by Eastern Presbytery, 1831, ord. Kilraughts, 1st August, 1832; ret. 1876; died 17th November, 1878; Clerk of Northern Presbytery; m.; 1 s. Rev. Charles Kirk (minister of Bready, 1866-1886), 2 d., Eliza, m. 20th December 1852, Wm Coffey, merchant, Ballymoney; Fanny, m. November 1873, Rev. John McKee, Penpont, Dumfriesshire.

Wallace, Robert
b. nr. Letterkenny, 20th December, 1823; y.s. of Daniel Wallace and Margaret Stewart; ed. Glasgow University, R.P. Theological Hall, Paisley, grad. Glasgow University, 1840; lic. by Western Presbytery, ord. Newry, 14th January, 1846; res. 1864; inst. Glasgow, 1864; died 4th September, 1880; m.1. Mary, d. Rev. Andrew Wilson, 2nd Dungannon; m.2. Frances, d. m. Rev. James Dick, Kellswater, 2 s., George, James.

Warnock, William
b. Greenshields, Ballymoney, 17th July 1882; s. of James Warnock and Agnes Carson; ed. Ballymoney Int. School, Queen's College, Belfast, R.P. Theological Hall, Belfast; grad. B.A. (R.U.I.) 1902; lic. by Northern Presbytery, 1905; ord. Killinchy, 31st October, 1905; res. 1908; inst. Dromara, 11th March, 1908; res. 1923; inst. Loanhead, Scotland, 11th December, 1923; res. 1929; inst Milford, Co. Donegal, 28th November, 1929; died 25th December, 1943; int. Milford; m. Mary Barker, L'derry; 3 s. Robert James Albert, William Barker Carson, Thomas Archibald; 2 d. Mary Violet, Agnes Eileen.

Watt, Robert John
b. nr. Coleraine, 1813; ed. Q.C., Belfast, R.P. Theological Hall, Scotland; lic. by Northern Presbytery, ord. College Street South, Belfast, 3rd July, 1839; res. 1841; inst. Stranraer Original Seceder, 4th May, 1842; Moderator of United Original Secession Synod, 1845; res. 1852; inst. Elgin Free High, 1852; died 16th September, 1862; m. 1840 d. of Dr Mawhinney, Belfast.

Watson, Robert Andrew
b. L'derry, 18th September, 1914; s. of Albert Watson and Jean; ed. Foyle College, L'derry, Magee College, T.C.D.; R.P. Theological Hall 1946-1949; grad. B.A. (T.C.D.), 1938; lic. by Western Presbytery, 27th July, 1949; ord. Greenock, 27th April, 1950; congregation dissolved, 1955; minister without charge, Western Presbytery, 1955-1991, died 6th July 1991; int. Ballyclare; m. Mary Finlay.

Walters, John
b. Milford, Co Donegal; s. of James M Walters; ed. Foyle College, L'derry, Magee College, L'derry, Trinity College, Dublin; R.P. Theological Hall, Belfast, 1924-1927; Princeton Theological College, U.S.A.; grad. B.A. (T.C.D.) 1925; lic. by Western Presbytery 1st June, 1927; ord. Bailiesmills, 26th October, 1927; inst. Knockbracken, 2nd November, 1927 (joint charge); ret. 7th May, 1968; Moderator of Synod, 1941; died 12th December 1970; m. Jessie; 1 d. Anne.

Wright, Alexander Reid
b. Craigs, Cullybackey, 3rd February 1910; s. of Hugh Wright and Annie Reid; ed. Ballymena Academy, Magee College, T.C.D.; R.P. Theological Hall, Belfast, 1931-1934; grad. B.A. (T.C.D.), 1932; lic. by Northern Presbytery, 23rd May, 1934; ord. Ballylaggan, 16th October, 1934; ret. 31st December, 1971; Moderator of Synod, 1944; author of Young Peoples Pages in "The Covenanter", 1935-1966, "Historical Sketch of Ballyclabber R.P. Church" (1947) and "Historical Sketch of Ballylaggan R.P. Congregation" (1941); died 17th March, 1983; int. Ballylaggan; m. Mary Carlisle McCollum, Inchmearn; 2 d. Irene, Lorna, m. Rev. Edward Donnelly; 1 s. David Hugh Alexander.

Wright, Hugh
b. Creevagh, Co Monaghan, 20th October, 1908; 2nd s. of Rev. James Renwick Wright and Elizabeth Reid; ed. Coleraine Model School, Coleraine Academical Institution, Magee College, T.C.D.; R.P. Theological Hall, Belfast, 1930-1932; R.P. Seminary, Pittsburgh 1932-1935; grad. B.A. (T.C.D.), 1930; lic. by Pittsburgh Presbytery, USA, 10th May 1932; ord. 'sine titulo' by Pittsburgh Presbytery, 10th August, 1934; s.s. Winnipeg 1932-35; inst. Winnipeg. 30th April 1936; res. 22nd July 1938; inst. Clarendon Street, L'derry, 10th November 1938; inst. Trinity Street, Belfast, 15th September, 1959; inst. Newtownards, 21st December, 1973; ret. 27th September, 1983; Moderator of Synod, 1946 and 1961; died 21st January, 1991; int. Knockbracken; m. Dorothea Macauley, d. Robert Macauley, Belfast, 15th june 1938; 3 d. Nancy, Rosemarie (died infancy), Edith; 1 s. James.

Wright, James Renwick
b. Craigs, Cullybackey, 5th July, 1879; s. of Hugh Wright; ed. Collegiate and Intermediate School, Ballymena, Queen's College, Belfast, R.P. Theological Hall, Belfast; grad. B.A. (R.U.I.); lic. by Eastern Presbytery, 1903; ord. Creevagh, 29th January, 1904; res. 1911; inst. Ballyclabber, 25th April, 1911; s.s. Ringrash; ret. 7th September, 1955; died 1st January, 1964; int. Agherton, Portstewart.; m. Elizabeth Reid, BA, d. of Alexander Reid, Glarryford; 3 s., Thomas Reid, Rev. Hugh, Rev. James Renwick; 1 d., Marie, wife of Norman Holmes, Ballymoney.

Wright, James Renwick
b. Coleraine, 6th May, 1918; 3rd s. of Rev James Renwick Wright and Elizabeth Reid; ed. Coleraine Model School, Coleraine Academical Institution; Magee College, T.C.D.; R.P. Theological Hall, Belfast, 1937-1939; R.P. Theological Seminary, Pittsburgh, 1939-40; lic. by St. Lawrence Presbytery April, 1939; ord. and inst. Ballymoney, 7th January, 1941; inst. Dromara, 7th January, 1953; res. 17th December, 1968; inst. Geneva R.P., Beaver Falls, Pa. U.S.A., 20th May, 1969; inst. Winchester R.P., Ks, 12th November, 1975; inaugurated Dean of Students and Prof. of New Testament Studies 19th September, 1978; ret. 1993; D.D. Geneva College, 1967; Moderator of Synod (R.P.C.N.A.), 1979; died 8th October, 2009; int. New Galilee R.P. cemetery, Pa., USA; m. Maureen Hamilton, daughter of Samuel Kelly, Ballymoney, 19th September, 1944; 2 s. Christopher, Jonathan.

Young, Robert
b. Kelso, Roxburghshire, 1732; ed. Associate Synod, Theological Hall; lic. by Associate Presbytery, joined Scottish Refd. Pres; ord. 1776 as missionary to Covenanters in North America; shipwrecked; landed at Glenarm; located for a time time at Cullybackey; itinerated in Cos. Antrim, L'derry and Donegal, esp. Cullybackey, Ramelton and Faughan;

died 9th November, 1794; int. Glendermott; m. 1777 Mary Dickson, Cullybackey; 3 s., John, Robert and Joseph; Joseph founded the Young Endowment, a Charity for girls in the City and Liberties of L'derry, by a bequest of £20,000.

Young, William

b. Milford, Co. Donegal, 26th September, 1909; s. of Samuel Young and Margaret Johnston; ed. Foyle College, L'derry, Magee College, T.C.D.; R.P. Theological Hall, Belfast, 1931-1934; grad. B.A. (T.C.D.), 1932; lic. by Western Presbytery, 16th May, 1934; ord. Wishaw, 24th October, 1934; inst. Stranraer, 8th May, 1946; inst. Grosvenor Road, Belfast, 4th September, 1956; Moderator of Synod 1958; inst. Dervock, 2nd February, 1973; ret. 29th April, 1980; died 8th August, 1983; int. Holywood; m. Elizabeth Barrie Farmer; 2 s., George, Samuel; 1.d. Gladys.

Fasti

of Irish born Ministers who have served in
the
Reformed Presbyterian Church of Scotland

Including extracts from the Irish Fasti relating to the R.P.C.S.

Blair, John Thomas Moffett
ord. Stranraer, 5th October 1932; inst. Glenmanus, Portrush, 17th October, 1944; inst. Airdrie, 17th October 1949; inst. Stranraer, 17th June, 1970; ret. 1978; died 1st April 1994; int. Ayr.

Boyd, Torrens
ord. Penpont, 1867; res. 1873; inst. Ringrash, Co. L'derry, 5th February, 1873.

Dick, James
ord. Wishaw, Scotland, 19th May, 1870; res. 1884; inst. Kilraughts.

Dickey, John Knox
ord. Bready, 28th September, 1911; res. 1919; inst. Stranraer (R.P.), 1919; res 1926; inst. Clarendon Street, L'derry, 4th February, 1926.

Gillespie, Alexander Patterson
ord. Rathfriland. 19th September, 1884; res. 1887; inst. Loanhead, Scotland, 17th February, 1887; emig. to U.S.A..

Gilmour, William James
ord. Loanhead, 4th October, 1932; inst. Nicholson Street, Glasgow, 11th February, 1941; inst. Cullybackey, 15th May, 1946.

Gregg, Andrew Cross
ord. Ballylaggan, 22nd May, 1890, res. 1897; inst. Loanhead, Scotland 12th February, 1897; res. 1922; inst. Greenock, 2nd November, 1921; editor "R.P. Witness", 1910-1940; died 13th September, 1949.

Guthrie, Archibald
ord. at Kilraughts, 12th September 1934, and designated missionary to Syria; res. November 1946; inst. Wishaw, 5th February 1947; Glasgow, "Editor, "The R.P. Witness", 1953-1966; "The Covenanter Witness", 1967 -1975; died 9th March 1975.

Kennedy, Samuel Guiler
ord. Wishaw R.P., Scotland, 12th December, 1889; res. 1896; inst. College Street South, Belfast, 5th February, 1896.

Martin, John
b. Laggan, Dumfriesshire; s. of Thomas Martin and Marion McMurdo, ed. Glasgow University; lic. by R.P. Presbytery of Edinburgh and Glasgow; ord. Rathfriland, 4th December, 1879; res. 3rd April, 1884; inst. Wishaw, 1884; res. 1888; inst. Stranraer, 1888; joined English Pres. Church; inst. Leeds; died Laggan, Drumfriesshire, 1900.

McKee, John
ord. Penpont, Scotland, 1873; res. 1891; inst. Dromara, 18th March, 1891, res. 17th December, 1897; inst. Wishaw, 1898; ret. 1930; died 5th December 1933.

Moffett, William James
ord. Milford, Co. Donegal, 12th October, 1905; res. 1916; inst. Greenock, Scotland, 1916; res. 1921; inst. Airdrie, 1st September, 1921; ret. 24th May, 1949; died 1st January, 1952, in Glasgow; Clerk of R.P. Synod of Scotland.

Reid, Samuel Lynas
ord. Stranraer 9th January, 1957; inst. Riverside, Newry, 19th December, 1969.

Russell, William
ord. Ballenon, 29th October, 1890; res. 31st October, 1905; inst. Paisley, Scotland, November, 1905; res. 23rd November, 1926; inst. Trinity Street, Belfast, 4th January, 1927.

Warnock, William
ord. Killinchy, 31st October, 1905; res. 1908; inst. Dromara, 11th March, 1908; res. 1923; inst. Loanhead, Scotland, 11th December, 1923; res. 1929; inst Milford, Co. Donegal, 28th November, 1929.

Watson, Robert Andrew
ord. Greenock, 27th April, 1950; congregation dissolved, 1955; minister without charge, Western Presbytery, 1955-1991, died 6th July 1991.

Young, William
ord. Wishaw, 24th October, 1934; inst. Stranraer, 8th May, 1946; inst. Grosvenor Road, Belfast, 4th September, 1956.

Currently the ministers of the Reformed Presbyterian Church of Scotland are from the Irish church. Several ministers who have served in Scotland are currently in pastoral charges in Ireland or in retirement.

Fasti

of Irish born Ministers who have served in the
Reformed Presbyterian Church
of North America

Including ordained ministers and licentiates of the
Reformed Presbyterian Church of Ireland who have
served in the R.P.C.N.A..

Brief historical sketch of the R.P.C.N.A.
with relevant facts relating to the following Fasti.

The first Reformed Presbyterian congregation in North America was organized in Middle Octorara (Lancaster County, Pennsylvania) in 1738. The first presbytery, organized by four Irish and Scottish Reformed Presbyterian ministers was formed 1774. At this time, Reformed Presbyterians were mostly concentrated in eastern Pennsylvania and northern South Carolina, but small groups of Reformed Presbyterians existed in Massachusetts, Connecticut, New York, western Pennsylvania, North Carolina, and Georgia. During the American Revolution, most Reformed Presbyterians fought for independence.

Since 1774, the denomination has undergone four major schisms.

1) In 1782, almost all of the church merged with the Associate Presbyterian Church to form the Associate Reformed Presbyterian Church, holding that the new situation of independence removed the reasons for political dissent. The few remaining members who refused to join the merger, including just two congregations, were reorganized into a presbytery in 1798.

2) In 1833, the church split, forming the New Light and Old Light R.P. Synods. The New Lights, who exercised political rights, grew for some years but suffered splits and went into decline, eventually merging in 1965 with the Evangelical Presbyterian Church to form the Reformed Presbyterian Church (Evangelical Synod), which in 1982 merged with the Presbyterian Church in America.

3) A third split, in 1840, resulted in two ministers and a few elders leaving to form the Reformed Presbytery (nicknamed the Steelites, after David Steele, their most prominent leader), which continues today. They held that the denomination itself had fallen away from its covenants and historical attainments by allowing occasional hearing, political activity, and membership in voluntary associations.

4) The main body of the RPCNA suffered another split, the "East End Split", in 1891, again on the matter of political activity and office-holding. Statistics reveal that

denominational membership suffered a net loss of 11% in 1891, most of whom joined the United Presbyterian Church.

From before the year 1800 the church took a strong stance against slavery and faithfully supported the North in the Civil War. This policy was a major factor in the decline of the denomination's South Carolina and Tennessee congregations, most members there moving to southern Ohio, Indiana, and Illinois.

Since 1980, the denomination has experienced growth, seeing an increase of approximately 25% in membership and 11% in the number of churches. The R.P.C.N.A. in 2008 had 6,334 members in 75 North American congregations, along with 238 more members in four congregations in Japan. The main areas of the church are in northeastern Kansas, central Indiana, and western Pennsylvania. The R.P.C.N.A. sponsors a university, Geneva College in Beaver Falls, Pennsylvania and also the Reformed Presbyterian Theological Seminary in Pittsburgh, Pennsylvania.

R.P.C.N.A. official published summary.

*** Indicates ordained ministers or licentiates of the
Reformed Presbyterian Church of Ireland**

Benaugh, George *
b. Drumlough, Rathfriland, County Down, 12th October, 1845; s. of George Benaugh and Mary Ann Dickson; ed. Crawford's Academy Warrenpoint, Q.C.B.; Princeton and McCormack Seminaries, grad. 1869; lic. by Chicago Presbytery, 3rd April, 1871; ord. and inst. Summit Hill, 1873, Pa.; inst. Philadelpia, 1877; inst. Mifflinown, Pa., 1880; inst. Camden, N.Y., 1885; inst. Lexington and Mansfield, Ohio, 1888; inst. Knockbracken, Co. Down, 1898; ret. 13th May, 1913; died 3rd December, 1919 in Belfast; int. Rathfriland; D.D. from New Windsor College, Maryland, 10th June, 1885; m. Nettie Androbus, of New London, Iowa, 6th February, 1880; d. Mary Elizabeth, wife of Henry C. Lyons, Newry.

Black, John
b. Ahoghill, Co. Antrim, 2nd October, 1768; s. of John Black and Margaret McKibben; ed. grad. Glasgow University, 1790; emig. 1797 to Philadelphia, suspected of being United Irishman; lic. by Refd Presbytery at Coldenham, New York, 24th June, 1799; ord. by Refd. Presbytery, 18th December, 1800, for West PA. centred in Pittsburgh; 1st Covenanter minister settled west of the Allegheny mtns.; 1820, appt. Prof. of Latin and Greek in Western University of Pa.; res. in 1832; President of Duquesne College one year; 1833, joined New School branch; remained pastor of a majority of his former congregation; died Pittsburgh, PA., 25th October, 1849.

Black, James Alexander
b. Dromore, Co. Down; s. of Samuel Black and Elizabeth Bell; emig. with parents 1841, Pittsburgh; ed. grad. Allegheny City College, 1862; lic. by Pittsburgh Presbytery, 23rd May, 1867; ord. and inst. by Pittsburgh Presbytery, 18th November, 1868, Clarksburgh, Indiana Co., P.A.; res. 11th April, 1882; appt. President Polytechnic Institute, Allegheny City, P.A.; inst. 9th February, 1886, Rehoboth, Wyman, Louisa Co., Iowa; m. 8th June, 1876, Tirzah M. Cannon, of New Alexandria, Pa.

Blackwood, James
b. Ardstraw, Co. Tyrone, 14th August, 1793; s. of Thomas Blackwood and Martha Akin; ed. grad. Glasgow University, 1814; lic. by Southern Presbytery, 10th May, 1822; emig. with family 1824, Belmont Co. Ohio; missionary West Pa. and Ohio; ord. by Pittsburgh Presbytery, 'sine titulo', 8th May, 1826 for this work; inst. Brush Creek, Locust Grove, Adams Co. Ohio, 12th April, 1827; res. 9th April, 1829, continued missionary work; inst. 24th May, 1834, Little Beaver, Austintown, Camp Run, Slippery Rock, Greenville and Sandy Lake in Beaver and Lawrence Cos. Pa.; continued at Slippery Rock and Camp Run; Moderator of Synod,1838; died nr. Portersville, Pa., 8th October, 1851; m. Jemima Calderwood, of Philadelphia, 18th August, 1833.

Blair, Robert Andrew
b. Drumsteeple, nr. Aghadowey, Co. L'derry, 11th May, 1876; s. of Neil Blair and Elizabeth Loughrey; father an elder, Ballylaggan; ed. matriculated as a student in the Royal University; grad. Geneva College, 1901; grad. R.P. Seminary Allegheny, 1904; lic. by Philadelphia Presbytery, 7thApril 7, 1903; ord. and inst. by Ohio Presbytery, Utica, Ohio, 12th October, 1904; res. 20th August, 1907; Missionary to China, Tak Hing Chau;

1908, compelled to return eye problems; 1909 -1912 , Field Secretary of Foreign Mission Board; 1912 to 1913 s.s. Olathe, Kansas; 1913 - 1916 Superintendent of the Jewish Mission, Philadelphia; 1916- 1917, Field Secretary of the Foreign Mission Board; inst. by Pittsburgh Presbytery, 2nd November, 1917, Slippery Rock (now Rose Point) Pa.; res.1923; inst. Parnassus, Pa. 1923; 1926 the sight of his remaining eye was taken; ret. 1945; Hon. D.D. Geneva College, 1934; died 17th January, 1960, Rose point, Pa.; m. Estella Giffen Garrett, Cleveland, Ohio, 8th November, 1905; 1.d. Anna E., 3.s. Robert , John L., Walter G..

Blair, Robert Andrew

b. Drumsteeple, nr. Aghadowey, Co. L'derry, 11th May, 1876; s. of Neil Blair and Elizabeth Loughrey; father an elder, Ballylaggan; ed. matriculated as a student in the Royal University; grad. Geneva College, 1901; grad. R.P. Seminary Allegheny, 1904; lic. by Philadelphia Presbytery, 7thApril 7, 1903; ord. and inst. by Ohio Presbytery, Utica, Ohio, 12th October, 1904; res. 20th August, 1907; Missionary to China, Tak Hing Chau; 1908, compelled to return eye problems; 1909 -1912 , Field Secretary of Foreign Mission Board; 1912 to 1913 s.s. Olathe, Kansas; 1913 - 1916 Superintendent of the Jewish Mission, Philadelphia; 1916- 1917, Field Secretary of the Foreign Mission Board; inst. by Pittsburgh Presbytery, 2nd November, 1917, Slippery Rock (now Rose Point) Pa.; res.1923; inst. Parnassus, Pa. 1923; 1926 the sight of his remaining eye was taken; ret. 1945; Hon. D.D. Geneva College, 1934; died 17th January, 1960, Rose point, Pa.; m. Estella Giffen Garrett, Cleveland, Ohio, 8th November, 1905; 1.d. Anna E., 3.s. Robert , John L., Walter G..

Calderwood, David *

b. Dunnygarron, Cullybackey, 14th September, 1891; s. of William John Calderwood and Sarah Jane Lowry; ed. Magee College, T.C.D.; R.P. Theological Hall, Belfast 1913-1916; grad B.A. (T.C.D.) 1914, M.A. 1917; lic. by Northern Presbytery, May, 1916; ord. Clarendon Street, L'derry, 2nd November, 1916; 4 months in France in 1918 Y.M.C.A.; res. 6th July, 1921; inst. by Colorado Presbytery, Denver, 21st September, 1922; inst. Seattle, Washington, 1925; inst. Los Angeles, 4th January, 1929; inst. St. Pauls Presbyterian Church, Los Angeles; appt. Minister of Education, Glendale Presbyterian Church, 1943; res. 1945; appt. Sec. California Branch Nat. Assoc. Evangelicals; joined Orthodox Presbyterian Church; inst. Grace O.P. Church, Los Angeles; died 29th March, 1970; m. Annie Mary King, Seattle, Washington; 2 s. Deryk David, Noel King.

Cannon, John

b. Dungiven, Co. L'derry, 19th November, 1784; s. of Hugh Cannon and Mary Thompson, (Presbyterian); emig. with parents 1787, to Westmorland Co. P.A.; 1788 joined Associate Refd. Church; ed. grad. 1810, Jefferson College; espoused Covenanter principles; Philadelphia Seminary; lic. by Middle Presbytery R.P. Church, 23rd May, 1815; ord. and inst. by Middle Presbytery, Greensburgh, Westmoreland Co. Pa. 16th September, 1816; Moderator of Synods of 1819 and 1833; died, at his home 2nd February, 1836; m. Martha Brown of Greensburgh, Pa., May, 1818; s. Rev Robert Brown Cannon.

Carlisle, Samuel

b. Ballybay, Co. Monaghan, 4th May, 1828; s. of Rev Samuel Carlisle and Letitia Craig; ed. Coleraine Academy, grad. O.C.B., 1847, Theological Hall, Paisley; lic. Northern Presbytery, 4th May, 1848; emig. ord. and inst. by New York Presbytery, 1st R.P. Cong.

Newburgh, New York, 15th November, 1849; Moderator of Synod, 1886; died 3rd July, 1887, Ocean Grove, N.J., int. Cedar Hill Cmty; m. Margaret Fenton of Newburgh.

Clarke, Alexander *
b. nr. Kilrea, Co. L'derry, 16th July, 1793; s. of William Clarke and Elizabeth Craig; ed. O.C.B., grad. Glasgow University, 1819, Theological Hall, Paisley; chosen by the Irish Synod as missionary to North American British Provinces; lic. and ord., 24th May, 1827; arrived St. John, New Brunswick, 23rd August, 1827, selected Amherst, Nova Scotia; He travelled extensively; est. 15 mission stations; Clarke and all his congregations joined General Synod (New School), 14th October, 1847; contd. Amherst, N.S., and the vicinity; Hon. D.D. University of Pa, 1856; Moderator of General Synod, 1856; died, 15th March, 1874; m. Catherine McMillan, of Belfast, 22nd May, 1821.
Cf. 'The Chignecto Covenanters,' by Eldon Hay, 1996.

Clyde, Charles
b. Ulster, 9th May, 1856; s. of Robert Clyde and Nancy Harrison; emig. 1865, Philadelphia; ed. Lexington Grammar School; theology under the Rev. David Steele; joined Reformed Presbyterian Church (Steelite); ord. by Reformed Presbytery 'sine titulo', 1884, ministered to scattered Presbytery; inst. Northwood, Ohio, 1887; joined R.P.C.N.A., rec. by Lakes Presbytery, 11th April, 1894, inst. Lochiel, Ontario, Canada, 8th July, 1897; died 7th December, 1901, Brodie, Ontario; m. 9 Children who moved to College Hill, Beaver Falls, Pa..

Clyde, Robert
b. Dervock, Co. Antrim, 6th May, 1851; s. of Robert Clyde and Nancy Harrison; family joined R.P. Church 1853; emig. 1865, Philadelphia; ed. studied 1874 under Dr. Steele, also New School Seminary, and Allegheny Seminary; lic. by Philadelphia Presbytery, 27th May, 1879; ord. by Iowa Presbytery, and inst. Elliota congregation, Canton, Fillmore Co., Minnesota, 12th February, 1886; res. 1890 and left the ministry; m. Bella Dougherty, of Philadelphia, 21st August, 1878.

Craighead, Alexander
b. Donegal, 18th March, 1707; s. of Rev. Thomas Craighead (Presbyterian Minister) and Margaret Craighead; emig. with family, 1715, Freetown, Massachusetts; 1721 removed to New Jersey. 1724, to White Clay Creek, Delaware, 1733, to Octorara, Lancaster Co., Pa.; ed. classical and theological education under his father; lic. by the Donegal (Pa.) Presbytery of Presbyterian Church, 16th October, 1734; first minister to preach west of the Susquehanna river, ord. and inst. Middle Octorara, Lancaster Co., Pa., 20th November, 1735; accompanied Whitefield on some tours; Sought to apply the S. L & Covenant, in the Church; 1742 withdrew from the American Presbyterian Church; joined the R.P., presided over General Meeting, built mtng. house in Octorara; 1743 with Covenanters of E. Pa. renewed the Covenants, opened correspondence with Refd. Presbytery of Scotland; He labored with great acceptance among the scattered societies for 7 years; 1749, returned to the Presbyterian Church,1749, removed to Virginia, later, North Carolina; died 12th March, 1766, nr. Charlotte, Mecklenberg Co., N.C..

Crawford, John
b. Carncullough, Dervock, Co. Antrim, 27th May, 1828; s. of James Crawford and Jane McAuley Crawford; ed.1845, O.C.B.., engaged in teaching, 1849, entered the Free Church

College of Edinburgh, under Dr. Cunningham; missionary in Edinburgh; R.P. Theological Hall, Paisley; emig. because of poor health 15th January, 1852, Philadelphia; studied under Drs. J. M. Willson and S. B. Wylie; lic. by New York Presbytery, 24th May, 1853, ord. by the Philadelphia Presbytery, inst. Baltimore, Maryland, 15th November, 1853; died 3rd September, 1856, Baltimore, Md.; int. Philadelphia; unm.

Cuthbertson, John

b. Ayr, Ayrshire, 3rd April, 1718; ed. theology under Rev. John McMillan, lic. by Refd. Presbytery, 16th May, 1745, ord. 'sine titulo' Braehead, 18th May, 1747, for work among the scattered societies of Scotland; Moderator of the Refd. Presbytery in 1750; with Rev. Thomas Cameron missionary to societies of Covenanters in Ireland; 1751 missionary to America, arrived New Castle, Delaware, 5th August, 1751; first Covenanter minister who came to America, settled Middle Octorara, Lancaster Co., Pa.; missionary tours through New York, Vermont, New Hampshire, Connecticut, New Jersey, Maryland, Virginia, and all parts of Pennsylvania, west to Ohio river; Winter of 1773, joined by Revs. Matthew Lynn and Alexander Dobbin, and organized the Refd. Presbytery of America, at Paxtang, Dauphin Co., Pa., 10th March, 1774; Ministered Middle Octorara; 1777 identified with cause of the colonies against British Gov.; September, 1778, without consulting or informing the Refd. Presbytery in Scotland, he began the conferences with the Associate Church, resulted in union, forming the Associate Reformed Church, 13th June, 1782; died 10th March, 1791; int. Lower Octorara; m. Sally Moore, Philadelphia, 25th February, 1756.

Dobbin, Alexander *

b. City of L'derry, 4th February, 1741; s. of John Dobbin, a 'pious sailor'; ed. grad. Glasgow University, 1771. Theological lectures in Glasgow; lic. by Refd. Presbytery of Ireland, 6th July, 1772, ord. 'sine titulo' Conlig, Co. Down, 20th August, 1772, as a missionary to the Covenanters in America; sailed with Rev. Matthew Lynn, from L'derry and landed in New Castle, Delaware, 13th December, 1773; He, with Revs. John Cuthbertson and Matthew Lynn, constituted the Refd. Presbytery of America, at Paxtang, Dauphin Co. Pa., 10th March, 1774; ministered at Rock Creek (Gettysburg), Adams Co, Pa.; involved in the union forming the Associate Reformed Church, 1782. continued at Rock Creek; died 1st June, 1809, Gettysburg; int. Marsh Creek graveyard; m.1. Isabella Gamble, of Co. Down, July, 1772; m.2. Mrs. Mary (Irvin) Agnew, of Adams Co., 1801.

Dodds, Josiah

b. Ballybay, Co. Monaghan, 3rd March, 1819; s. of John Dodds and Elizabeth McKee; emig. with family 1819, Dodds, Lucesco, Westmoreland Co. Pa., 1829; removed to Butler Co.; ed. under the Rev. Hugh Walkinshaw, grad. 1842, from Western University of Pa.; Allegheny and Cincinnati Seminaries; lic. by Pittsburgh Presbytery, 13th April, 1846, ord. and inst. by Lakes Presbytery, Beech Woods, Preble Co., Ohio, and Garrison, Fayette Co., Indiana, 6th October, 1847; res. 10th October, 1865, missionary in the West for two years, principally at Winchester, Jefferson Co., Kansas; inst. Winchester 7th November, 1868, res. 18th October, 1876. inst. Sylvania, Dade Co., Missouri, 9th May, 1878; ret. 1891; died 24th February, 1896, Topeka Kansas; int. Winchester cmty.; m.1. Matilda Cannon, of Greensburgh, Pa., 28th June, 1847; m.2. Mary Milligan, of Fayetteville, Indiana, 29th March, 1853; m.3. Belle Torrence, of Northwood, Ohio, 12th August, 1857; s. Rev. Josiah Boggs Dodds.

Donnelly, Thomas
b. nr. Donegal town, Co. Donegal, 13th January, 1772; s. of Thomas Donnelly and Nancy Moore; ed. grad. Glasgow University, 1790; emig. spring 1791, Chester District, South Carolina. grad. Dickinson College, 1794, studied theology under Rev. William King; lic. by Refd. Presbytery, Coldenham, Orange Co., New York, 24th June , 1799, returned to South Carolina; ord. and inst. Rocky Creek congregation, later known as the 'Brick Church', and Bethesda congregation, Chester District, South Carolina, 3rd March, 1801. ministered also to societies of Covenanters in Tennessee, North Carolina and Georgia; opposition to slavery caused many members to migrate to the free States of Ohio, Indiana and Illinois; Remained in the South, and continued to minister to the last of the Covenanters in the Carolinas; Moderator of Synod, 1818; died 27th November, 1847, Rocky Creek, Chester District, S.C.; m. Agnes Smith, of Chester, S.C. 6th March, 1801; a staunch opponent of slavery.

Edgar, George Alexander
b. Belfast, 5th December, 1865; s. of William Edgar and Sarah Moore; College Street South R.P.; emig. 1881, Cedarville, Ohio; ed. Indiana University, grad. Geneva College, May, 1890. grad. Seminary in Allegheny, March, 1894; lic. by Pittsburgh Presbytery 12th April, 1893; ord. and inst. Olathe, Kansas, 26th June, 1894; res. 20th August, 1907; inst. Rehoboth, Wyman, Iowa, 8th May, 1908; res. 13th August, 1912; inst. St. Louis, Missouri, 10th September, 1912; res. 17th September, 1915; appt. Superintendent of the Knox Academy, Selma, Alabama, September, 1915; ret. ill-health, January, 1921; Hon. D.D. Geneva College; Moderator of Synod, 1918; died 10th February, 1927, Winona Lake, Indiana; int. Olathe, Kansas; m. Mrs. Elizabeth Montgomery (Adams) Wylie, of Kansas City, Kansas. 1st May, 1900.

Edgar, Samuel
b. nr. Rathfriland, Co. Down, January, 1872; s. of Samuel Edgar and Sarah McMullan (Both Scottish); emig. Boston; joined 1st Boston R.P.1889.ed. Geneva College. grad. R.P. Seminary in Allegheny, 1903; Princeton Seminary; lic. by New York Presbytery 6th May, 1902; ord. and inst. by Colorado Presbytery, La Junta, Colorado, 9th June, 1904; res. 1907; Latakia, Syria, 1907-1915; imprisoned by Turks 1915; 1915-16 s.s. Wyman, Iowa; inst. Greeley, Colorado, 21st June, 1917; res. 15th April, 1918; 1918 -1919 Red Cross Work in Palestine and Syria; Foreign Mission again from 1919 to 1921; returned home; inst. Eskridge, Kansas, 7th September, 1922; res. 13th September, 1925; inst. Santa Ana, California, 8th October, 1925; ret. 1945; Hon. D.D. Geneva College, 1939; Moderator of Synod, 1938; died 23rd September, 1968, Santa Ana California; m. Jennie M. Faris of Peckham, Colorado, 26th October, 1904; 3 s. Gifford (died in Syria), Rutherford F., and William Donald.

Ewing, Gordon Thompson *
b. nr. Portglenone, Co. Antrim, 17th July, 1798; s. of John Ewing and Mary Thompson (Anti-burgher Seceders); ed. under Rev John Bryce, and grad. O.C.B., 1821; emig. 1822, Philadelphia; befriended Rev Samuel Wylie, and went with him to Kaskaskia, Illinois, opened a classical school; espoused R.P. principles, studied theology under Rev Samuel Wylie; 1824, Philadelphia Seminary; lic. by Pittsburgh Presbytery, 9th May, 1825; ord. and inst. by Pittsburgh Presbytery, Canonsburgh, Washington Co., Pa., 23rd October, 1827; res. 16th May, 1830, ill-health returned to Ireland late 1830; 1831, called to L'derry; but engaged as s.s., 1831-40; inst. Grange, Co. Tyrone, 20th July, 1840; res. 9th November,

1841, returned to America, joined New School branch;. inst. 2nd Pittsburgh (Bayardstown), 9th September, 1842; Moderator of General Synod, 1847; a constant sufferer from malaria for many years, in March, 1848, he embarked for New Orleans, Louisiana, intending a voyage to New York; died 21st March, 1848, on board the steamer "General Pike," 100 miles above New Orleans; m. Margaret Black, of Pittsburgh, 13th March, 1828.

Fisher, John

b. Cremore, Co. Armagh, 10th October, 1797; s. of Robert Fisher and Jane Porter; emig. June 1820, Coldenham, Orange Co., New York, teacher; ed. Montgomery Academy, Philadelphia Seminary; lic. by Philadelphia presbytery, 16th April, 1828; ord. and inst. by Northern Presbytery, congs. of York, Livingston Co., Rochester, New York, 21st July, 1831; res. Rochester, 17th April, 1835; died, 22nd July, 1845, York, New York; m. Catherine Balfour, of York, New York, 16th May, 1831; a zealous advocate of the principles of the Covenanter Church esp. in 1833.

Gailey, Francis

b. Killilastian, Co. Donegal, 14th March, 1802; emig. 1816, to Orange Co., New York, encouraged by Rev. J. R. Willson; ed. Academy of Coldenham, theology privately under Dr. J. R. Willson; lic. by the Northern Presbytery, 14th May, 1830; suspd. 1839; contd. to preach and formed the "Safety League."; pub. American Reformed Covenanter in 1839; died 21st May, 1872, in Bellevue Hospital; m. Jane Wylie, of Baltimore, Maryland, 9th July, 1847.

Galbraith, John

b. Edenmore, Co. Antrim, 6th April, 1818; s. of James Galbraith and Margaret McClure; emig. 1832, Burgettstown, Washington Co., Pa.; ed. grad. Western University of Pa. 1838, theology in the Allegheny Seminary, lic. by Pittsburgh Presbytery, 1st June, 1842. ord. and inst. congs. Union, Pine Creek and Lovejoy, Valencia, Butler Co., Pa., 29th June, 1843; cont. from 1870 of North Union, Pittsburgh; ret. 8th October, 1889; died 30th September, 1904; Moderator of the Synod 1874; m. Sarah Wylie, of Elizabeth, Pa. 11th July, 1843; s. Rev. Samuel Renwick Galbraith.

Gault, Matthew Augustine

b. Coleraine, Co. L'derry, 2nd May, 1845; s. of John Gault and Martha Adams; emig. Brockport, Monroe Co., New York; 1852, to Waukesha, Waukesha Co., Wisconsin; ed. Monmouth College in 1870, Allegheny Seminary; lic. by Pittsburgh Presbytery, 15th April, 1874; ord. and inst. by Iowa Presbytery, Lind Grove, Mediapolis, Des Moines Co., Iowa, 20th May, 1875; res. 4th October, 1877, s.s. Long Branch congregation, Blanchard, Page Co., Iowa, inst. 1st October, 1880, res 25th October, 1882; Secretary of the National Reform Association; res. 1892; inst. Bloomington, Indiana, June, 1893; res. 1895; editor of the 'Christian Cynosure', of Chicago, Illinois; inst. Wahoo, Nebraska, September, 1901; res. 22nd October, 1906; inst. Oakdale, Illinois, 14th June, 1907; died 18th December, 1913; m. Maggie P. Turner, of Waukesha, Wisconsin, 17th September, 1871

Gayley, Samuel Maxwell

b. Creevy, Co. Tyrone, 4th June, 1802; s. of Andrew Gayley and Margaret Crawford; emig. May, 1823, Philadelphia, connected with R. P. Church; ed. Philadelphia Seminary, lic. by

Philadelphia Presbytery, 4th April, 1828. s.s. Conococheague, Pottsville and Mauch Chunk, in E. Pa.; ord. Mauch Chunk, Wilmington, Delaware, 25th December, 1832; 1833 joined New School branch; joined Presbyterian Church, 13th June, 1837; inst. Rockland, Delaware; died 19th December, 1862.

Gibson, John

b. Ballymena, Co. Antrim, 14th August, 1791; s. of Rev. William Gibson and Rebecca Mitchell; emig.1797, Philadelphia; 1799, removed to Ryegate, Caledonia Co., Vermont; ed. University of Vermont, Philadelphia Seminary; lic. by Middle Presbytery, 19th May, 1817, ord. and inst. by Middle Presbytery, Baltimore, Maryland, 15th December, 1818; 1833, joined the Presbyterian Church; 1858, s.s Belleville, Illinois; in 1862, at Mt. Vernon; 1866, Sparta, Illinois; 1868, Cincinnati, Ohio; Moderator of Synod, 1821; died 3rd June,1869; b. of Rev. W. J. Gibson; m. Elizabeth Jamieson, of Baltimore, Maryland, in 1821.

Gibson, Robert

b. Ballymena, Co. Antrim, 1st October, 1793; s. of Rev. William Gibson and Rebecca Mitchell; emig. 1797, Philadelphia, 1799, removed to Ryegate, Caledonia Co., Vermont; ed. Philadelphia Seminary; lic. by Middle Presbytery, 5th June, 1818; ord. and inst. by Pittsburgh Presbytery, Little Beaver, New Galilee, Beaver Co., Pa., 6th September, 1819; res. ill-health 16th October, 1830; inst. 2nd New York City, 18th May, 1831; 1837, visited Ireland; Moderator of Synod, 1834; died 22nd December, 1837, New York City; m.1. Mary A. Harvey, of Philadelphia, 1817; m.2. Mary A. Lindsay, of Philadelphia, 1827.

Gibson, William *

b. nr. Knockbracken, Co. Down, 1st July, 1753; s. of Robert Gibson and Susannah McWhirr; joined R.P. ed. grad. Glasgow University,1775, theology in Edinburgh; lic. by Refd. Presbytery of Ireland, 19th May, 1781; ord. and inst. by Refd. Presbytery congs. of Kellswater and Cullybackey, Co. Antrim, Ireland, 17th April, 1787; emig. Philadelphia, 18th October, 1797; s.s. Coldenham, New York, and in Vermont; with Rev. James McKinney and ruling elders, constituted the Refd. Presbytery of America, at Philadelphia, May, 1798; inst. Ryegate, Caledonia Co., Vermont, 10th July, 1799; inst. 13th April, 1815, Canonsburgh, Washington Co., Pa., 23rd October, 1817, res. ill-health, 27th May, 1826; s.s. Paterson, New Jersey; 1836, s.s city of New York; Moderator of first Synod, 1809, and 1816; died 15th October, 1838, New York; m. Rebecca Mitchell, of L'derry; s. Rev. John Gibson, Rev. Robert Gibson.

Gillespie, William John

b. Ballynahinch, Co. Down, 3rd. October, 1841; s. of John Gillespie and Sarah Gillespie (Seceders); ed. classical school Wishaw, Scotland; emig. 14th May, 1857, Newburgh, New York joined R.P. church; ed. grad. Westminster College, 1866; Allegheny Seminary; lic. by Pittsburgh Presbytery, 15th April, 1868; ord. and inst. by Illinois Presbytery, Old Bethel, Sparta, Randolph Co., Illinois, 13th October, 1869; joined United Presbyterian Church, 6th August, 1870; inst. Sparta, Illinois, 11th September, 1870, res. 14th August, 1877; inst. Charles Street, New York, 30th August, 1877, res. 16th June, 1879; inst Jordan's Grove, Randolph Co., Illinois, 16th December, 1879, res. 24th October, 1882; inst. Sparta, Illinois, 8th January, 1883, res. 31st May, 1886; inst. Mission, Leavenworth, Kansas, 5th June, 1886; Chaplain of the National Home for Disabled Volunteer Soldiers; m. Jennie Wier, of Sparta, Illinois, 1st October, 1872.

Graham, David *
b. Coleraine, Co. L'derry, 8th September, 1779; s. of Thomas Graham and Mary De Witt; ed. grad. Glasgow University, 1799, Theological Hall, Paisley; lic. by Refd. Presbytery of Ireland, 9th March, 1804; ord. and inst. Magherafelt, Co. L'derry, 16th October, 1805; went to London, 1807, was deposed by Refd. Presbytery of Ireland, for abandoning his charge; emig. 8th February, 1808, city of New York; restd. by Northern Presbytery, at Milton, Northumberland Co., Pa., 12th August, 1809; 1810, called to Canonsburgh, Pa., depd. by Middle Presbytery, 20th August, 1811; identified with Seceder Church, Butler Cos., Pa.; admitted to the practice of law, 9th November, 1820; died 13th September, 1839, New York, ; m. Mary Hazleton, of L'derry, 16th March, 1807.

Graham, William
b. nr. Ballybay, Co. Monaghan, 7th July, 1826; s. of John Graham and Dorothy Martin; emig. December, 1847, city of New York, engaged in business for many years; ed. grad. University of New York, 1859; theology under Rev. Andrew Stevenson; lic. by New York Presbytery, 1st November, 1859; ord. and inst. by New York Presbytery, 1st Boston, Massachusetts, 11th July, 1860; died 15th March, 1893, Boston; m.1. Elizabeth Bell, of New York City, 26th March, 1856; m.2. Mary A. Dickson, of Ryegate, Vermont, 3rd December, 1862.

Guthrie, Thomas Cathcart
b. nr. Broughshane, Co. Antrim, 7th August, 1796; s. of Hugh Guthrie and Margaret Cathcart; ed. early training by Rev. W. J. Stavely, of Kellswater; emig. 1817 for health, ed. Pittsburgh Academy, grad. Western University of Pa., 1823; Philadelphia Seminary; lic. by Pittsburgh Presbytery, 14th April, 1825; ord. and inst. by Pittsburgh Presbytery, to congs. of Pine Creek, Union and Camp Run, Bakerstown, Allegheny Co., Pa. 26th April, 1826; 1833, identified with New School branch; res. 23rd May, 1855; inst. Mount Pleasant, Westmoreland Co., Pa., 9th June, 1856; with cong., connected with United Presbyterian Church, 10th October, 1859, res. 24th May, 1864; Hon. D.D. Franklin College, 1843; Moderator of General Synod, 1844; died 22nd March, 1876, Sparta, Randolph Co., Illinois; m.1. Elizabeth Caskey, of Pittsburgh, Pa. 30th December 30, 1828, m.2. Mrs. Nancy (Gilleland) McLean, of Bakerstown, Pa. 26th January, 1837; m.3. Mary Faun, of Allegheny City, Pa. 1st June, 1849.

Hamilton, Joseph *
b. Belraugh, Co. L'derry, 13th June, 1842; s. of Joseph Hamilton and Susannah Logan; ed. Belfast Academy, grad. Q.C.B.1861, Theological Hall, Belfast; lic. Northern Presbytery, 30th January,1866; ord. and inst. by Northern Presbytery, Garvagh, Co. L'derry, 7th November, 1867; res. 6th August, 1872; emig. 1873, rec. by Rochester Presbytery, 30th May, 1873, supplied esp. Canadian vacancies; suspended by the Rochester Presbytery, 5th October, 1875.

Hawthorne, Hugh
b. Kilkinamurry, Co. Down, 17th June, 1805; s. of John Hawthorne and Mary Graham; ed. under Rev. John Stewart, grad. from R.B.A.I. 1828. Theological Hall, Paisley; emig. May, 1830, Theology under Rev. S. B. Wylie, Philadelphia; lic. by Philadelphia Presbytery, 17th May, 1831; joined Dutch Reformed Church, 8th November, 1834, supplied vac. Albany, and New York; He was drowned while bathing in a river in New York, 16th July, 1836.

Hawthorne, John *

b. Kilkinamurray, Co. Down, 7th December, 1795; s. of John Hawthorne and Mary Graham; ed. R.B.A.I., grad. Glasgow University, 1816, Theological Hall, Paisley; lic. by Southern Presbytery, 10th March, 1821; ord., and inst. Ballenon, 7th May, 1822; res. 28th October, 1845; emig. April, 1847, with his family, for Muskingum Co., Ohio; died 14th May, 1847of a fever, in quarantine at Quebec; m. Ann E. Boggs, of Ballylane, 1823.

Hutchenson, Robert

b. Loughgilly, Co. Armagh, 24th April, 1810; s. of James Hutchenson and Sarah Martin (Seceders); emig. 1829 Cambridge, Guernsey Co., Ohio, joined R.P. Church; ed. Allegheny Seminary; lic. by Pittsburgh Presbytery, 8th May, 1839; ord. 'sine titulo' by Pittsburgh Presbytery, as Home Missionary, 10th September, 1841; inst. Brush Creek, Adams Co., Ohio, 29th September, 1842, res., 21st May, 1856; inst. Grove Hill, Bremer Co., Iowa, 17th April, 1863; res. 8th May, 1867; 1869, North-West Missions; died 1st April, 1880, Washington, Iowa; m.1. Jane Walkinshaw, of Lucesco, Pa., in 1840; m.2. Mrs. Jane (Coulter) Andrews, of Princeton, Illinois, 15th November, 1865.

Johnson, Robert *

b. Killygore, Cloughmills, Co. Antrim, 17th November, 1810; s. of Robert Johnson and Margaret; grad. R.B.A.I. 1836, Theological Hall, Paisley; lic. by Northern Presbytery, 17th May, 1839; ord. and inst. to mission cong. of Manchester, England, 3rd August, 1842, res. 9th April, 1849; emig. rec. by R.P. Synod, North America, 23rd May, 1849; inst. Toronto, Canada, 4th November, 1852, res. 10th April, 1859; inst. Vernon, Waukesha Co., Wisconsin, 7th November, 1859, res. 17th December, 1867; inst. Kossuth, Des Moines Co., Iowa, January 7, 1868, res. ill-health, 27th July, 1875; died 27th July, 1879, Kossuth, Iowa; unm.

Kennedy, George

b. Limavady, Co. L'derry; s. of Rev. James Kennedy and Eliza Conn; emig. with parents, New York 1870; ed. grad. Columbia College1874, Allegheny Seminary; lic. by New York Presbytery, 16th May, 1877; ord. and inst. by Lakes Presbytery, United Miami cong., Northwood, Logan Co., Ohio, 23rd May, 1878, res. 15th June, 1882; app. chair of Greek in Geneva College, 9th September, 1882, served for 36 yrs. until death; D.D. Geneva College, 1904; killed by a streetcar, died 22nd May, 1918, Pittsburgh; int. Beaver Cmty. Beaver, Pa.; m. Fannie Coverdale, 1891; 2 s. Miles Coverdale, George Conn; 3d. Elizabeth Conn, Caroline Mary and Catherine Christina.

Kennedy, James *

b. Drumreagh, Co. Antrim, 15th August, 1818; s. of George Kennedy and Mary Paul; ed. Bryce's Academy, R.B.A.I, 1840, Theological Hall, Paisley; lic. by Northern Presbytery, 10th May, 1842; ord. and inst. by Western Presbytery, Newtonlimavady, 18th May, 1843; res. 2nd August, 1870; inst. 4th New York City, New York, 13th November, 1870; Moderator of Irish Synod 1846, American Synod in 1875; grad. D.D. (Geneva), 1886; appt. Prof, in R.P. Theological Seminary in 1887, declined appointment on account of age and attachment to pastoral ministry; ret. 30th October, 1894; died 26th January, 1898, at daughter's home, St.John, New Brunswick; int. Covenanter burial ground, Bronxville; m. Eliza Conn, of Coleraine, 9th May, 1848; s. Rev. George.
pub. "Tekel" (1858), "Assurance of Grace and Salvation" (1877), "Christ in the Song";

Kennedy, Joshua

b. Newtownlimavady, Co. L'derry, 22nd August, 1815; s of James Kennedy and Catharine Cannon; emig.1823, Shady Grove, Franklin Co., Pa.; ed. Green Castle Academy, grad. Union College, 1841, Allegheny Seminary; lic. by Illinois Presbytery, 12th May, 1844; ord. and inst. by New York Presbytery, Conococheague, Fayetteville, Franklin Co., Pa., 5th November, 1845. In 1852; res. 1st May, 1860, during war, Missionary and Chaplain in Fernandina, Florida; inst. Bovina, Delaware Co., New York, 11th January, 1865, res. ill-health 20th May, 1885; died 15th October, 1891, Bovina; m. Mary J. Bell, of Carlisle, Pennsylvania, 8th October, 1847; His ministry was an active and adventurous one. He rode 70,000 miles horseback; preached on 2,452 days; baptized 1,806 persons; and married 240 couples.

King, William *

b. Donegal, Co. Donegal, 6th January, 1747; ed. grad. Glasgow University, 1782, Theology, Stirling; lic. by Refd. Presbytery of Scotland, 16th March, 1784, preached in Coleraine, Co. L'derry, for seven years; ord. 'sine titulo' by the Refd. Presbytery of Scotland, at Wishaw, 4th June, 1792, Missionary to America; settled Chester District, South Carolina; settled at 1794 Beaver Dam S.C. congregation; invited to organize the Refd. Presbytery in Alexandria, Virginia, May, 1798, but on account of serious illness he was not able; died 24th August, 1798, at his house in Chester District, S.C.; m. Nancy Neil, of Chester, S.C., September, 1794.

Lawson, James Reid *

b. Rathfriland, Co. Down, 23rd May, 1820; s. of James Lawson and Elizabeth Reid; ed. R.B.A.I. 1841, Theological Hall, Paisley; lic. by Southern Presbytery, 4th March, 1845; ord. 'sine cura' by Southern Presbytery, 18th September, 1845, a Missionary to the British North American Provinces; settled in South Stream, now Barnesville, Kings Co., New Brunswick, in the spring of 1846; res. 17th October, 1856; inst. Boston, Massachusetts, 20th November, 1856, res. 22nd October, 1857. He returned to Barnesville, N.B., res., 12th April, 1882; died 4th July, 1891, Barnesville; m. Margaret Hastings, of St. John, N.B., 1st July, 1851.

Little, John *

b. Ouley, nr. Rathfriland, Co. Down, 17th June, 1823; s. of James Little and Esther Allen; ed. grad. R.B.A.I., 1843, Theological Hall, Paisley; lic. by Southern Presbytery, 8th March, 1848. emig. 1848, ord. and inst. by New York Presbytery, 3rd New York City, 5th June, 1849; suspended by New York Presbytery, 20th April, 1852; received by Presbyterian Church, Presbytery of the City of New York, 9th February, 1853; died 2nd January, 1855; unm.

Littlejohn, John Martin

b. Glasgow, 15th February, 1865; s. of Rev. James Littlejohn (Garvagh); ed. Glasgow University, Original Seceder Hall, R.P. Theological Hall; lic. Northern Presbytery, 1886; ord. Creevagh, 7th September, 1886; res, 1888; grad, M.A. (Glasgow), 1889, B.D. (Glasgow), 1890, and LL.B. (Glasgow), 1892; emig. 1892 because of ill-health; Ph.D. Columbia University, 1893; rec. by Philadelphia Presbytery; 1895, under Kansas Presbytery, President of Amity College, College Springs, Iowa; 1889, res. ill-health; 1899, The American School of Osteopathy in Kirksville, Missouri; 1900 in Chicago, M.D.,1900; under Iowa Presbytery, develops the science, theory and practice of osteopathy; 1913 returns to U.K., Thunderley, Essex, certified under, R.P.C.S.; establishes the British School of Osteopathy; died 8th December, 1947.

Littlejohn, William *
lic. Northern Presbytery, emig. 1889, Pennsylvania; rec. by Pittsburgh Presbytery, 1889; ord. and inst. 3rd December, 1889, by Iowa Presbytery, Lind Grove, Mediapolis, Iowa; res. 1893; inst. North Cedar, Denison, Kansas, by Kansas Presbytery, 27th June, 1893; res. 9th November, 1896; joined United Presbyterian Church.

Lusk, Robert
b. nr. L'derry City, 8th March, 1781; s. of William Lusk and Elizabeth Holliday; emig. with parents 1792, Cumberland Co., Pa.; 1804 entered Academy of Greensburgh, Pa., grad. Jefferson College,1810. Philadelphia Seminary; lic. by Middle Presbytery, 9th May, 1814; ord. and inst. by Middle Presbytery, Conococheague, Chambersburgh, Franklin Co., Pa., 16th June, 1816; res. 15th October, 1823; inst. Walnut Ridge, Washington Co., Indiana, 7th October, 1824; Moderator of the Synod of 1817; left the R.P. Church, 24th June, 1840, joined the Reformed Presbytery; died 14th December, 1845; m.1. Margaret Thomson, of Conococheague, Pa., in 1816; m.2. Mary Reid, of Walnut Ridge, Indiana, in 1824. .

Lynd, John
b. Knockaduff, Aghadowey, Co. L'derry, 2th March, 1850; s. of Andrew Lynd and Rosa Gilmore; ed. Aghadowey Classical School, Coleraine Academy, grad. Magee College, 1871. R.P. Theological Hall, Belfast; emig. April, 1873, grad. 1st Hons. Mental and Moral Sc., D.D., Geneva College Pa.; lic. by New York Presbytery, 20th May, 1873; ord. and inst. by Philadelphia Presbytery, Baltimore, Maryland, 4th December, 1873, res. 6th November, 1877; appt. chair of Greek and English Literature in Beaver College, Northwood, Ohio, also inst. Belle Centre, Logan Co., Ohio, 5th January, 1879; res. the chair at the removal of the College, 26th May, 1880; inst. Rushsylvania, Logan Co., Ohio, 12th August, 1880; res. 14th April, 1885; inst. Ballylaggan Co. L'derry, 5th June, 1885; res. 1889, inst. Dublin Rd., Belfast, 16th April, 1889; appt. Prof. of Hebrew and Biblical Criticism, Theological Hall, 1901-1921; ret. 26th June, 1923; Moderator of the Irish Synod of 1886; died 27th June, 1926, at Alsager, Cheshire; int. Ballylaggan; m. Isabel (Belle) Purvis, of Baltimore, Maryland, 8th April, 1875. 2 s. Tom, William, 1 d. Sally.

Lynn, Matthew *
b. Corkermain, Carncastle, Co. Antrim, 10th August, 1731; s. of Matthew Lynn; 1757, ord. a ruling elder; ed. grad. Glasgow University, 1760; lic. by the Refd. Presbytery of Scotland, 16th July, 1761; ord. at the organization of the Refd. Presbytery of Ireland, at Vow, Co. Antrim, inst. to societies of Bannside, Limavady and Aghadowey, 21st August, 1763; helped to form congregations at Ballylaggan, Drimbolg and Garvagh; fruits of his ministry seen in development of Covenanting cause at Bready, 1765, Faughan 1770, and Ramelton; appt. to accompany Rev. Alexander Dobbin as Missionary to America; arrived New Castle, Delaware, 13th December, 1773; Revs. Lynn, Cuthbertson and Dobbin, organized the Refd. Presbytery of America, at Paxtang, Dauphin Co. Pa., 10th March, 1774; assigned to Paxtang, Dauphin Co., and Stoney Ridge, Cumberland Co., Pa.; joined Associate Reformed Church at its formation, 1st November, 1782; 1783, inst. A.R.P. congs. Green Castle, Chambersburg, West Conococheague and Great Cove, Franklin Co., Pa.; res. 13th March, 1798; died 21st April, 1800, Green Castle, Franklin Co., Pa.; int. graveyard at

Brown's Mills; m. Jennett Fulton, of Co. Antrim (cousin of Rbt Fulton. of steamboat fame), 1769.

Madden, Campbell *
b. Coleraine, Co. L'derry, 8th September, 1795; ed. Coleraine Academy, grad. Glasgow University,1816; lic. by Northern Presbytery, 1st June, 1819; emig. Autumn 1820, Chester District, South Carolina; grad. College of Physicians and Surgeons, in Lexington, Kentucky, M.D.1st Hons.,1821; ord. and inst. by Southern Presbytery, Beaver Dam, Chester District, S.C., 18th June, 1822, also served as M.D.; died 12th August, 1828, Chester District, S.C.; m. Margaret Cathcart, of Chester, S.C., in 1821.

Martin, William *
b. Ballyspallan, nr. Ballykelly, Co. L'derry, 16th May, 1729; 1st s. of David Martin; ed. grad. Glasgow University, 1753. Theological Hall under Rev. John McMillan; lic. by Refd. Presbytery of Scotland, 10th October, 1756; ord. at Vow nr. Rasharkin, the first Covenanter minister ord. in Ireland, inst. to societies in Cos. Antrim L'derry and N. Down, 2nd July, 1757; 1760, served Co. Antrim at Kellswater; emig. with large body of people, 1772, Rocky Creek, Chester District, South Carolina; the first Covenanter minister settled in the South. In 1774, preached at Catholic, S.C.; dismissed 1777, continued preaching 1781 and resumed his charge; 1785, dismissed, 1793 restored; member of the Cmte. of the Refd. Presbytery of Scotland, for the church in America; preached widely, N.C. S.C. and Georgia; deposed 12th March, 1801; died 25th October, 1806; m. 1. Mary, died Ballymoney; 2. Jennett Cherry of Co. Antrim, d. Nancy; 3. Susanna Boggs, S. Carolina. Cf. 'Scots Irish Migration to South Carolina, 1772'. by Jean Stephenson 1971.

McClelland, Daniel *
b. Bovevagh, Co. L'derry, 1736; emig. America, returned to Ireland, where he studied theology; lic. by Refd. Presbytery of Scotland, 21st December, 1763; he preached for a time in Ireland; ord. 'sine titulo' by Refd. Presbytery of Ireland, at Laymore, nr. Ballymena, 13th July, 1765, as a Missionary to America; 1766, settled in Connecticut; joined Newcastle Presbytery, Synod of New York and Philadelphia; 1767 preached in Eastern Pa.; 1768, returned to New England; Remaining events unknown, probably drifted from the Church.

McConachie, Robert
b. Co. Antrim, 7th January, 1899; s. of James McConachie and Anne J. Neill; emig. Philadelphia, joined 2nd Philadelphia 1923; ed. Nyack Missionary College, 1927-1931; R.P. Seminary 1931-1934; lic. by Philadelphia Presbytery, August, 1932; ord. By Philadelphia, 30th August, 1934; inst. Toronto, Ontario, October, 1934; res. April, 1939; inst. Stafford, Kansas, October, 1939; res. April, 1943; inst. Toronto, Ontario, August, 1943; res. March, 1946; inst. Santa Ana, California, April, 1946; res. June, 1954; joined United Presbyterian Church; inst. Burlington, Washington, U.P.C.N.A., June, 1954; ret. March, 1963; died February, 1965 at daughter's home, Santa Clara, Ca.; m. Anne J. Kennedy, of Birmingham, Alabama, 26th June, 1931; 2 d. Barbara, Judith.

McConnell, Thomas
b. Portglenone, Co. Antrim, 27th April, 1819; s. of Thomas McConnell and Jane McConnell was born in Portglenone; emig. 1837, Allegheny, Pa.; ed. classical studies under Rev. Hugh Walkinshaw, grad. Duquesne College; lic. by Pittsburgh Presbytery, 27th October,

1847; preached in vacancies 1848, ret. ill-health 1849; died 3rd May, 1850, West Elizabeth, Pa.; m. Mary J. Anderson, of Canonsburgh, Pa., 10th February, 1848.

McCracken, Joseph

b. Rathfriland, Co. Down, 21st October, 1825; s. of William McCracken and Elizabeth Hood McCracken; emig. 1832, York, Livingston Co., New York; ed. Temple Hill Academy, grad. Union College,1848; 1849, Theological Hall, Paisley; lic. by Rochester Presbytery, 13th May, 1853; ord. by Illinois Presbytery at Linton, Iowa, 29th October, 1856; inst. Clarinda, Page Co. Iowa, 6th July, 1857; res. 16th October, 1858; inst. St. Louis, Missouri, 14th October, 1859; res. 2nd September, 1874; appt. chair of Mathematics in Geneva College, Northwood, Ohio; res. 26th May, 1877; inst. Southfield, Birmingham, Oakland Co., Michigan, 15th June, 1878; Moderator of the Synod of 1873; ret. 9th May, 1903; died 19th February, 1905, York, New York.; m. Harriet H. Rowan, of Argyle, New York, 15th September 15, 1857.

McCullough, Boyd

b. Rathfriland, Co. Down, 25th March, 1825; s. of William Boyd and Mary Moffett; emig. 1832, Beech Woods, Jefferson Co., Pa.; ed. studied under Rev. James Milligan, grad. Duquesne College,1848; Cincinnati and Northwood Seminaries; lic. by Lakes Presbytery, 16th April, 1852; ord. and inst. by lakes Presbytery to congs. Novi, Oakland Co., and Detroit, Michigan, 19th September, 1855; res. 14th May, 1871; 1871-72 preaching tour of British Isles; supply preaching 3 yrs.; joined U. P. Church, 13th August, 1875, s.s. Caledonia, Minnesota, and Pepin, Wisconsin; 1886, s.s Beech Tree, Pa.; m. 1. Julia A. Johnston, of Northwood, Ohio, 19th November, 1850; m. 2. Mrs. Emily C. (Jameson) Johnston, of Belle Centre, Ohio, 8th December, 1885.

McFall, David

b. nr. Dervock, Co. Antrim, 12th March, 1846; s. of James McFall and Ann Dunlap; McFall; emig. 1867, city of Allegheny, Pa.; ed. grad .Westminster College in 1869; Allegheny Seminary; lic. by Pittsburgh Presbytery, 12th April, 1870; ord. and inst. by Pittsburgh Presbytery , Oil City, Pa., 18th May , 1871; res. 8th April, 1873; inst. 2nd Boston, Mass., 11th July, 1873; Chaplain, for 12 years of Middlesex County Jail; died 29th December, 1889, Boston; m. Clara B. Milligan, of Allegheny City, Pa., 16th October, 1873.

McFall, Thomas

b. nr. Dervock, Co. Antrim, 23rd August, 1848; s. of James McFall and Ann Dunlap; emig. 1867, city of Allegheny, Pa.; ed. Westminster College, grad. Geneva College 1875, Allegheny Seminary; lic. by Pittsburgh Presbytery, 8th April, 1879; ord. and inst. by New Brunswick and Nova Scotia Presbytery, congs. Cornwallis and Horton, Somerset, Kings Co., Nova Scotia, 25th August, 1881; Hon. D.D. Geneva College, June 1928; died 14th January, 1929, Somerset, N.S.; m. Anna M. Lyons, of Philadelphia, Pa., 16th September, 1879; s. Robert, d. Mary.

McFarland, Armour *

b. nr. Cookstown, Co. Tyrone, 8th March, 1808; s. of Patrick McFarland and Eliza Knox; ed. grad. M.A. Hons. Glasgow University,1828. Theological Hall, Paisley; lic. by Western Presbytery, Ireland, 21st October, 1830; emig. May, 1831, West Bedford, Coshocton Co., Ohio; ord. and inst. by Ohio Presbytery Utica, Licking Co., 3rd Ohio, October, 1837, also inst. Jonathan's Creek, Muskingum Co., Ohio, 6th October, 1847; res. Utica, 23rd May, 1855 for Jonathan's Creek; Middle Wheeling, West Virginia, added 4th April, 1866; res. Middle Wheeling, 12th April, 1873, and ret. Jonathan's Creek, 12th April, 1876; died 4th April, 1894, nr. Zanesville, Ohio; m. Sarah McCune, of Utica, Ohio, 22nd March, 1842.

McFeeters, James
b. Raphoe Co. Donegal, 1st January, 1848; s. of Thomas McFeeters and Mary Fletcher; emig. 1850, Jamestown, Mercer Co., Pa.; ed. Adamsville Academy, grad. Westminster College in 1870.Allegheny Seminary; lic. by Pittsburgh Presbytery, 8th April, 1873; ord. and inst. by Pittsburgh Presbytery congs. Manchester and Parnassus, Westmoreland Co., Pa., 19th June, 1874; Brookland, 16th November, 1886; res. 18th December, 1888; inst. 2nd Philadelphia, 17th January, 1889; ret. 1st February, 1921; Moderator of Synod 1894; died 24th December, 1928, at daughter's home Hetherton, Michigan; m. Nannie C. Dill, of Wyman, Iowa, 25th February, 1875.

McGarragh, James *
b. Donaghadee, Co. Down, July, 1752; ed. grad. Glasgow University,1781; studied under Rev. William Stavely; lic. Refd. Presbytery of Scotland, at Bready, Co. L'derry, 20th August, 1783;He preached with much acceptance to the scattered societies throughout Ulster for several years; accepted call to S. Carolina, ord. Bready, 28th August, 1789; 1791, Beaver Dam, a branch of the Rocky Creek congregation, Chester District, S. C.; suspended 24th June, 1795; deposed 5th February, 1801; school teacher; died 6th September, 1816; int. Paul's graveyard, nr Mount Prospect, Chester District, S. C.; m.1. Elizabeth Clark, of Co. Down, m.2.

KcKee, David
b. Ballybay, Co. Monaghan, 10th April, 1821; s. of David McKee and Jane Smith; emig. 1836, Crawford Co., Pa.; ed. Mercer Academy, grad. Jefferson College 1847, Cincinnati Seminary; lic. by Pittsburgh Presbytery, 9th April, 1851. He was a Professor of Greek in Westminster College, two year; ord. and inst. by Philadelphia Presbytery, 4th Philadelphia, 5th July , 1854; res. 4th August, 1859; inst. Clarinda, Page Co., Iowa, 20th September, 1862; established churches at Blanchard, Iowa, Superior, Nebraska, and in other places; Moderator of the Synod,1885; died 27th September, 1893, Clarinda; m. Mary E. Gregg, of Allegheny City, Pa., 3rd September, 1856.

McKee, Robert
b. Ahoghill, Co. Antrim, 13th May, 1798; emig. New York City; ed. theology in the Philadelphia Seminary; lic. by Northern Presbytery, 9th August, 1825; s.s. Fayetteville, Lincoln Co., ord. and inst. by Northern Presbytery, congs. Lansingburgh and Troy, New York, 29th December, 1830; received by Presbyterian Church, Presbytery of Albany, 16th May, 1835, 8th Presbyterian Church in Albany, New York,; died 13th July, 1840, Albany, New York; m. Hannah Thomson, of Conococheague, Pa. in 1820.

McKinney, James *
b. Kilrea, Co. L'derry, 16th November, 1759; s. of Robert McKinney and Elizabeth McIntyre; ed. grad. Glasgow University 1778; full course in medicine and theology; lic. by Refd. Presbytery of Ireland, 19th May, 1783; ord. and inst. Dervock, Co. Antrim, 14th October, 1783. emig. 1793; Missionary to scattered Societies from Vermont to the Carolinas; with the Rev. William Gibson and ruling elders, constituted the Refd.

Presbytery of America, at Philadelphia, May, 1798; congs. Galway and Duanesburgh, New York; res. Duanesburgh, New York, 4th April, 1802, inst. Rocky Creek, Chester District, South Carolina; died 16th September, 1802, int. Rocky Creek; m. Mary Mitchell, of Co. L'derry, 1794. author "A View of the Rights of God and Man"

McKinney, Samuel

b. Galway, Co. Galway, 10th March, 1807; s. of Samuel McKinney (br. of Rev. James McKinney) and Margaret Findley; emig. 1813, Hawkins Co., Tennessee; ed. grad. University of Pennsylvania, 1832, theology under Rev. S. B. Wylie, at Philadelphia; lic. Northern Presbytery, 10th June, 1832; ord. and inst. by Ohio Presbytery, Elkhorn, Oakdale, Washington Co., Illinois, 15th April, 1835; res. 24th May, 1840; Prof. in Denmark College, Tennessee; 1843, President of West Tennessee College; 1844 connected with the Presbyterian Church; 1850 President of Austin College, Huntsville, Texas, ret. 1875; died Huntsville, Texas, 27th November, 1879; m. Nancy W. Todd, of Oakdale, Illinois, 4th July, 1836.

McMaster, Gilbert

b. Saintfield, Co. Down, 13th February, 1778; s. of James and Mary Crawford; emig. 1791, Franklin Co., Pa.; ed. Franklin Academy 1798, Jefferson Academy, Canonsburgh, Pa.1802, grad. Medicine 1805, physician in Mercer, Pa.; lic. Refd. Presbytery, 7th October, 1807; ord. and inst. by Northern Committee congs. Galway and Duanesburgh, New York, 8th August, 1808; res. Galway branch, 10th May, 1818, for Duanesburgh; 1833, joined New School remained pastor of majority; res. 17th April, 1840; inst. Princeton, Gibson Co., Indiana, 5th May, 1840; Hon. D.D. Union College in 1828; Moderator of the Synods of 1811 and 1827, and General Synod of 1851; ret. 31st March, 1846; died 17th March, 1854, New Albany, Indiana; m. Jane Brown, of Canonsburgh, Pa. 13th June, 1803.

McMaster, John

b. Donegore, Co. Antrim, 1st March, 1808; s. of Hugh McMaster and Eleanor Barr; emig. 1811, Pittsburgh, connected with R.P. under Rev. John Black; ed. Pittsburgh Academy, grad. Western University of Pa.1827, theology under Rev. John Black; lic. by Pittsburgh Presbytery, 8th April, 1830; ord. and inst. by Western Presbytery, Schenectady, New York, 26th January, 1832; 1833, joined New School, remained pastor of a portion of his charge; res. 16th April, 1837; inst. Walnut Hill, Marion Co., Illinois, 4th November, 1837; res. 13th April, 1846; inst. Princeton, Gibson Co., Indiana, 4th June, 1846, which joined U. P. Church, 30th August, 1870; Hon. D.D. Jefferson College,1864. Moderator of the General Synods, 1845 and 1866; died 11th July, 1874; m.1. Joanette McMaster, of Duanesburgh, New York, 15th November, 1832; m.2. Mary Milburn, of Walnut Hill, Illinois, 22nd March, 1841; m.3. Margaret Sterne, of Princeton, Indiana, 5th June, 1862.

McMillan, Gavin

b. Dervock, Co. Antrim, 6th February, 1787; s. of Hugh McMillan and Jane Harvey; emig. 1787, Chester District, South Carolina; father elder in Rocky Creek; ed. 1810, under Rev Thomas Donnelly, Classical School of John Orr, grad. Hons. South Carolina College, Columbia, 1817; theology under Rev. S. B. Wylie, Philadelphia; lic. by Philadelphia Presbytery, October 13, 1821; ord. and inst. by Pittsburgh Presbytery, Beech Woods, Morning Sun, Preble Co., Ohio, 7th May, 1823; 1833, joined New School branch, pastor of a portion of his charge; Moderator of the General Synods, 1839 and 1861; died 25th

January, 1867, Morning Sun, Ohio; m. Rosanna Reynolds, of Ryegate, Vermont, 4th February, 1824.

Montgomery, Andrew
b. Connor, Co. Antrim, 2nd July, 1824; s. of James Montgomery and Mary Francie; emig. March, 1846, New York City; ed. grad. Geneva College,1853; Northwood Seminary; lic. by New York Presbytery, 9th November, 1854; preached throughout Church 8 years; rec. by Columbia Presbytery of Presbyterian Church, 10th June, 1862; s.s. Congregational Church of Jefferson, Schoharie Co., New York, for several years. In 1868, s.s. to the Presbyterian Church of Jewett, N.Y., 1873 s.s. in Ct.; May, 1880, s.s Minnesota; m. Mary C. Avery, of Jefferson, New York, in 1864.

Neill, James
b. Aghadowey, Co. L'derry, 16th March, 1811; s. of Matthew Neill and Jane Black; ed. grad. Glasgow University, 1840, Theological Hall, Paisley; emig. May, 1840; ed. Allegheny Seminary; lic. by Pittsburgh Presbytery, 7th April, 1842; ord. and inst. by Lakes Presbytery, Southfield, Oakland Co., Michigan, 18th May, 1843; res. 6th October, 1851. s.s. Iowa, vacancy and mission stations; died 15th January, 1880, Hopkinton, Iowa; m. Emeline McCartney, of Norwich, Ohio, 30th May, 1843.

Neill, William
b. Garvagh, Co. L'derry, 16th June, 1801; parents Seceders; emig. with parents, Farmington, Belmont Co. Ohio; ed. Franklin College; lic. by Refd. Dissenting Presbytery, 13th May, 1829; ord. and inst. 19th April, 1831, societies of Three Ridges, Short Creek and Forks of Wheeling, in West Virginia, and Miller's Run in Washington Co., Pa., 18th October, 1831; rec. into R.P. Church, by the Western Subordinate Synod, 14th October, 1839; joined the Associate Church, rec. by the Chartiers Presbytery of that body, 5th September, 1849; died, 14th May, 1862.

Nevin, John
b. Carnaff, Dervock 1805; s. of Robert Nevin and M Dunlop; lic. by Northern Presbytery; ord. Liverpool, 23rd September, 1835; emigrated 1839 to U.S.A; rec. by General Synod (New School) Reformed Presbyterian Church, inst. Shenango, Pa.; died 24th August, 1866, Hill Prairie, Marissa, Illinois.

Newell, James Robert
b. Belfast, 3rd March, 1831; s. of Thomas Newell and Elizabeth Gregg; ed. grad. Q.C.B., 1849; emig. 1850; teacher in Baltimore, Maryland; 1853, appt. Prof. Westminster College, Allegheny City, Pa.; 1861 Professor of Languages in Allegheny City; founded Newell Institute, Pittsburgh; ed. Allegheny Seminary; lic. Pittsburgh Presbytery, 23rd May, 1867; joined Presbyterian Church, 1871, chosen Pres. of Mt. Auburn Female Seminary, Cincinnati, Ohio; died 8th November, 1874; m. Christiana W. Sproull, of Allegheny City, Pa., 22nd July, 1856.

Newell, John *
b. Belfast, 18th August, 1824; s. of Thomas Newell and Elizabeth Gregg; ed. grad. R.B.A.I., 1845. Theological Hall, Paisley; lic. by Eastern Presbytery, Ireland, 9th October,1849; emig. 1850; ord. and inst. by Rochester Presbytery, Syracuse, New York, 7th May, 1851; res. 26th May, 1853; 1853, Presidency of Westminster College, Allegheny

City, Pa.; res. 1860, returned to Ireland; inst. Newtownards, Co. Down, Ireland, 8th May, 1861; res. 10th May, 1867; inst. Manchester, England, 14th August, 1867; returned to U.S. May, 1871, taught in Newell Institute, Pittsburgh; Moderator of the Synod of Ireland in 1862; died 20th September, 1875, Wilkinsburgh, Pennsylvania; m. Harriet Finlay, of Buffalo, New York, 20th May, 1851. 8 children.

Orr, Robert Gamble *

b. Brigh, Co.Tyrone, 8th July, 1787; 3s. of Robert (or James) Orr and Elizabeth Gamble; ed. grad. Glasgow University, 1810, Theological Hall, Stirling; lic. by Southern Presbytery 16th March, 1813; ord. and inst. by Northern Presbytery, Limavady, 31st August, 1815; res.1827; emig.1832, U.S.A.; 1833, joined New School branch; preached at Ogdensburgh, New York; died 12th June, 1835, Paterson, New Jersey; m. 2d.

Reilly, John

b. Ballybay, Co. Monaghan, 7th August, 1780; emig. October, 1797, Philadelphia, Pa., teacher, Darby and Frankford, nr. Pa.; ed. theology under Rev. Dr. S. B. Wylie; lic. by Middle Presbytery, 24th May, 1809; ord. 'sine titulo' by Middle Presbytery, 23rd February, 1813, Missionary to South Carolina; inst. Beaver Dam in Chester District, and Wateree in Fairfield District, South Carolina, 8th October, 1813; died 27th August, 1820, Beaver Dam, S.C.; m. Jane Weir, of Philadelphia, Pa.

Robinson, Samuel

b. Dervock, Co. Antrim, 1780; s. of John Robinson and Sarah McElroy Robinson; emig. 1791, Chester District, South Carolina; ed. Philadelphia Academy, Philadelphia Seminary; lic. by Middle Presbytery, 9th May, 1814; ord. and inst. by Western Presbytery, Cincinnati, Ohio, 10th October, 1818; depsd. 20th August, 1821; rest. by Associate Refd. Church; s.s. in A.R.P. Cincinnatti; joined New School Branch; preached Cincinnati, and lectured in the Mechanic's Institute; died 15th August, 1845, nr. Oxford, Preble Co., Ohio; m.1. Margaret Miller, of Philadelphia, Pa., m.2.?, m.3. Mrs. Camp, of Cincinnati, Ohio.

Scott, George

b. Creevagh, Co. Monaghan, 26th July, 1805; s. of William Scott and Agnes Henry; emig. 1822, Philadelphia, opened a classical school; ed. theology under Rev. S. B. Wylie; lic. by Philadelphia Presbytery, 14th April, 1830; ord. and inst. by. Pittsburgh Presbytery, Little Beaver, New Galilee, Beaver Co., Pa., 19th April, 1831; 1833, joined New School; ministered to portion known as Darlington; res. 10th October, 1863; joined Presbyterian Church, 7th October, 1868; inst.1878 New Brighton, Pa.; Hon. D.D. Monmouth College, 1864; Moderator, General Synod,1852; died 16th December, 1881; m.1. Mary Brown, of Greensburgh, Pa., 18th June, 1832; m.2. Duisa A. Forbes, of Petersburgh, Ohio, 28th November, 1843; m.3.. Mrs. Maria C. Lindsley, of New York City, 20th May, 1873.

Shanks, Walter Moffat

b. Ouley, Banbridge, Co. Down, 12th October, 1842; s. of Samuel Shanks and Agnes Rea; emig. city of New York; ed. grad. Lafayette College1873; Allegheny Seminary; lic. by New York Presbytery, 17th May, 1876; s.s. Detroit and Fairgrove, Michigan; 1881, s.s. Douglas Water, Scotland; inst. Lanark, Scotland; m. Isabella G. McQueen, of West Hebron, New York, 1st January 1, 1878.

Sharpe, Robert James

b. Ahoghill, Co. Antrim, 11th December, 1835; s. of John Sharpe and Sarah Simpson; emig. as child, Mahoning, Indiana Co., Pa.; ed. grad. Allegheny City College, 1861, Allegheny Seminary; lic. by Pittsburgh Presbytery, 12th April, 1865; ord. and inst. by Philadelphia Presbytery, 3rd.Philadelphia, Pa. 6th April, 1866; res. 10th April, 1879; continued as s.s.; died 11th March, 1913, Bellvue, Pa.; int. Round Hill, Cmty. Elizabeth, Pa.; m. Martha J. Withrow, of Elizabeth, Pa. 5th May, 1859; 2s. 6.d.

Shaw, David Jamison

b. Knockbracken, Co. Down, 14th May, 1821; s. of James Shaw and Susannah Patterson; emig. 1832, New Alexandria, Pa.; ed. Academy of Elder's Ridge, grad. Geneva College,1853; Northwood Seminary; lic. by Lakes Presbytery, 12th April, 1854; ord. and inst. by Illinois Presbytery, Bloomington, Monroe Co., Indiana, 22nd May, 1856; ret. 1891; s.s. Clarkesburg Pa.; died 11th February, 1907, New Alexandria, Pa.; m. Martha J. Hartin, of Belle Centre, Ohio, 13th November, 1854.

Shaw, James William

b. nr. Ardstraw, Co. Tyrone, 6th November, 1812; s. of William Shaw and Martha Gormley; emig. 1824, West Hebron, Washington Co., New York; ed. 1837 Coldenham Academy; Lafayette College; Coldenham and Allegheny Seminaries; lic. by Southern Presbytery, 11th April, 1843; ord. and inst. by New York Presbytery, Coldenham, Orange Co., New York, 29th May, 1844; res. ill-health, 26th October, 1881; died 27th November, 1886, Coldenham, New York; m.1. Margaret J. Burnside, of Pittsburgh, Pa., 28th February, 1843; m.2. Elizabeth M. Finley, of Little Britain, New York, 1st July, 1845. s. Rev. Samuel Gormley Shaw.

Sloane, William

b. nr. Larne, Co. Antrim, 12th May, 1787; s. of William Sloane and Jane Robinson; ed. Larne Academy in 1808. teacher; emig. 1817; theology under Rev. Dr. J. R. Willson, Coldenham, New York; lic. by Northern Presbytery, 4th April, 1820; ord. and inst. by Northern Presbytery, Topsham, Orange Co., Vermont, 14th October, 1820; res. 17th April, 1829; inst. congs. Greenfield and L'derry, Ohio, 16th November, 1829; res. 23rd October, 1838; inst. Elkhorn congregation, Oakdale, Illinois, 13th September, 1840; res. illhealth, 9th May, 1858; died 3rd December, 1863; m. Mary McNeice, of Carnmoney, Ireland, in 1816. s. Rev. James Renwick Willson Sloane D.D.

Sommerville, Robert McGowan *

b. Grand Pre, Nova Scotia, 14th October, 1837; s. of Rev. William Sommerville and Sarah B. Dickie; ed. grad. Q.U.B. 1860, Theological Hall, Belfast; lic. by Eastern Presbytery, Ireland, 3rd January, 1861; ord. and inst. by New Brunswick and Nova Scotia Presbytery, co-pastor with father, congs. Horton and Cornwallis, Nova Scotia, 16th October, 1861; 1862 inst. Wolfville, built a meeting house; 1866, Inspector of Schools for Kings Co., Nova Scotia; res. 13th November, 1873; s.s. Cincinnati, Ohio; inst. 2nd New York City, 14th December, 1875; Moderator of Synod, 1889; ret. 17th September, 1912; died 3rd February, 1920; m. Elizabeth Chipman, of Cornwallis, Nova Scotia, 13th September, 1865.

Sommerville, William *

b. Ballyroney, Co. Down, 1st July, 1800; s. of William Sommerville and Jane Kirk; ed. grad. Glasgow University,1820, Theological Hall, Paisley, Scotland; lic. by Southern Presbytery, 5th December, 1826; ord. 'sine titulo' by Southern Presbytery, 31st May, 1831, Missionary to the British North American Provinces; settled Cornwallis Valley, in Nova Scotia; minister to presbyterians Grand Pre, Horton Township, King's Co., 16th May, 1833; inst. add. cong. Cornwallis 9th May, 1835; died 28th September, 1878, Somerset, Kings Co., N. S.; m.1. Sarah B. Dickie, of Amherst, Nova Scotia, in 1832; m.2. Mrs. Jane E. (Caldwell) Woodworth, of Grand Pre, Nova Scotia, September, 1854. s. Rev. Robert McGowan Sommerville.

Stavely, Alexander McLeod *

b. Corkey, Co. Antrim, 9th June 1816; 4th. s. of Rev. Dr. William John Stavely (Kilraughts) and Jane Adams; ed. O.C.B., grad. Edinburgh University, 1835, Theological Hall, Paisley, lic. by Northern Presbytery, 16th March, 1839; ord. by Northern Presbytery 'sine titulo' 12th May, 1841, Missionary to St. John, New Brunswick; res. 16th June, 1879; preached in vacancies in Ireland; inst. Ballyclare Co. Antrim, 10th December, 1884, s.s. Larne; ret. November 1898; died 9th July 1903; m. Margaret Cameron, 2nd d. of Ewen Cameron, St John's, 21st April 1851(2?), ; 3 d., Lizzie Cameron, m. Professor James McMaster, Magee College; Jane Adams, m.1. Dr Hamilton, Leeds; m.2. Rev. J. B. Armour, Ballymoney; Annie.

Steele, David

b. Upper Creevagh, Co. Donegal, 2nd November, 1803; s. of David Steele and Sarah Gailey; ed. 1820 Academy of L'derry; emig 1824 Huntingdon, Pa.; grad. Western University of Pa.,1827, theology under Rev. Dr. John Black, Pittsburgh; lic. by Pittsburgh Presbytery, 8th April, 1830; ord. and inst. by Ohio Presbytery, Brush Creek, Adams Co., Ohio, 6th June, 1831; Withdrew, from R.P.C.N.A., organized the Reformed Presbytery, 24th June, 1840; 1859 removed to Hill Prairie, Illinois; October, 1866, he removed to Philadelphia, Pa.; 1885, he removed to Galesburgh, Illinois;1886, returned to Philadelphia; Hon. D.D. Western University of Pa., 1884; died 29th June, 1887, Philadelphia ; m. Eliza Johnston, of Chillicothe, Ohio, 4th May 4, 1831.

Stevenson, Andrew

b. Ballybay, Co. Monaghan, 10th January, 1810; Son of John Stevenson and Isabella Brown Stevenson; 1831, chosen by Synod to accompany the Rev. William Sommerville to British North American Provinces; Missionary in New Brunswick; 1833, opened classical school, Philadelphia; ed. theology under Revs. J. R. Willson and James Christie; lic. Southern Presbytery R.P.C.N.A., 15th May, 1839; ord. and inst. Southern Presbytery, 2nd New York City, 14th November, 1839; ret. ill-health 17th May, 1875; Hon. D.D. University N. Y. City, 1865; Moderator of Synod, 1869; died 24th June, 1881, New York; m. Anna M. Willson, of Coldenham, New York, 10th February, 1840.

Stewart, James Wylie

b. Ballybay, Co. Monaghan, 24th August, 1794; s. of John Stewart and Mary Wylie; ed. grad. R.B.A.I. 1815. Theological Hall, Stirling; lic. by Southern Presbytery, 3rd December, 1816; emig. May, 1823, ord. and inst. by Northern Presbytery, Argyle now West Hebron, Washington Co., New York, 13th October, 1825; res. 5th April, 1832; 1833 joined New School branch; joined Dutch Reformed Church, 9th June, 1835; inst.

Battenville, Washington Co., New York; Principal of the Jackson Academy; 1838, Principal of the Academy of Warwick, Orange Co., New York; joined Presbyterian Church, 16th October, 1844; 1845 inst. Union Church, of Philadelphia; died 1st March, 1849; m.1. Ruth Gifford, of New York, 1827; m.2. Elizabeth Willard, of Salem, New York, 1835.

Stewart, Robert Miller *
b. Ballynaloob, Co. Antrim, 5th April, 1824; s. of William Stewart and Elizabeth Beggs; ed. grad. R.B.A.I., 1843., Theological Hall, Paisley; lic. by Northern Presbytery, 3rd February, 1847; Missionary in Connaught; London prize for proficiency in Gaelic; ord. 'sine titulo' by R.P. Synod 12th July, 1849, Missionary to the North American British Provinces; 1849 mission station of Wilmot, Annapolis Co., Nova Scotia, also Margaretville and Lawrencetown for over thirty years; res. 26th May, 1881, and supplied vacancies in U.S.A.; died 29th September, 1899, Wilmot, N.S.; m. Margaret Morrison, of Melvern Square, N.S., 7th November, 1855.

Stott, John *
b. nr. Cremore, Co. Armagh, 17th May, 1808; s. of Thomas Stott and Jane Hamilton; ed. grad. R.B.A.I., 1830, studied medicine; Theological Hall, Paisley; lic. by Northern Presbytery, 9th March, 1834; ord. and inst. by Western Presbytery, Convoy, Co. Donegal, 8th July, 1835; res. 16th October 16, 1850; emig. 1851; rec. by Synod, 28th May, 1851; inst. Princeton, Gibson Co., Indiana, 13th October, 1851, suspd. 2nd June, 1868; formed independent organization, preached without ecclesiastical connection, practiced medicine, Princeton, Indiana; Moderator of Synod of 1865; m. 13th March, 1842, Eliza., d. of Wm. Black Aughigalt.

Stuart, Alexander Charles
b. nr. L'derry City, 17th July, 1823; s. of Charles Stuart and Matilda Buchanan, member of Secession Church; ed. grad. O.C.B., 1843, Theological Hall of the Original Seceder Church, Edinburgh; emig spring of 1847, St. John, New Brunswick, joined R.P. Church; lic. by New Brunswick and Nova Scotia Presbytery, 26th September, 1847; preached St. John, Mill Stream, Campbell, New Brunswick; 1850, preached New York, Philadelphia; 1852, Montreal, Canada, joined United Presbyterian Church of Canada; m. Eleanor Middleton, of Manorcunningham, 15th August, 1844.

Teaz, John
b. nr. L'derry City, 1st July, 1849; s. of Ezekiel Teaz and Lavinia Cromie; emig. June, 1869, Brooklyn, New York; grad. Brooklyn Lay College, 1877. Allegheny Seminary; lic. Pittsburgh Presbytery, 12th April, 1881. for missionary work; 4 yrs Central Board of Missions in the Maritime Provinces and the West; ord. and inst. by Illinois Presbytery, Church Hill, Coultersville, Randolph Co., Illinois, 7th July, 1885; June, 1888; Southern Mission, Selma, Alabama, 1890-91; 1891, joined United Presbyterians, inst. Kansas City, Missouri; res. entered business.

Walkinshaw, Hugh
b. Broughshane, Co. Antrim, 15th June, 1803: s. of John Walkinshaw and Mary Henry (Presbyterian); was born near Broughshane; 1819, emig. Belmont Co., Ohio; ed. grad. Franklin College, 1827; theology under, Rev. Dr. John Black, Pittsburgh, and Rev. Dr. S. B. Wylie, Philadelphia; lic. by Philadelphia Presbytery, 17th June, 1832; ord. and inst. by

Pittsburgh Presbytery, Brookland, Lucesco, Westmoreland, Co., Pa., 15th April, 1835; died 19th April, 1843; m. Lydia J. Sproull, of Lucesco, P.a., in 1835.

Wallace, James

b. Lisadier, Co. Armagh, 10th March, 1810; s. of Rev. Robert Wallace and Margaret King; emig. 1811, Philadelphia; 1814, to Norwich, Muskingum Co., Ohio; ed. grad. Franklin College,1834, Coldenham Seminary; lic. by Southern Presbytery, 10th May, 1838; ord. and inst. by Western Presbytery, Northwood, Ohio, 13th July, 1840, Old Bethel, Sparta, Randolph Co., Illinois; res. 15th May, 1867; appt. secretary National Reform Association; Moderator of Synod, 1862; died 1st May, 1877, St. Louis, Missouri; m.1. Sarah Wright, of Adamsville, Ohio, in 1840; m.2. Mrs. Mary J. (Sloane) McClurkin, of Warriston, Illinois, 17th April, 1855; m.3. Mrs. Mary B. (Murdock) Trumbull, of Rochester, New York, in 1861.

Wallace, Robert

b. Loughgilly, Co. Armagh, 14th December, 1772; s. of David Wallace and Mary Brown (Anti-Burgher Seceders); 1794, joined Ballylane R.P.; ed. grad. Glasgow University, 1810; emig. 1811, Philadelphia, Pennsylvania; ed. Philadelphia Seminary; lic. Middle Presbytery, 9th May, 1814, ord. by Middle Presbytery at Pittsburgh, Pa.; inst. congs. Licking and Chillicothe, Ohio, 12th October,1814; a pioneer Missionary in Ohio; res. Licking branch, 10th May, 1820, contd. Chillicothe; inst. Salt Creek (now New Concord), Norwich, Muskingum Co., Ohio, 9th October, 1823; died 19th July, 1849; m.1. Margaret King, of Co. Armagh, 1796; m.2. Mrs. Isabella (McCreary) McCartney, of Cambridge, Ohio, October, 1839. s. Rev. John Wallace.

Wallace, John

b. Lisadier, Co. Armagh, 25th December, 1800; s. of Rev. Robert Wallace and Margaret King; emig. 1811, Philadelphia; ed. grad. Western University of Pa., 1829; theology under Rev. Dr. John Black, Pittsburgh; lic. by Pittsburgh Presbytery, 4th April, 1832; ord. by Ohio Presbytery; inst. congs. Muskingum and Tomica, Dresden, Muskingum Co., Ohio, 14th April, 1833; res. 4th April, 1855; joined Associate Refd. Church, rec. 2nd Presbytery of Ohio, 27th October, 1857; 1858 joined United Presbyterian Church, inst. Adamsville, Crawford Co., Pa., 6th May, 1862; res. 1st May, 1866; returned to R.P. Pittsburgh Presbytery, 16th October, 1866; died 7th January, 1880; m.1. Jane E. Wylie, of White Cottage, Ohio, 1st June, 1837; m.2. Eleanor George, of White Cottage, Ohio, 4th April, 1849.

Williams, Matthew

b. Ballymena, Co. Antrim, 17th July, 1768; parents Seceders. Church; emig. 1794, Ligonier Valley, Westmoreland Co., Pa.; joined Associate Refd. Church; ed. grad. Jefferson Academy, 1801; 1802 joined R.P.; theology under Rev. Dr. John Black, Pittsburgh; lic. by Reformed Presbytery, 20th September, 1804; 1805, missionary Butler Co., Pa.; ord. by Middle Committee of the Reformed Presbytery, inst. united societies of Pine Creek, Union and Deer Creek, Butler Co., Pa., 18th May, 1807; died 11th September, 1828, Pine Creek, Pa.; m. Elizabeth Parkhill, of Elizabeth, Pa., 1807.

Wilson, William
b. Findrum, Co. Donegal, 25 December, 1803; s. of John Wilson and Lilly A. Wilson; emig. with parents, 1823, New York City; ed. grad. Union College, 1828, Philadelphia Seminary; lic. by Philadelphia Presbytery, 14th April, 1830; ord. 'sine titulo' by Philadelphia Presbytery, Home Missionary, 16th June, 1831, Milton, Northumberland Co., Pa., 6th August, 1832; 1833, joined New School branch; Principal Milton Academy, res. 13th April, 1837. He returned to the city of New York, and, in 1838; inst. Cincinnati, Ohio, 13th July, 1839; susp. 14th October, 1847, org. independent "Church of the Covenanters."; returned to New School body, 17th May, 1854; Chaplain in Union Army; died 9th September, 1873; Cincinnati, Ohio; Moderator General Synod, 1843; m. Anna Campbell, of Cincinnati, Ohio, 1853

Wright, Alexander
b. Craigs, Co. Antrim, 25th December, 1831; s. of William Wright and Eliza Laughlin; emig.1843, E. Pa.; ed. grad. Lafayette College, 1862. Allegheny Seminary; lic. by Pittsburgh Presbytery, 23rd May, 1867; died 21st November, 1869 of consumption visiting relatives, Vernon, Waukesha Co., Wisconsin; um.

Wright, Hugh *
b. Creevagh, Co. Monaghan, 20th October, 1908; 2nd s. of Rev. James Renwick Wright and Elizabeth Reid; ed. Coleraine Model School, Coleraine Academical Institution, Magee College, L'derry, Trinity College, Dublin; R.P. Theological Hall, Belfast, 1930-1932; R.P. Seminary, Pittsburgh 1932-1935; grad. B.A. (T.C.D.), 1930; lic. by Pittsburgh Presbytery, USA, 10th May 1932; ord. (sine titulo) by Pittsburgh Presbytery, 10th August, 1934; s.s. Winnipeg 1932-35; inst. Winnipeg. 30th April 1936; res. 22nd July 1938; inst. Clarendon Street, L'derry, 10th November 1938; inst. Trinity Street, Belfast, 15th September, 1959; inst. Newtownards, 21st December, 1973; ret. 27th September, 1983; Moderator of Synod, 1946 and 1961; died 21st January, 1991; int. Knockbracken; m. Dorothea Macauley, d. Robert Macauley, Belfast; 3 d. Nancy, Rosemarie (died infancy), Edith; 1 s. James.

Wright, James Renwick *
b. Coleraine, 6th May, 1918; 3rd s. of Rev James Renwick Wright and Elizabeth Reid; ed. Coleraine Model School, Coleraine Academical Institution; Magee College, L'derry; Trinity College, Dublin; R.P. Theological Hall, Belfast, 1937-1939; R.P. Theological Seminary, Pittsburgh, 1939-40; lic. St. Lawrence Presbytery April, 1939; ord. and inst. Ballymoney, 7th January, 1941; inst. Dromara, 7th January, 1953; res. 17th December, 1968; inst. Geneva R.P., Beaver Falls, Pa. U.S.A., 20th May, 1969; inst. Winchester R.P., Ks, 12th November, 1975; inaugurated Dean of Students and Prof of New Testament Studies 19th September, 1978; ret. 1993; D.D. Geneva College, 1967; Moderator of Synod (R.P.C.N.A.), 1979; died 8th October, 2009; int. New Galilee R.P. cemetery, Pa., USA; m. Maureen Hamilton, daughter of Samuel Kelly, Ballymoney, 19th September, 1944; 2 s. Christopher, Jonathan.

Wylie, Samuel
b. Moylarg, Co. Antrim, 19th February, 1790; s. of Andrew Wylie and Elizabeth Wylie; emig. 1807, Philadelphia; ed. grad. University of Pennsylvania, 1811. Philadelphia Seminary; lic. by Middle Presbytery, 23rd May, 1815; 1817, explored new fields for missionary operations in the West; ord. 'sine titulo' at Synod, in Pittsburgh, 26th May,

1818, Missionary S. Illinois, Randolph, and parts of St. Clair and Washington Cos.; inst. Bethel, Eden, Randolph Co., Illinois, 19th June, 1821; 1833, joined New School branch; res. 20th February, 1870; Hon. D.D. Washington and Jefferson College in 1868; Moderator of the Synod 1830, General Synod, 1850; died 20th March, 1872, Sparta, Illinois; m.1. Margaret Millikin, of Philadelphia; m.2. Mrs. Margaret (Black) Ewing, of Pittsburgh.

Wylie, Samuel Brown
b. Moylarg, Co. Antrim, 21st May, 1773; s. of Adam Wylie and Margaret Brown; ed. grad. Glasgow University, October, 1797; teacher, Ballymena, emig. USA. alleged connection with United Irishmen October, 1797, Philadelphia, Pennsylvania; 1798 Tutor in the University of Pa.; theology under Rev. William Gibson; lic. by Refd. Presbytery, Coldenham, New York, 24th June, 1799; ord. 'sine titulo' by Refd. Presbytery, at Ryegate, Vermont, 25th June, 1800, the first Covenanter minister ordained in America; accompanied Rev. James McKinney through the South to abolish slavery; inst. Philadelphia, 20th November, 1803; appt. Prof in new Theological Seminary in Philadelphia, 1810; res. 1817, appt. 1823; res. 1828; appt. Professor of Latin and Greek University of Pa., 17 yrs., 1833 joined New School branch; Hon. D.D. Dickinson College, 1815; Moderator Refd. Presbytery1800, 1801; died 13th October, 1852, Philadelphia; m. Margaret Watson, of Pittsburgh, 5th April, 1802.

Members of the Eastern Reformed Presbyterian Synod, Ireland who served in The 'New School Branch',

General Synod of the Reformed Presbyterian Church in America.
Bole, John
b. Scotland, 1821; orphaned in early life; ed. Glasgow University; Theological Hall under Andrew Symington; emig. U.S.A. 1853; ord . and inst. 24th December, 1853 by Northern Presbytery of General Synod of R. P. Church, Ryegate Vermont. res. 2nd June, 1862, inst. Linenhall Street, Belfast; 1863; returned to U.S.A. 1869, inst. West Barnet, Vermont. ret. 1886; d.1906; m. 1853, Marion Brown, niece of Dr. Symington, 7 children four of them born in Ryegate, one in Glasgow, and two in Belfast; s. 1. John d. in childhood, William McClure, Andrew Symington, served as a Congregational minister, first in Turner, Maine, then in Coventry, Vermont, and finally in East Hardwick.

Chestnut, Robert. W.
Minister of General Synod of Reformed Presbyterian Church of North America from Duanesburg, N.Y.; s.s. Cullybackey, between 1902-1905.

Moffett, Joseph
b. Broughshane, Co. Antrim, 22nd July, 1844; 3rd s. of Robert Moffett; attended Cullybackey, E.R. Synod; ed. Galway, Belfast, Philadelphia, D.D.; emig. 1870, Philadelphia; lic. Presbytery of Philadelphia, General Synod; ord. and inst. by Pittsburgh Presbytery, General Synod, Darlington and New Galilee, Pa., September, 1870; returned to Ireland, 1873; inst. Gortlee, 3rd September, 1874; 1902, joined with cong. General Assembly; res. October, 1907; preached supplies Edinburgh, Church of Scotland; D.D.; m. Miss. Lizzie Beck of Belfast, 1876; 3 d. Margaret, Eliza, Emma; 2 s., Rev. Dr. Joseph Moffett of Crown Court, Church of Scotland, London; John Rick.

Fasti

OF

THE EASTERN REFORMED

PRESBYTERIAN SYNOD

Including those ministers who entered the Synod and

those who were later ordained or installed.

1842-1902

THE DIVISION OF 1840
RESULTING IN THE FORMATION OF THE
EASTERN REFORMED PRESBYTERIAN SYNOD

The matter of the Covenanter's relationship with civil government sadly affected the three Reformed Presbyterian Churches in the 19th Century, resulting in division in the American Church in 1833, the Irish Church in 1840 and the Scottish Church in 1863.

In 1830 Thomas Houston of Knockbracken accepted the invitation of the Synod to publish and circulate a magazine throughout the Church, and issued the first copy in December 1830, which he called *'The Covenanter.'* The magazine, which contained articles of a practical and devotional nature, was warmly welcomed throughout the church. In March, 1831, Houston began a series of articles on 'The Magistracy.' Mr. Houston who wrote the articles, believed that scripture taught that a magistrate, that is an officer of civil government, must be a Christian in order to administer the law for the glory of God and for the public good.

As the articles in *'The Covenanter'* on continued, the matter was raised in the Synod of 1831. Rev. John Paul, the minister of Loughmourne and Carnmoney, entered a period of public correspondence with Houston on the power of the civil magistrate in matters of religion and charged the editor of *'The Covenanter'* with advocating 'persecuting principles.'

A crisis was reached at the Synod of 1832 when Mr. Houston framed a libel against Mr. Paul for 'slander' and 'misrepresentation'. It was hoped that peace would be made between the two parties by the Synod of 1833 at Moneymore. A measure of resolution was arrived at. However, in 1835, a report from the American Synod of the Reformed Presbyterian Church was discussed. This report dealt with the question whether members of the Church should exercise the elective franchise to vote and take active part in civil government. The American Church was divided on the issue and many congregations had left forming the General Synod, in 1833. By the Synod of 1836 a proposal was adopted approving the principle of the national establishment of religion, but disapproving of the existing civil and religious establishments. Rev. Paul, supported by three ministers and four elders, dissented from this decision.

The controversy continued for the next four years. The majority party led by Mr. Houston issued a long statement in 1837 on Civil Government that did not please Mr. Paul and his supporters. It was becoming increasingly evident that reconciliation between the two parties was impossible. Mr. Paul and his adherents, most of whom were members of the Eastern Presbytery, requested the Synod in 1839 adopt the Testimony of the Scottish Reformed Presbyterian Church and Terms of Communion that had been recently modified. Synod adopted the Testimony of the Scottish Church, but rejected their Terms of Communion. Against this decision the Eastern Presbytery dissented. A deadlock was reached. When the Synod met at Moneymore in 1840, the Eastern Presbytery entered a protest against the various decisions of Synod on the subject of the civil magistrate and declined the authority of the Synod. The document was signed by five ministers and twelve ruling elders. They, along with the congregations they represented, withdrew from the jurisdiction of the Reformed Presbyterian Synod forming the two Presbyteries of Belfast and Derry and on the 18 October, 1842 were constituted as the Eastern Reformed Presbyterian Synod. This section of the Reformed Presbyterian Church had a separate history of some sixty years. At its strongest, it consisted of ten congregations. Some new congregations were established from divisions within congregations. Some of these failed due to the lack of the supply of Gospel ordinances. The division also affected the Covenanter congregation in Liverpool which being unable to be supplied by the Belfast Presbytery, joined the Scottish R. P. Church and later the English Presbyterian Church.

Friendly relations were maintained through the years, but the two Synods never found common ground for reunion. In 1902, the Eastern Reformed Presbyterian Synod decided to join the General Assembly of the Presbyterian Church in Ireland. Half of their congregations, led by their members, took independent action and returned to the fellowship of the Reformed Presbyterian Synod of Ireland.

Ministers of the

Eastern Reformed Presbyterian Synod of Ireland, 1842-1902

Alexander, Jacob
b. L'derry; s. of Rev. John Alexander, Faughan and Linenhall Street; inst. 1844 Londonderry, (Waterside), E.R.P.; res. 1854.

Alexander, John
b. near L'derry, 1773; elder br. of Rev. Josias Alexander; ed. Scotland; lic. 1803; ord. Faughan and L'derry; res. 1825; inst. Linenhall Street, Belfast, 1826; joined Eastern R.P. Synod, 1840; Prof. of Theology in Eastern R.P. Church, 1841-1852; ret. 1850; died 22nd August 1852; Jacob Alexander, Waterside R.P. Church, was a son; Samuel Quigley, was a son-in-law.

Austin, Hugh
b. Cullybackey; inst. Eskylane; minister 1849-1853; died in 1853.

Bartley, John Robert
b. Co. Cavan, 1855; ed. B.A. L.L.B. (T.C.D.); had ministered in Canada; under care of Presbytery of Carrickfergus, General Assembly; inst. Botanic Ave., 21st February, 1899; res. 1902; rec. by General Assembly; inst. Tralee, 10th March, 1903; died 10th October, 1918, as a result of the sinking of the S.S. Leinster, torpedoed in Irish Sea; he was on the way to visit his son, Sgt. William Bartley in a London hospital.

Beck, John Fritz
b. Belfast; s. of Dr. Frederick Beck, (Belfast); ed. grad. M.A. and M.D., Divinity Hall Edinburgh, R.P.C.S.; lic. by the Belfast Presbytery of the Eastern Synod; ord. Milford, 13th January, 1870; ret. 1900.died 1901?; m. 1868, Kate; s. Fred K. Patterson.

Bole, John
b. Scotland, 1821; orphaned in early life; ed. Glasgow University; Theological Hall under Andrew Symington; emig. U.S.A. 1853; ord . and inst. 24th December, 1853 by Northern Presbytery of General Synod of R. P. Church, Ryegate Vermont. res. 2nd June, 1862, inst. Linenhall Street, Belfast; 1863; returned to U.S.A. 1869, inst. West Barnet, Vermont. ret. 1886; d.1906; m. 1853, Marion Brown, niece of Dr. Symington, 7 children four of them born in Ryegate, one in Glasgow, and two in Belfast; s. 1. John d. in childhood, William McClure, Andrew Symington, served as a Congregational minister, first in Turner, Maine, then in Coventry, Vermont, and finally in East Hardwick.

Close, William
b. 17th January, 1822 lic. by Belfast Presbytery, E.R.P. Synod; ord. and inst. 7th November, 1848 Loughmourne; s.s. Eskylane, 1864 - 1873; received with cong. into General Assembly 1893; ret. 3rd August, 1897; died 12 May 1899; int. Loughmourne; m. Eliza Kinear; s. Robert; d. Mary.

Chestnut, Robert. W.
Minister of General Synod of Reformed Presbyterian Church of North America from Duanesburg, N.Y.; s.s. Cullybackey, between 1902-1905.

Fallon, Andrew
b. Ballymoney, 1870; lic. Route Presbytery; ord. 22nd February, 1899; sought union with General Assembly; res.1902.; Presbyterian Church, Clapton, London, 1902-1907; Howard Street Presbyterian Church, North Shields, 1907-1925; m. Ella, b. Donegal; d. Reeba Katrine.

Gamble, William
b. nr. Ballykelly, 1763; s. of Robert Gamble; ed. Scotland; lic. by Refd. Presbytery, 1785; ord. Ballygay and Gortlee, Co. Donegal, 23rd July, 1788; died 6th August, 1839 at Greenhill, Letterkenny; m. Miss Art, Stranorlar; author "The Glory of Christ", N.B. "Brief Biographical Sketches", Ferguson.

Henry, Robert Mitchell
s. of Rev. William Henry, Newtownards and Gortlee; inst. Linenhall Street, Belfast, 1853; res. 4th May, 1858, later became a Baptist minister; s. Paul Henry, painter Laureate of The Irish Free State; Robert, M Henry, Prof. Q.U.B.

Henry, William
b. Macosquin, 1789; e.s. of Thomas Henry; ed. Glasgow University, R.P. Theological Hall, Paisley; grad. M.A. (Glasgow), 1811, D.D., Indiana University (1st Irish R.P. minister to rec. D.D. from U.S.A.), 1835; lic. by Northern Presbytery; ord. Newtownards, 1813; withdrew with part of his congregation (Ann Street) and joined Eastern R.P. Synod in 1842; res. 1843; inst. Gortlee, 1843; died 7th August 1852; int. at Gortlee; m.; 1 s,, Rev. Robert M. Henry; 1 d., Mrs McFarland, who had 2 S., Sir John Henry McFarland, M.A., L.L.D., Chancellor of Melbourne Univ., Robert Arthur Henry McFarland, Headmaster of Campbell College, Belfast; pub. "The Warning to Sardis" 1848, pub. "The Funeral Sermon for Rev. J.A. Alexander, 1823.

Houston, Clarke
b. Maghera, 1787; youngest. s. of Clarke Houston, merchant; ed. Glasgow University, R.P. Theological Hall, Paisley; lic. by Eastern Presbytery, 1st November, 1811; ord. Limavady, 1814; res. 1815; inst. Cullybackey, 1818; he and congregation joined Eastern R.P. Synod in 1842; grad. D.D. (hon. caus.); Clerk of R.P. Synod, 1827-1840; died 13th November, 1852, at Newcastle-on-Tyne; 2 weeks after the death of his son, Rev John Clarke Houston, minister of Clavering Place U.P Church, 2 d.

McVicar, John Galway
b. Belfast; s. of John McVicar, merchant; lic. 29th Septmeber, 1848 by Pennsylvania Presbytery, General Synod; returned to Ireland 1849; ord. Ann Street, Newtownards (Eastern R.P. Cong.) 10th December, 1850; res. 1853; inst. Cullybackey, 9th August 1853; res. 15th September, 1859, and withdrew from R.P. Church; joined Baptist Church and organised the new church in Hill Street, Ballymena, 1860; res. 1862; October, 1862, formed the first Brethren assembly in Ballymena; 1870, assoc. with Upper Clapton, London, Brethren assembly; died 5th January, 1900; m. 1850 d. of Wm Montgomery, Belfast.

Marcus, John Paul

inst. Ballymoney , 1850; cong. met in old Town Hall; ran a classical school; died in the ministry 1876.

Moffett, Joseph

b. Broughshane, Co. Antrim, 22nd July, 1844; 3rd s. of Robert Moffett; attended Cullybackey, E.R. Synod; ed. Galway, Belfast, Philadelphia, D.D.; emig. 1870, Philadelphia; lic. Presbytery of Philadelphia, General Synod; ord. and inst. by Pittsburgh Presbytery, General Synod, Darlington and New Galilee, Pa., September, 1870; returned to Ireland, 1873; inst. Gortlee, 3rd September, 1874; 1902, joined with cong. General Assembly; res. October, 1907; preached supplies Edinburgh, Church of Scotland; D.D.; m. Miss. Lizzie Beck of Belfast, 1876; 3 d. Margaret, Eliza, Emma; 2 s., Rev. Dr. Joseph Moffett of Crown Court, Church of Scotland, London; John Rick.

Moffett, Samuel

b. Broughshane, 1846; ed. Queen's College Belfast, Divinity Hall, Edinburgh; inst. Eskylane 1876-1917. joined General Assembly, 1903; died 8th October, 1918; m. Margaret ?.; s. Robert, s. Thomas, d. Rita, d. May, s. Bertie.

Moody, Joseph Archibald

b. Cullyvenny, Coleraine; s. of John Moody (member of Ballylaggan); ed. Queen's College, Belfast, Theological Hall, Belfast; lic. by Northern Presbytery; ord. Convoy, 20th October, 1858; res. 1860; inst. Cullybackey (Eastern Refd. Synod), 1st November, 1860; died 4th February 1898.

Patton, Samuel

b. L'derry City, 1832; lic. July, 1859; ord. and inst. Londonderry, (Waterside), 1859 to 1908; July 1908 resigned from Waterside and s.s. of Gortlee. later joined General Assembly; m. Miss Dunn, d. 1. Eliza Jane, 2. Katherine.

Paul, John

b. Tobernaveen, Antrim, 1777; s. of John Paul; ed. Glasgow University, R.P. Theological Hall; lic. by Irish Refd. Presbytery at Garvagh, 1803; ord. Loughmourne, 11th September, 1805; grad. D.D. (Union, U.S.A.) 1836; res. from R.P. Synod of Ireland, 1840; joined (with his cong.) Eastern Refd. Synod at its formation 1842; author "Refutation of Arianism"; died 16th March, 1848; m. 1807 Rachel Smith, Ballyearl, Carnmoney; 1 d. m. Rev. D Stewart Bates, Glasgow.

Robinson, John

lic. by Northern Presbytery, R.P.C.I. Synod; ord. Gortlee, 4th October, 1859; ran a Classical School in Letterkenny; died 31st December, 1866; int. Gortlee; m. 1855, d. of John Berryhill.

Smith, Matthew

Ann Street, Newtownards, 1848-1850.

Stewart, George
  b. Letterkenny; inst. Eskylane, 6th August, 1856; res. 18th July, 1859 joined the General Assembly.

Stewart, Hugh
Ann Street, Newtownards, inst. 20th November, 1855; res. 2nd May, 1887; remained as s.s. later joined General Assembly; died, 22nd April, 1903.

Stevenson, Samuel Bole
b. Lack, nr. Letterkenny, 1818; ord. by Western Presbytery, Milford, 1839; joined the Derry Presbytery of the Eastern Reformed Presbyterian Synod; ministered, Milford and Bridge End, Ramelton; res. September, 1869; inst. Linenhall Street, Belfast, in 1875, the congregation removed to a new building in Botanic Avenue, where he served from 1875-1898; died 1898.

Congregations of the
Eastern Reformed Presbyterian Synod, 1842-1902

Derry Presbytery

Gortlee, Letterkenny

Waterside, Londonderry

Milford

Bridge End, Ramelton

Belfast Presbytery

Linenhall Street, Belfast, later Botanic Avenue after 1875.

Cullybackey

Loughmourne and Carnmoney

Ann Street, Newtownards

Ballymoney, met in Old Town Hall

Eskylane

Under Care of Synod

Liverpool.(later Shaw Street, Everton)

THE RECORDS OF THE
REFORMED PRESBYTERIAN CHURCH
OF IRELAND

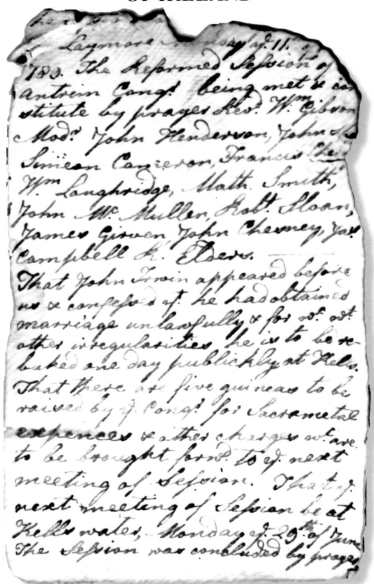

Page from the session book of the Antrim Congregation, dated Laymore 1789.

In the possession of Public Record Office of Northern Ireland

NOTES ON PRIMARY AND SECONDARY SOURCES

At the final meeting of the Reformed Presbytery of Ireland, held at Maghera, County Londonderry, on 7 November 1810, a suggestion was made that a history of the rise and progress of the Covenanter Church in Ireland ought to be written. Rev. William Stavely, the longest-serving of the ministers in the denomination at that time, was asked to prepare something on this. Whether Stavely ever got round to writing this history is unclear; certainly nothing has survived to show that he did. Had it, our understanding of the Reformed Presbyterian Church in its formative years would be much greater than it is now. As it is, our knowledge of the Irish Covenanters in the first half of the eighteenth century is limited in the extreme. There are a few references to Ireland in the minutes of the General Meeting of Societies in Scotland from this period, though these are of a fairly broad nature.

RECORDS OF CONGREGATIONS

The fullest list of Reformed Presbyterian records currently available can be found in *Guide to Church Records*, produced by the Public Record Office of Northern Ireland (PRONI) and originally published by the Ulster Historical Foundation in 1994. An updated *Guide* is currently available in PRONI. PRONI has originals or microfilmed copies of records from around thirty individual congregations. The records can include registers of baptisms, marriages and, though much less often, burials/deaths. None of these date from before 1830 which is fairly late. Many of the R. P. marriage registers date from no earlier than the 1860s. The scattered nature of the few congregations in the latter part of the eighteenth century would certainly have militated against proper record-keeping. In the early eighteenth century Covenanters in Ireland often had to travel to Scotland or wait for a visiting Scottish minister before children could be baptised or marriages performed.

In some cases the lack of early records was due to the accidental destruction of them. The 'negligence and disobedience of a female servant' resulted in the loss of some of the records of the Bready congregation in a fire in the home of the clerk of session on 9 September 1868. Other records were destroyed deliberately. One nineteenth-century Reformed Presbyterian minister became convinced that infant baptism was contrary to

Scripture and left his congregation, but not before he had destroyed many of the baptismal registers.

Other documents found among Reformed Presbyterian records in PRONI include session minutes, committee minutes, communicants' rolls and accounts. Session minutes are often the earliest records of a particular congregation, in many cases predating registers of baptism and marriages. The earliest session minutes are those for the Antrim congregation comprising what are now the separate congregations of Cullybackey and Kellswater. These cover the period from *c.*1789-1802 and 1806-09. A volume covering part of the intervening period can be found in the Presbyterian Historical Society Library. Other early session minutes in PRONI include those for Drimbolg, near Tamlaght O'Crilly, beginning in 1809, the former Grange congregation, which date from 1812, and Ballenon, which date from 1820. An examination of the earliest session book for the Antrim congregation reveals much about the Covenanters at the end of the eighteenth century. The session book is in a very fragile condition and parts of it are difficult to read, but nonetheless it contains a remarkable insight into the life of the congregation at this time.

The records for Ballenon include registers of admissions, 1849-67, and departures, 1849-68. Among the Londonderry records is a list of members from 1848 with details of baptisms, marriages, deaths and emigrations. The records for Limavady (originally known as Broadlane) include names of persons admitted to membership, 1896-1982, removed from membership, 1896-1933 and emigrations, 1887-93. Among the Rathfriland records are lists of members with details of emigrations, deaths and marriages, 1884-1944. A list of names is recorded in a pledge book of the Total Abstinence Association, 1869-1906, found among the Newtownards records.

The Kilraughts records include a renewal of the National Covenant of Scotland and the Solemn League and Covenant signed by the elders and others, 1855. Printed financial reports for individual congregations can also be found which will name those paying the stipend. The records for Knockbracken include annual reports from 1869-1959 (with gaps) as well as testimonials of the congregation to the Rev Thomas Houston, printed in 1840. The records of Londonderry include minutes of the building committee, 1856-9, established to oversee the construction of the new church in Clarendon Street.

PUBLICATIONS

The best account of the Reformed Presbyterian Church is Professor Adam Loughridge's *The Covenanters in Ireland*, first published in 1984 and reprinted in 1987. Professor Loughridge was regarded as the principle authority on the history of the Church and was instrumental in creating a Church History Committee. He also served as Honorary Secretary of the Presbyterian Historical Society. An earlier history is a volume entitled *Reformed Presbyterian Testimony: Part II Historical* (1939). A lively account of several of those who played a major role in the denomination in the late 1700s is Rev. Samuel Ferguson's *Brief biographical sketches of some Irish Covenanting ministers who laboured during the latter half of the eighteenth century* (1897). It includes a list of ministers, licentiates and students under the care of the presbyteries from 1757 to 1857 (around 90 names). Histories of the American and Scottish Churches include W. M. Glasgow, *A History of the Reformed Presbyterian Church of America* (1888) and Matthew Hutchison, *The Reformed Presbyterian Church of Scotland, 1680-1876* (1893). Also Johannes G. Vos, *The Scottish Covenanters* (1940) is still available and is an excellent overview of Covenanter history. Several congregations have published histories, often issued to coincide with important anniversaries. These histories are invaluable as they often contain factual information garnered from a whole range of sources that are not readily available.

BIBLIOGRAPHY OF PUBLISHED CONGREGATIONAL HISTORIES

'The Covenanters in Ireland', by Rev. Professor Adam Loughridge. 1984.

Ballenon: '"The Bog Edge Meetin" Historical sketch of Ballenon Reformed Presbyterian Church 1820-1991', by Rev. James A. Ritchie. 1991.

Ballyclabber: 'Historical Sketch of Ballyclabber Reformed Presbyterian Congregation', by Rev. A. R. Wright. 1947.

Ballyclabber: 'Everything in its season. A History of Ballyclabber Reformed Presbyterian Church, 1947-1997', by M. E. and T. Donnelly. 1997.

Ballyclare: 'The Covenanters in Ballyclare. A History of Ballyclare Reformed Presbyterian Church', ed. by Joseph Kennedy. 2007.

Ballylaggan: 'Historical Sketch of Ballylaggan Congregation', by Rev. A. R. Wright, published in 'The Covenanter', January 1941.

Cullybackey: 'A Short History of the Reformed Presbyterian Congregation, Cullybackey', by William Shaw. 1912.

Cullybackey: 'The Covenanters at Cullybackey, 1789-1989', by Rev. Professor Adam Loughridge. 1989.

Dervock: 'A Covenant Heritage, Historical Sketch of Dervock Reformed Presbyterian Church, 1783-1983', by Rev. J. D. Trevor McCauley. 1983.

Dromara: 'Centenary Story of Dromara Reformed Presbyterian Church, 1874-1974' by Rev. Robert Hanna. 1974.

Dromore: 'Brewery Lane. A Brewery with a Covenanting Connection', by Rev. Professor Robert McCollum, in Dromore and District Local Historical Group Journal, Volume 3. 1993.

Dublin Road: 'A Century of Christian Witness in Dublin Road, Belfast 1889-1989', by Mr Tom Hamilton. 1989.

Faughan: 'Planted by a River. 200 years of Covenanter Witness at Faughan Bridge, 1790-1990', by Trevor Magee. 1990.

Glenmanus: 'A century of Witness at Glenmanus', by Rev. Professor Adam Loughridge. 2000.

Gortlee: A History of Gortlee, in 'Letterkenny, Congregations, Ministers and People, 1615-1960', by A. J. Weir, Trinity Presbyterian Church. 1960.

Kellswater: 'Kellswater Reformed Presbyterian Church, Co. Antrim, A Short History', by Robert Buchanan. 1989.

Kilraughts: 'Two Hundred Years of Witness. The Story of Kilraughts Covenanting Church', by Rev Prof Adam Loughridge, 1983.

Newry: 'The Reformed Presbyterian, Covenanter, Congregation of Newry, Historical Sketch, 1845 to 1984, in two parts', by Rev. Professor T. B. McFarlane and Rev. Samuel L. Reid. 1984.

Rathfriland: 'A Story Worth Telling, Historical Sketch of Rathfriland Reformed Presbyterian Church: 1777-1977', ed. by Rev. David Magee. 1977.

Newtownards; 'A Covenant Community. History of Newtownards Reformed Presbyterian Church', by Trevor McCavery. 1997.

Histories of Missionary and other Work.

'The Theological Hall Centenary, 1854 - 1954', Reformed Presbyterian Church of Ireland, 1954.

'A Brief History of Colonial Mission Work in Canada and Australia by The Reformed Presbyterian Church of Ireland', by Rev. Hugh Wright. 1958.

'A Brief History of the Irish Mission of the Reformed Presbyterian Church of Ireland', by Rev. Samuel R. Archer. 1970.

'James Martin, Pioneer Medical Missionary in Antioch', by Isobel Lytle. 2003

'A School of the Prophets, the History of the Reformed Theological College Belfast 1854-2004', by Rev. Professor F. S. Leahy. 2004.

'Woman's Missionary Union, 1932-1982 and Missionary Associations from 1824', by Kathleen R. Wright. 1982.

Biographies of R. P. ministers

'Brief biographical sketches of some Irish Covenanting ministers who laboured during the latter half of the eighteenth century', by Rev. Samuel Ferguson, 1897.

'Homer Teaz - Student, Preacher, Soldier', by Rev. Ezekiel Teaz. 1920

'William Staveley', ed. Eull Dunlop, 1993.

'R. J. McIlmoyle', ed. Eull Dunlop. 1991.

'Josias A Chancellor', by Rev. John McDonald. 1895.

Article by Dr. William Roulston, adapted from his article in
'Familia'. Ulster Genealogical Review Vol. 24. 2008. Used with permission.

THE DISTINCTIVE PRINCIPLES OF THE REFORMED PRESBYTERIAN OF IRELAND

Reformed Presbyterians hold common ground with larger Reformed Churches on many points of doctrine and practice. They share their adherence to the form of Church Government with Presbyterians all over the world. They accept the Westminster Confession of Faith and the Larger and Shorter Catechisms as a summary of the Christian faith and in doing so have fellowship with Christians everywhere who hold fast the Reformed tradition. However, they maintain a separate existence as a denomination because they hold distinctive doctrines and practices regarded to be in accordance with the teaching of the Word of God. The distinctives come under four headings;

1. They believe that Covenanting is a Scriptural practice and that the Scottish Covenants of 1638 and 1643 are of continuing obligation.
2. They believe in the supreme authority of Christ over the nation.
3. They teach the supreme and exclusive Headship of Christ over His Church.
4. They proclaim the Lordship of Christ which must apply to every sphere of life.

The first of these four principles is the only one that is peculiar to the Reformed Presbyterian Church; the other three are emphasised to a greater or lesser degree by other evangelical churches, but the Reformed Presbyterians have applied them in such a specific manner that they are a distinctive element of the Church's Testimony.

THE PRINCIPLE OF COVENANTING

The Reformed Presbyterian Church of Ireland accepts and teaches that the Scottish Covenants of 1638 and 1643 laid a continuing obligation upon succeeding generations. This principle was maintained, not only by the Reformed Presbyterian Churches of Scotland, Ireland and the United States of America, but by the Associate or Secession Church of Scotland and Ireland. However the Reformed Presbyterian Church maintained this witness alone from 1690 to 1733, when the first Secession from the Church of Scotland took place and therefore claims direct descent form the Covenanters of the Scottish Second Reformation.

Covenanting is an occasional duty to be performed by Christian Churches or nations as circumstances require and it is expedient to renew such Covenants, although their continued obligation does not depend on their renewal. The unfaithfulness of the majority in this nation does not free the minority in the Church or the nation from Covenant obligation.

In times when the Church felt that there was an increase in error or laxity in principle, it was deemed advisable to call the attention of members to the historic Scottish Covenants, to reaffirm their teaching and to adapt and apply their message to the needs of the day. The Covenants were renewed at Aughensaugh, near Douglas in South-West Scotland, in 1712. This renewal of the Covenants by the Scottish Church was cordially approved by the covenanters in Ireland. A second renewal of the Covenants took place at Crawfordjohn in 1745 as a matter of thanksgiving.

A special meeting of the Irish Synod was held for the purpose of Covenant renovation in 1853. The official Testimony of the Church looked on this act of Covenant-renovation as the forerunner of blessing, associating with it the successful establishment of the Theological Hall the following year, the revival of the Irish Mission and of missionary interest generally in the Church, and the increase given for the support of the ministry. The Act of Covenant-renovation was undertaken again at Ballymoney in 1901 and at Belfast in 1911 and most recently in 1990 at Creevagh, Co. Monaghan..

THE SUPREMACY OF CHRIST OVER THE NATION

Reformed Presbyterians hold firmly the doctrine of the sole Headship of Christ over the nation. In Erastianism the civil government claims authority over the Church. The Scottish Reformation was anti-Erastian in character and the Reformed Presbyterian Church maintains this attitude. The nation as well as the Church had been given to God in Covenant, as the Covenants were civil and ecclesiastical bonds and therefore these bound the nation and the Church in loyalty to King Jesus. The Church owes allegiance to none but Christ and thus the Revolution settlement of 1690 is opposed as it was Erastian in character. The 'Regium Donum' introduced in 1672 by Charles II, was seen as a bribe from a Covenant-breaking nation.

However the principle of an establishment or a national Church is not opposed. Both Church and the State are divine institutions, each independent and supreme in its own sphere, the Church to teach the Christian Doctrine and the State to establish the Church by suitable legislation and to provide for its financial support out of national resources. Reformed Presbyterians maintain the Doctrine of Christ's Headship over the Nation, not merely because he is God, and therefore the Sovereign Lord of all, but because it is part of His office as Mediator. This is embodied in the Church's Testimony, which establishes that the Scriptures are the only rule for the conduct of civil affairs. The Word of God is not only the standard for all matters ecclesiastical, but also the supreme guide for all the relationships and activities of life. The Civil Magistrate is not the servant of Society, but the minister of God to men for good. All legislation should therefore be based on the Moral Law of God.

Reformed Presbyterians have been challenged that they interfere with the rights and liberties of men, but the rights of man ought never to be in conflict with the rights of God. This position is, in effect, a challenge to the modern secular state's right to exist in God's world. Members of the Church regulate their attitude to the State in the light of Christ's Headship over the Nation. They bare responsibility as citizens, working for the good of the community, paying taxes and serving in the armed forces of the Crown. But they have refrained from exercising the elective franchise as an act of dissent from and protest against the fact that the law and constitution of the United Kingdom make no acknowledgment of the Sovereignty of Christ over the Nation and do not give the Moral Law of God a supreme place in legislation. Covenanters also insist on Christian qualifications for legislators.

A modification of this position was approved by Synod in 1982.
Covenanters should vote only for candidates who recognize the Kingship of Jesus Christ. This means those candidates who :

(a) give evidence of consistent Christian character;
(b) promise to frame all their policies in accordance with the Word of God and to resist all pressures of political expediency and party discipline which might compromise such obedience;

(c) make an explicit declaration of dissent from all within their sphere of government which is contrary to the Word of God and pledge themselves to work for public and national recognition of Christ;

(d) refuse, where applicable, to take the present oath of allegiance, and make instead an affirmation of loyalty which would specifically safeguard their primary loyalty to Jesus Christ.

THE HEADSHIP OF CHRIST OVER THE CHURCH

The Doctrine of the Headship of Christ over His Church is one that is accepted in theory by all the Reformed Churches. Its application, however, regulates the doctrine, discipline and worship of the Church. Christ is the head of His Church and every detail of the Church's life must be in line with the teaching of Scripture. The Westminster Confession of Faith and the Larger and Shorter Catechisms are subscribed as they are fully Scriptural in their teaching. The Presbyterian form of Church government is plainly outlined in the New Testament. The medium of praise for the Church of the New Testament is the Psalms of the Old Testament Church. These divinely inspired praises are appointed for the worship of God and are therefore superior to any other merely human compositions. Psalms should be sung unaccompanied, since instrumental music in the Old Testament was used in connection with the Temple ritual and sacrifices which were symbolic and temporary.

THE LORDSHIP OF CHRIST OVER ALL OF LIFE

Reformed Presbyterians hold that the Headship of Christ affects every detail of an individual's life and character. Acknowledgement of Christ's headship guides believers in their behaviour as members of families, as employers/employees in the workplace and as active members in society. They testify against oath-bound secret societies on the grounds that sworn secrecy was contrary to the teaching of Scripture and to the example of Jesus Christ who advocated openness in life and conduct. Honouring Christ is an important part of personal godliness and will find expression in a heartfelt obedience to His will as set forth in the Scriptures of the Old and New Testaments.

Adapted from Prof. Adam Loughridge, in 'The Covenanters in Ireland'

INDEX
OF CONGREGATIONS

464

HISTORICAL PUBLICATIONS FROM CAMERON PRESS

James Martin

PIONEER MEDICAL MISSIONARY IN ANTIOCH

A Thrilling Account of Faith and Courage

by

Isobel Lytle B.A.

A School of the Prophets

the history of the
Reformed Theological
College
Belfast
1854 - 2004

by F. S. Leahy

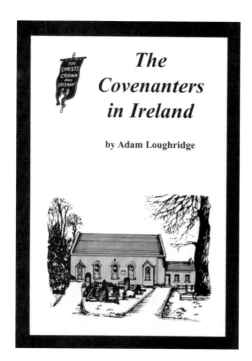

For Christs Crown and Covenant

The Covenanters in Ireland

by Adam Loughridge

Currently available from
The Covenanter Book Centre
www.covenanterbooks.com